Bilinguality and
Bilingualism

Bilinguality and Bilingualism

JOSIANE F. HAMERS
Professor of Psycholinguistics, Laval University

MICHEL H. A. BLANC
Emeritus Reader in Applied Linguistics and Bilingualism
Birkbeck College, University of London

The right of the
University of Cambridge
to print and sell
all manner of books
was granted by
Henry VIII in 1534.
The University has printed
and published continuously
since 1584.

CAMBRIDGE UNIVERSITY PRESS

CAMBRIDGE

NEW YORK   PORT CHESTER   MELBOURNE   SYDNEY

Published by the Press Syndicate of the University of Cambridge
The Pitt Building, Trumpington Street, Cambridge CB2 1RP
40 West 20th Street, New York, NY 10011, USA
10 Stamford Road, Oakleigh, Melbourne 3166, Australia

Originally published in French as *Bilingualité et bilinguisme*
by Pierre Mardaga, Editeur 1983
and © Pierre Mardaga, Editeur, Liège, Bruxelles

Revised edition first published in English by Cambridge University Press 1989 as
Bilinguality and Bilingualism

English translation © Cambridge University Press 1989
Reprinted 1990

Printed in Great Britain at the University Press, Cambridge

British Library cataloguing in publication data
Hamers, Josiane F.
Bilinguality and bilingualism
1. Bilingualism. Psychosocial aspects
I. Title   II. Blanc, Michel H.A.
III. Bilingualité et bilingualisme. *English*
306'.4

Library of Congress cataloguing in publishing data
Hamers, Josiane F.
[Bilingualité et bilingualisme. English]
Bilinguality and bilingualism / Josiane F. Hamers,
Michel H. A. Blanc. – Rev. ed.
   p.   cm.
Translation of: Bilingualité et bilingualisme.
Bibliography.
Includes indexes.
ISBN 0 521 33279 6.   ISBN 0 521 33797 6 (pbk.)
1. Bilingualism.   I. Blanc, Michel. II. Title.
P115.H3613 1986
404'.2 – oc19   86–11841 CIP

ISBN 0 521 33279 6 hard covers
ISBN 0 521 33797 6 paperback

CONTENTS

v

FOREWORD TO THE FRENCH EDITION

Twenty years ago no one could have written such a book as this. Back then bits and pieces of a general theme were only beginning to emerge here and there. The field was wide open though no one had a clear idea what or where the field itself was. Some of us saw the early starts as extensions of one branch or another of the behavioural sciences, for those making the early research explorations came from various academic backgrounds – experimental psychology, linguistics, social psychology, anthropology, sociology, area studies, information-based studies, or communication and speech. None of us had the training to write such a book because we were all tied too closely to one or perhaps two of the basic behavioural sciences.

What was required to make a book of this sort possible was, first, a new generation of scholars trained to cross discipline boundaries; second, time for numerous bits and pieces to come to light to give an outline of a field of study; and third, time for a set of social conditions to shape themselves so as to make the study of bilingualism and of bilinguals something more than an academic preoccupation.

This is a splendid book not only because it is beautifully written and carefully documented, but also because it discovers and stakes out a rich and robust field of study that some of us presumed was there but none of us really recognized. To discover the terrain, it took a particular combination of talents and experiences that Josiane Hamers and Michel Blanc happen to have. Their interdisciplinary experiences are evident throughout this book. Josiane Hamers came to McGill University for graduate training in the early 1970s after a complete classical education in Belgium in the behavioural sciences and experimental psychology. McGill was then as now an active centre that not only appreciated her inquisitiveness about the psychology, neurology and social psychology of bilingualism and bilinguals but also encouraged it. While learning, she taught the rest of us as much as she learned. Michel Blanc brings a different set of talents and experiences to this important book, and his own flawless bilinguality and biculturality, like Josiane's, include a special knowledge of languages and cultures. He came to the disciplines of psycholinguistics and sociolinguistics from a literary, linguistic and ethnographic background and from teaching and research experience in second-language teaching. Together the authors cross numerous disciplines and they do so with comfort and ease because they have been research contributors all along the line.

As a consequence, the field they present to us is real and extensive. For example, they take the reader through the psychological and cognitive aspects of bilingualism to the exciting promises of the neurosciences which in turn are enriched because of their current fascination with the bilingual condition. At the same time, they integrate and elucidate the experimental, the social psychological and the ethnographic aspects of bilingualism with examples drawn from various corners of the world. In fact, it is the cross-cultural applicability of the principles of bilingualism that they propose, including the role language plays in personal identity, that convinces the reader of the promise of the new field of study that they present in this book. The national and international features of language, the challenges of linguistic planning, the contact of languages within each social system become clear and understandable because one set of theoretical principles applies to data gathered from a wide array of nations. The authors are equally convincing as they apply their principles to three real-life topics in the final chapters: the bilingual education of children, the learning or acquisition of second languages, and the translation of information across languages.

Without subtracting a thing from the effort and the skills of the authors, the times have helped shape this work in important ways. We are living in a world where language is tightly linked to personal identity which in turn is tightly linked to nationality. It is a world where a neglect of this language-based identity provokes sentiments of separatism and independentism. It is a world of immigrants and emigrants, where questions of maintaining or abandoning one's home language affect education policies in all immigrant-receiving nations. It is also a world where the most advanced nations realize that they can no longer be ignorant of the languages and cultures of other peoples on this very small planet. Josiane Hamers and Michel Blanc have intelligently capitalized on the times and their book is a very important contribution to human understanding.

Wallace Earl Lambert
Department of Psychology
McGill University, Montreal

PREFACE

This English edition is an updated and completely revised version of a book by the same authors originally published in French under the title *Bilingualité et bilinguisme* (P. Mardaga, 'Psychologie et Sciences Sociales' series, 129, Brussels; Hamers & Blanc, 1983). Though broadly based on the French original, the present work is not a translation. Few chapters have remained intact, one has been deleted, some conflated, others split up. The new Chapter 1 combines the material originally shared between Chapters I and II. Chapter III has been divided into Chapters 2 and 3; the latter, entitled 'The social and psychological foundations of bilinguality', presents a much-revised and expanded social psychological model of bilingual development. The former Chapter V has been divided into two, now Chapters 5 and 6, corresponding to the first and second parts of the original chapter respectively. Chapter VI is now Chapter 7, the original Chapter VII having been deleted and some of its contents developed elsewhere in the book. Chapters 8–10 cover pretty much the same ground as in the French version.

In updating and revising the French edition we have benefited from the wealth of publications on bilingualism since 1983; we have also taken into account the public and personal comments and criticisms addressed to the original work, although on the whole we have been greatly encouraged by these comments and criticisms. Lastly, we have learned from our own research findings and this new book is the fruit of three years of continuing dialogue between the two authors. If there is a difference between this English edition and the original French version, it is essentially one of focus and emphasis: the present book attempts to present the state of the art in the study of languages in contact from a multidisciplinary point of view and offer the reader our own syntheses and theoretical models based on the evidence available, rather than to cover the ground. What we have lost in detailed descriptions we hope to have gained in explanatory power. Let the reader be the judge of this.

We gratefully acknowledge the encouragement and comments of our colleagues Wally Lambert, Hugo Baetens Beardsmore, Richard Clément, Richard Bourhis and Rodrigue Landry. We thank the Canadian High Commission in London, and in particular Michael Hellyer, for their financial assistance; Rob Kennedy for his technical advice and Birkbeck College for their unstinting hospitality; Penny Carter and Rosemary Morris for their editorial skill and patience; and last, but not least Dr Sanchez Romate for his vital support throughout the writing of this book. We of course accept full responsibility for its shortcomings.

Michel H. A. Blanc and Josiane F. Hamers
London and Quebec
September 1987

Introduction

In this book we attempt to present the state of the art on the principal issues of bilingualism and languages in contact. Our approach is multidisciplinary in so far as we study the various phenomena at different levels of analysis: we analyse languages in contact first in the language behaviour of the individual, next in interpersonal relations, and finally at the societal level where we consider the role of language in intergroup relations.

Each level of analysis requires specific disciplinary approaches: psychological at the individual level, social psychological at the interpersonal level and sociological at the intergroup level. We discuss only those theoretical constructs which either have been empirically confirmed or for which empirical verification is possible. We have rejected unsound and unverifiable models, or if we mention them, it is to stress their theoretical and methodological flaws. We have also rejected data that is not based on theoretical assumptions, as well as theories based solely on anecdotal evidence; we have not relied either on models constructed on the grounds of evidence stemming from isolated case-studies. However, we do not ignore this evidence provided that it can confirm experimental data, or if it is the only available evidence, as for example in the study of bilingual aphasics. Typologies of bilingualism are mentioned only when they are based on theoretical grounds and have therefore a predictive character: we consider a typology useful only in so far as a new classification of phenomena permits a better understanding of the psychological, sociological and linguistic processes and their interplay when languages are in contact.

In the first seven chapters we analyse theoretical models and research data in various disciplines as well as the methodological issues relating to them. Sometimes we propose a new interpretation or a modification of the existing one. The last three chapters address applied domains of languages in contact, namely bilingual education, second-language learning and interpretation and translation. Although throughout the book we are interested in the psychological and social behaviour of the bilingual speaker, we rarely detail linguistic descriptions specific to languages in contact, such as interference, borrowing, mixing and fusion. This would have lengthened our main analysis; we refer the

1

reader to the work of linguists such as Haugen (1950), Weinreich (1953), Clyne (1967), and Poplack, Sankoff & Miller (1987) among others.

It must be borne in mind that in English there is an ambiguity in the term *language*, which sometimes refers to a general communication process, rule-governed and shared by all humans (in French *langage*) and sometimes to the code of a specific speech community with its own rules (in French *langue*) (see also Le Page & Tabouret-Keller, 1985). As he reads on the reader will probably become aware that *language* does not necessarily have the same meaning in the different chapters. In the early chapters on the individual's language behaviour we use a more 'focussed' definition of language, i.e. it is defined as an abstract entity distinct from others, whereas in the later chapters we sometimes refer to a 'diffuse' definition, i.e. distributed on a continuum (see Le Page, 1978). In yet other chapters we take 'language' to mean a linguistic code used by a group of speakers who stand in a similar relationship to it and perceive it to be different from other linguistic codes.

Our main concern is the identification of universals of behaviour when two or more languages are in contact. The phenomenon of language behaviour cannot be studied in isolation, as it is in constant interaction with other phenomena, namely with culture. Although language is part of culture there is no simple cause-and-effect relation between them; rather, they are in constant interplay. When a chapter focusses on one or the other aspect, it must be kept in mind that one aspect of language behaviour, e.g. interpersonal features, cannot be explained if other dimensions, e.g. intergroup relations, are ignored. This focussing, therefore, is a momentary simplification which enables us to analyse the phenomenon more closely. Similarly, when we use a dichotomization, e.g. compound versus coordinate bilinguality, it must be understood as two extreme poles on a continuum rather than as two distinct entities.

In trying to understand behavioural processes there is a danger of reifying such conceptual constructs as language, culture, society, cognition, frames, scripts, etc. Because we view these concepts only as theoretical constructs which should enable us to understand human behaviour better and are convinced that they do not exist in the absence of human behaviour, we have tried to avoid their reification. It is in this spirit that all constructs used throughout the book must be understood.

In Chapter 1 we propose a number of definitions which are useful for subsequent discussions. We also identify some dimensions which enable us to classify bilinguals in discrete categories. Then we discuss measures that have been developed to assess bilingualism at the individual and the societal level.

Chapters 2 and 3 address the issue of bilingual development. The empirical research data on the bilinguistic, neuropsychological, cognitive and sociocultural dimensions of the ontogenesis of bilinguality are discussed in Chapter 2. Chapter 3 deals more specifically with the social and psychological foundations of bilingual development: after analysing the nature of language behaviour and development we stress the role of social networks and socialization. To end the chapter we propose a social cognitive model of bilingual development.

Chapter 4 examines the psychological mechanisms relevant to bilingual information processing, i.e. decoding, encoding and the representational mechanisms, in particular memory. The dual-coding model is discussed at some length. We further give a brief review of the bilingual's non-verbal behaviour and close this chapter with a discussion of aphasic bilinguals and the relevance of clinical data for our understanding of bilingual processing.

The next two chapters deal with the social psychological dimensions of bilinguality. In Chapter 5 we examine the relationship between culture, identity and language behaviour in a multicultural environment. After a discussion of the interdependency between language and culture, we analyse the bilingual's cultural identity and the social psychological processes which determine inter-ethnic interpersonal relations. Chapter 6 addresses the issue of the interaction between interpersonal relations and linguistic behaviour: in the first part speech-accommodation theory and its consequences for bilinguistic behaviour and bilingual speech mode are discussed, while in the second part we describe communication strategies specific to intercultural interactions, such as code selection, speech modification, code-switching and code-mixing.

The relations between multiculturalism and intergroup relations are discussed from a sociolinguistic and social psychological standpoint in Chapter 7. The role of language in intergroup behaviour is approached from different perspectives: language as a symbol and instrument of group identity, the concept of ethnolinguistic vitality and the interface between language and ethnicity in a multicultural setting. We then discuss language-planning policies and their consequences for groups and individuals. In the second part of this chapter we review the different types of sociolinguistic variations that arise from languages in contact: bilingual speech repertoires, diglossia, language shift, pidginization, creolization and decreolization. We analyse their implications for language behaviour and linguistic theory.

The last three chapters deal with fields of application of bilingual theorizing. Chapter 8 reviews the educational problems arising from a language contact situation: educational language planning and development of literacy, bilingual education for the majority children, bilingual programs for the ethnic minority children, bidialectal education and community bilingual education. In Chapter 9 we analyse the psycholinguistic foundations which underlie L_2 learning and teaching methodology. The processes of acquisition of a second language are discussed and compared with those of L_1 acquisition. After reviewing some of the theories on which different teaching methodologies are based, i.e. contrastive analysis, error analysis and interlanguages, we describe a number of psychological processes relevant to L_2 teaching which might provide useful guidelines in developing language-teaching methods:

communicative competence, aptitude and memory in L_2 acquisition, communication modes, cognitive styles and affective processes such as attitudes towards L_2. In Chapter 10 a different domain of application which calls for bilingual competence is analysed, that is, interpretation and translation. We try to understand how the different psychological processes involved in these tasks interplay with the necessary bilingual skills.

Language contact is a widespread phenomenon which deserves our attention as it involves a large and growing proportion of the world population; it is a complex phenomenon which requires several levels of analysis and hence several disciplines, each with its own theoretical and methodological approaches. Several disciplines have made considerable contributions to our knowledge of this phenomenon. But a better understanding of languages in contact calls not only for a multidisciplinary approach but for an interdisciplinary integration of these diverse disciplines (Blanc, 1987a). One of the major problems of an interdisciplinary approach is the integration of the macrological and the micrological levels of analysis. Because of the enormous methodological and theoretical difficulties, very few scholars have attempted it, and even fewer succeeded. If at times our discussions lack an interdisciplinary scope, it is because the state of the art does not allow it yet.

This book is meant for all those who are interested in language behaviour: psychologists, psycholinguists, sociologists and sociolinguists, linguists, pedagogues, educators, administrators who have to plan bilingual education, language teachers, interpreters and translators. We do not address the questions of communication disorders in bilinguals, speech therapy or bilingual behaviour in exceptional children, neither do we discuss the issue of contacts between a natural spoken language and a natural sign language. Fascinating though these issues are, they are beyond the scope of the present book. However, professionals working with bilinguals might find some useful insights in the present book in so far as it offers them general principles of bilingual behaviour.

Even though we felt it necessary sometimes to give complex technical details, we have tried to avoid the unnecessary use of technical jargon, and when we could not avoid it we tried to define it in a way accessible to all readers, regardless of their disciplinary background, and notes are provided for some chapters. Some of the most important terms and concepts we use are defined in a Glossary at the end of this book. This, we hope, will further help the reader unfamiliar with certain terms and concepts. Throughout this book we use the masculine form as a generic term, unless otherwise specified; *he*, *him* and *his* refer therefore to a person, regardless of gender.

Given the magnitude of the problem, some analyses may have escaped us. We apologize to the authors we have unconsciously left out and to those we have misinterpreted, either because we had to summarize their view in a few sentences or because we had to synthesize approaches and disciplines with which we are not familiar. We will be rewarded if this book informs the reader on problems of languages in contact. We hope that *she* or *he* will have a better grasp of these problems after reading this book. Our goal will have been attained if this reading provokes many challenging questions. However, we do not necessarily provide the answers, as they are not known in the present state of the art.

1

Dimensions and measurement of bilinguality and bilingualism

The aim of this book is to critically review the state of the art in the field of *languages in contact*. By languages in contact we understand the psychological state of an individual who uses more than one language[1] as well as the use of two or more codes in interpersonal and intergroup relations. We distinguish between bilinguality and bilingualism. Bilinguality is the psychological state of an individual who has access to more than one linguistic code as a means of social communication; the degree of access will vary along a number of dimensions which are psychological, cognitive, psycholinguistic, social psychological, social, sociological, sociolinguistic, sociocultural and linguistic (Hamers, 1981). The concept of bilingualism, on the other hand, includes that of bilinguality (or individual bilingualism) but refers equally to the state of a linguistic community in which two languages are in contact with the result that two codes can be used in the same interaction and that a number of individuals are bilingual (societal bilingualism).

1.1 Definitions

The concept of bilingualism seems at first sight to be non-problematical. According to the Webster Dictionary (1961) bilingual is defined as 'having or using two languages especially as spoken with the fluency characteristic of a native speaker; a person using two languages especially habitually and with control like that of a native speaker' and bilingualism as 'the constant oral use of two languages'. In the popular view being bilingual equals being able to speak two languages perfectly; this is also the approach of Bloomfield (1935), who defines bilingualism as 'the native-like control of two languages' (p. 56). In contradistinction to this definition which includes only 'perfect bilinguals', Macnamara (1967a) proposes that a bilingual is anyone who possesses a minimal competence in one of the four language skills, i.e. listening comprehension, speaking, reading and writing in a language other than his mother tongue. Between these two extremes one encounters a whole array of defini-

6

tions, as for example the one proposed by Titone (1972), for whom bilingualism is 'the individual's capacity to speak a second language while following the concepts and structures of that language rather than paraphrasing his or her mother tongue' (p. 11).[2]

All these definitions, which range from a native-like competence in two languages to a minimal proficiency in a second language, raise a number of theoretical and methodological difficulties. On the one hand, they lack precision and operationalism: they do not specify what is meant by native-like competence, which varies considerably within a unilingual population, nor by minimal proficiency in a second language, nor by obeying the concepts and structures of that second language. Can we exclude from the definitions of bilingual someone who possesses a very high competence in a second language without necessarily being perceived as a native speaker on account of a foreign accent? Can a person who has followed one or two courses in a foreign language without being able to use it in communication situations, or again someone who has studied Latin for six years, legitimately be called bilingual? Unless we are dealing with two structurally different languages, how do we know whether or not a speaker is paraphrasing the structures of his mother tongue when speaking the other language?

On the other hand, these definitions refer to a single dimension of bilinguality, namely the level of proficiency in both languages, thus ignoring non-linguistic dimensions. Even recently Paradis (1986: xi), while suggesting that bilinguality should be defined on a multidimensional continuum, reduces the latter to linguistic structure and language skill. When definitions taking into account dimensions other than the linguistic ones have been proposed, they too have been more often than not limited to a single dimension. Baetens Beardsmore (1982) has listed some thirty-five definitions and typologies of bilingualism, very few of which are multidimensional.

We have no intention of reviewing all the definitions or typologies that have been proposed for bilingualism; instead we will mention only those which are operational and can be applied in empirical research or those which are based on a theoretical construct. It must be borne in mind that when qualifiers are used to describe bilingualism or bilinguality, they generally focus on one single dimension of these phenomena which are thereby viewed from a particular angle. If we use some of the classifications put forward by researchers it is because they appear to be relevant to the dimension under study; however, we must not lose sight of the fact that bilinguality and bilingualism are multi-dimensional phenomena and must be investigated as such. In the past failure to take into account simultaneously other dimensions in addition to linguistic ones has all too often led to incomplete or erroneous interpretations of these phenomena.

1.1.1 Dimensions of bilinguality

We have found the following dimensions relevant: relative competence, cognitive organization, age of acquisition, exogeneity, social cultural status and cultural identity. (For a summary of these see Table 1.1.)

The dimension of competence enables us to take into account the relative nature of bilinguality, since it focusses on the relationship between two linguistic competences, one in each language. A distinction has been made between the *balanced* bilingual who has equivalent competence in both languages and the *dominant* bilingual for whom competence in one of the languages, more often the mother tongue, is superior to his competence in the other (Lambert, 1955). Balanced bilinguality should not be confused with a very high degree of competence in the two languages; it is rather a question of a state of equilibrium reached by the levels of competence attained in the two languages as compared to monolingual competence. Equivalent competence should not be equated with the ability to use both languages for all functions and domains. Dominance or balance is not equally distributed for all domains and functions of language; each individual has his own dominance configuration.

Regardless of the state of equilibrium, bilinguality may differ on other dimensions. For example, age and context of acquisition may lead to differences in cognitive functioning. Ervin & Osgood (1954) distinguished between *compound* and *coordinate* language systems: in a compound system two sets of linguistic signs come to be associated with the same set of meanings, whereas in a coordinate system translation equivalents in the two languages correspond to two different sets of representations. This distinction is schematized in Figure 1.1.

This distinction, often misinterpreted in the literature, has to do with a difference of cognitive organization and not to a difference in the degree of competence, or a difference in the age or context of acquisition. Although there is a high correlation between the type of cognitive organization, age and context of acquisition, there is no one-to-one correspondence between the form of cognitive representation and the age of acquisition; indeed, an individual who learned both languages as a child in the same context is more likely to have a single cognitive representation for two translation equivalents, whereas one

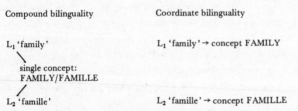

Figure 1.1 Schematic representation of the compound–coordinate distinction (adapted from Ervin & Osgood, 1954)

Table 1.1 Summary table of psychological dimensions of bilinguality

	Dimensions		Comments*
A.	According to competence in both languages	1. balanced bilinguality	$L_{A/1}$ competence = $L_{B/2}$ competence
		2. dominant bilinguality	$L_{A/1}$ competence > or < $L_{B/2}$ competence
B.	According to cognitive organization	1. compound bilinguality	$L_{A/1}$ unit equivalent to $L_{B/2}$ unit = one conceptual unit
		2. coordinate bilinguality	$L_{A/1}$ unit = conceptual unit 1
			$L_{B/2}$ equivalent = conceptual unit 2
C.	According to age of acquisition	1. childhood bilinguality	$L_{B/2}$ acquired before age 10/11
		(a) simultaneous	L_A and L_B = mother tongues
		(b) consecutive	L_1 = mother tongue; L_2 acquired before 11
		2. adolescent bilinguality	L_2 acquired between 11 and 17
		3. adult bilinguality	L_2 acquired after 17
D.	According to presence of L_2 community in environment	1. endogenous bilinguality	presence of L_2 community
		2. exogenous bilinguality	absence of L_2 community
E.	According to the relative status of the two languages	1. additive bilinguality	$L_{A/1}$ and $L_{B/2}$ socially valorized → cognitive advantage
		2. subtractive bilinguality	L_2 valorized at expense L_1 → cognitive disadvantage
F.	According to group membership and cultural identity	1. bicultural bilinguality	double membership and bicultural identity
		2. L_1 monocultural bilinguality	$L_{A/1}$ membership and cultural identity
		3. L_2 acculturated bilinguality	$L_{B/2}$ membership and cultural identity
		4. deculturated bilinguality	ambiguous membership and anomic identity

* For an explanation of L_A, L_B, L_1, L_2, see p. 10.

who learned a L_2 in a context different from that of his mother tongue will probably have a coordinate organization, that is, he will have separate representations for two translation equivalents. However, for operational purposes, age and context of acquisition are often used in order to identify the two types of bilinguals. This misinterpretation is often made, even by specialists in bilingual studies who, while noting the relation between age and context of acquisition and type of bilinguality, forget that the distinction refers essentially to differences in semantic organization in the bilingual (see, e.g., Fishman, 1964; Gumperz, 1964a and Dodson, 1983). It must be stressed that this distinction is not absolute but that different forms of bilinguality are distributed along a continuum from a compound to a coordinate pole; a bilingual person can at the same time be more compound for certain concepts and more coordinate for others. This distinction is further explored in Chapter 4.2.1.

The age of acquisition plays a part not only in respect of cognitive representation but also in other aspects of the bilingual's development, particularly his linguistic, neuropsychological, cognitive and sociocultural development. Age of acquisition combines with other data from the subject's language biography, such as context of acquisition and use of the two languages. Indeed age and context often go together; for instance, early acquisition of two languages often occurs in the same family context, while later acquisition of the second language often takes place in a school context distinct from a family context for the first language.

A distinction must first be made between *childhood bilinguality*, *adolescent bilinguality* and *adult bilinguality*. In the first of these bilingual experience takes place at the same time as the general development of the child; in other words this bilingual experience occurs at the time when the various developmental components have not yet reached maturity and can therefore be influenced by this experience. In childhood bilinguality one must distinguish (a) *simultaneous early* or *infant bilinguality*, when the child develops two mother tongues from the onset of language, which we call L_A and L_B, as for example the child of a mixed-lingual family; and (b) *consecutive childhood bilinguality*, when he acquires a second language early in childhood but after the basic linguistic acquisition of his mother tongue has been achieved. In this case and in all other cases of consecutive bilingual acquisition we refer to the mother tongue as L_1 and to the second language as L_2. While the development of simultaneous bilinguality takes place through informal, unintentional learning, consecutive childhood bilinguality may occur informally, as in the case of the child of an immigrant family, but may also result from intentional learning, as in certain bilingual educational programs.

According to whether the speech communities of both languages are present or not in the child's social environment we will speak of *endogenous* or *exogenous* *bilinguality*. An endogenous language is one that is used as a mother tongue in a community and may or may not be used for institutional purposes, whereas an exogenous language is one used as an official, institutionalized language but has no speech community in the political entity using it officially. Examples of exogenous languages are English or French in West, Central and East African countries; a Benin child from Cotonou, speaking Fon at home and going to a school where French is the exclusive language of instruction will develop an exogenous bilinguality in Fon and French.

In respect of cognitive development the type of bilinguality is also dependent on the sociocultural environment, in particular the relative status of the two languages in the community. According to whether the two languages are socially valued in his environment, the child will develop different forms of bilinguality. If the two languages are sufficiently valued the child's cognitive development will derive maximum benefit from the bilingual experience, which will act as an enriching stimulation leading to greater cognitive flexibility compared to his monolingual counterpart; on the other hand, if the sociocultural context is such that the mother tongue is devalued in the child's environment, his cognitive development may be delayed in comparison with a monolingual peer's; in extreme cases, the bilingual child may not be able to make up for this delay. The former type of bilingual experience has been called *additive bilinguality*; the latter *subtractive bilinguality* (Lambert, 1974). This distinction relates to the conceptual–linguistic consequences of the sociocultural context of bilingual development.

Finally, bilinguals can be distinguished in terms of their cultural identity. A bilingual may identify positively with the two cultural groups that speak his languages and be recognized by each group as a member: in this case he is also *bicultural*. This cultural identity integrating two cultures is probably, at the socio-affective level, the analogue of additive bilinguality at the cognitive level. A balanced biculturalism often goes hand in hand with a balanced bilinguality. However, this is not always necessarily the case: in multilingual societies, for example, a multiple cultural membership can coexist with varying degrees of dominant bilingual competence. A high bilingual competence does not always mean a cultural identity with dual cultural membership; a person may become a fluent bilingual while remaining *monocultural* and identifying culturally with one of the groups only. Bilingual development can also lead a person to renounce the cultural identity of his mother-tongue group and adopt that of the second-language group, in which case he will become a L_2 *acculturated bilingual*. Sometimes, however, the bilingual may give up his own cultural identity but at the same time fail to identify with the L_2 cultural group and as a result become anomic and *deculturated* (Berry, 1980).

Bilinguality can also be described in terms of language use. Weinreich (1953) and Mackey (1962) define bilingualism as the alternate use of two or more languages by the same individual. However, use is not a dimension but the expression of one or more dimensions of bilinguality. The notion of use means that the bilingual individual has the capacity to call on either language, and this implies that he must have a minimal competence in both languages. Use will tell us whether a bilingual person is more or less dominant in one or the other of his languages for a specific domain or topic. Dodson (1981) proposes the term *preferred language* to account for choice of language in a particular situation.

1.1.2 *Dimensions of bilingualism*

Sociolinguists have shown how monolingual behaviour varies according to a number of parameters such as, e.g., role relation, relative status of speakers and languages, topic, domain etc. (see, e.g., Ervin-Tripp, 1964; Fishman, 1965, 1972; Labov, 1966). It can be assumed that these variables apply to language contact situations and that the state of bilinguality interacts with these. The bilingual's language behaviour will vary according to whether he interacts with a monolingual or a bilingual interlocutor in a unilingual, bilingual or multilingual environment.

When a person bilingual in L_X, L_Y encounters a monolingual interlocutor in a unilingual community speaking L_X, he will follow the social and linguistic norms of the L_X community. If he encounters a bilingual person like himself (L_X, L_Y) in a similar setting, they can follow the unilingual norms of either community or they can create their own set of language norms, as the community defines only the monolingual behaviour norms of L_X.

In a multilingual community, on the other hand, there exists a set of norms defining bilingual behaviour. For a bilingual community to exist there must be at least two languages commonly used by some members of the community. Either the community is composed of two groups speaking two different languages as their mother tongue, along with a small number of bilinguals speaking both languages or a small number of both groups speaking a third common language, used as a *lingua franca*; or, as in the case of an exogenous language, some members of the community speak a second language that has no or few native speakers in the community. Any of these languages may be an *official language* of the community.

Every bilingual community is situated between the two poles of a continuum, ranging from a set made up of two unilingual groups each containing a small number of bilinguals, to a single group with a more or less large number of members using a second language for specific purposes. At one pole most speakers in each group use only one language for all functions, whereas at the other a varying number of speakers use both languages but for different purposes. One can distinguish the following typical cases:

(1) *Territorial bilingualism*, in which each group finds itself mostly within its own politically defined territory, with the two (or more) languages having official status in their own territory; the official status of the other national

language(s) will vary considerably from country to country. Examples of territorial bilingualism can be found in Belgium, Switzerland, the Soviet Union, Spain and Canada, each country applying the principle of territorial bilingualism in its own way. (For further details see Chapter 7.1.1.)

(2) Another case of bilingual communities can be found in multilingual countries of Africa and Asia where, beside the native languages of indigenous ethnic groups or nations, there exist one or more languages of wider communication cutting across these groups and nations and native to none or few of them; this can be either a lingua franca like Swahili in Eastern and Central Africa and Tok Pisin in Papua New Guinea or a superposed language imposed by political decision making which introduces an exogenous language, normally inherited from a colonial past and used only in certain official domains, as is the case with French or English in several African countries.

(3) Finally, a bilingual community can be described as diglossic, that is, two languages are spoken by a variable section of the population, but they are used in a complementary way in the community, one language or variety having a higher status than the other and being reserved for certain functions and domains. Examples of diglossic bilingualism are the use of Spanish and Guaraní in Paraguay and of French and Creole in Haiti; in these cases both languages have a significant group of native speakers in the community.

   Let us stress that monolinguality is more commonly found in economically dominant groups whereas the members of minority or subordinate groups tend to be bi- or multilingual. Minority does not necessarily imply numerical inferiority, but refers rather to a subordinate status in the community. However, a subordinate group can use its numerical superiority to impose its own language norms through *language planning* legislation which aims at ending the subordinate status of that group; in this case the formerly dominant group will undergo a *minorization* process.
   To the extent that a community's ethnolinguistic duality is officially recognized, the community sets up a number of institutions in order to manage the use of both languages. Inside these institutions either members of the different language groups use one language, which can be a language of the community, a lingua franca, or an exogenous language; or several languages from the community can be used to a varying extent, as for example when two members of different language groups speak to each other in their respective languages; in this case each understands but does not necessarily speak the other's language, or if they do not understand each other's language they make use of an interpreter.
   The various dimensions of bilinguality and bilingualism which we have briefly defined bring out the multidimensional nature of these phenomena. We have called upon notions taken from a variety of disciplines: psychology,

psycholinguistics, sociolinguistics, sociology and linguistics. Bilingualism must be approached as a complex phenomenon which simultaneously implies a state of bilinguality of individuals and a state of languages in contact at the collective level. Therefore, this phenomenon should be studied at several levels of analysis: individual, interpersonal, intergroup and societal. Even though the several disciplines involved in the study of bilingualism have developed different methodologies, they all share the problem of operationalizing and measuring the concepts they make use of. In the next section we will discuss some of the measures developed by the various disciplines to quantify the dimensions of bilinguality and bilingualism.

1.2 *The measurement of bilinguality and bilingualism*

In this section we will critically evaluate the measures developed for the assessment of bilinguality and bilingualism. A scientific approach to the study of languages in contact calls for the development of measures relevant to the adopted conceptual framework: conceptualization and operationalization of concepts must precede their measurement. To conceptualize is to build a mental representation by organizing previous knowledge logically in such a way that some of its features will appear as relevant. To operationalize a concept is to identify those salient features that can be quantified by a specific methodology; normally one measures only the most salient dimensions of a concept. To measure is to compare certain quantities with a standard; an event must be quantified in order to be compared with other events. In order to operationalize a concept its definition will often be reduced to what a test measures. The quantification of a concept, however, should not be confused with the concept itself.

For example, a concept like that of *language competence* is multidimensional and difficult to operationalize. If one considers that the command of pronunciation, grammar and vocabulary is relevant to *linguistic competence*, which is one aspect of language competence, one will introduce tests of pronunciation, grammar and vocabulary in the measurement of that competence. These tests, however, measure only some aspects of linguistic competence and do not cover all aspects of language competence.

In the next section we will review some of the measures developed for bilinguality and bilingualism; without attempting to give an exhaustive list of all measures developed and used in the field, we will try to abstract the basic principles underlying these measures. If a measure has been developed for the specific purpose of assessing languages in contact, we will discuss it in some detail; if it has been developed for another domain, we will only discuss the rationale for its application to the measurement of bilinguality and bilingualism.

1.2.1 *The measurement of bilinguality*

The measurement of bilinguality must take into consideration the definition of bilinguality, that is, it should assess a psychological state and therefore account for its specificity. If bilinguality is defined as a psychological state of the individual who has access to more than one linguistic code, one might think it sufficient to measure two separate monolingual states to obtain an adequate measure of bilinguality. This is indeed the assumption upon which the majority of measures of bilinguality have been constructed. Now there are reasons to believe that the bilingual is more than the sum of two monolinguals and that his behaviour displays some unique characteristics. Unfortunately, at present theorizing about the bilingual's specific behaviour is still in its infancy and we therefore lack an adequate methodology to capture the specificity of bilingual behaviour.

We will now discuss the following measures of bilinguality: the comparative approach; tests of bilingual competence; behavioural measures; language-biography questionnaires; judgements of language production and measures of the cognitive and affective correlates of bilinguality.

1.2.1.1 Comparative measures

The most frequently used technique for measuring the various dimensions of bilinguality consists in taking measures in each of the bilingual's two languages and comparing them. However, a direct comparison between measures in two languages is extremely difficult even when it is possible. For instance, for us to be able to compare language competence in two languages there must exist measures of language competence in each language and these two sets of measures must be comparable. A measure of language competence implies that we have a clear definition of what a native speaker's competence in that language is. Because there are such wide variations between the competence of native speakers of the same language, it is extremely difficult to identify and thus to operationalize the salient features of a native competence. Moreover, native competence is not necessarily synonymous with a high level of competence; as we have already pointed out, a concept like balanced bilinguality is defined by an equilibrium between two native-like competences.

A way round the methodological difficulty of comparing behaviours in two languages consists in making a double comparison: the monolingual competences of a bilingual speaker are compared with monolingual standards in each language. As a consequence of this approach we no longer need the same operational definition of native speaker's competence in the two languages. If, for example, in a series of language tests a bilingual's scores in two languages are in the first percentile, we can conclude that he is highly competent in both languages and that his bilinguality is relatively balanced. Note that the measures used do not need to be similar for each language, since the comparison occurs at the level of a statistical distribution of the competences of native speakers. Such an approach enables us to avoid the problem of directly comparing behaviour in one language with that in another.

This comparative approach is the only valid one when bilinguality is measured on the 'additive–subtractive' dimension. In this case the conceptualization of the dimension implies that a comparison is made between cognitive measures obtained for bilinguals and monolinguals: the cognitive advantages or disadvantages of additive and subtractive bilinguality are measured in respect of monolingual populations (see 1.2.1.5).

1.2.1.2 *Measures of language competence*

Can language competence be measured and if so how?

1.2.1.2.1 *Tests of competence in the mother tongue*

The impossibility of defining native-language competence (Jakobovits, 1970) makes the construction of valid and reliable measures of language competence extremely problematic. This difficulty, however, has not prevented psychometricians from designing such tests. Let us mention, for example, the Peabody Picture Vocabulary Test (Dunn, 1959) measuring receptive vocabulary, Reynell's syntactic complexity test (Reynell, 1969) and the numerous language tests included in traditional test batteries. All these tests measure one aspect of language competence in the mother tongue, but it is far from evident that the particular aspect measured is the most relevant dimension. Is it even justifiable to measure separate skills which supposedly make up language competence? Some tests attempt to capture the unitary nature of competence, for instance, cloze tests;[3] Oller (1979) claims that they are a procedure for testing the learner's internalized system of grammatical knowledge (p. 344). The main value of the cloze procedure lies in its predictive power of language competence as measured by a battery of other tests.

However, these tests do not measure some aspects of communicative competence, such as knowledge of illocutionary rules and appropriate use of linguistic rules in communication settings (Hymes, 1971; Canale & Swain, 1980). Unfortunately, tests of communicative competence are even less developed than those of linguistic competence, especially in mother-tongue assessment.

Whatever their shortcomings, tests of competence in the mother tongue are useful, as they are the only means of assessing the bilingual's competence and comparing it with that of his monolingual counterpart.

1.2.1.2.2 *Tests of competence in a second language*

These tests are designed to measure the level of competence in the second language reached by non-native speakers of that language. They are of limited usefulness for the measurement of bilinguality, as we cannot compare them with tests of mother tongue competence; nonetheless, they are of interest in that they enable us to define levels of dominance in bilinguals, especially at an early stage in the development of bilingual competence. For example, two L_1-dominant bilinguals can be distinguished as to their proficiency in L_2 by means of these tests, which are useful for the identifying of stages in the development of a consecutive bilinguality resulting from a L_2 teaching program.

In second-language testing there is a large number of tests of linguistic competence (for an annotated list of tests of first and second language see Savard, 1977). To date very few tests of communicative competence in L_2 have been developed (however, see Morrow, 1977; criteria for the construction of truly communicative tests have been defined by Porter, 1983).

1.2.1.2.3 Behavioural measures

The difficulty of measuring bilingual competence by means of traditional language tests has led experimental psychologists to design measures which allow a direct comparison between the two languages. These measures are based on the following principle: whenever a task involves a certain degree of verbal competence a balanced bilingual's performance should be the same whatever the language used in performing the task. A difference in the performance between a task in L_A/L_1 and the same task in L_B/L_2 will indicate a dominance in one of the languages. Implicit in this principle is the idea that the relation between L_A/L_1 and the given task is the same as the relation between L_B/L_2 and that task.

(1) Reaction or latency-time measures. This technique, widely used in experimental psychology, measures verbal fluency in both languages. In these tasks a bilingual subject is asked to verbally either decode or encode or both; his reaction time to the task in each language is measured. Equal reaction times in the two languages indicate a state of balanced bilinguality. Reaction times have been used as a measure of bilinguality in the following tasks:

(a) Verbal decoding, non-verbal encoding: for example, a subject will be asked to react to oral instructions in both languages by pressing one of two keys; if the reaction times to the same instruction in the two languages are equal, subjects will be classified as balanced (Lambert, 1955). Another test consists of measuring the reaction time taken for recognizing a word presented through a tachistoscope; if the reaction time for the recognition of words in L_A/L_1 is equal to the reaction time to the translation equivalents in L_B/L_2, one will infer that the bilinguality of the subject is balanced. Using this technique, Lambert, Havelka & Gardner (1959) found significant correlations between these measures and traditional linguistic measures of bilinguality.

(b) Non-verbal decoding, verbal encoding. In this technique the subject is asked to respond verbally in one and then in the other language to non-verbal stimuli: for example, a subject is asked to name in each language pictorially presented objects (Ervin, 1961) or colours (Hamers, 1973). A difficulty with this type of measure is that the stimuli might not have the same cultural value in each language; for example, in a colour-naming task the two cultures may have different ways of classifying and naming colours, as in the case of English, Bassa and Shona (Gleason, 1961).

(c) Verbal decoding, verbal encoding. Here one finds the many tests of reading aloud in both languages. According to Macnamara (1969), speed of reading aloud in both languages is assumed to be a good predictor of bilingual competence. Also in this category are tests of word completion in each language; for example, a bilingual subject is given the beginning of potential words (e.g. the digraph co-) and he has to produce as many words as possible in both languages starting with those letters (for example, English: cob, cock, coin, colt, combination, con, convention, cooperative, copper, cottage, country, court; French: combien, combinaison, comme, comment, commerce, conduite, côte, côté, côtelette, courage, couvent, couvert) (Lambert, 1955).

For all their ingenuity some of these tests come up against a number of problems relating to differences between languages. The main question is one of identity of the task in the two languages; for some pairs of languages it is impossible to find comparable tasks, e.g. completing words starting with the same digraph implies two languages which not only use the same script but also share a cognate vocabulary. Other tasks are not equal in the two languages, either because of the frequency distribution of the translation equivalents or because the decoding processes seem to be different in each language. In this vein, Meara (1984) has demonstrated that while in English the beginning of a word is the most important cue for decoding, in Spanish it is the middle syllable. Non-verbal reaction times to verbal stimuli in different languages seem also to be different regardless of the degree of balance of a subject. For example, it seems that decoding English stimuli is systematically faster than decoding French even for fluent bilinguals dominant in French, as experiments by Treisman (1964) and Hamers (1973) have shown. Decoding tests must therefore be used with caution as a measure of bilingual balance.

(2) Completion and word-detection tests. The same completion test as described above can be used, but the measure is the number of words produced in one language compared with the number of words produced in the other language. Lambert, Havelka & Gardner (1959) demonstrated that there are significant correlations between results obtained through this technique of measurement and traditional measures of language competence. In another

technique developed by the same authors, a bilingual subject is asked to recognize in both languages as many words as possible in a string of nonsense syllables. For example, a French–English bilingual is asked how many French and English words he can recognize in the string DANSONODENT. This test is subject to the same limitations as the previous ones; it can only be used with two languages that have a common graphemic system and have similar graphemic strings. As Baetens Beardsmore (1982) has commented, this type of puzzle may favour the subordinate language since the subject will concentrate on his weaker language at the expense of the stronger; and one might wonder about the validity of this type of technique as a measure of bilingual competence.

(3) Verbal association tests. Verbal association tests in two languages have been used to measure balance or dominance. A subject is asked to give as many associations as possible to a stimulus word, in the same language as that stimulus, in a given time; this test is repeated for the translation equivalents in the other language. The difference between the total number of words obtained in each language divided by the highest total number or words given in one of the languages gives an index of *verbosity* (Lambert, 1955). This technique is based on the assumption that the more a learner becomes competent in L_2, the more likely he is to give a high number of associations to L_2 words and the more closely these associations will resemble those of the native speakers of L_2.

(4) Interlingual verbal flexibility. Other behavioural tests attempt to measure the bilingual's ability to manipulate the two languages simultaneously. Examples are the tests of speed of translation; according to Lambert, Havelka & Gardner (1959) such a measure is not a good index of the degree of bilingual competence. The same holds for the ability to switch from one language to another without translating (Macnamara, 1969). It is assumed that these tests call upon a different skill from that of bilingual competence. This assumption is supported by clinical data: indeed, in some cases of aphasia a bilingual can lose some aspects of his competence in both languages without losing his ability to translate (Paradis, 1980).

(5) Use of interlingual ambiguity. Another test developed for measuring the degree of bilingual balance consists in reading aloud a list of cross-language ambiguous words, e.g. *pipe, chance* and *silence* in English and French (Lambert, Havelka & Gardner, 1959). The underlying hypothesis here is that the more balanced a subject is, the less he will decode these words as belonging to one language to the exclusion of the other, and he will obtain equal scores for both languages. This test has been shown to correlate with other measures of bilingual balance. However, its use is limited to languages that have an extensive

lexicon in common. Another difficulty comes from the fact that these ambiguous words have very different frequency distributions in each language and it may be that it is the characteristics of the word that condition decoding in one language rather than in the other.

Because of the insufficient operationalization of concepts like dominance and balance which imply a comparison between two competences, it is premature to want to assess bilinguality on the basis of one type of measure only. We have argued that traditional tests of language competence measure a few aspects of this competence, but give us no answer as to how to compare competences in the two languages with each other. Behavioural measures, on the other hand, have the advantage of being simple and easy to administer, and of permitting direct comparisons; but they rest on the assumption that certain tasks are performed in a similar way in either language. It seems therefore that combining the two kinds of measure should improve the method of quantifying bilingual proficiency. Before discussing further improvements in quantification we will first consider the measurement of the compound–coordinate dimension of bilinguality.

1.2.1.3 Measures of compound–coordinate bilinguality

As we saw in 1.1.1, the distinction between the compound and coordinate bilingual is one of semantic representation; it implies that for the coordinate bilingual there is a greater semantic independence between his two linguistic codes, while for the compound there is greater semantic interdependence between the two codes. How can the degree of semantic independence and interdependence be measured?

We have seen that this dimension is closely linked to the context of acquisition of the two languages. Therefore, this information can be used to differentiate between compound and coordinate bilinguals who have reached the same level of proficiency in both languages. Some techniques which differentiate between compounds and coordinates and have been used for the purpose are: semantic satiation and semantic generalization (Lambert & Jakobovits, 1960; Jakobovits & Lambert, 1961, 1967; Lambert & Segalowitz, 1969); semantic distance (Lambert, Havelka & Crosby, 1958); core-concepts technique (Lambert & Rawlings, 1969; Arkwright & Viau, 1974); word-association technique (Lambert & Moore, 1966). (For more details of these measures see Chapter 4.1.1.)

1.2.1.4 Language biographies, self-evaluation and judgement of bilingual production

Language biographies provide information on the age and context of acquisition of both languages, their past and present use, their number, the varieties spoken, the degree of literacy, etc. The age, context and use are cues to the type of bilinguality developed by the subject. For example, a person who has acquired two languages in the home from infancy, has received his education in both his languages and uses them both regularly at home and at work has most probably developed a balanced and compound bilinguality. On the other hand, a bilingual whose mother tongue is a foreign language in the society where he lives, who has been educated in a language other than his mother tongue, who used his first language only with his family, but has never learned to read or write in it and has ceased to use it altogether, is likely to be a coordinate bilingual, dominant in his L_2. This information, however useful, relates to a declared behaviour as perceived by the subject and not to an actual observable behaviour and should therefore be used in combination with other measures.

Other measures frequently used to evaluate bilingual competence are self-evaluation and evaluation scales. The differential scores between the self-evaluations of proficiency in the two languages are good predictors of the degree of bilingual competence. Evaluation of proficiency in both languages by native speakers of each language can be used as a reliable measure of balanced bilinguality; it is however more difficult to use in order to evaluate the proficiency of dominant bilinguals, since it seems less reliable for judging proficiency in a language spoken in a non-native way. Self-evaluation and judgement by native speakers are generally done by assessing a number of language skills on a three-, five- or seven-point scale ranging from nil to native-like.

1.2.1.5 *Measures of bilingual specificity*

Except for the measures that call upon a simultaneous use of the two languages, such as translation and verbal flexibility, we have so far examined only measures in which the bilingual's behaviour is viewed as the sum of two monolingual behaviours. A bilingual probably also develops patterns of behaviour that are unique to his state of bilinguality (Grosjean, 1985a). For example, when bilinguals communicate with each other they can make simultaneous use of the resources of each of their languages by e.g. borrowing words from one language while using the other (loan words) or by developing mixed or switched codes which are governed by their own specific rules. The study of these specific codes has only just begun. Let us mention Poplack's (1980) attempt to correlate the degree of balance of bilinguals with a high level of competence in rule-governed code-switching. In the same vein, Lavandera (1978) has drawn attention to the inadequacy of monolingual measures to try to evaluate speech production in a bilingual communication situation. The bilingual's total repertoire can be fully exploited by him only in situations in which he can call upon the resources of his two languages and strategies spe-

cific to language contact (see Chapter 6.2). The development of tests designed
to capture the bilingual's specific competence is an urgent task for researchers.
But first a major effort of conceptualization and operationalization is required
(Grosjean, 1985a).

The specific linguistic behaviour of a bilingual has often been mistaken for
interference. Indeed, considered from the angle of monolingual norms code-
mixing and code-switching might seem deviant (Weinreich, 1953). It must be
stressed that the notion of interference, if often used, has never been more
clearly defined than as the inappropriate use by a speaker of elements or rules
of one language while using the other. However, the use of a mixed code is
inappropriate only in terms of the monolingual norm. The concept of interference is used extensively in second-language learning methodology and refers to learning processes in which the L_2 learner inappropriately transfers
units of his first language to the second. In a traditional language-teaching
methodology interference is perceived as a main source of errors in L_2. To this
day there is no operational definition of the concept in interference, still less
techniques to measure it. The only attempts are limited to frequency counts of
elements often arbitrarily identified as interferences.

Even if interference, as defined above, is an expression of the lack of linguistic competence in a dominant bilingual's weaker language, it is by no means
proven that it is characteristic of the balanced bilingual. On the contrary,
according to Ben-Zeev (1977a), one of the specific mechanisms developed by a
balanced bilingual is precisely the use of strategies to avoid interference from
one language with the other. Unfortunately, to date we have no reliable
measures to capture these specific cognitive and communicative strategies.

1.2.1.6 Measurement of cognitive correlates of bilinguality

A considerable amount of empirical evidence suggests that there exists a correlation between the development of bilinguality and cognition. The results of
these studies are apparently contradictory in so far as they show either a cognitive advantage or a cognitive disadvantage of bilingual development as compared to monolingual development. These research results are discussed in
detail in Chapter 2.3. Because the concepts of cognitive advantage and disadvantage are defined by reference to monolinguals, the only way to demonstrate one or the other is by comparing bilinguals with monolinguals.
Depending on which aspect of cognitive development is assumed to be affected
by bilingual experience, an experimental design is used to which the results of
verbal and non-verbal intelligence tests, verbal creativity, verbal flexibility,
divergent thinking, verbal transformations, symbol substitutions, etc., are
compared. We refer the reader to the classic study by Peal & Lambert (1962)
as an example of an experimental design using a large array of measures in
order to assess cognitive differences between bilinguals and monolinguals.

1.2.1.7 Measurement of affective correlates of bilinguality

There is always a cognitive and an affective aspect to development. The affective component of bilingual development has to do with the relationships between the bilingual individual and his two languages. Since language is a social phenomenon all affectivity towards it is not limited to the language but applies also to the individuals and groups who speak that language.

(1) One relevant affective aspect of bilingual behaviour concerns value judgements towards languages and their speakers. The most commonly used technique to measure value judgements consists of using Lickert-type evaluation scales, in which subjects are asked to express their degree of agreement or disagreement with a number of statements relating to the languages and their speakers. Such scales have been developed to measure attitudes towards languages and their speakers, motivation to learn or speak a second language, anxiety and confidence in the use of L_2: in other words, all social psychological mechanisms relevant to the affective processes of bilinguality. Among the numerous evaluation scales developed for the measurement of the affective dimensions of bilinguality, we will mention those developed by Gardner & Lambert (1959, 1972), Gardner & Smythe (1975) and Clément (1978).

(2) Another technique adapted to the measurement of the affective dimensions of bilinguality is the semantic differential (Osgood, Suci & Tannenbaum, 1957). As this technique measures the evaluation of a concept it is possible to use it in a differential way and obtain a measure of the relative evaluation of two languages or two groups of speakers. An interesting application of the semantic differential as an affective measure of bilinguality can be found in the *matched guise* technique (Lambert, Hodgson, Gardner & Fillenbaum, 1960). This technique enables the researcher to measure value judgements towards languages and speakers without having to ask direct questions of the subjects. One objection to the technique is that it ignores all the elements relevant to communication with the exception of voice characteristics.

(3) Of equal importance in the affective domain are the measures of the bilingual's cultural identity. Unlike the bilingual's language competence, which can be viewed as a distinct entity for each of his languages, his cultural identity can be conceptualized only as a single entity which is the outcome of his bilingual/bicultural experience. Even more than in the case of bilingual competence it is not enough to consider two monocultural identities. It is essential to have a technique capable of capturing the specificity of the bilingual's cultural identity. Techniques developed for measuring cultural identity, such as multidimensional scaling, ethnic dolls, role playing, etc., have all been adapted to the measurement of the bilingual's cultural identity (see Chapter 5.2).

1.2.2 Measurement of bilinguality in cultural minorities

The measures of bilinguality previously mentioned are not applicable to all situations of languages in contact; and in particular, there are difficulties when we try to use them in a cultural-minority situation. This is especially critical in the case of the education of cultural-minority children because they follow curricula in the language of the majority, which is usually their weaker language; now psychometric tests of academic proficiency are usually administered in the majority language. As pointed out by, among others, Cummins (1984a), psychometric tests of academic language proficiency are not appropriate for the assessment of minority children because these children have not reached the level of development required for these tests to be valid. Furthermore, results of psychometric tests, e.g. verbal and non-verbal intelligence tests, obtained with minority children who do not have a sufficient linguistic competence in the language of instruction cannot be compared with norms obtained for a different population. (For a fuller treatment of these issues see Chapter 8.5.)

There is also the problem of the cultural differences between the different groups. For example, if one wants to measure knowledge of vocabulary and the minority child is presented with pictures of familiar objects in the majority culture, as in the Peabody Picture Vocabulary Test (Dunn, 1959), but unfamiliar in the child's culture, lack of response by a minority child has no assessment value. Although attempts have been made to construct culture-free measures applicable to all children, it has proved impossible to eliminate the cultural bias from tests without impairing their validity as measures. (See Samuda, 1975; Samuda *et al.*, 1980.)

In the case of the child from an immigrant community one solution sometimes put forward is to use norms from the culture of origin; this, however, raises other problems, as the child either is no longer familiar with, or has never been exposed to, that original culture. Sometimes the child's experience of the language and culture of origin may be limited to a small community, even to the immediate family circle. Another solution, allegedly culture-fair, that can be used when the minority group is sufficiently large is to establish group norms; here the problem is that if the minority group is socially disadvantaged, the group norms will then be depressed and results will not be comparable to majority results. It is impossible in these conditions to use these tests diagnostically. (For a discussion of some of these issues see N. Miller, 1984.)

Even if we could design valid psychometric tests, these would still not be capable of measuring the specificity of the minority child's bilingual behaviour, since they would have been developed for monolingual children in each community. The minority child is therefore doubly disadvantaged: on the one hand, the tests used in his case are not adapted to his particular situation, and on the other, there exist no measures capable of assessing the specific character of his bilinguality. Recently, researchers have begun to attempt to capture this specificity by resorting to ethnographic/sociolinguistic approaches; it is too early to evaluate the impact of these new approaches on the assessment of bilingual competence. (For more details, see Rivera, 1983, 1984.)

In this section our main objective has been to highlight the problems raised by the use of psychometric tests for the assessment of the competence of children exposed to languages and cultures in contact. In the present state of our knowledge, there are no obvious solutions to these problems. (For a particular discussion of the issues of academic evaluation of minority children in North America see Samuda, 1975; Samuda *et al.*, 1980.)

1.2.3 Measurement of societal bilingualism

Few methodologies have been designed specifically for the study of languages in contact at the societal level, and even fewer measures have been developed for the quantification of collective bilingual phenomena. Researchers in this area normally make use of more general social science methodologies such as census techniques, polls and surveys as well as applying the methods of sociolinguistics and of the ethnography of communication. Let us note also that most of these methodologies are essentially descriptive in nature and only permit us to make rather crude predictions about collective behaviour in language-contact situations. However, even this descriptive approach is useful to the extent that it enables us to analyse covariations between linguistic and sociological phenomena.

The study of societal bilingualism can be carried out at several levels of analysis ranging from the macro-sociological to the micro-sociological.[4] These two approaches differ mainly in that at the macro-sociological level the researcher operates with large samples, even whole populations, and as a result, can only ask questions of a very general kind and easy to analyse, whereas the micro-sociological approach uses in-depth methods of data collection and analysis, thereby reducing the size and representativity of the samples. For this reason the former approach allows mainly questions on reported behaviour, while the study of actual behaviour demands a more micro-sociological methodology.

1.2.3.1 Censuses

A frequently used instrument to obtain data on language use is the population census, or rather those questions in it that ask for information on the mother tongue(s), the patterns of language use including all language(s) known by the respondents, and the degree of competence in those languages. Because of their magnitude censuses are usually initiated by governments as part of language-planning policies, and as such cover a territory defined by political boundaries. Unfortunately political boundaries are not necessarily coextensive with linguistic and cultural ones. For example, political boundaries in West Africa or in Europe divide linguistic communities which cut across a number of countries; another example is the Canadian census which informs us on the use of French north of the 47th Parallel but tells us nothing about the Franco-Americans of New England.

However, even if censuses were conducted in all countries sharing the same linguistic communities, the results would most probably not be comparable because the basic concepts are not defined in the same way. The concept of *mother tongue* is a case in point: for instance, the Canadian census defines the mother tongue as 'the first language learned in childhood and still understood': in India, on the other hand, it was defined in the 1961 census as the language spoken in childhood by the respondent's mother. Now this definition raises a difficulty in the case of children of mixed-lingual families where the mother's tongue is not the most commonly used language (Pattanayak, 1981). Furthermore, census questions are often vague, ambiguous or worded differently from context to context and from census to census. For example, the question on the mother tongue in the singular does not account for the case of simultaneous infant bilinguals who acquired two mother tongues. The answers from respondents are equally unreliable: they can be ambiguous or mistaken, and respondents may deliberately or unconsciously conceal their linguistic habits or language attitudes. Great care, therefore, should be taken when interpreting or using census data.

For all their flaws and shortcomings census data are nonetheless indispensable: they are the only data of this kind collected on a nationwide scale and at regular intervals, and within limits they enable us to describe patterns of language use in a population. The lack of linguistic census data, as in the case of Belgium where the linguistic questions have been prohibited since 1947, hampers research on language behaviour at the societal level.

Censuses also permit us to calculate changes in time and space in the patterns of language use, linguistic diversity, language maintenance and shift, assimilation and acculturation in ethnolinguistic communities. By comparing answers to questions on mother tongue and language use it is possible to calculate the assimilation rate of a group. To estimate language shift in a given population, Roy (1980) uses the following formula:

$$\frac{L_{MX} - L_{UX}}{L_{MX}} \times 100$$

where L_{MX} refers to the proportion of mother-tongue speakers of L_X and L_{UX} to the proportion of respondents who declare using L_X as their language of use in the home. For the Canadian province of New Brunswick she calculated that on the basis of the 1971 census the rate of assimilation to English by the population of French mother tongue was 7.7 ([34.0 − 31.4] / 34.0 × 100).

Another measure of societal bilingualism that has been developed on the basis of language-census data is the index of linguistic diversity. To measure the degree of intercommunication between different ethnolinguistic groups in a given community Greenberg (1956) calculated an index (H) of linguistic diversity on a continuum ranging from total lack of intercommunication to complete intercommunication; this index gives the probability that two members of a population taken at random share a common language. Using a refined index, Lieberson (1964) showed that the probability of one Algerian and one European living in the Algeria of 1948 sharing a common language, i.e. able to communicate with each other, was just over two in ten.

An extension of the Greenberg–Lieberson measure is Kuo's (1979) index of communicativity designed to calculate the potential of a particular language to act as a means of communication between two speakers in a given society. Whereas the former measures linguistic diversity or intercommunication regardless of the languages involved, Kuo's index evaluates the communication power of a given language. Taking Singapore in 1978 as an example, he shows that there are almost two chances in five that two randomly drawn adults would be able to communicate in English with each other. He also suggests that the index can measure the importance of a given language as a medium for intergroup communication.

It must be stressed that indices of linguistic assimilation, diversity and communicativity are mere statistical constructs which tell us little about real intergroup and interpersonal communication needs and practices in a multicultural setting. For a more detailed account of index measures on the basis of census data, see Fasold (1984).

1.2.3.2 Surveys

Surveys differ from censuses in that they are based on a sample of the total population and are specially designed to collect linguistic- and language-behaviour data. Although they inform us mostly on reported behaviour they sometimes include information on actual behaviour. The following are the most commonly used types of survey:

(a) geolinguistic surveys which describe the geographic distribution of languages and their variations in a given space; one example is The Linguistic Composition of the Nations of the World (Kloss & McConnell, 1974, in progress).

(b) linguistic atlases presenting in a cartographic and analytic form information stemming from censuses and geolinguistic surveys, such as the geographic atlas of the languages and ethnies of India by Breton (1976).

(c) ethnolinguistic studies of multilingual communities like, for example, the Survey of Language Use and Language Teaching in Eastern Africa (Polomé, 1982), which covers several countries, the various sociolinguistic surveys in Singapore (Andersen, 1985), or the Linguistic Minorities Project (The other languages of England, 1985), a survey conducted in selected urban areas of England.

(d) inquiries into language behaviour commissioned by governments in multilingual nations, such as the Royal Commission on Bilingualism and Biculturalism in Canada (1967–70) and the inquiry on the status of the French language in Quebec (Gendron, 1972).

Whether they deal with whole populations or large samples, the afore-mentioned techniques have their limitations in that they do not permit the use of sensitive instruments and refined quantification, such as numerous, precise and detailed questions or the recording of actual language behaviour in a great variety of situations. Other methodological approaches, such as socio-linguistic studies or the ethnography of communication, enable us to use more sophisticated measures and analysis, but because of the complexity of their use they are limited to small samples.

1.2.3.3 Sociolinguistic and ethnographic methods

Sociolinguists study language variation by examining the social distribution of the variants of a number of linguistic variables, as for example Labov's (1966) study of the covariation between the variants of a phonological variable and social class and stylistic variables. (For a critical review of sociolinguistic meth-odology see Wardhaugh, 1986.) These techniques, which have been developed for the study of intralingual variation, can be applied to the investigation of situations of language contact. However, to date very few studies have been carried out in multilingual communities; for an application of the methodo-logy to a multilingual context we refer to Labov (1978).

Another sociolinguistic approach is that of Le Page & Tabouret-Keller (1985) in their investigation of language use and attitudes in multilingual communities in Belize and St Lucia. In this field study they collected data on the language behaviour of children and their families by means of question-naires (reported behaviour) and recorded interviews (reported and actual be-haviour). As in the Labovian approach they correlate a number of linguistic variables with sociological ones; but, unlike Labov (1966), they do not use pre-established sociological categories; instead, they examine the covariation of social, cultural, social–psychological, etc., factors with language behaviour.

Finally, the methodology of the ethnography of communication observes small and well-defined multilingual communities in minute detail, calling upon anthropological techniques like participant observation of small groups. Many ethnographic studies limit themselves to case studies, as for example when language behaviour is observed in one single family. A detailed analysis of the ethnography of communication methodology is given in Saville-Troike (1982).

To sum up, although there exist numerous measures of collective bilingualism, most of these are still lacking in sophistication. They are restricted to the description of phenomena and give us only frequencies of occurrence of language variation for a given population. The main reason for this state of affairs is probably the lack of theoretical constructs that are predictive of the different forms taken by societal bilingualism.

1.3 Conclusion

In this chapter we have attempted to review critically some of the problems arising from the definitions and measurements of bilinguality and bilingualism. In a first part we distinguished between the individual and the societal level and defined the relevant dimensions of each. We pointed out the multi-dimensional character of these phenomena by calling successively on a variety of disciplines: psychology, psycholinguistics, etc. Bilingualism is a global phenomenon which involves simultaneously a psychological state of the individual and a situation of languages in contact at the interpersonal level and the collective level. A situation of languages in contact can occur at the societal level without implying the bilinguality of individuals, and conversely, individuals can be bilingual without the existence of collective bilingualism.

In a second part we gave an overview of several relevant measures either developed specifically, or adapted from more general social science methodologies, for the study of bilinguality and bilingualism. In our discussion of the measures of bilingual competence we made a distinction between those which reduced this competence to the sum of two monolingual ones and those attempting to evaluate the specificity of bilingual behaviour. We also emphasised the importance of using a variety of measures in order to capture a state of bilinguality. We drew attention to the problems created by the use of psychometric measures in the educational assessment of bilingual children from ethnolinguistic minorities. At the societal level we reviewed a variety of measures which can be used to describe a collective situation of languages in contact.

The main aim of the present chapter has been to draw the reader's attention to the difficulties inherent in the attempt to define and quantify languages in contact at all levels of analysis as well to the absence of adequate measures and the lack of refinement of existing ones. However, we have to use these measures, as they are the only ones available in the present state of the art. Even if some of the measures are still crude it is preferable to use them rather than to reject quantification altogether or to attempt to obtain precise measures with a rubber band. It is therefore in this critical frame of mind that the following chapters should be read.

2

The ontogenesis of bilinguality

Since the beginning of the century scholars from a variety of disciplinary backgrounds, such as psychologists, linguists, neurologists and educators, have paid attention to the development of bilinguality; in the past two decades, however, there has been a research explosion on the subject. During the first half of the century two types of studies were prominent: (a) carefully documented child biographies, such as those by Ronjat (1913) and Leopold (1939–49) and (b) comparative psychometric studies of school tests obtained from bilingual and monolingual children. Whereas the first biographies generally pointed to a harmonious development of the bilingual child, the early psychometric studies, such as for example the studies by Pinter & Keller (1922) and Saer (1923), indicated a developmental delay in bilingual children as compared with monolingual peers. This apparent contradiction and the so-called negative consequences of bilinguality will be further discussed in the section on the relationship between bilinguality and cognitive and sociocultural development.

These two types of approach are still used today; however, the present methodologies applied to the study of bilingual development are more sophisticated and employ more accurate techniques. For example, rather than simply describe the language development of young bilinguals, scholars attempt to analyse their language in terms of modern theoretical constructs in child language; bilingual development will be described according to developmental psycholinguistic aspects such as the acquisition of interrogation or negation. At the same time, more attention is paid to the control of factors like the socio-economic status of the subjects, their level of proficiency in the language used for testing or their degree of bilinguality. The lack of such controls invalidates the conclusions reached in the earlier studies, which attributed poor school results to the children's bilingual experience. Present-day psychometric studies are more careful in concluding to bilinguality as a cause of developmental outcome.

In this chapter we will review the present state of the art in the study of bilinguality, in terms of linguistic development, its neuropsychological foundations and its relation to the cognitive and sociocultural growth of the child; in particular, we shall attempt to assess the empirical evidence regarding the positive consequences of a bilingual experience for the child's cognitive development. In the next chapter we will propose a social psychological model of bilingual development.

As far as the linguistic development of the bilingual child is concerned, in the present chapter we will discuss only *early simultaneous bilinguality*, since it enables us to observe the consequences of the simultaneous acquisition of two languages (L_A and L_B) on the period of language development from birth to the age of 4/5 years. The linguistic aspects of *consecutive bilinguality* (L_1 and L_2) will be dealt with in Chapter 9.1 when we discuss the alleged analogy between mother-tongue and second-language acquisition. For the other aspects of bilingual development both simultaneous and early consecutive bilinguality will be examined in the present chapter.

The first description of the linguistic development of a bilingual child is that of the French psychologist Ronjat (1913), who made detailed records of his son Louis's language behaviour from birth to the age of 4;10 (four years and ten months); the Ronjats, who lived in Paris, were a mixed-lingual family in the sense that the father was a native speaker of French, the mother and the nanny native speakers of German. The family adhered to Grammont's Principle according to which each adult uses exclusively his or her mother tongue with the child. Ronjat's observations can be summarized as follows: a bilingual upbringing has no adverse effect on the child's overall development; the phonology, grammar and lexis of both languages develop in parallel; very early on the child becomes aware of the existence of two distinct linguistic codes and acts as interpreter; he rarely mixes the two languages and mixing tends to disappear as the child grows up; finally, far from delaying the cognitive development of the child, an early bilingual experience fosters a more abstract conception of language. Ronjat concludes that in a mixed-lingual family a child develops normally and in a harmonious way.

The most detailed biography of bilingual development is Leopold's (1939–49), in which the author describes the language acquisition of his daughters in a German–English mixed-lingual family where the one parent–one language rule was observed. His conclusions are in agreement with Ronjat's: there are no developmental or linguistic disadvantages; from the start of the acquisition of syntax, the morphology and vocabulary of both languages are separated; mixing is only occasional; soon after the age of three the child discriminates between the languages according to her interlocutor. Leopold also comments on some advantages of early bilinguality, such as a sustained attention for content rather than form and a greater capacity for dissociating the word from its referent. But the author remains imprecise as to his standards of comparison and his conclusions are sometimes difficult to justify on empirical grounds.

Whatever their merits such detailed biographies have their shortcomings (many more have been written since Leopold's; for a review of some case-studies of simultaneous bilingual acquisition, see McLaughlin, 1984): when the first observations were made there were no scientifically sound theoretical constructs on language development and child language was viewed as an impoverished imitation of adult language. Their contribution to the study of bilingual development is therefore limited to that of well-documented descriptive diaries and contains no information on the developmental psycholinguistic processes relevant to bilinguality. We had to wait until the sixties to witness a renewal of interest in the subject with a number of studies on bilingual development based on general theoretical models of language acquisition.

2.1 Bilinguistic development

The theoretical advances in the study of language acquisition since the sixties have resulted in novel approaches to the investigation of bilingual development. A number of scholars have examined certain specific linguistic dimensions of bilingual acquisition, in an attempt to answer some important questions, such as: Is it possible to distinguish stages in bilinguistic development? If so, how far do they coincide with the developmental stages of monolingual acquisition? Is the bilinguistic development delayed compared with the monolingual one? How do certain characteristics that are unique to bilingual behaviour like, for instance, code-mixing or loan blends develop? How far are the two linguistic systems differentiated (or not) in the early stage of language acquisition? These approaches, going far beyond the early biographical descriptions, enabled researchers to generate a number of hypotheses and assumptions concerning the development of bilinguality.

Although the majority of studies of bilinguality in the young child focus on speech production, a few investigators have looked at early perception. Eilers, Gavin & Oller (1982), for example, analysing the perception of phonemes by 4–8 month-old infants raised in bilingual (Spanish–English) or monolingual (English) environments, found that the former appeared to discriminate[1] better than the latter not only between English and Spanish phonemes, but also between the phonemes of English and those of Czech, a language to which they had never been exposed. The authors interpret these results as possible evidence that a richer linguistic input from the environment may foster a better development of the relevant skills, in this case phonemic discrimination. From a longitudinal observation of children from mixed-lingual families in Montreal, it also appears that infants at the prelinguistic stage, i.e. before the production of the first word, are capable of discriminating between the intonation patterns of French and English (Goodz, 1984, 1985). Thus it seems that an infant exposed to a bilingual environment may develop perceptual skills which will enable him to distinguish between his two languages. Whether this will later facilitate the separation of the two languages at the production stage remains a question to be explored.

2.1.1 Stages of bilinguistic development

Since Brown's (1973) pioneering work in developmental psycholinguistics in the late sixties, in which he identified successive stages[2] in the child's linguistic development, a number of attempts have been made to analyse bilinguistic development in terms of stages. In a longitudinal study of question forms produced by 2–4-year-old French–English children living in Quebec City Swain (1972) found that the formulation of polar questions (i.e. questions requiring a yes or no answer) followed an order of increasing complexity, irrespective of the language used: first intonation and the question tag *eh*[3] are used; the second to appear are special-purpose question morphemes, first *ti*[3] and then *est-ce-que*; in a third stage the constituents are rearranged in the utterance, e.g. inversion of verb and subject pronoun.

Analysing the evolution of negation in children acquiring simultaneously Spanish and English, Padilla & Lindholm (1976) observed that it followed the same pattern as the one proposed by Klima & Bellugi (1966) for monolingual English children. But this was not the case for the acquisition of wh-questions. Studying the acquisition of English grammatical morphemes by her daughter exposed from birth to Chichewa (a Bantu language) and English, Chimombo (1979) found no significant correlation between the order of their acquisition and the one observed by Brown (1973) for monolingual English children. More recent observations of bilinguistic development also analyse it in terms of stages, but these are no longer essentially related to models of grammatical development in one language. Rather they are concerned with identifying the specificity of bilingual acquisition.

2.1.2 Is there a lag in bilinguistic development?

Years ago Ronjat (1913) and Leopold (1939–49) raised the question of a possible delay in linguistic development induced by the exposure to two languages. Both concluded that there was no observable delay and that bilingual and monolingual acquisition followed the same pace. Comparing thirty-five bilingual children in Montreal with matched monolingual counterparts, Doyle, Champagne & Segalowitz (1977) observed that if the former produced their first word at the same age as the latter, other aspects of language acquisition appeared to follow different developmental curves. During their second year bilingual children seem to possess a less extended receptive vocabulary, as measured by the Peabody Picture Vocabulary Test (Dunn, 1959), than their monolingual counterparts but greater verbal fluency as measured by the Reynell Developmental Language Scales (Reynell, 1969).

Comparing the age of acquisition of polar questions by her bilingual subjects with that observed by Klima & Bellugi (1966) for monolingual English subjects and by Grégoire (1947) for monolingual French subjects, Swain (1972) noticed a delay in bilinguistic development: for example, *est-ce-que* is acquired at 3.2 years by bilingual compared with 2.6 for monolingual francophones; inversion in the English interrogative is acquired by the age of 3.8 by bilingual and at 3.2 by monolingual anglophones. Swain interprets this as characteristic of the bilinguistic development, since the child concentrates on specific aspects of its dual linguistic system, rather than as an overall delay in his linguistic development. Apparently conflicting evidence comes from a study by Padilla & Liebman (1975), who compared the data from three Spanish–English bilingual children aged between 1.5 and 2.2 with, on the one hand, monolingual Spanish data (Gonzáles, 1970), and on the other, monolingual English data (Brown, 1973). Calculating a MLU (mean length of utterance)[2] for Spanish, English and mixed utterances Padilla & Liebman conclude that there is no delay in the acquisition of the two languages.

These two sets of data, however, are only superficially contradictory. From an analysis of the available data on bilinguistic development it appears that certain aspects of linguistic development follow a monolingual pattern closely while others do not. Moreover, bilinguistic development is characterized not only by a possible lag but also by linguistic behaviour specific to the bilingual speaker, such as mixings and loan blends.

2.1.3 Linguistic mixing

When we refer to mixing in bilinguistic development we include the use of elements from language B in an utterance in language A (code-mixing) as well as the alternation between language A and language B in the same utterance (code-switching) (see Chapter 6.2). These elements may be lexical, syntactic or semantic. The notion of mixing is close to that of interference (see 1.2.1.5), that is, a deviation from the norm in each language due to familiarity with two languages. However, mixing is not necessarily a matter of interference but may be the expression of a strategy specific to the bilingual speaker. According to Grosjean (1985a) bilinguals use a bilingual speech mode with other bilinguals who share their languages and with whom they normally mix languages (code-switching, code-mixing and borrowing).

It would seem that mixing is an integral part of bilinguistic development. It is mentioned in almost all biographies and studies. The majority of mixings are lexical in nature, with nouns as the most frequently substituted words (e.g. *Dónde está la clock?* (Swain & Wesche, 1973; Cornejo, 1975; Lindholm & Padilla, 1978; Redlinger & Park, 1980). Many mixings are 'lexical reduplications' or 'spontaneous translations', as when a translation equivalent is supplied as a synonym (for example, *another one, un autre*); spontaneous translations would suggest that the child is aware of the mixing and is deliberately using it as a communication strategy, and when the situation requires, acts as an interpreter (Swain & Wesche, 1973). A phenomenon related to mixing is *loan blending*, that is borrowing a word from the lexicon of the other language and grammatically adapting it to the language used in the utterance, as e.g. the verb *mailer* used in a French utterance; in this example the French suffix *-er* is added to the English word *mail* in order to conform with French verb-formation rules. Mixing is not exclusively lexical but may also occur at other levels, as in the example *est-ce que you give it to her?* (Swain, 1972), where a French question morpheme precedes an English sentence.

Although probably all bilingual children mix codes, it must be noted that this mixing occurs with a low frequency: according to Swain & Wesche (1973), Lindholm & Padilla (1978) and Redlinger & Park (1980) only 2–4% of utterances of infant bilingual productions are mixings; they are always present in early bilingual speech but their frequency tends to decrease as the child grows older. What role mixing plays in bilinguistic acquisition is still very little known. According to Swain (1971) it is a manifestation of a creative process used in the acquisition of language. The child may use mixing either because he lacks the equivalent in the appropriate language or because the mixed utterance expresses the intended meaning more adequately. Goodz (1984) observed that language mixing in the child is related to the mixing produced by the parents: at the onset of the child's speech production parents will use every possible communication strategy, including mixing; at a later stage, however, they might revert to a separation between the languages, especially if they notice a lag in the production of one of the child's languages. Mixing raises the whole issue of differentiation between the two languages.

2.1.4 *Differentiation of linguistic systems*

At what point in their development do bilingual children use their two codes as separate systems? The evidence on this question seems to be contradictory. On the one hand Swain (1972) formulates the following hypothesis: the child first develops linguistic rules common to both languages which would then function as two codes of one language; the bilingual child must develop differentiation strategies which will enable him to distinguish between the two languages. She further suggests that the child develops a common system for rules shared by two languages and separate systems for specific rules. Lags in the acquisition of some linguistic rules are attributed to the fact that the bilingual child has to develop differentiation strategies. The less frequent use of language mixing as the child grows older would be a manifestation of his improved capacity to keep his two languages separate.

Volterra & Taeschner (1978; also Taeschner, 1983) suggest that increased differentiation between linguistic systems follows a number of stages specific to bilinguistic development. From a longitudinal observation of two children acquiring Italian and German between the ages of 1;2 and 3;6, they distinguish three stages. Stage 1 involves the acquisition of a unified lexical system including words from both languages with few translation equivalents. For example, a child first learned the Italian *occhiali*, which was associated with her father's glasses, and later the German, *Brille* associated with drawings by her mother, but in this first stage she would not use them as translation equivalents; although there is some evidence that the child is 'aware' that the two words are translation equivalents she will not 'use' them as such, but say one or the other according to the context. In Stage 2 the child differentiates between the lexical systems but applies the same syntactic rules to utterances in either language: for instance, she expressed possession with the genitive case (as in German) in both Italian and German, e.g. *Giula Buch*; *Lisa bicicletta*. In Stage 3 the child has attained full differentiation between the two systems; e.g. *Giula Buch*; *i capelli di Lisa*.

The existence of an early undifferentiated stage has been questioned by Padilla & Liebman (1975), who maintain that differentiation between the two systems is established at a much earlier age and that the child is capable of keeping the two phonological systems separate as soon as these develop. The data on prelinguistic phonetic discrimination (see above, p. 33) would add support to this view. According to Padilla & Liebman a unified but complementary lexicon does not necessarily imply an undifferentiated system: rather it might reflect the developing communicative strategies of the child who makes use of all the resources at his command.

The whole issue of whether or not bilinguistic development goes through an undifferentiated stage first cannot be resolved in the present state of our knowledge. Only some psycholinguistic aspects have so far been investigated with a very small number of subjects; from what we know of early language development it might also be expected that large individual differences will exist among children developing with two or more languages. Furthermore, most researchers have so far neglected other factors relevant to bilinguistic development, in particular the role played by the environmental linguistic input and by the interactional setting in which acquisition takes place, which vary greatly from one case to the other.

2.1.5 The role of linguistic context in bilinguistic development

A widespread notion among parents and educators interested in bilingual development is concerned with the separation of languages in terms of the adult models: the assumption is that separate contexts will enhance bilinguistic acquisition, whereas a mixed context will hinder acquisition and induce confu-

sion and interference. This assumption, also known as *Grammont's Principle*
(Grammont, 1902), implies that the home environment should introduce a
strict 'one language = one person' correspondence. This idea has been
adhered to by most bilingual-child biographers but there is no proof of its psycholinguistic reality. Ronjat (1913) adopted it at the instigation of Grammont
and considered it as a proven rule rather than as a hypothesis. The few studies
that have investigated its role did not find any support for it. Bain (1976) did
not observe any effect of the application of the Grammont Principle on the
cognitive functioning of bilingual children; Doyle, Champagne & Segalowitz
(1977), studying the impact of language mixing in mixed-lingual families on
the bilingual child's vocabulary, failed to find significant differences between
children whose parents followed the principle and those whose parents did not.
It seems that Grammont's Principle is not as strictly observed as parents pre-
tend: Goodz (1984) found that the observance of the principle was linked to
the stage of bilinguistic development reached by the child; when the situation
called for parental attention to formal features of language, the 'one parent–
one language correspondence' would be adhered to, but the parents would
relax the observance of the rule as the child's bilinguistic development
evolved.

Far more important for the development of bilinguality than Grammont's
Principle seem to be the role of social networks and the linguistic models they
provide the child. Arnberg (1984) has shown that it is not sufficient for a child
living in a mixed-lingual family to receive a speech input from one parent
only, especially if that parent's language is exogenous, i.e. not spoken as a first
language by the speech community. Only if the child has close contacts with
the community of his parent's language, by either making prolonged stays in
the parent's country of origin or interacting with peers speaking the exogenous
language in his environment, or both, will he be able to become a balanced bilingual. We will return to the importance of social networks for bilingual development in Chapter 3.2.

2.1.6 The role of social context in bilinguistic development

It must be borne in mind that at a very early age the bilinguistic environment
does not necessarily expose the child to similar linguistic experiences. Because
in most of the studies on bilinguistic acquisition the parents of the observed
children tended to keep to Grammont's Principle, the linguistic environment
in which both languages are acquired varies as a function of the social roles of
the adults around the child.

The importance of social interaction for bilinguistic development has been
stressed by Goodz (1984, 1985) in her studies of the differences between mater-
nal and paternal speech in the bilingual family. She distinguishes five stages in
the bilingual child's linguistic development in which parent–child interaction

plays a crucial role. In the first two Stages (1 and 2, covering the first year), during which the adults provide bilinguistic input, the child becomes capable of discriminating between the two languages and pays attention to their specific prosodic features. In Stage 3 parents respond to the child by repeating, recasting and expanding the child's utterences, often using both linguistic systems; semantic and pragmatic features are stressed rather than formal ones and this brings about a higher frequency of code-mixing. As the child develops his comprehension and production the parents make greater demands on the child with regard to formal aspects, thus accentuating differences between the languages (Stage 4). As the child becomes proficient in both languages parents once again adopt a more flexible attitude.

If, as the currently available evidence on bilinguistic development suggests, the bilingual child is capable of evolving strategies unique to his bilingual experience, it follows that this experience will have consequences for his cognitive growth. In 2.3 we will discuss the cognitive consequences of bilinguality, but we will first raise the question of the possible consequences of bilinguality for the child's neuropsychological development.

2.2 *Neuropsychological development of bilinguals*

Evidence from the neuropsychology of language suggests that bilinguals develop different neurological strategies of information processing according to their history and context of acquisition of both languages. Empirical evidence stemming from clinical work with polyglot aphasics[4] (see Chapter 4.4) has since the last century suggested that there might exist a cerebral organization specific to the bilingual (Minkowski, 1963). Numerous studies on polyglot aphasia (for a review see Paradis, 1978, 1983) point to the fact that loss of one language and its subsequent recovery occur in a different way from the loss and subsequent recovery of the other language. This evidence might suggest that there is a different cerebral organization for each of a bilingual's languages (Vaid & Lambert, 1979) and that the anatomical bases for the two languages only partially overlap (Vaid, 1983). It would however be dangerous to generalize from clinical evidence to normal behaviour and one must turn to the recent neuropsychological literature on bilingual brain organization to understand the bilingual's cerebral functioning.

Cerebral control of language behaviour is characterized by functional asymmetry,[5] which is a product of neuropsychological maturation. Cerebral lateralization develops in early childhood – most researchers agree that its first manifestations can be observed around 4–5 years – though the claim for some biological basis is well founded (Corballis, 1980). Generally speaking, the majority of the population has a dominant left hemisphere which exercises a contra-lateral control, i.e. on the right side of the body (most humans are right-handed) and also controls most of linguistic behaviour. Concordance between hemispheric dominance for motricity and for language is however not complete: whereas 96% of right-handers do have a left-hemispheric control for language, 70% of left-handers also have the language control centres in the left hemisphere (Milner, 1975). Right-hand preference is therefore a good indicator of left-hemispheric dominance for language, whereas left-hand preference is not.

The very notion of cerebral dominance must not be taken as absolute, but rather as a greater specialization of one or the other hemisphere for a given task. Bogen (1969), for example, describes the left hemisphere as logical, convergent, analytic, sequential and propositional[6] and the right hemisphere as intuitive, divergent, holistic, parallel and appositional.[6] At the same time, hemispheric specialization is not exclusive; each hemisphere may be capable of processing information in the other's typical mode (Witelson, 1977). Therefore, both hemispheres will have different degrees of involvement in information processing according to the nature of the linguistic task. Thus, one might expect that for the vast majority of the population the left hemisphere will have a greater involvement in linguistic information processing. The right hemisphere will also be involved to a limited extent: according to Schneiderman (1986), right-hemisphere participation in normal language acquisition is that of a limited, specialized role in the perception, retention and basic comprehension of new language stimuli; it also performs a complementary function in that it facilitates processing by the left hemisphere.

In the last two decades researchers in the neuropsychology of language have developed a number of methodologies and techniques in order to assess language hemispheric functioning and there has been a growing scientific literature on cerebral lateralization of language in bilinguals (for a review of methodological issues see Obler, Zatorre, Galloway & Vaid, 1982). Specific techniques most frequently referred to in this field are: (1) tachistoscopic techniques to present visual information to either the left or the right hemisphere (LH or RH); (2) the dichotic[7] listening technique to verify the dominance of one or the other hemisphere for auditory processing; (3) evoked potentials, an electro-encephalographic technique which measures the cortical activity of each hemisphere. It must be understood that because of the contra-lateral neurological connections of the human body right-ear advantage and right-visual field advantage correspond to left-hemispheric dominance. For reasons of clarity we will in this section refer only to the hemispheric dominance (LH or RH).

The literature on cerebral dominance in bilinguals is far from presenting a clear, unified picture of how they process language. Whereas most scholars agree that bilingual experience has some influence on brain functioning, they disagree on the nature of the neuropsychological consequences of this experience. Whereas some researchers contend that bilinguals and monolinguals are equally lateralized, many researchers suggest that bilinguals are more bilateral than monolinguals (Albert & Obler, 1978). However, whereas this might be the case for dominant bilinguals, there is also some evidence which shows that balanced infant bilinguals evince a greater lateralization (Shanon, 1982). It should come as no surprise, therefore, that in this field we have to deal with a large amount of apparently contradictory evidence; this state of uncertainty is to be attributed to the high number of factors influencing the functioning and development of neuropsychological processes. However, researchers are still capable of raising a number of relevant questions on the relation between bilinguality and brain functioning.

The vast majority of experimental studies on the neuropsychological functioning of bilinguals attempt to answer one or more of the following questions: (a) is the neuropsychological development of bilinguals different from that of monolinguals? (b) Do bilinguals process information in their different languages in a similar way or do they develop specific brain mechanisms for each of their languages? (c) Does the age of acquisition play a significant role in determining cerebral dominance in bilinguals? (d) Does the level of competence in the second language influence the hemispheric involvement in language processing? (e) Is the context of acquisition of and exposure to a second language relevant in determining the degree of lateralization? (f) What role do structural differences between languages play in determining the use of both hemispheres? (g) What effect does a difference in script between languages have on brain functioning in bilinguals?

2.2.1 Comparing bilinguals and monolinguals

A direct comparison between the neuropsychological functioning of bilinguals and monolinguals has been made in a number of studies. For example, Barton, Goodglass & Skai (1965) found no differences of lateralization between Hebrew–English bilinguals and English monolinguals responding to a tachistoscopic task of word-recognition presented in the right or the left visual field; both groups had a LH advantage. Tzeng, Hung, Cotton & Wang (1979) found that Chinese–English bilinguals and Chinese monolinguals had similar reaction times to a word-recognition task of English and Chinese words. No differences were found between English–Portuguese bilinguals and English monolinguals, who both showed a LH advantage (Soares & Grosjean, 1981). Simularly, Soares (1984) confirmed that there were no differences between bilinguals and monolinguals; their speech production was equally disrupted when a concurrent task interfered in the left hemisphere. In the same vein, Albanese (1985) found no difference in lateralization between L_1 and L_2 among French–English bilinguals, regardless of their levels of proficiency and the nature of the task. All these studies indicate that LH dominance for language, observed in monolinguals, is equally present in bilinguals.

However, some studies seem to contradict the previous conclusion. Walters

& Zatorre (1978) argue that bilinguals show a greater degree of heterogeneity in their hemispheric organization than monolinguals. Indeed a number of studies mention a greater RH involvement in bilinguals (e.g. F. W. Carroll, 1978a; Vaid & Lambert, 1979; Galloway, 1980; Sussman, Franklin & Simon, 1982). However, the studies mentioning a greater RH involvement and those showing no differences between bilinguals and monolinguals differ in terms of population characteristics such as age of onset of bilinguality and L_2 proficiency. This suggests that a number of factors which are likely to influence the cerebral organization of the bilingual have to be taken into account.

2.2.2 *Language-specific cerebral organization of bilinguals*

On the basis of their research in neuropsychology Penfield & Roberts (1959) put forward the hypothesis that one and the same cerebral mechanism is responsible for the processing of the bilingual's two languages. This hypothesis has been verified by Hamers & Lambert (1977), who concluded that the two hemispheres played a similar part in processing, regardless of the language. In their experiment balanced French–English bilinguals had to respond to a tachistoscopically presented language-recognition task; the results showed that the difference in processing of the two hemispheres is the same for the two languages. This finding was confirmed by Gordon (1980), who found no differences in lateralization for the two languages for English–Hebrew subjects responding to a dichotic listening task; a strong lateralization for one language is highly correlated with a strong lateralization for the other, regardless of the age of acquisition of L_2, the level of competence in L_2 and the uses of the two languages. His conclusion has, however, been challenged by a number of researchers who stress the relevance of the age of acquisition of bilinguality for cerebral organization.

2.2.3 *Age of acquisition of bilinguality and laterality*

The age of acquisition of bilinguality or of L_2 appears to be a relevant factor in the development of laterality which will also determine the relative role of the two hemispheres in verbal information processing. Generally speaking, cerebral dominance is more precocious when the child experiences enriching early stimulation (Bever, 1970; Geffner & Hochbert, 1971). Multilingual experience in early childhood seems to bring forward the onset of cerebral dominance. One study using a dichotic listening technique with 6-, 7- and 8-year-old Hebrew–French–English trilinguals showed that these children developed laterality earlier than English monolingual counterparts matched for socioeconomic background and intelligence (Starck, Genesee, Lambert & Seitz, 1977).

More important even than the speeding up of lateralization is the way bilingual experience will influence the relative importance of each hemisphere for verbal information processing. In one experiment conducted at McGill University (Genesee, Hamers, Lambert, Mononen, Seitz & Starck, 1978) evoked potentials were measured during a language-recognition task for three groups of balanced French–English bilinguals different in respect of age of acquisition (infant, childhood and adolescent bilinguality), but not in terms of their competence in both languages and their language use. The results showed that the three groups used different cerebral strategies and thus called on different neuropsychological mechanisms for a similar task: infant and childhood bilinguals relied more on LH processing than did adolescent bilinguals, who relied more heavily on RH. The authors interpreted these results as an indication that early bilinguals rely more on semantic strategies in verbal processing than late bilinguals.

This interpretation was confirmed by another experiment (Vaid & Lambert, 1979) in which early and late bilinguals had to process semantically congruent and incongruent[8] stimuli. F. W. Carroll (1978b), using dichotic measures with English–Spanish bilinguals with different language histories, also concluded that the age of bilingual experience was a crucial factor in determining the role played by the left hemisphere in language processing. Shanon (1982) also demonstrated that balanced bilinguals who had developed early childhood bilinguality were more LH dominant than fluent but not balanced bilinguals who had learned L_2 at a later age. From these experiments it can be argued not only that hemispheric processing depends on the task, but that the strategies of processing are neither the same for the different types of bilinguals nor controlled in the same way. For example, early bilinguals call upon both hemispheres for a semantic analysis (Vaid & Lambert, 1979) but they also prefer LH processing strategies to a strategy under the control of the right hemisphere (Genesee *et al.*, 1978).

These findings raise the question of the optimal age for L_2 learning: as bilingual experience at an early age may lead to a preference in processing strategies, L_2 learning might be different for children, adolescents and adults. The question of optimal age for L_2 learning will be further dealt with in Chapter 9.1.5.

Although generally speaking one might expect greater reliance on the left hemisphere among early than among late bilinguals, not all experiments conducted with early bilinguals point to a greater LH involvement. For example, in one of her experiments F. W. Carroll (1978a) found greater RH involvement in the processing of English by early Navajo–English bilinguals than by English monolinguals. However, her Navajo subjects, who were dominant in Navajo, did not show the same pattern in processing Navajo. Competence in the two languages will thus also play a role in determining the type of cerebral strategy bilinguals use.

2.2.4 Bilingual competence and hemispheric dominance

A differential use of the two hemispheres has been mentioned for L₁ and L₂ in
the scientific literature (for a review see Vaid, 1983). This observation and the
fact that L₁ and L₂ acquisitions occur in a different context prompted Galloway & Krashen (1980) to postulate the *stage hypothesis*: they suggested that
there is an intermediary stage at the beginning of the acquisition of L₂ during
which the right hemisphere might have greater involvement in language processing; as a consequence of an increased competence in L₂, cortical activity
during language processing might be shifted to the left hemisphere. In support
of this hypothesis Silverberg, Bentin, Gaziel, Obler & Albert (1979) found a
greater RH involvement in the acquisition of reading in L₂ for Hebrew-
speaking children who had learned English for only two years than for comparable children who had received four to six years of English instruction.
Obler (1981) suggests that non-fluent second-language learners will call upon
a common strategy in which they rely heavily on key words and 'guess' the
meaning from the linguistic and the non-linguistic context; intonation
patterns, which are processed by the right hemisphere, are part of this context.
Furthermore, learners in the beginning stages of L₂ acquisition may be more
exposed to drills and to formulaic language, the processing of which will involve the RH.

    The stage hypothesis, however, has received only limited support from other
studies. Schneiderman & Wesche (1980), using a dichotic listening technique
with anglophones learning French in a formal setting, found that although
lateralization was more pronounced for English than for French, there was no
increase in lateralization for the second language concomitant with an increased competence in that language. Galloway (1980) demonstrated that
Spanish-speaking Mexicans who learned English in an informal context had
the same LH dominance for Spanish and English; Rupp (1980) reported a
greater LH involvement for L₂ in Vietnamese children learning English; and so
did Rogers, Ten Houten, Kaplan & Gardiner (1977) with Hopi children
learning English. As Albanese (1985) points out, the stage hypothesis predicts
a large RH involvement at the beginning stage of learning L₂ and a decrease in
RH involvement with increasing proficiency, but this is unsupported by empirical evidence. So far, the stage hypothesis has received support only for learning
to read in L₂ (Vaid, 1983).

2.2.5 Hemispheric dominance and language acquisition context

The context in which L₂ is acquired may also influence the development of
laterality. According to Vaid (1983) there will be greater RH involvement in
L₂ as compared with L₁ if L₂ is learned informally; and conversely, there will
be greater LH involvement in L₂ than in L₁ if L₁ is learned formally. Although

a number of experiments support this statement (Albert & Obler, 1978; F. W. Carroll, 1980; Gordon, 1980) it may be oversimplified in the sense that the type of formal learning will also influence the hemispheric involvement. It is indeed possible that certain L_2 teaching methods may call for a greater LH involvement than others (Krashen, Seliger & Hartnett, 1974). Hartnett (1975), for example, demonstrated a greater LH processing in L_2 learned through a deductive method, but a greater RH involvement when an inductive method was used. Thus, even in formal learning hemispheric involvement may be influenced by the particular teaching methodology.

2.2.6 Language differences and lateralization

The assumption that structural differences between languages may involve both hemispheres to different degrees has also been advanced. One study (Rogers *et al.*, 1977) suggests that Hopi–English bilinguals make greater use of the right hemisphere in processing elements of Hopi than in processing English. They explain this by the fact that Hopi is an appositional[6] language which depends more on RH strategies. Whereas this conclusion is also supported by some studies with American Indian bilinguals (Hynd & Scott, 1980 and Scott, Hynd, Hunt & Weed, 1979 with Navajo–English bilinguals; Vocate, 1984 with Crow–English bilinguals), it is invalidated by other studies (F. W. Carroll, 1978a and Hynd, Teeter & Stewart, 1980 with Navajo–English bilinguals).

However, are these differences between hemispheric functioning really attributable to structural differences between languages, since in all these cases the language-learning experiences are dissimilar? For example, it is evident from the experiments by Rogers *et al.* (1977) and by Scott *et al.* (1979) that the experience with the two languages is very different indeed. It is impossible to attribute differences in laterality development to structural differences between languages unless one can control the conditions under which both languages are learned.

2.2.7 Script differences and cerebral dominance

In bilingual speakers whose languages differ in their degree of sound–symbol correspondence between the spoken and the written language, it may be hypothesized that different patterns of hemispheric functioning will occur. Generally speaking, it may be assumed that the more phonetic the script, the greater the LH involvement (Vaid, 1983). Sugishita, Iwata, Toyokura, Yoshioka & Yamada (1978) reported in Japanese commissurotomy patients a RH impairment for reading Japanese in kana (a syllabic script), while the ability to read in kanji (an ideographic script), which is supposedly controlled by the left hemisphere, remained intact. Hemispheric differences between processing of kana and kanji scripts have also been observed in normal Japanese subjects in studies using evoked potential measures (Hink, Kaga & Suzuki, 1980) and in tachistoscopic studies (Endo, Shimizu & Hori, 1978). These demonstrated a LH superiority for the kana script and a RH superiority for the kanji script. These findings were also confirmed in a study by Hatta, 1981. RH involvement has also been reported for Chinese script (Vaid, 1983; Hasuike, Tzeng & Hung, 1986). RH superiority in Japanese and Chinese subjects applies only in the case of written material, as LH superiority is reported in dichotic studies with Japanese and Chinese monolinguals (Bryson, Mononen & Yu, 1980).

Differences in modes of writing must affect semantic organization, as for example the difference between a phonetic and an ideographic script, in order for these differences to impinge on brain functioning. More surface differences, like the opposite directionality of two phonetic scripts, do not seem to lead to different processing strategies. This is confirmed by a number of studies with written Yiddish and English (Mishkin & Forgays, 1952; Orbach, 1953), with written Hebrew and English (Barton, Goodglass & Skai, 1965; Gaziel, Obler & Albert, 1978; Shanon, 1982), and with Urdu and Hindi (Vaid, 1983), which all reported a similar LH laterality for both languages. Although there may exist a small scanning effect on cerebral processing, it is overridden by other factors.

If the whole body of literature on lateralization in bilinguals does not entitle us to draw a unified picture of their brain functioning, it nonetheless appears that age of bilinguality and childhood experience in learning different languages are relevant factors in determining hemispheric preferences. Herbert (1982) proposed the following explanation for the higher degree of bi-lateralization of bilinguals mentioned in a number of studies (see Albert & Obler, 1978 for a review): according to Corballis & Morgan (1978) the right hemisphere would be more involved in delayed acquisition; because of the de-lay in maturation between both hemispheres, the left one being slightly ahead and predisposed for language acquisition, early language acquisition should rely essentially on the left hemisphere; in the case of late language acquisition, the difference in maturation between both hemispheres would be lessened and a greater RH involvement would be possible. This interpretation would account for the evidence mentioning greater RH processing. Most studies on the processing of bilinguals deal with consecutive, dominant bilinguals; the few studies referring to early, balanced bilinguals mentioned greater LH pro-cessing (Genesee *et al.*, 1978) and a more pronounced laterality (Shanon, 1982).

Cognitive strategies that are used in the analysis of verbal material and de-termine the role of each hemisphere are dependent on early language experi-ences. While it is not evident that structural differences between languages lead to differential functioning, different types of script used for the written mode appear to call on different strategies. This means that bilinguals biliterate in two languages using different scripts will call upon different strategies in each of their languages. Even if no clear picture of bilingual brain functioning emerges, the knowledge that early language experience will shape informa- tion-processing strategies in later life has important implications for language- teaching methodologists, for parents who want to raise their children in more than one language and for educators who have to introduce children to liter- acy in a language other than the mother tongue.

2.3 Bilinguality and cognitive development

The relation between bilinguality and cognitive development has only recently been the object of scientifically sound and rigorous investigation. This relation must be viewed in the wider framework of the relationship between language and thought in contemporary theories of behaviour. Whether one considers that language plays an important role in the development of thought or whether both are seen as developing independently from each other will in- fluence the extent to which bilinguality is considered as a relevant factor for the development of cognitive processes.

For Vygotsky (1962) language plays an essential role in cognitive develop- ment, at least from the time the child has attained a certain level of language competence. Language, first developed as a means of social communication, is later internalized and becomes a crucial tool in the shaping of cognitive pro- cesses relevant for the elaboration of the abstract symbolic system which will enable the child to organize thought. In the same vein, Bruner (1975a) pro- poses that the child develops conceptual–linguistic abilities; language comes to play an increasingly powerful role as an implement for knowing; language per- mits productive, combinatorial operations in the absence of what is repre- sented (Bruner, 1973b). According to Vygotsky (1962), being able to express the same thought in different languages will enable 'the child to see his language as one particular system among many, to view its phenomena under more general categories, and this leads to awareness of his linguistic opera- tions' (p. 110). Viewing bilinguality in this framework of metalinguistic awareness, Segalowitz (1977) suggests that the internalization of two languages rather than one will result in a more complex, better-equipped 'mental calculus' enabling the child to alternate between two systems of rules in the manipulation of symbols. Analysing the cognitive nature of metalinguis- tic awareness Bialystok & Ryan (1985a) argue that bilingual children may have a greater cognitive control in information processing and that this pro- vides them with the necessary foundation for metalinguistic ability. However, before we discuss any further the role of metalinguistic competence in bilin- guality and propose a theoretical model of bilinguality (see Chapter 3) we will first review the existing empirical evidence.

It is against this general theoretical background that we must try to interpret the empirical evidence on the cognitive correlates of bilingual development. If, as Macnamara (1970) suggests, bilinguality does not 'have any effect upon the development of the basic, common, cognitive structures' (p. 33), then it becomes irrelevant to raise questions about the intellectual functioning of the bilingual (Cummins, 1973). If, on the other hand, we adopt the theoretical stand that language development and cognitive growth are intimately connected, then we must determine how relevant bilingual development is for intellectual growth and account for the empirical evidence concerning the cognitive development of the bilingual child.

2.3.1 *Early studies*

The early studies on the relation between bilinguality and cognitive development, sometimes undertaken in order to demonstrate the negative consequences of bilingual development, supported the idea that bilingual children suffered from academic retardation, had a lower IQ and were socially maladjusted as compared with monolingual children. Suffice it to mention the studies by Pintner & Keller (1922), who reported a 'linguistic handicap' in bilingual children, and Saer (1923), who spoke of 'mental confusion' to describe the bilingual's cognitive functioning. For a critical review of these early studies we refer the reader to Darcy (1953) and Peal & Lambert (1962).

One tentative explanation of the early research results is that of Macnamara (1966), who attributes the lag in verbal intelligence on the part of bilinguals to a 'balance effect'. According to him proficiency in L_1 diminishes as proficiency in L_2 increases, so that the sum of the two linguistic proficiencies cannot be superior to the monolingual's proficiency. This construct postulates that all bilingual development leads to a diminished functioning in the two languages. It does not account for the fact that many bilingual children achieve a high level of competence in both languages and can, as we shall see later in this chapter, surpass their monolingual counterparts in each language.

A number of methodological criticisms may be levelled at these early studies: the bilingual subjects were often not comparable with the monolingual controls in terms of socio-economic background or proficiency in the language of testing; the very notion of bilinguality was not adequately defined and tests were often administered in the subjects' weaker language. These variables have been better controlled in more recent studies which make use of more elaborate experimental designs.

2.3.2 *The relation of bilinguality to intelligence*

In an early experiment (Arsenian, 1937), which controlled for age, sex, socio-economic group and measurement of bilingualism, no negative correlation was found between bilinguality and intelligence for American-born Jewish children. But one had to wait until the late fifties in order to come across the first of a series of rigorous experimental studies. Peal & Lambert (1962), comparing English–French bilingual elementary-school pupils in Montreal with their monolingual counterparts in each language, found that the former scored higher on tests of verbal and non-verbal intelligence. Besides matching the groups for age, sex and socio-economic level, the authors also controlled them for language proficiency: they calculated a 'balance score' on the basis of tests of vocabulary and association as well as a self-evaluation scale in the two languages; bilingual subjects had to achieve high scores in both languages in order to qualify, whereas monolinguals had to have very low scores on one of the languages. The bilingual group scored significantly higher than the monolinguals controls for most of the measures. Peal & Lambert suggested that the higher scores of the bilinguals on intelligence measures could be attributed to greater mental flexibility and a greater facility in concept formation; they attributed this to their ability to manipulate two symbolic systems and thus analyse underlying semantic features in greater detail.

Ronjat (1913) and Leopold (1939–49) had already drawn attention to the bilingual child's cognitive and verbal flexibility without being precise about its nature. However, since the Peal & Lambert study numerous empirical studies in different countries and with different language combinations have detailed the various aspects of the cognitive advantages of the bilingual child; greater ability in reconstructing perceptual situations (Balkan, 1970, with French–English bilinguals); superior results on verbal and non-verbal intelligence, verbal originality and verbal divergence tests (Cummins & Gulutsan, 1974, with English–Ukrainian bilinguals in Western Canada); a greater sensitivity to semantic relations between words (Ianco-Worrall, 1972, with English–Afrikaans bilinguals; Cummins, 1978 with English–Irish bilinguals); higher scores on Piagetian concept-formation tasks (Liedtke & Nelson, 1968, with English–German bilinguals); and better performance in rule-discovery tasks (Bain, 1975, with English–French bilinguals in Western Canada; Bain & Yu, 1978, with French–Alsatian bilinguals in France, German–English bilinguals in Germany and English–French Canadian bilinguals in Germany).

Bilinguals also show a greater degree of divergent thinking (Scott, 1973, with French–English bilinguals in Montreal; Carringer, 1974 with English–Spanish bilinguals). In the same vein, Torrance, Gowan, Wu & Aliotti (1970) found Chinese–English bilingual children in Singapore to be superior to monolinguals on originality and elaboration tests of the Torrance Test of Creative Thinking. Gorrell, Bregman, McAllistair & Lipscombe (1982) found that Spanish–English and Vietnamese–English bilinguals outdid monolinguals on traditional psychometric school tests (WISC-R Block Design). Ben-Zeev (1972; 1977a) observed that English–Hebrew bilinguals had a greater facility in solving non-verbal perceptual tasks and in performing grouping tasks. Bilinguals are also better in verbal-transformation and symbol-substitution tasks (Ekstrand, 1980, with Swedish–Finnish bilinguals). To sum up, the cognitive advantages linked to bilingual experience seems to be mainly at the level of a higher creativity and reorganization of information. Further, some recent research indicates that the cognitive advantages of bilinguality might extend to non-verbal tasks; Powers & López (1985), for example, observed that 4-year-old bilinguals outperform monolinguals not only in following complex instructions but also in perceptual–motor coordination.

These observations have been confirmed by a number of more recent studies of bilingual children who speak various combinations of Indo-European and non-Indo-European languages in Third World as well as Western countries. Whereas there are some indications that creativity differences between bilinguals and monolinguals might be universal and thus attributable essentially to the child's bilingual experience, some aspects of creativity seem to be influenced by cultural particularities. Okoh (1980), comparing the development of bilingual children in Nigeria (bilingual in Yoruba and English) and Wales (Welsh–English) with matched monolinguals in both countries, found that the bilinguals, aged 9–11, generally scored higher on measures of divergent thinking and verbal creativity, but that on non-verbal creativity tests the Welsh bilinguals scored significantly higher than the Nigerian bilinguals, who did not differ from the monolinguals. Cultural variations in the type of cognitive tasks on which bilinguals show an advantage have also been noted in a study comparing Spanish–English and Vietnamese–English bilinguals (Gorrell *et al.*, 1982).

Okoh's conclusions that bilingual children may be potentially more creative than monolinguals are supported by experiments in India, conducted with bilingual and monolingual children from the same tribal cultural background. Kond bilingual children in the State of Orissa, speaking Kui (a Dravidian tribal language) and Oriya (the Indo-European State language) scored significantly higher than matched Kond children monolingual in Oriya on measures of metalinguistic ability, Raven's Progressive Matrices and Piagetian conservation (Mohanty & Babu, 1983; Pattnaik & Mohanty, 1984). Furthermore, the bilinguals were also better at detecting syntactic ambiguity (Babu, 1984). The authors interpret these results as a manifestation of a higher metalinguistic ability and cognitive flexibility developed by the bilinguals; thus, bilingual experience may result in the development of a greater ability to reflect on language.

Several authors have demonstrated that even when bilinguals and monolinguals are equated for cognitive functioning, the former may possess better verbal abilities. A number of studies already mentioned (e.g., Ben-Zeev, 1972, 1977a; Okoh, 1980; Mohanty & Babu, 1983; Babu, 1984; Pattnaik & Mohanty, 1984) report bilinguals as being superior in a variety of verbal tasks: analytic processing of verbal input; verbal creativity; awareness of the arbitrariness of language and of the relation between words, referent and meaning;

and perception of linguistic ambiguity. Evidence from studies of bilingual education by immersion also point in the same direction: bilingual pupils achieve better results than their monolingual counterparts in tests of complex syntactic structure and in mother-tongue composition (Swain & Lapkin, 1982); they are better in mother-tongue syntax (Tremaine, 1975) and a variety of other linguistic measures (Barik & Swain, 1978); they are also more adept at analysing structural ambiguity (Cummins & Mulcahy, 1978). In a similar vein, Kessler & Quinn (1982, 1987) reported that bilingual children performed better on problem-solving tasks than their monolingual counterparts; they interpret these results as evidence of greater metalinguistic competence and better-developed creative processes.

However, not all recent studies report a cognitive advantage associated with bilinguality. A few mention an intellectual handicap. Tsushima & Hogan (1975) found lower scores on tests of verbal ability among 10–11-year-old Japanese–English bilinguals than among monolinguals matched for non-verbal intelligence. In a UNESCO investigation in Sweden Skutnabb-Kangas & Toukomaa (1976) found that Finnish migrant children, of average non-verbal IQ, attending Swedish comprehensive schools, were considerably below Finnish and Swedish norms in their literacy skills in L_1 and L_2. They further observed that those children who migrated at age 10 achieved a level in both languages fairly comparable to those norms, whereas children who migrated at an earlier age did not. They also found that the extent to which the mother tongue was developed prior to migration was related to achievement in both languages; from these findings they postulated that competence in the mother tongue had to be sufficiently established before the child could successfully acquire a second language.

Negative effects of bilingual development have also been reported together with positive results for the same children, according to the type of task they are asked to perform. Ben-Zeev (1977b) found that while Spanish–English bilingual children showed some delay in terms of vocabulary and grammatical structure when compared with monolingual English-speaking peers, at the same time they were better at verbal transformations, analysis of structural complexity, classification and non-verbal tasks requiring perceptual analysis. It must be noted that those studies mentioning negative effects cannot be faulted on the ground of methodological weakness; for this reason we must find an explanation which takes into account the negative as well as the positive consequences of early bilingual experience. In other words, we must inquire into the nature of the advantages and disadvantages linked to bilinguality.

2.3.3 *The nature of the bilingual's cognitive advantages*

Most of the studies reporting the positive consequences of bilingual experience also report that bilinguals seem to develop a higher awareness of the arbitrary nature of the linguistic sign. Genesee (1981b) suggests that this increased capacity of the bilingual for dissociating a signifier from its signified could be a manifestation of a more general cognitive ability to analyse the underlying conceptual characteristics in information processing. This conclusion might however be premature. The empirical evidence on the cognitive development of bilinguals is far from giving us a complete picture of those cognitive aspects that might benefit from a bilingual experience. It is reasonable to assume that not all thought processes are enhanced by bilingual experience and that those cognitive tasks which rely more on language will benefit most from that experience.

Ben-Zeev (1977a) has put forward the following hypothesis concerning the cognitive advantages accruing from an early bilingual experience: it would seem that the bilingual child develops a strategy for analysing the linguistic input which enables him to overcome the potential interference arising from a bilingual environment. She distinguishes four mechanisms for resolving interference at the structural level of language: (1) a greater capacity for language analysis; (2) sensitivity to feedback cues from surface linguistic structure and/or verbal and situational context; (3) maximization of structural differences between languages; and (4) neutralization of structure within a language. These four mechanisms, developed in the first place to respond to a bilingual environment, will be generalized to other information-processing tasks and will thus benefit the overall cognitive growth of the child.

Negative consequences of bilingual experience have been described in terms of a cognitive deficit. The notion of 'semilingualism' has been used to describe the child who fails to reach monolingual proficiency in literacy skills in any language and might be unable to develop his linguistic potential (Skutnabb-Kangas & Toukomaa, 1976). 'Semilingualism' is defined as a linguistic handicap which prevents the individual from acquiring the linguistic skills appropriate to his linguistic potential in any of his languages. It does not imply failure to communicate in ordinary everyday situations, since children labelled as 'semilingual' are judged to be quite fluent; but this fluency is alleged to be only superficial and to mask a deficit in the knowledge of the structure of both languages.

The use of 'semilingualism' as an explanatory device has been criticized on the following grounds: first, the notion is ill-defined; 'linguistic potential' is unexplained; in addition, the deficit is measured only by comparison with standardized norms obtained through traditional psychometric tests and academic results (Brent-Palmer, 1979). From these, no conclusion can be drawn as to the existence of a linguistic/cognitive deficit; rather, there is enough counterevidence which suggests that sociocultural factors are responsible for poor normative linguistic achievement and scholastic results (Troike, 1984). Many immigrant groups who also come from a different cultural background, but who do not have to face depressed socio-economic conditions, perform linguistically and cognitively at least as well as monolinguals. As Troike (1984) points out, if a linguistic handicap resulting from bilingual experience were responsible for poor results on linguistic tests and academic tasks, then the Hispanic Americans, who are socio-economically more deprived than the White Americans from Anglo-Celtic background but less so than the Black Americans, should perform worse on language tests than both these mono-lingual groups; this is however not the case: the Hispanics perform worse than the Whites but better than the Blacks. It becomes difficult, then, to implicate language proficiency alone as an explanatory factor for poor performance (for a further discussion, see Chapter 8.5).

Cummins (1976, 1979, 1981) attempted to explain the contradictory posit-ive and negative results in the following way: One has to assume, first, a *de-velopmental interdependence hypothesis* and, second, a minimal *threshold of linguistic competence hypothesis*. The first hypothesis suggests that competence in a second language is a function of competence in the mother tongue, at least at the be-ginning of exposure to the second language. The threshold hypothesis implies that a first-language competence threshold has to be crossed in order to avoid cognitive deficit linked to childhood bilinguality and that a second-language competence threshold must be passed if bilinguality is to positively influence cognitive functioning. This is schematized in Figure 2.1.

According to Cummins the twofold threshold hypothesis explains the apparently contradictory results from the different studies. The first threshold must be reached in order to avoid an intellectual handicap as a consequence of childhood bilingual experience; if this lower threshold is not attained, a below-

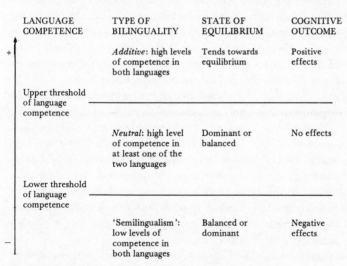

Figure 2.1 Cognitive effects of different types of bilinguality (adapted from Cummins, 1979, 230)

normal level of competence in both languages might result. Above the first threshold and below the second a handicap will be avoided. But it is only when the second threshold is passed that bilingual experience can have a positive effect on cognitive processing and that competence in both languages tends towards balance. Empirical evidence in support of this construct is given in a number of studies. For example, Duncan & De Avila (1979) found that Hispanic minority schoolchildren in the USA who had developed high levels of proficiency in L_1 and L_2 performed significantly better than monolinguals and other non-proficient bilinguals from the same cultural sample on cognitive tasks. Similarly Hakuta & Diaz (1984) found that fluent bilinguals performed better on cognitive tasks than their non-fluent counterparts. The levels of language competence cannot be determined in absolute terms, rather they 'vary according to the children's stage of cognitive development and the academic demands of different stages of schooling' (Cummins, 1979, 230). The level of language competence seems to act as an intervening variable and play a crucial role in determining the effect of bilingual experience on future cognitive development.

Cummins's other hypothesis, that of developmental interdependence, postulates that the level of competence in L_2 is partly a function of the competence developed in L_1 at the start of exposure to L_2. When certain language functions[9] are sufficiently developed in L_1 it is likely that massive exposure to L_2 will lead to a good competence in L_2 without detriment to competence in L_1. A high level of competence in L_1 is thus related to a high level of competence in L_2. In support of this hypothesis Cummins (1984a) reports, for example, on the Carpinteria Spanish-language preschool program in California: Spanish-speaking preschool children who scored much lower on a school readiness test compared with English-speaking peers were exposed to a variety of language-enriching experiences in their mother tongue; at elementary school entry these children outperformed Spanish-speaking controls in both English and Spanish and compared favourably with English controls on readiness skills.

Although Cummins did not develop the idea that the interdependence is bidirectional, there is empirical support in favour of this from a study of Swedish children learning English as a second language in Sweden (Holmstrand, 1979): it was found that elementary-school children who already had a high competence in their mother tongue and who started to learn a foreign language at an early age would improve their competence in mother tongue more than peers who did not have exposure to a foreign language. This evidence suggests that the interdependence hypothesis works in both directions and that language training in one language might be helpful for attaining a higher level of competence in the other language.

According to Cummins (1984a), instruction that develops first-language literacy skills is not just developing these skills, it is also developing a deeper conceptual and linguistic competence that is strongly related to the development of general literacy and academic skills. In other words, there is a common cognitive proficiency underlying behaviour in both languages. The interdependence or common underlying proficiency principle implies therefore that experience with either language can promote development of language-cognitive skills, given proper motivation and exposure to both languages.

But what does Cummins mean by language proficiency? It is conceptualized in such a way that the developmental interrelationships between academic performance and language proficiency in both L_1 and L_2 can be explained (Cummins, 1984b). Note that this model is proposed only in relation to the development of academic skills in bilingual education and is not necessarily appropriate to other skills and other contexts of bilingual development. The author suggests that cognitive academic proficiency can be conceptualized along two independent continua: the first relates to the degree of contextual support available for expressing and receiving meaning (from context-embedded to context-reduced); the second refers to the degree of cognitive involvement in the verbal activity (from cognitively undemanding to cognitively demanding). Thus, a verbal task may be cognitively demanding or not and, at the same time, be more or less context-embedded. Many of the linguistic demands of the school rely on context-reduced and cognitively demanding language behaviour. Most of the studies reporting negative consequences of early bilingual experience are concerned with measures of context-reduced and cognitively demanding behaviour of children who may not have developed the necessary underlying proficiency.

In other words, when bilingual development does not result in cognitive advantages it is always in cases where the children did not possess the skills prerequisite for literacy. It might well be that here we are dealing with a literacy or a metalinguistic problem, not a linguistic competence threshold: metalinguistic awareness is different from ordinary linguistic communication in the sense that it calls on different cognitive skills, and bilingual children differ from monolingual children on literacy and metalinguistic tasks (Bialystok & Ryan, 1985a, 1985b). This issue will be further discussed in Chapter 3.1.8.

Cummins's model is relevant in so far as it attempts to explain apparently contradictory evidence; it is also useful in providing a model for bilingual education (see Chapter 8.5). However, it lacks explanatory adequacy. On the one hand, it remains silent on the issue of simultaneous bilinguistic development and its cognitive correlates. On the other hand, it fails to explain why some children attain the upper threshold, while others never reach the lower one. It may also be an oversimplification to define the threshold levels on the basis of purely language criteria (McLaughlin, 1984). Furthermore, Cummins is vague about his definition of a cognitively demanding task. Finally, cognitive development is also influenced by sociocultural factors apart from language (Hamers & Blanc, 1983).

2.4   The sociocultural context of bilinguality

Lambert (1974, 1977) suggests that the roots of bilinguality are to be found in several aspects of the social psychological mechanisms involved in language behaviour, particularly in the relative social status of both languages and in its perception by the individual. He was the first to draw attention to the fact that different types of bilinguality may result according to the sociocultural context in which bilingual experience occurs. He distinguishes between an *additive* and a *subtractive* form of bilinguality. In its additive form bilingual development is such that both languages and both cultures will bring complementary positive elements to the child's overall development; this situation is found when both the community and the family attribute positive values to the two languages; the learning of an L_2 will in no case threaten to replace L_1.

Subtractive bilinguality, on the other hand, develops when the two languages are competing rather than complementary; this form will evolve when an ethnolinguistic minority rejects its own cultural values in favour of those of an economically and culturally more prestigious group. In this case, the more prestigious L_2 will tend to replace L_1 in the child's repertoire. This happens, for example, when a minority child is schooled through an L_2 socially more prestigious than his own mother tongue. The degree of bilinguality will 'reflect some stage in the subtraction of the ethnic language and the associated culture, and their replacement with another' (Lambert, 1977, 19). This subtraction will manifest itself at several levels and will influence intellectual development and personality; language competence which first developed via the mother tongue will be affected.

Lambert's views explain why a cognitive advantage linked to bilingual experience is found primarily either among bilingual children from mixed-lingual families or among children from a dominant social group who receive their schooling through the medium of a less prestigious L_2, while the subtractive form is met among children from ethnolinguistic minorities schooled through a dominant, more prestigious L_2. In the additive case, the two languages receive important positive values from the community and consequently from the child himself, whereas in the subtractive condition L_1 is little valorized compared with L_2. Lambert's model insists on the role played by the sociocultural environment in the development of bilinguality. It accords with a more general view of child development: for Bruner (1966) the cultural environment plays a major role in the child's growth once the symbolic stage is reached; culture then serves as a catalyst for cognitive growth.[10] It is therefore crucial to focus on the cultural environment in which bilingual development occurs and to understand its role in the development of bilinguality.

By pointing out the relevance of the sociocultural environment Lambert stresses the role played by social psychological mechanisms in the development of bilinguality, particularly those involved in the internalization of societal values (this will be further discussed in Chapter 5.2). Lambert also introduces the notion of an interdependence hypothesis, but at the level of the internalization of social cultural values and language statuses: it is the relative status between the two languages and its internalization that will determine the nature of bilinguality.

There is ample empirical evidence to support the sociocultural interdependence hypothesis. For example, Long & Padilla (1970) and Bhatnagar (1980) demonstrated that pupils obtained superior academic results when their low-status L_1 was valorized and fully used in the home than when L_1 was neglected in the home in favour of L_2. Similarly, Dubé & Herbert (1975) found that school results and language proficiency in both languages improved when the mother tongue was valorized and used in the school system. There is also ample evidence, stemming from research on immersion programs (see Chapter 8.4.2) that when a child is a member of a dominant ethnolinguistic group, for whom L_1 is valorized in the community, schooling through the medium of L_2 may be a way to develop high bilinguistic skills, possibly with positive cognitive effects.

However, Lambert's approach is based essentially on correlational evidence; his theoretical construct lacks explanatory adequacy in respect of developmental processes and the development of the social psychological mechanisms involved in shaping cognitive growth. The equation 'bilinguality = cognitive advantage' or 'bilinguality = cognitive deficit' may be too simple. Both equations are possible: under the right conditions bilingual experience may have positive effects on cognitive processes; under adverse social cultural conditions bilingual experience may hinder cognitive growth. We still know very little about the social psychological mechanisms that will intervene between the social cultural environment and intellectual functioning. Lambert's model draws attention to the existence of a relationship but it does not explain how this relationship develops.

The identification of all the conditions that are favourable to an additive form of bilinguality is still a long way off. If it seems that these conditions are dependent on the relative status of each language in the child's environment, to what extent is the child's perception of these social factors more important than the factors themselves? To what extent can an additive form of bilinguality develop in a subtractive context? In other words, how determining is the sociocultural context for the outcome of bilinguality and how far can the individual develop strategies and social psychological mechanisms that can modify the influence of the social context? Further research is needed on the causal link between social psychological roots of bilinguality and their cognitive outcome; that is to say, all the environmental factors which enable the child to reach the competence necessary for developing additive bilinguality have to be identified. Finally, we still lack an adequate theoretical model that can take into account social and individual factors and attempt to explain their causal relationship.

2.5 Conclusion

In this chapter we have attempted to present the different facets of bilingual development, by looking at its linguistic manifestations, its neuropsychological functioning and its cognitive consequences. Several questions were raised about bilinguistic development. Are there stages in bilinguistic development? Is there a lag in this development compared with that of the monolingual child? Are the two linguistic systems differentiated and what is the role of linguistic mixing? How relevant are the linguistic and social contexts in bilinguistic development? Next, we analysed the neuropsychological aspects of bilingual development. How does the bilingual brain function compared with the monolingual brain? How does the age of onset of bilinguality and bilingual competence impinge on laterality for language? Does the context of language acquisition influence hemispheric dominance? Do language and script differences affect language lateralization? Finally, we inquired into the cognitive consequences of bilingual experience. What is the relation between bilinguality and intelligence? Are there any cognitive advantages or disadvantages to early bilinguality and what is their nature?

The answers to these questions, as we have seen, are still vague and partial. The empirical evidence is often contradictory, and few theoretical constructs are sufficiently developed to account for these contradictions. Models are very often incomplete and at this stage are more descriptive than explanatory. A number of methodological questions can also be raised about the empirical evidence itself: abusive generalizations from limited or biased data base, e.g. one or few children; vague definition of degree of bilinguality and lack of control of bilingual experience; lack of control of co-varying factors; validity of measures; confusion of independent and dependent variables, which raises the issue of the direction of causality. This last problem, for instance, has been discussed by McNab (1979). She argues that there is no evidence that becoming bilingual leads to cognitive advancement because, by selecting balanced bilingual subjects, one might introduce a bias in favour of more intelligent children, and that non-balanced children might score lower on cognitive functioning measures to begin with. This criticism has been recently countered by improvements in statistical methodology which allow for testing of alternative causal models. Hakuta & Diaz (1984) in their study of Spanish-dominant bilingual children found that more balanced children scored higher on non-verbal intelligence tests; a stepwise multiple regression analysis enabled them to demonstrate that the model which claims that degree of bilingualism affects non-verbal intelligence fits the data better than the model claiming the reverse directionality.

In spite of some methodological shortcomings, which should and can be overcome as the most recent research demonstrates, an empirical approach is the only way to go on unravelling the complexities of bilingual development. Only a large body of sound experimental data will enable scholars to perfect the necessary theoretical constructs, thus giving us a better insight into the ontogenesis of bilinguality.

3

The social and psychological
foundations of bilinguality

In the present chapter we propose a theoretical approach to bilingual development which attempts to take into account the many dimensions of bilinguality. Such a framework must first be congruent with current theoretical developments on the nature of language behaviour; secondly, it must also explain how the child comes to internalize language behaviour in his immediate and wider environment; thirdly, it must account for the relationships between the social psychological and the cognitive dimensions of bilinguality; and fourthly, it must fit the existing empirical evidence on bilingual development. Before we can discuss the processes by which the internalization of language behaviour occurs and propose our model, a number of theoretical issues regarding the nature of language behaviour and development must first be raised (Hamers & Blanc, 1987).

3.1 *The nature of language behaviour and development*

To understand the role played by language in the child's development we consider that the following points are relevant: (1) language is at once a means of communication, an organizer of knowledge and an object of analysis; (2) language is stored as a social and a propositional representation; (3) its internalization is an active process; (4) language forms develop to fulfil already existing functions; (5) the child organizes interactive events into scripts; (6) to develop language the child must be exposed to an adequate model; and (7) from being highly contextualized language becomes more and more decontextualized.

Language is part of the semiotic or symbolic function, that is, of the various ways in which individuals represent to themselves the outside world and their own actions and experiences. A representation is a stylized model of the world (Charniak & McDermott, 1985) which comes into existence through the individual's experience. This experience is partly unique to the individual and partly shared with others. Representation of higher-order knowledge involves a semiotic function which is at one and the same time individual and social.

60

Without this semiotic function thought could not be expressed either for the benefit of others or for self (Piaget & Inhelder, 1966). Unlike other aspects of the semiotic function, which can to a large extent be initiated by the child himself as a means of representing the external world (for example, imitation), language must first be socially transmitted to the child. Language is also a social structure, existing in society and shared by members of a linguistic community, and a social attribute on which the community confers values; it exists in the individual as a social representation, that is, as knowledge organized in and by the individual but shared with others in the society.

3.1.1 Functions and representations

Language has a dual function: it is used both as a means of communication between people and as an individual tool for organization of knowledge. These two aspects are interrelated: both communication and cognition develop from birth onwards; higher-order cognition develops through interpersonal interaction (Bruner, 1975a) and is shaped by the values, attitudes and norms of our social environment. Thus representations of knowledge are created and re-created at the social as well as the individual level (Forgas, 1981). Social cognition is therefore not limited to individual information processing; it includes collective cognitive processes, since it must be recognized that societies, communities and groups are also engaged in the creation, processing and definition of knowledge (Berger & Luckman, 1967). Language is also an object of analysis: an individual develops metalinguistic knowledge, that is, knowledge about language. At the same time he uses cognitive organization to analyse language and he manipulates language for the organization of knowledge.

Although all mental representations are to a certain extent social in nature, some representations rely more heavily on the physical characteristics of the world and partly exist without the intervention of a structured society.[1] In Bruner's (1975b) classification of representations into echoic, iconic and symbolic modes, the first two rely more on the child's perception and organization of his knowledge of the physical world, whereas the last type of representation is heavily dependent on culture and language. In a similar vein, Andersen's (1983) distinction between temporal, spatial and propositional representations also suggests that different modes of organizing knowledge depend to a varying extent on the different physical, social or cultural characteristics of the outside world. The organization of higher-order knowledge draws on these different modes, but mainly on propositional or symbolic representations which use relational categorizations of experience to store and organize information. The evidence from research on memory processes, for example, suggests that complex information is stored in terms of meaning, and thus relies heavily on language (Paivio & Begg, 1981).

Once knowledge is represented in a propositional form it is important to distinguish between unanalysed and analysed knowledge (Bialystok & Ryan, 1985b); this is similar to Piaget's (1954) distinction between figurative and operative representations. In both kinds of knowledge the proposition is the same, that is, a propositional representation consists of a predicate–argument structure (Miller & Johnson-Laird, 1976); in other words, meaning is the same in both. In unanalysed knowledge, however, the subject uses information routinely without intentional manipulation and with little awareness of the structures and the rules of the proposition; whereas in analysed knowledge the subject has access to the structure, which he can transform in order to re-organize knowledge. Our knowledge of and about language varies according to the degree to which it is analysed (Bialystok & Ryan, 1985b).

3.1.2 Social representations

One part of an individual's representations of knowledge is unique to him and derives from his interactions with the physical world, whereas the other part is shared with members of society. Because these shared representations are transmitted over generations, they result from the sum of similar physical and social experiences and include also the collective values attributed to these representations. Thus social representations are the sum of the knowledge shared by a collectivity; they are systems of practices, ideas, attitudes and values. Because all higher-order representations have a social component, the individual's organization of complex human knowledge will depend to a great extent on social interaction and its two salient characteristics, culture and language (see Moscovici, 1984).

Knowledge of language and about language is part of social cognition; it is experienced only in interaction with others who use language in its various functions. The representation of language has a social and a propositional character. The social representation of language also includes a code for social exchange, a way of organizing knowledge via a linguistic code in such a manner that it is accessible to others.

3.1.3 The internalization of language

As language becomes internalized as an organizer of knowledge it frees itself from the situational context, i.e. it becomes more and more decontextualized;[2] its formal aspects move away from the rules of language used in everyday communication. In so doing, language evolves into autonomous codes which create their own rules. However, language must necessarily remain a socially shared tool to permit the transmission of knowledge (Moscovici, 1984). But as language in its cognitive function becomes more autonomous and thus moves further away from its social function and form, the communication of knowledge becomes more complex in the sense that it calls upon a higher number of intermediate steps to build a bridge between language as a cognitive organizer and language as a means of communicating knowledge. In order to communicate ideas it is necessary to use language in a socially decontextualized form, that is, the speaker has to make all the elements of knowledge fully explicit in the text[3] while making optimal use of shared knowledge and shared representations.

The child can only become cognizant of the shared social knowledge and representations through interaction with members of his social environment: 'the construction of social meanings is an interactive process that begins at birth' (Nelson, 1981, 97). Language evolves in the physical and social interactions between the infant and adults. According to Bruner (1975a; Bruner & Sherwood, 1981) the child, through a highly structured interaction with the adult involving the development of joint attention, action and communication, develops a mastery of the rules of social interaction, that is, of culture and language. In order for the child to learn how to use language in its multiple functions, he must create for himself a functional representation of language; put in simple terms, the child must learn what he can do with language.

3.1.4 The development of language functions

Although the communicative and the cognitive functions of language are closely interrelated, it is accepted that language develops first in its communicative function and that it will not develop in its cognitive function without social interaction. The child must first acquire knowledge of the functional aspects of language; he must then develop the cognitive skills necessary for using language as a functional tool of communication (Bruner, 1975b). In order to develop language as a tool of communication he must learn to master both the non-linguistic (for instance turn-taking) and the linguistic communicative skills.

Once language is used as a communicative tool, it evolves into a tool of cognitive functioning: the child can develop what Bruner calls 'analytic competence', that is, the conceptual–linguistic abilities involving 'the prolonged operation of thought processes exclusively on linguistic representations (and) propositional structures' (Bruner, 1975b, 72). The cognitive function of language refers to a general psychological process by which the child appropriates language as an organizer of knowledge, i.e. in classification, hierarchization, inferencing, etc.; it may include written language skills, but should not be confused with them. The cognitive function of language is a prerequisite for the acquisition of reading and writing and will in turn be enhanced by them. As soon as linguistic communication develops, both the communicative and the cognitive functions are present and interrelated. This is because communication is not merely exchanging signals that stand in a one-to-one relationship with specific objects, actions and events. Linguistic communication has a cognitive component: it essentially involves exchanging conceptual information. Language used in social interaction will thus provide the child with an enlarged data base for constructing his knowledge and will help him recognize certain parameters as relevant to problem solving. The extent to which the adults, in their interactions with the child, manipulate language in problem solving will enable him to develop language in this function.

Language development is dependent upon a number of prerequisites, including socialization processes, the development of the functions for which language will be used, and the existence of language-behaviour models in the child's environment. We view socialization as a complex set of learning processes including the development of social scripts, the building up of social, cultural or ethnic identity, the internalization of social values, and the motivational processes involved in learning or using a language; these processes will shape the child's construction of his shared representation of language (Hamers & Blanc, 1982). They will be further discussed in 3.2.

Before the child can learn the functional and formal rules of language, he must first begin to acquire the functions served by communication; he must also develop some conceptual knowledge about the world. The child develops these functions through cooperative action with the adults around him, that is through joint attention and joint action. For example, the child will first learn that he can act upon others ('instrumental function') and at a later stage that he can use language for this function. According to Halliday (1975), a child who is learning his first language is 'learning how to mean'. In this sense, language is not just a device for generating structures, it is a semantic potential relating meaning to the functions that language is made to fulfil in the life of the growing child. He will only develop a specific linguistic structure if it can serve a given function for communicating with others or for organizing knowledge. In turn language becomes a constructive element in the development of functions (Karmiloff-Smith, 1979). Similarly, the child first develops concepts that will later be used linguistically; for example, he will learn the concepts of 'agent' or 'attribute' before he is able to express them in linguistic form. The mastery of language then acts as a catalyst which in turn amplifies the development of already existing functions. According to Bruner (1971) and Wells (1981) such an amplifier, because of its potential role in the organization of the child's experience, is essential for shaping his cognitive capacities. This constant dynamic interaction between language and cognitive functioning will shape both the cognitive and linguistic development of the child.

3.1.5 Language and scripts

Through his interaction with others the child will learn communicative procedures, such as the rules of dialogue and grammar, in highly concrete situations. Before acquiring these procedures, however, the child must first be able to organize his knowledge of interactional events. The representation of events, called 'scripts' by Schank & Abelson (1977) and Nelson (1981) and 'formats' by Bruner & Sherwood (1981), is derived from, and applied to, social contexts. A script is 'an ordered sequence of actions appropriate to a particular spatial–temporal context, organized around a goal' (Nelson, 1981); it is however not episodic but serves as a generalized model valid for all instances of a class of events.

It is through scripts that children learn how to get things done with the help of others; that they learn about the complex structure of interpersonal interaction and how to use language in this interaction even before they have mastered formal linguistic rules (Bruner & Sherwood, 1981). Because scripts serve as a guide to routine encounters in social interactions, they are highly dependent on shared social representations, conventions, norms and language. A shared script is also an economical device for communication as it presupposes shared knowledge of goal and actions which no longer have to be made explicit in the act of communication. Furthermore, a script requires a relatively high level of abstraction as it calls for classification, grouping and the recognition of relations; in other words, a script is highly dependent on the cognitive organization of knowledge and hence on language. In turn scripts form 'basic building blocks' for subsequent cognitive development (Nelson & Gruendel, 1981).

3.1.6 *The onset of language development*

The various aspects of language will only develop if an adequate model of language behaviour is present in the child's environment and used in interaction with him. By adequate model we mean a functional and formal model through which the child is introduced to the use of specific forms of language for specific functions. Because of the social attributes of language, the functions that are the most used and valorized with the child are those which he is the most likely to develop.

When the child begins to develop linguistic forms, in a first stage there is a one-to-one correspondence between form and function and the child recreates language, in functional terms, using his own forms and rules. In a second stage the child's utterances begin to be plurifunctional and words from the adult language can be identified in his speech. It is also at this stage that he begins to separate his utterances into two main categories of functions: he uses language on the one hand to satisfy his communicative needs; on the other hand he makes use of language as a cognitive organizer. This usually coincides with a dramatic increase in vocabulary and with the development of dialogue; the child's utterances evolve from holophrases (one-word utterances) into more complex linguistic structures which combine words in a rule-governed way.

From this functional base the child is now ready to develop the linguistic forms and rules approximating to adult language (Halliday, 1975).

3.1.7 Decontextualized language

Children will first develop language in familiar social interactions for which they construct scripts; language in the early stage is physically and socially contextualized. By this we mean that children, and adults interacting with them, use linguistic units for which the referent is present. This is evidenced, for example, by the deictic use of utterances, such as the 'verbal pointing' adults use at a very early stage in children's language development, and the frequency of children's first utterances and adult utterances referring to the objects present in the immediate environment. These utterances take their meaning from the configuration of the various physical and social elements in the situation; this meaning is shared by the child and the other persons present. The meaning of a linguistic unit can thus be viewed as the shared social representation of its referent.

As the child grows older language is used in more decontextualized ways and he learns to use it as an active organizer in thought processes. It must be stressed that the mere mastery of a language for everyday communication is not sufficient to guarantee that it will be used in the organization of knowledge. To exploit the potential cognitive power of language a child has to develop 'an enhanced awareness of the symbolic properties of linguistic representations: the realization that the meaning and implications of a message depend upon the precise linguistic formulation of that message and upon the internal relations and consistency between its constituent parts, rather than upon any necessary correspondence between the message and the perception or memories of the extralinguistic context(s) to which the message might apply' (Wells, 1981, 252).

Decontextualized language, that is language in which the transmission of the meaning depends on linguistic rather than situational information, finds its ultimate realization in written texts. In written language we find the same differences between the processes of encoding (writing) and of decoding (reading) as those found in oral language between production and comprehension; however, the task of creating decontextualized written texts is not only different from, but also cognitively and linguistically even more complex than, that of comprehending them, as every element of the message has to be produced by the writer and expressed in the text. Although decontextualized language is not confined to the written mode, since cognitively and linguistically complex messages can be produced orally, it is more characteristic of writing; however, not all written language is independent of the context of situation, nor does it necessarily imply a high degree of complexity of the message (as for example in some forms of letter writing, advertising and popular journalism).

In order for a child to acquire decontextualized language, an adequate model must be present in his environment; that is, decontextualized language must be used around and with the child. This development seems to be promoted through a number of shared language-related activities concerned with problem solving between adult and child, such as extended conversations about meanings that are made explicit; being read to; looking at and talking about books. Familiarity with decontextualized oral language seems to be of the utmost importance for the learning of written skills (see Wells, 1985a).

In literate societies education through schooling stresses the decontextualized use of language and more particularly reading and writing; children who as preschoolers learned the purposes and mechanics of decontextualized language are the ones who will have the greatest advantage in the attainment of literacy at school (Wells, 1985a; Torrance & Olson, 1985). It is not the mere fact of being ablt to read and write that facilitates the use of decontextualized and symbolic language, but rather the purpose, i.e. the use of language in cognitive organization, for which the child has learned these skills (Scribner & Cole, 1981). Furthermore, as Luria (1976) has shown, when a traditional society modifies its economic, social and cultural goals and becomes more cognitively oriented with the introduction of literacy, the scope of the functional representation of language will move from being context-bound communicative to become context-free cognitive.

However, if in a literacy-oriented society the child has not been prepared to use decontextualized language before schooling, he will experience difficulties in learning how to use language as a cognitive organizer for academic tasks, whether oral or written. In order to compensate for this lack of preliterate skills it appears that it is necessary to promote interactive adult–child literacy-related activities (Tizard, Schofield & Hewison, 1982). Now what is true in a monolingual situation applies *a fortiori* to a bilingual situation where, on the one hand, the minority home language may be devalued and, on the other, the child is expected to develop the cognitive function of language in a different tongue which he either does not know or knows only in its communicative function.

3.1.8 *A cognitive model of language development*

A comprehensive model of language development should take into consideration the several aspects of language development we have just discussed. In other words, it should account for the functional and representational aspects of language, for the internalization processes in language development, and for the change from contextualized to decontextualized language with its consequences for language processing. Bialystok & Ryan (1985a, b) propose a framework which takes into account the interrelationship between different language-use domains as well as the internal structure of each of these domains. The type of language tasks required by these situations are: (1) 'conversational' tasks in which language is put to an interactive use; (2) the 'literacy' use of language which requires a decontextualized use of language and often calls upon new modes of information processing, including reading and writing; and (3) the 'metalinguistic' tasks in which the subject has to attend to language forms, to speak, think and comment about language and to be conscious of his ability to manipulate language.

According to Bialystok & Ryan two cognitive dimensions associated with structuring and accessing knowledge are necessary to define these different levels of language behaviour. First, the dimension of 'analysed knowledge' through which the subject has access to the structure and manipulation of his representations; and, secondly, the dimension of 'cognitive control', which is responsible for selecting and coordinating the required information within a given time and space. The different language tasks vary along these two dimensions: simple conversational tasks demand a low degree of analysis of knowledge and of cognitive control, while the ability to solve metalinguistic problems requires high levels of information processing in terms of both the manipulation of knowledge and the control exercised over the selection of appropriate information: 'the decrease in contextualization from conversational to metalinguistic tasks increases the need for analysed knowledge, while the increase of the requirement to focus on form increases the need for cognitive control' (Bialystok & Ryan, 1985a, 233).

For the child, developing language and cognition means progressing from little-analysed knowledge and limited cognitive control to more analysed knowledge on which he gradually exercises greater control in terms of attention, selection and priorities. As far as knowledge of language is concerned, the more it is analysed, the more its form is likely to differ from language used in everyday conversation interaction. When Moscovici (1984) argues that, in the internalization process, language moves away from the form it has in everyday communication, it should be understood that this happens along these two dimensions: language undergoes more and more transformations through cognitive manipulation, while at the same time the individual has to establish more control procedures to deal with the task. This cognitive model of language processing is schematized in Figure 3.1.

But metalinguistic skills are not only required for reaching a certain level of abstraction; they are also necessary for communicating abstract thought. However, the metalinguistic skills required for this type of communication are not necessarily the same as those for analysing linguistic input. A speaker who wants to convey information must take his interlocutor into consideration. He must therefore modify and reorganize his language in such a way that he makes use of knowledge, scripts and meanings shared with his interlocutor. These metalinguistic skills interact with social cognition to produce a language of communication which is different from the language of everyday com-

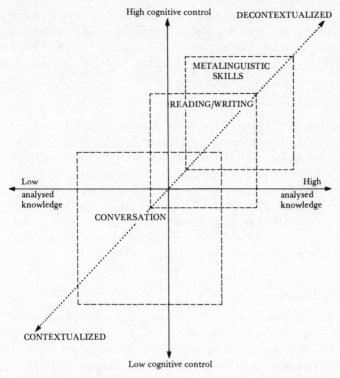

High cognitive control DECONTEXTUALIZED

METALINGUISTIC
SKILLS

READING/WRITING

Low
analysed
knowledge

High
analysed
knowledge

CONVERSATION

CONTEXTUALIZED

Low cognitive control

Figure 3.1 Schematized model of the cognitive dimensions of language processing (adapted from Bialystok & Ryan, 1985a)

munication. They find their more elaborate expression in literacy skills, such as reading and writing, in which information processing cannot rely on contextual clues.

To sum up, the child must appropriate social language around him, analyse and control it cognitively and process analysed language in a communicable form. Therefore the child's representation of language must include all the functions of language used and valued by society at large and by the significant members of his social network. This shared representation determines how he will: (1) use language as a means of communication; (2) appropriate language as a cognitive organizer; (3) analyse language and (4) process language in such a way that he can communicate knowledge to his interlocutor. Whatever the pattern of language use in his environment, the child must acquire three competences, that is, communicative, analytic, and metalinguistic competence, in addition to linguistic competence in one or more languages, in order to develop a general competence in language. Social representation of language is shared with other members of a community and includes, at the individual level, shared meanings and scripts, and social cognitive processes which play a major role in the development of language use and competence in language. These processes are particularly relevant when the child's language experience includes more than one language.

3.2 Language, social networks and socialization

Language is present in its different aspects in the child's environment and will be used to a varying extent and for different functions by speakers with and around the child in his social network. By social network we understand the sum of all the interpersonal relations one individual establishes with others over time. The relevance of a network, centred on the individual, lies in the fact that, on the one hand, it provides the child with functional and formal linguistic model(s) and with shared scripts, and, on the other hand, it transmits to the child the system of societal values, attitudes and perceptions relating to the language(s) and their users (Blanc & Hamers, 1987).

3.2.1 The role of social networks

All social network studies, whether they relate to language or not, have shown that close-knit, territorially based social networks act as norm-enforcement mechanisms by exerting pressure on their members to adopt the network norms, values and behaviour, including those pertaining to language (Milroy, 1980). The break-up of such a structure, for example the loosening of kinship and peer-group ties and the establishment of new links outside the original network, are the social mechanisms whereby norms and values change and the individual develops new group loyalties and adopts new language norms and behaviour. More specifically, close-knit network structure is associated with the maintenance of non-standard linguistic norms, whereas a loosened structure tends to be associated with changing norms and a shift towards a legitimized standard language.

In the early years the child is normally surrounded by a close-knit personal network which is often territorially based and consists of clusters of relations where ties of kinship and friendship predominate: first, the older generation of parents and relatives and the contemporary generation of siblings and peers; then, as he grows older, his personal network widens to include neighbours, school peers and teachers. The kinds of norms, values and language model to which the child is exposed and which he will internalize depend on (1) whether there is one or more functional and formal model(s) of language around the child; (2) whether his network is homogeneous or heterogeneous, that is, all its members have a similar language behaviour or some members have a different language behaviour from others; and (3) whether there are competing values and norms or not.

It is through his immediate social network that he becomes cognizant of the wider social system of intergroup relations, of the place of his network and community within that system and of the values attributed to, and the status conferred upon, the languages or language varieties and their functions. It is also through his social-network environment that he is exposed to a model or models of language and language behaviour; he internalizes the different kinds of social behaviour which are central to him, learns about the social behaviour of outgroups and builds his own social representations of language; these social representations in turn determine how and for what functions he will use his linguistic knowledge.

3.2.2 *Socialization and language development*

In the process of socialization[4] the child internalizes the system of social values and norms pertaining to language as his own and constructs his social representations of language. Socialization is a complex set of learning processes by which the child learns to become a member of his group and through which he builds social representations. The social representation of language comprises shared meanings, social scripts, and the internalization of social values, which plays an essential role in the development of cultural identity. These social cognitive processes will, in turn, determine the motivational processes for learning or using a language in its different functions. Socialization occurs through the interaction between the child and the members of his social network with whom he has frequent and important interactions. Socialization is thus seen as the interface between a particular social network, which is part of a larger social structure but with its own pattern of language use, and the individual's social representations, which will shape the child's relation to language and languages.

In the socialization process the psychological mechanisms relevant to language development are:

(i) *identification*, whereby a child identifies with other persons and practises the roles associated with those persons; as the child tends to behave like the persons around him, the models from which he learns language play an important part in the language-development process;

(ii) *internalization*, in which the child makes his own the social values associated with the behaviour prevalent in his community; this is not a passive process as it involves a reorganization of values in terms of the child's own experience; some of these values are more specifically linked to language, e.g. the social perception of a particular language, accent or literate usage, thus making a community language, a social group accent or literate usage into social markers;

(iii) *the development of social, cultural or ethnic identity*, by which the child is enabled, through social–psychological mechanisms like social comparison, categorization and distinctiveness, to build his own social identity and define himself as a member of certain social groups, distinct from others in terms of values and norms (Tajfel, 1974); when language, or certain aspects of language, like accent for example, are used as social markers, the child will recognize these markers as part of his self-image and thus as part of his own social, cultural or ethnic identity; in the case of the coexistence in the community of several languages or varieties which are differentially valued, the child will internalize these differences in the building up of his own cultural identity; according to whether he perceives himself as belonging to a more or less valued group, he will perceive himself and his language(s) as having greater or lesser value (see Chapter 5.2).

Shared meanings, shared representations, scripts, and cultural identity are the outcome of these mechanisms. They are begun in primary socialization, which normally occurs in the family, and continued during secondary socialization. In primary socialization cultural forms for expressing basic social behaviour are internalized from the models of significant others (Mead, 1934) and become *the* only conceivable world for the child (Berger & Luckman, 1967). It provides him with rule-governed and institutionalized programs for everyday life, i.e. scripts. In secondary socialization the child internalizes the rules of institution-based worlds, such as the school, and he becomes aware of social structures and their symbolic systems. Secondary socialization will also play an important if less emotionally loaded role in the development of the child's identity. If a major change occurs in a person's life, such as moving to another cultural environment, secondary socialization is more susceptible to modification than primary socialization (see Chapter 5.2.4).

3.2.3 The social basis of language development

Language development cannot be envisaged outside the social and cultural context in which it takes place. It is rooted in the child's social interaction with the significant others in his social network who present him with a model or models of language behaviour. This social network around the child is part of a larger social structure and it mediates between him and the culture, and transmits to the child not only knowledge about the social structure but also the value system which determines the status and relevance of language. The shared representations and scripts which are basic to language processing arise in the interaction between the child and the significant others around him. The representations of language the child will construct are highly dependent on the shared social representations in his environment. The child will internalize those language functions that are valorized and used with him; it is through the socialization process that he becomes cognizant of functions and representations.

Interaction with others, and in particular child-rearing practices, determine both language and cognition and hence the way in which language and cognition will interact in the child's development. According to Vygotsky (1978), the process of internalization of higher psychological functions, including language, consists of a series of transformations: an operation that occurred initially externally in interaction with the outside world will become internalized; furthermore, these transformations from an interpersonal process to an intrapersonal one are the result of an accumulation of developmental events and the internalization is linked with changes in the rules governing that operation.

Cognitive appropriation of language is dependent on the functional and formal language models around the child. These are transmitted through the social network centred on the child, who develops an awareness of their relative values in the society. He will further develop an awareness that other formal and functional models of language behaviour exist with a relatively greater or lesser social value in the same society; however, these other models and their attributed values may not be central to his own network and therefore, though he may recognize them as having a greater social value than his own, he will not perceive them as being part of his own personal make-up. If changes occur in his social network which introduce new forms and functions of language, as, for example, when he goes to school, this will influence his own relationship to language according to how far he perceives the change to be important in his own social network and thus central to himself (Hamers & Blanc, 1982).

The positive valorization of all or some of the values linked to the formal and functional aspects of language will help to elaborate and trigger off a motivational process for learning and using those aspects of language. These processes will first enable the child to develop a competence in the communicative function of language; by developing this competence he will valorize even more language as a communicative tool, thereby being further motivated to learn and use it in that function. Secondly, and provided he is exposed to an adequate functional model, the child will also develop a competence in the cognitive function of language; the same social psychological processes are at work here: the child must be exposed to, valorize, and be motivated to learn and use language in its cognitive function. The socially valorized and successful use of language in this function will act as a feedback on the child's valorization and motivated processes, thus prompting the child to make further use of language for this function. Thus, the two main functional aspects of language, that is the communicative and the cognitive, develop through a number of mediational mechanisms, provided that there is an adequate environment in which the child can pick up the necessary cues from his own social network.

Thus, language development has its roots in the social interactions which determine to what extent the child appropriates language both as a cognitive tool and as a social attribute. Once the child has appropriated language for organizing knowledge, he must learn to use it in order to communicate this knowledge in a variety of social interactions, including writing; to this end, he must develop new social forms of language appropriate to new communication situations. Since the social attributes of language play such a major role in this process, the social context is determining for language development. This will be all the more so in the case of languages in contact in society and in the child's network, where social attributes of the different languages and varieties vary according to the existing power relations.

3.3 The development of bilinguality

As we pointed out in Chapter 1.1, the development of bilinguality involves the acquisition of two (or more) linguistic codes perceived as socially distinct by the linguistic community. In this final section we raise the problem of how far this linguistic duality affects the child's overall development. More specific- ally, we ask the following questions: (1) To what extent are the child's social and propositional representations of language modified by an early bilingual experience? (2) To what extent are the child's social cultural and social psychological correlates of language affected by this experience? (3) To what extent is the use of language in cognitive organisation influenced by early bi- lingual experience? and (4) How and to what extent are the child's language behaviour and cognitive development influenced by his bilinguality? For each of these questions we also have to ask how far the child's two language systems are independent from each other and how far they are interdependent.

3.3.1 The bilingual child's language representation

The child who develops bilinguality must learn two sets of linguistic rules (see Chapter 2.1) as well as their appropriate use in social interactions and in the organization of knowledge. In the case of simultaneous bilinguality, as for example in the mixed-lingual family which valorizes both languages as a means of socialization, the child learns that one class of social interactions cor- responding to one set of scripts can make use of two sets of linguistic rules according to a number of situational variables, such as interlocutor, topic and context. He also learns to associate a given function of language with two sets of linguistic rules. If the child develops all functions in both his languages, he will value these functions and the languages used for them.

From the empirical data available on simultaneous bilingual development it appears that children are not only capable of switching from one set of linguistic rules to another, in a socially appropriate manner, at an early stage of language development and long before they have mastered all the rules of adult language; they are also aware of the existence of two distinct codes (Ronjat, 1913; Leopold, 1939–49; Swain, 1972; Fantini, 1985). An infant bilingual spontaneously translates for two adults each of whom speaks one of his languages, thus establishing equivalences between his two languages (Swain & Wesche, 1973). Ths ability to use either code for similar interactions is proof that the child is capable of equating the interactional rules of his two languages before he has acquired adult-like language competence and is aware of at least certain dimensions of the social context of language use.

Thus, as the child starts acquiring two languages, he develops a representation in which the two languages are differentiated in terms of not only their formal aspects but also the functions they serve in interactions. He also internalizes the degree to which the two languages are interchangeable; that is, the child learns whether both languages can be used to address the same or different interlocutors, to fulfil the same or different functions in the same or different social contexts. Therefore, the relativization of the languages at all levels of representation is built into his representation of language. If only one language is used for a specific function, e.g. the cognitive one, how will this affect his representation of language? If he perceives that language is a cognitive organizer independently from the specificity of the codes, he may be able to transfer a function acquired in one language to the other. Evidence on this point is still scanty, although it may be inferred from a number of studies of older bilingual children that transfer occurs. For example, Da Silveira (1988) observed that Benin children, bilingual from early childhood in Fon and French, but using only the latter for cognitive functioning, who scored high on cognitive–linguistic tasks in French also scored equally high on these tasks in Fon, although they had never before performed similar oral tasks in this language.

In the case of early consecutive bilinguality the child first develops a language representation in which there is only one language. When the child is introduced to a second language at an early age, this may have the following effects on his representation of language:

(1) If he has already developed a full functional representation of language, that is for communicative, cognitive and metalinguistic purposes, it may be relatively easy for him to transfer these skills to the new language; he will then have a functional representation in which the two languages are interchangeable for all functions. This interchangeability will in turn enhance his metalinguistic awareness (see 3.3.4). This is evidenced by studies of immersion programs (see Chapter 8.4.2), in which it is shown that children transfer cog-

nitive functioning acquired in L_1 to the new L_2 at school and, conversely, transfer newly acquired cognitive skills in L_2 to their L_1 (Cummins, 1984a; Harley, Hart & Lapkin, 1986). These observations also extend to immigrant children who have developed academic skills in their L_1 before entering school in the host-country language (Skutnabb-Kangas & Toukomaa, 1976; Cummins, Swain, Nakajima, Handscombe, Green & Tran, 1984).

(2) If, on the other hand, the child has not developed the cognitive function of language when he is introduced to L_2 at school, no transfer is possible; he is however expected to acquire this function and at the same time learn a relatively new language. He is thus confronted with two new difficult tasks, a cognitive and a linguistic one. If, in addition, language is little valorized in its cognitive function in the home and L_1 is not valorized in the child's environment, he will have great difficulty in acquiring the analytic function of language and transferring it to his L_1, because he lacks the necessary functional and social representations. Empirical evidence for this can be found in Chapter 2.3. Note, however, that this lack of cognitive development is not a necessary outcome: provided that the cognitive function of language is sufficiently valorized in the home through interactions with adults, the child may be better able to develop this cognitive function, while acquiring literacy skills in L_2 (Tizard, Schofield & Hewison, 1982); or else, provided that the child is first introduced to literacy skills in his mother tongue at school, he may later transfer these skills to his L_2 (Lambert, 1977; Dolson, 1985).

3.3.2 *The social determinants of bilinguality*

The child shares a social representation of language with members of his community and more specifically with members of his social network. If two or more languages are present either in society at large or in his immediate environment, the child will develop a shared representation which relativizes the different languages. As a result of power relations between social groups, a multilingual society confers different status upon languages by valorizing them to varying extents for socially desirable activities, by institutionalizing them as such and by conveying attitudes about them. The dominant group will legitimize its language and impose it as the norm on subordinate groups, who will either accept it or try to challenge it (see Chapter 7.1.1). The child's social network will usually reflect the societal values of the languages and transmit them to the child. The child will develop shared representations of the languages which will include the status, values and attitudes transmitted by his social network; he will thus more or less valorize his own mother tongue(s) relatively to the other languages around him. In a minority group a child may acquire a mother tongue to which negative values may be attached by his socializers, and he will therefore internalize these values and develop relatively negative attitudes towards his own language.

If the child belongs to a dominant group which does not attach value to the other languages in the society, and if none of these languages is used in early socialization, then the child is likely to remain monolingual. If, on the other hand, the majority child is exposed to another language in his network, the type of bilinguality he develops will depend on the relative use of the languages and on the kind of shared representation his network transmits, that is, on the extent to which the language has status, is valorized for its different functions and is valued as a social attribute.

The situation is totally different for the child of a subordinate group. The dominant language, which is imposed by the society, will to a greater or lesser extent be used in the child's social network. It is therefore likely that the child will acquire some communicative proficiency in that language. Generally speaking, the more prestigious L_2 is more valorized both in society and around the child, while the lower-status L_1 is devalorized in society and often, though not necessarily, in the child's network; but even when it is valorized it will often be limited to the communicative function. If the child starts schooling through his L_2 this will further valorize the dominant language in its cognitive function; on the other hand, if he is taught totally or partially in his L_1 this will valorize his mother tongue for cognitive functioning, thereby enabling him to perceive it more favourably.

Valorization of L_1 and of literacy in the child's social network are both crucial for the development of literacy skills. Landry & Allard (1985) have demonstrated that, in a French-speaking minority setting in New Brunswick, the more the parents valorized the mother tongue, the better the children achieved at school. The authors conclude that negative perceptions of his mother tongue by the minority child can be avoided if L_1 is valorized in the child's social network. If, in addition, the school valorizes the child's mother tongue, this will reinforce the child's positive perception of his language. Similarly, the valorization of literacy skills *per se* may also have a positive effect on the child's representation of language: Clay (1976), for example, observed that in New Zealand English-medium schools Samoan children were more successful in learning to read than Maori children; the author attributes these results to the greater valorization of literacy in the Samoan community.

3.3.3 Language and cognitive organization in the bilingual

As we suggested in Hamers & Blanc (1982), the use of language as a cognitive organizer is developed by the bilingual child at three different levels: two levels specific to each language and one abstract level common to both languages, which we called 'L'. In 3.1.1 we argued that language is stored in the form of propositional representations, that is, as relational categorizations; we further argued that propositional representations are related to the general characteristics of language and independent from the specificity of a given language. We therefore propose that the bilingual has propositional representations which are common to both his languages and that he uses this common pool in organizing knowledge. Cummins's (1981) model of 'common underlying proficiency', discussed in Chapter 2.3.3, also suggests that the bilingual develops a literacy-related proficiency common to both languages and that the two languages are interdependent at deeper levels of processing.

When a bilingual child has well-developed propositional representations his organization of knowledge will be independent of the specific characteristics of his languages and it is likely that he will be able to use his two languages interchangeably to communicate this knowledge. On the other hand, if a child has not learned to use language as a cognitive organizer to a significant extent, introducing him to a second language will not promote this function. Thus, the development of propositional representations and the ability to use language as a cognitive organizer must be viewed as psycholinguistic processes that are independent of the specific characteristics of the languages. Bilingual experience may, however, interact with these psycholinguistic processes.

3.3.4 Bilinguality and cognitive development

How does early bilingual experience impinge on cognitive development? The nature of the bilingual child's cognitive development and the empirical evidence have already been discussed in Chapter 2.3. From this discussion it appears clearly that early bilingual experience enhances cognitive functioning when the child has the opportunity to develop all functions of language and provided that both languages are highly valorized. In this case, early bilingual experience seems to promote a number of cognitive and metalinguistic abilities: originality, creativity, divergent thinking, problem solving, symbol substitution, rule discovery, sensitivity to linguistic cues, disambiguation and verbal flexibility. All these abilities are related to the two cognitive processes of analysis and control. Metalinguistic competence results from the ability to analyse language and to exercise cognitive control on language (Bialystok & Ryan, 1985a, b). What the bilingual child develops are general cognitive mechanisms of information processing; once these mechanisms have been set in motion, the child is able to apply them to all information-processing tasks, even to non-linguistic ones.

The final question that remains to be answered is: if early bilingual development enhances cognitive development, why is it that not *all* bilingual experience leads to cognitive enhancement? Positive cognitive consequences of early bilingual experience are almost invariably associated with positive parental attitudes towards both languages and towards literacy. On the other hand, when negative consequences are reported for bilingual experience, they invariably refer to a sociocultural setting which has the following characteristics: (1) the child comes from a socially disadvantaged subordinate group; (2) he speaks a mother tongue which is little valorized in the society at large; and (3) he is schooled through a prestigious L_2 while the school system tends to ignore or denigrate his mother tongue. So far we have no clear evidence that these negative consequences imply that the child's cognitive processes are less developed; rather, there is plenty of evidence that these children underachieve at school. This has prompted a number of scholars (e.g. Cummins, 1984a) to blame the educational system for this underachievement. There is no doubt that sociocultural factors are responsible for poor linguistic and scholastic results: witness the many immigrant groups who also come from different cultural backgrounds but do not have to face depressed socio-economic conditions, and who perform linguistically and cognitively at least as well as monolinguals (Troike, 1984).

Because positive consequences of bilingual experience result from the enhancement of cognitive functioning, and negative consequences stem from the social conditions in which the bilingual experience takes place, a general model of bilinguality should bring together both the cognitive aspects and the social aspects of bilingual development. We attempt this integration in the next section.

3.3.5 The social cognitive foundations of bilinguality

In order to construct a theoretical framework to account for the development of bilinguality it is necessary to integrate the different levels of analysis of language development from which to view the different situations where languages are in contact in the child's early years. In other words, we should analyse bilinguality from both a cognitive and a social perspective; but we must also attempt to combine them in one theoretical framework that is consistent with the existing empirical evidence.

As we have already pointed out, Lambert (1974, 1977) was the first to draw attention to the effect of the relevant status of two languages on their internalization and to the cognitive consequences of this internalization for the child (see Chapter 2.4). Because the cognitive appropriation of language depends upon the functional and formal models in the child's social network, the child has to be exposed to these models in order to develop the cognitive function that will enable him to analyse and control language. When two languages are present in the child's environment, at least one of them must be used to fulfil the cognitive function. The sooner the child develops an analysed representation of language, the easier it will be to apply these cognitive skills to both his languages and the more likely it is that he will be able to use this knowledge in cognitive operations.

The ideal situation, then, is when the child develops the cognitive literacy-related functions of language at an early age and his linguistic skills in both languages simultaneously. If simultaneous infant binguality is paired with an early development of the cognitive function of language, it is likely that it will evolve into an additive form of binguality. In early consecutive binguality, provided the monolingual child has developed a functional representation of language before schooling, he may soon be able to transfer this representation to the new language he is acquiring; if the child can soon exploit his binlingual skills for his cognitive functioning, then he might also be able to develop an additive form of binguality. In both cases, the two languages have been equally valorized around and by the child.

A subtractive form of binguality, however, will only develop if (1) the language skills the child possessed in his L_1 are relatively devalorized compared with a more prestigious L_2; (2) he has not fully developed the cognitive function of language in L_1 before he is schooled, and (3) he is introduced to the cognitive function of language exclusively in an L_2 in which he has at best a limited knowledge. Because all three conditions have to obtain before subtractive binguality can develop, early simultaneous bilingual experience, where the two languages are more or less equally valorized, will not lead to subtractivity.

The distinction between additive and subtractive binguality may then be considered on a continuum resulting from two independent dimensions, one dealing with the development of the cognitive function of language, the other with the relative valorization of the languages. This is schematized in Figure 3.2. At the additive end of the continuum the cognitive function of language is well developed and both languages are highly valorized; the child has not only developed a functional representation of language, but, because he valorizes both languages to the same extent, he will perceive them as interchangeable; this will in turn facilitate the development of his skills for analysing and controlling language processing, hence enhancing his overall cognitive functioning. At the other end of the continuum we find a subtractive form of binguality. In this case, a child who in the first place did not develop the cognitive literacy-oriented aspects of language in his devalorized L_1 is then required to do so in a new, more valorized language.

Thus, the use of two languages around and with the child who is developing his cognitive skills in language, that is, the ability to analyse language and control linguistic cues, will enhance these skills. For children who have an early experience in analysing language, the bilingual experience is likely to promote their cognitive control to the point where they are able to solve metalinguistic problems (Bialystok & Ryan, 1985b). Empirical evidence (see Chapter 2.3.3) indicates that bilingual children are more advanced than monolinguals on an array of metalinguistic tasks. For children who develop simultaneous infant binguality, the very situation of being confronted with two interchangeable languages, i.e. two labels for one concept, at a time when they are developing a

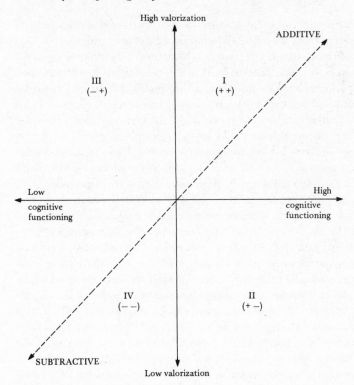

High valorization

ADDITIVE

III
(− +)

I
(+ +)

Low
cognitive
functioning

High
cognitive
functioning

IV
(− −)

II
(+ −)

SUBTRACTIVE

Low valorization

Figure 3.2 The sociocultural and cognitive dimensions of the additive–subtractive continuum

functional representation of language as a cognitive tool, may push them towards developing their analysed knowledge about language. For the child, developing an early representation that language is a cognitive organizer and that his two languages are interchangeable may facilitate the general development of analysed knowledge in all areas. This representation will be facilitated if the child's environment valorizes both languages equally. For children who began to acquire a representation of language as a cognitive organizer through their L_1 and are then introduced at an early age to an L_2, this may have similar effects: the introduction of a new language to which they can apply their analytical ability will also prompt them to develop their metalinguistic skills further, thereby enhancing their ability to analyse knowledge.

Why is it then that not all children who have an early bilingual experience develop an additive form of bilinguality? First, it is a necessary condition that bilingual experience should interact with the ability to analyse knowledge in order to enhance the child's cognitive development; if this ability is not developed or poorly developed a bilingual experience will have little impact on it. As far as cognitive development is concerned, children in this situation will not be very different from their monolingual peers; the only difference is that they acquire proficiency in a L_2. Second, it is important that children perceive their two languages as interchangeable, that is, that they perceive that both languages can perform the same functions. Even though a child may have developed the necessary cognitive functions, he may still perceive that one of his languages is not suited for these functions and will, therefore, not valorize it and use it for this purpose. This could be, for example, the case of certain diglossic situations where one of the languages is restricted to an everyday communication function; however, we lack empirical evidence on this point and it might well be that a child is able to perceive the interchangeability of his codes, even though they are not used in this way in his environment. At this stage we do not know if the cognitive valorization of language extends to all the languages a child is exposed to or if it is limited to specific languages.

Subtractive bilinguality occurs when a minority child who has a socially devalorized language as his mother tongue, and who has limited cognitive skills in language, is schooled through a more prestigious language in which he has no or only a limited proficiency. As the child has not developed the cognitive skills of language his bilingual experience can have no positive affects. But why is it that in this situation he will be less successful at cognitive tasks than his monolingual peer who also lacks these cognitive skills? First, because of the low value attached by society to his L_1 it will be more difficult for this child to see the two languages as interchangeable and therefore to use them for socially valorized activities. Secondly, schooling will reinforce this perception by introducing him to cognitive tasks exclusively in the majority language; he might then perceive the L_2 as the only language suitable for cognitive functioning. Thirdly, whereas in language development it seems necessary for the child to develop a function before he can acquire the linguistic form to express it, the child is here required to learn new forms of language for a language function he has not developed. The negative cognitive result of bilingual experience can in this case be attributed to the adverse sociocultural and educational context in which the minority child develops bilinguality. In the subtractive form of bilinguality it is therefore the context which stops the child from developing his cognitive potential.

The preceding discussion suggests that, for a bilingual child, there is a degree of interdependence, both at the social affective level and at the level of cognitive processing. In other words, the bilingual child is not just the sum of two monolinguals but develops specific psycholinguistic mechanisms in which both languages are interrelated to different degrees. This 'interdependence hypothesis', which is beginning to receive some empirical support (Clément & Hamers, 1979) will be further discussed in Chapter 4.1 and 4.2 in relation to information processing by, and representations in, the bilingual, and in Chapter 5.3 in respect of ethnolinguistic attitudes. More recently, the question

or on the processing of mixed-language texts. The most common techniques are: (1) the use of bilingual adaptations of the Stroop (1935) test, in which the subject is required to attend to one characteristic of a stimulus word in one language while the word is presented in the other language; (2) the bilingual picture–word interference technique in which the subject has to attend to a picture in one language while an incongruent word is presented in the other language; (3) the cross-language version of the flanker technique in which a target word is presented simultaneously with a word-to-be-ignored (Shaffer & Laberge, 1979); and (4) the processing and the reading of mixed-language continuous texts.

The *Stroop* technique was first developed to verify the possible interference between semantic and physical characteristics of a stimulus word. In its original form a subject is presented with a series of colour words, e.g. *red, green*, written in different-coloured inks; the task consists in naming the colour of the ink while ignoring the meaning of the word. For example, the correct response to the word *red* written in green ink is GREEN. A subject will produce more errors and take more time to name the colours when the stimulus word is a colour name such as *red*, than when the stimulus-word meaning is unrelated to colours, such as the word *chair*; the most common error is to respond to an incongruent stimulus, i.e. a word denoting a colour different from the ink in which it is written (such as *red* written in blue), by reading the stimulus word instead of naming the colour of the ink. This technique allows us to measure the possible interference of a highly automatized verbal decoding process on the required encoding process. A large number of studies, using techniques adapted from the Stroop paradigm (see Dyer, 1972; 1973), confirm that semantic features of a stimulus word impinge in a powerful way on the verbal encoding of physical characteristics.

Preston (1965) adapted the Stroop technique to assess if the same amount of interference would occur when two languages interplayed in the encoding/decoding processes. In the bilingual version the subject is required to respond to the colour of the ink in one of his languages while the colour word is presented in his other language. For example, the correct response to the English word *red*, written in green ink, is the French word VERT. According to Lambert (1972) this technique enables us to assess the interference caused by simultaneously activating the decoding process in one language and the encoding process in the other language and compare it with the intralingual interference. If a switch mechanism is operating between the bilingual's two language systems then colour words presented in the language different from the one in which the response is encoded should not interfere with the colour-naming task. Testing the degree of interference between colour and word in monolingual and bilingual conditions with three groups of balanced bilinguals (French–English, German–English and Hungarian–English), Preston & Lambert (1969) observed that the interference in the bilingual condition was only slightly

has also been raised of a possible linguistic interdependence which will be examined in Chapter 6.2 when we come to discuss code alternation in the bilingual.

3.4 Conclusion

In this chapter we inquired into the nature of language behaviour and its implication for language development. We showed how the child develops language in interaction with others in his social environment and appropriates it for communication and for cognitive functioning. Through the development of a number of psychological processes, such as scripts, social and propositional representations and cognitive processing, the child becomes able to process language which is more complex and more decontextualized. We then proposed a cognitive model of language development centred around the dynamic interaction between language and cognition. We further discussed the social nature of language development, stressing more specifically the relevance of social network characteristics and of socialization processes for the internalization of language.

In the second part of the chapter we examined the development of bilinguality in the light of the processes in language development. We tried to understand how both the social dimension of valorization and the development of the cognitive function of language interact to determine which type of bilinguality, additive or subtractive, a child will develop.

From our discussion of additive and subtractive bilinguality it appears that social factors are chiefly responsible for the negative consequences of bilingual experience, whereas additive bilinguality will result from the development of the cognitive function of language in a favourable social environment. Therefore, in favourable conditions, that is, when the development of the cognitive function of language and the valorization of both languages are assured, bilinguality should be promoted as early as possible. If, on the other hand, these conditions do not obtain, care should be taken to modify the subtractive context before introducing the child to a second language. Education should consider the sociocultural context in which the child develops bilinguality and should valorize the less prestigious language and culture in the community. In this case, education should aim at increasing competence in the first language, especially the literacy-oriented skills, without however isolating the child in a cultural ghetto. This issue will be further discussed in Chapter 8.

4

Information processing in the bilingual

As we have already mentioned, any theorizing on the bilingual's behaviour has to be integrated into more general theories of language behaviour and development. Although theories of language behaviour[1] differ greatly in terms of the mechanisms postulated, there is good agreement that an adequate model of language processing must have certain characteristics. First, there must be a peripheral means of analysing sensory input; secondly, as speech is temporal, all models dealing with speech perception have provisions for a memory system. Thirdly, all models of language processing agree that verbal decoding ends and verbal encoding starts with cognitive structures functioning at some level different from the linguistic level, and that verbal behaviour can be explained only in its relationship with these cognitive structures. Fourthly, all models also agree that different levels of processing verbal material have to be distinguished and that these levels exist for both the decoding and the encoding processes. Between the perceptual and the cognitive levels, a third level has to be postulated to account for the transformation of messages from their outer verbal forms to their underlying cognitive structures, or, in encoding, from cognitive structures to verbal forms (Hamers, 1973).

A theory of language behaviour must account for the bilingual's specific behaviour, particularly for the psychological mechanisms which will enable him to function alternatively in one or the other language while at the same time having an extended control on the possible interference; it must equally explain the capacity a bilingual has to encode in one language while simultaneously decoding in the other language as interpreters, for example, do. Finally a model of the bilingual's processing must be informative about the existing relation between the bilingual's two codes for every mechanism relevant to language processing.

In the first part of the present chapter we will discuss how the bilingual has access to, organizes and stores his two languages and propose theoretical frameworks for language processing and representation, which we consider as two separate but interrelated psycholinguistic mechanisms. We will then briefly discuss the bilingual's non-verbal behaviour and finally we will give a

short overview of the state of the art on language processing by aphasics.

4.1 Language processing in bilinguals

Psycholinguistic research on bilinguals deals essentially with the relation between the bilingual's two linguistic codes and several psychological mechanisms involved in language processing. In the present section we analyse the necessity of postulating either the existence of two independent psychological mechanisms, one for each language (independence hypothesis) or the existence of a single mechanism common to both linguistic codes (interdependence hypothesis) at different levels of information processing. More specifically we will review the degree of interdependence between the bilingual's two languages for: (1) different mechanisms of information processing, namely verbal perception, decoding, encoding and production in the two languages and (2) language representation in bilinguals, that is, cognitive organization and memory at different levels of representation. We describe briefly some of the most used experimental techniques and discuss empirical data in terms of the independence–interdependence hypothesis.

4.1.1 Encoding, decoding and the switch mechanism

When a bilingual is presented with verbal material his first task is to identify the language in which this material is presented (Hamers & Lambert, 1972). Which processing mechanisms enable a bilingual to identify in an unambiguous way the language of verbal stimuli? Are these pre-attentive processes as suggested by Macnamara & Kushnir (1971)? Or does the bilingual first have to process all verbal input, as put forward in Treisman's (1969) theory of information processing? In order to explain the ease with which a bilingual, functioning in one of his languages, can suddenly switch to his other language, Penfield & Roberts (1959) suggested the existence of a switch mechanism: when one linguistic system is in operation this would automatically shut the other one out. This single-switch hypothesis implies the existence of two psycholinguistic systems, one for each language, and a certain degree of independence between two sets of language-specific information processors. The existence of language-specific processors versus a common mechanism is the major debate in psycholinguistic research on bilinguals.

4.1.1.1 The single-switch hypothesis

In order to test the switch hypothesis a number of experimental techniques have been developed and adapted: they rely either on the use of interfering distractors presented in the other language during processing in one language

smaller than in the monolingual condition and that the most common error was to give the translation of the stimulus word (e.g. ROUGE for the incongruent stimulus word *red* written in green ink). They interpreted these results as evidence against the existence of a switch mechanism.

4.1.1.2 Differences in inter- and intralingual interference

However, if no input switch is postulated, the small but consistent difference between the monolingual and the bilingual condition must be explained. This difference was reported in several studies using different adaptations of the bilingual Stroop task, with various groups of balanced bilinguals and language combinations (Dalrymple-Alford & Budayr, 1966; Dalrymple-Alford, 1968 and Dalrymple-Alford & Aamiry, 1970 for English–Arabic and English–French; Dyer, 1971 for English–Spanish; Hamers & Lambert, 1972, 1974 for French–English and Dutch–French; Biederman & Tsao, 1979 for Chinese–English; Kiyak, 1982 for Turkish–English). One possible explanation is to attribute it to the physical difference between the stimulus word and its translation equivalent: Preston & Lambert (1969) demonstrated that interlingual and intralingual interference were almost equal when a stimulus word was physically similar to its translation equivalent (e.g. *red* and ROT) but that intralingual interference was greater than interlingual interference when the two words were different (e.g. *black* and SCHWARZ).

Further support for this explanation comes from studies by Hamers & Bertrand (1973) who, using a language-named task in which subjects had to attend to the language in which the name of different languages was spoken (e.g. they had to respond FRANCAIS to the French word *néerlandais*), found that more interference occurred when the translation equivalents were similar (as with *français* and *frans* than when they were different (as with *Dutch* and *nederlands*); by Biederman & Tsao (1979) in a Chinese version of the Stroop task using different ideographic scripts; and by Fang, Tzeng & Alva (1981), who found interlingual interference to be higher when the two languages shared the same script (Spanish–English) than when they had different scripts (Chinese–English and Japanese–English).

Furthermore, the degree of interlingual interference depends also upon the bilingual's proficiency in both languages. Magiste (1985) observed that, for Swedish–German bilinguals who had attained different degrees of dominance in one or the other language, the dominant language caused more interlingual interference than the weaker language; this is equally true for a Stroop task and for a bilingual dichotic listening[3] task (Magiste, 1986). This may be congruent with other results which found relatively more interlingual interference from the dominant language than from the weaker language. Ehri & Ryan (1980), for example, observed that in a picture–word interference task

Spanish–English bilinguals would display greater interlingual interference from Spanish than from English.

4.1.1.3 A two-switch model?

However, can we conclude on the basis of experiments done with single words that no input switch exists? Rather than rejecting the switch hypothesis Macnamara (1967b) proposed a two-switch model: one switch for the verbal input controlled by the environment and an independent output switch under the subject's control. This mechanism would allow the bilingual to encode in one language while decoding in the other. Thus the two languages would be simultaneously activated but independent from each other. In support of this approach Macnamara and his colleagues (Macnamara, 1967b; Macnamara, Krauthamer & Bolgar, 1968; Macnamara & Kushnir, 1971) cite results from studies using mixed-language reading. They found that, in reading a mixedlingual text, bilingual subjects would take time for switching from one language to another; they estimated both the input and the output switch to be around 0.2 seconds.

Although this interpretation was supported by one other study (Kolers, 1966), Macnamara's two-switch model has been criticized by several authors. Dalrymple-Alford (1985) argues that no clear conclusion can be drawn from the fact that it takes time to switch languages in a mixed-lingual text. The estimate that the input switch is close to 0.2 seconds cannot be sustained, as there is a wide within- and between-experiments variation in the time observed. Furthermore, the time taken for switching can be accounted for in a different way: alternating languages within sentences in an artificial way must generate unfamiliar syntactically anomalous patterns and this could probably account for slower responding times. I. Taylor (1971), using a slightly modified version of the mixed-language reading task, demonstrated that when the subject controls the point of switching no time is taken up by changing languages. In a similar vein, Chan, Chau & Hoosain (1983) observed that, with two languages as different as Chinese and English, no time was taken for switching when the switch occurred at natural boundaries (as defined by bilinguals who code-switch in a natural setting). They conclude that natural code-switching does not take time for bilinguals familiar with code alternation and that there is no need to postulate the existence of an input switch.

Grosjean (1985a) and Grosjean & Soares (1986) recently attempted to identify some of the features in which bilingual speech modes might differ from monolingual ones. They observed that recognition of code-switched words depends on (1) general factors such as word properties (e.g. frequency of the word), preceding context and listener's pragmatic and cognitive knowledge; and (2) specific code-switching factors which are either psychosocial (speaker's habits and attitudes, listener's perception and situation) or linguistic (e.g.

density of code-switching in text or phonotactic characteristics) in nature. (For a further discussion of code-switching, see Chapter 6.2.3.)

If, as Macnamara suggested, an input switch really operates at a pre-attentive level, it does not account for the interlingual interference observable in the Stroop tasks. Further proof against the existence of an input switch comes from an experiment by Guttentag, Haith, Goodman & Hauch (1984). Using a cross-language flanker technique, they found that a different-language distractor has a similar effect to a same-language distractor. Goodman, Haith, Guttentag & Rao (1985) also argue against a voluntary input switch: they observed that the meaning of a distractor affects picture-naming in balanced bilingual children and in beginning-second-language learners as soon as they can read the distractor. Furthermore, several bilingual decoding tasks do not take more time than monolingual ones: responses to two-word signals are unaffected by language mixing (Dalrymple-Alford & Aamiry, 1967); reading mixed-language lists does not take more time than reading unilingual lists (Dalrymple-Alford, 1985); categorizations of words in one language are made equally fast in categories labelled in the same as in a different language (Caramazza & Brones, 1980) and mixing languages does not affect the judgement of comparisons (Desrochers & Petrusic, 1983).

The input-switch hypothesis is also disconfirmed by experiments in which a continuous text was used. In bilingual dichotic listening tasks[3] a subject is unable to attend to a message in one language received in one ear while ignoring a message in the other language, received in the other ear (Treisman, 1964; Moore, Macnamara & Tucker, 1970; Magiste, 1986). If a switch mechanism was operating at a pre-attentive level no interference from the distracting message would occur.

4.1.1.4 *The output-switch model*

Rather than postulating a switch mechanism, Treisman (1969) suggested that all characteristics of verbal input are analysed regardless of the language used. Treisman's approach has received empirical support from a number of studies. Looking at the errors produced in several Stroop-like interference tasks, Hamers & Lambert (1972, 1974) and Hamers (1973) concluded that the incorrect responses almost always corresponded to the stimulus word which was either read, repeated (in an auditory version) or translated; however, the language in which the response was expected was almost always correctly chosen. From these studies it was concluded that: (1) an output switch operating somewhere in the on-line output processing had to be responsible for the correct choice of the language in which to encode the response; (2) there was no evidence for a similar switch operating in the input processing; and (3) the major source of interference stemmed from semantic similarity between the stimulus word and a possible but incorrect response.

Further proof that bilinguals control their language of output but that they cannot avoid decoding in both languages comes from experiments using cross-language semantically ambiguous words (Hamers & Lambert, 1974). When bilinguals are presented with written words that can be part of both their languages but have different meanings in each language (e.g. the words *chat* and *pain* in French and English) they react to them as to homographs in one language: frequency and grammatical class are more powerful factors than language for identifying the meaning of the word. That is, when a bilingual was, for example, presented with the English words *chat* and *ail* in an English word list he would give the translation equivalents of the most common associations to the words *chat* and *ail* in French (e.g. DOG to the word *chat* in the English list). His language of response was however almost always correct. Professional translators trilingual in French–English–German would also often mistakenly translate these words in the list; for example, the word *chat* in the English list would often be translated into KATZE, that is, the German word for its French meaning. Hamers & Lambert interpret these results as proof that no switch mechanism is triggered off at the input level and that bilinguals decode all verbal material for meaning.

In summary, then, the experiments mentioned above show that there is a certain degree of independence between decoding and encoding mechanisms but fail to prove the existence of a switch mechanism in decoding at the semantic level. We cannot, however, exclude the possibility that a switch mechanism may occur at more surface levels of processing. One study (Caramazza, Yeni-Komshin & Zurif, 1974) tested the two-switch model at the phonological level: the authors concluded that, at the phonological level, a switch mechanism had to be postulated for the input as well as for the output process. However, we lack further empirical evidence on that point and the question remains: if there is an input switch, where along the on-line processing of language will it be activated? Altenberg & Cairns (1983) showed that in a lexical decision task both sets of phonotactic constraints are simultaneously active during processing by a bilingual, even though the task calls for one language only.

Mack (1986) argues that language interdependence is not limited to the semantic level but already exists at the syntactic level: she found that, in a laboratory setting where they were required to do rapid on-line processing, French–English bilinguals recognized grammatically incorrect English sentences that followed French word order as correct more often than did monolinguals. She concludes that there is no decoding switch mechanism operating but that bilinguals cannot avoid the interaction of their linguistic knowledge when decoding in one language and thus that keeping the languages functionally separated must occur further on in the on-line processing. She further suggests that a model for verbal decoding in the bilingual must include a mechanism of functional linguistic interdependence. Because the bilingual cannot suppress the automatic activation of one language in rapid on-line pro-

has also been raised of a possible linguistic interdependence which will be examined in Chapter 6.2 when we come to discuss code alternation in the bilingual.

3.4 *Conclusion*

In this chapter we inquired into the nature of language behaviour and its implication for language development. We showed how the child develops language in interaction with others in his social environment and appropriates it for communication and for cognitive functioning. Through the development of a number of psychological processes, such as scripts, social and propositional representations and cognitive processing, the child becomes able to process language which is more complex and more decontextualized. We then proposed a cognitive model of language development centred around the dynamic interaction between language and cognition. We further discussed the social nature of language development, stressing more specifically the relevance of social network characteristics and of socialization processes for the internalization of language.

In the second part of the chapter we examined the development of bilinguality in the light of the processes in language development. We tried to understand how both the social dimension of valorization and the development of the cognitive function of language interact to determine which type of bilinguality, additive or subtractive, a child will develop.

From our discussion of additive and subtractive bilinguality it appears that social factors are chiefly responsible for the negative consequences of bilingual experience, whereas additive bilinguality will result from the development of the cognitive function of language in a favourable social environment. Therefore, in favourable conditions, that is, when the development of the cognitive function of language and the valorization of both languages are assured, bilinguality should be promoted as early as possible. If, on the other hand, these conditions do not obtain, care should be taken to modify the subtractive context before introducing the child to a second language. Education should consider the sociocultural context in which the child develops bilinguality and should valorize the less prestigious language and culture in the community. In this case, education should aim at increasing competence in the first language, especially the literacy-oriented skills, without however isolating the child in a cultural ghetto. This issue will be further discussed in Chapter 8.

4

Information processing in the bilingual

As we have already mentioned, any theorizing on the bilingual's behaviour has to be integrated into more general theories of language behaviour and development. Although theories of language behaviour[1] differ greatly in terms of the mechanisms postulated, there is good agreement that an adequate model of language processing must have certain characteristics. First, there must be a peripheral means of analysing sensory input; secondly, as speech is temporal, all models dealing with speech perception have provisions for a memory system. Thirdly, all models of language processing agree that verbal decoding ends and verbal encoding starts with cognitive structures functioning at some level different from the linguistic level, and that verbal behaviour can be explained only in its relationship with these cognitive structures. Fourthly, all models also agree that different levels of processing verbal material have to be distinguished and that these levels exist for both the decoding and the encoding processes. Between the perceptual and the cognitive levels, a third level has to be postulated to account for the transformation of messages from their outer verbal forms to their underlying cognitive structures, or, in encoding, from cognitive structures to verbal forms (Hamers, 1973).

A theory of language behaviour must account for the bilingual's specific behaviour, particularly for the psychological mechanisms which will enable him to function alternatively in one or the other language while at the same time having an extended control on the possible interference; it must equally explain the capacity a bilingual has to encode in one language while simultaneously decoding in the other language as interpreters, for example, do. Finally a model of the bilingual's processing must be informative about the existing relation between the bilingual's two codes for every mechanism relevant to language processing.

In the first part of the present chapter we will discuss how the bilingual has access to, organizes and stores his two languages and propose theoretical frameworks for language processing and representation, which we consider as two separate but interrelated psycholinguistic mechanisms. We will then briefly discuss the bilingual's non-verbal behaviour and finally we will give a short overview of the state of the art on language processing by bilingual aphasics.

4.1 Language processing in bilinguals

Psycholinguistic research on bilinguals deals essentially with the relationship between the bilingual's two linguistic codes and several psychological mechanisms involved in language processing. In the present section we analyse the necessity of postulating either the existence of two independent psychological mechanisms, one for each language (independence hypothesis) or the existence of a single mechanism common to both linguistic codes (interdependence hypothesis) at different levels of information processing. More specifically, we will review the degree of interdependence between the bilingual's two languages for: (1) different mechanisms of information processing, namely, verbal perception, decoding, encoding and production in the two languages; and (2) language representation in bilinguals, that is, cognitive organization and memory at different levels of representation. We describe briefly some of the most used experimental techniques and discuss empirical data in terms of the independence–interdependence hypothesis.

4.1.1 Encoding, decoding and the switch mechanism

When a bilingual is presented with verbal material his first task is to identify the language in which this material is presented (Hamers & Lambert, 1977). Which processing mechanisms enable a bilingual to identify in an unambiguous way the language of verbal stimuli? Are these pre-attentive processes[2] as suggested by Macnamara & Kushnir (1971)? Or does the bilingual first have to process all verbal input, as put forward in Treisman's (1969) theory of information processing? In order to explain the ease with which a bilingual, functioning in one of his languages, can suddenly switch to his other language, Penfield & Roberts (1959) suggested the existence of a switch mechanism: when one linguistic system is in operation this would automatically shut the other one out. This single-switch hypothesis implies the existence of two psycholinguistic systems, one for each language, and a certain degree of independence between two sets of language-specific information processors. The existence of language-specific processors versus a common mechanism is the major debate in psycholinguistic research on bilinguals.

4.1.1.1 The single-switch hypothesis

In order to test the switch hypothesis a number of experimental techniques have been developed and adapted: they rely either on the use of interfering distractors presented in the other language during processing in one language or on the processing of mixed-language texts. The most common techniques are: (1) the use of bilingual adaptations of the Stroop (1935) test, in which the subject is required to attend to one characteristic of a stimulus word in one language while the word is presented in the other language; (2) the bilingual picture–word interference technique in which the subject has to attend to a picture in one language while an incongruent word is presented in the other language; (3) the cross-language version of the flanker technique in which a target word is presented simultaneously with a word-to-be-ignored (Shaffer & Laberge, 1979); and (4) the processing and the reading of mixed-language continuous texts.

The *Stroop* technique was first developed to verify the possible interference between semantic and physical characteristics of a stimulus word. In its original form a subject is presented with a series of colour words, e.g. *red, green,* written in different-coloured inks; the task consists in naming the colour of the ink while ignoring the meaning of the word. For example, the correct response to the word *red* written in green ink is GREEN. A subject will produce more errors and take more time to name the colours when the stimulus word is a colour name such as *red,* than when the stimulus-word meaning is unrelated to colours, such as the word *chair*; the most common error is to respond to an incongruent stimulus, i.e. a word denoting a colour different from the ink in which it is written (such as *red* written in blue), by reading the stimulus word instead of naming the colour of the ink. This technique allows us to measure the possible interference of a highly automatized verbal decoding process on the required encoding process. A large number of studies, using techniques adapted from the Stroop paradigm (see Dyer, 1972; 1973), confirm that semantic features of a stimulus word impinge in a powerful way on the verbal encoding of physical characteristics.

Preston (1965) adapted the Stroop technique to assess if the same amount of interference would occur when two languages interplayed in the encoding/ decoding processes. In the bilingual version the subject is required to respond to the colour of the ink in one of his languages while the colour word is presented in his other language. For example, the correct response to the English word *red,* written in green ink, is the French word VERT. According to Lambert (1972) this technique enables us to assess the interference caused by simultaneously activating the decoding process in one language and the encoding process in the other language and compare it with the intralingual interference. If a switch mechanism is operating between the bilingual's two language systems then colour words presented in the language different from the one in which the response is encoded should not interfere with the colour-naming task. Testing the degree of interference between colour and word in monolingual and bilingual conditions with three groups of balanced bilinguals (French–English, German–English and Hungarian–English), Preston & Lambert (1969) observed that the interference in the bilingual condition was only slightly smaller than in the monolingual condition and that the most common error was to give the translation of the stimulus word (e.g. ROUGE for the incongruent stimulus word *red* written in green ink). They interpreted these results as evidence against the existence of a switch mechanism.

4.1.1.2 *Differences in inter- and intralingual interference*

However, if no input switch is postulated, the small but consistent difference between the monolingual and the bilingual condition must be explained. This difference was reported in several studies using different adaptations of the bilingual Stroop task, with various groups of balanced bilinguals and language combinations (Dalrymple-Alford & Budayr, 1966; Dalrymple-Alford, 1968 and Dalrymple-Alford & Aamiry, 1970 for English–Arabic and English–French; Dyer, 1971 for English–Spanish; Hamers & Lambert, 1972, 1974 for French–English and Dutch–French; Biederman & Tsao, 1979 for Chinese–English; Kiyak, 1982 for Turkish–English). One possible explanation is to attribute it to the physical difference between the stimulus word and its translation equivalent: Preston & Lambert (1969) demonstrated that interlingual and intralingual interference were almost equal when a stimulus word was physically similar to its translation equivalent (e.g. *red* and ROT) but that intralingual interference was greater than interlingual interference when the two words were different (e.g. *black* and SCHWARZ).

Further support for this explanation comes from studies by Hamers & Bertrand (1973) who, using a language-named task in which subjects had to attend to the language in which the name of different languages was spoken (e.g. they had to respond FRANCAIS to the French word *néerlandais*), found that more interference occurred when the translation equivalents were similar (as with *français* and *frans* than when they were different (as with *Dutch* and *nederlands*); by Biederman & Tsao (1979) in a Chinese version of the Stroop task using different ideographic scripts; and by Fang, Tzeng & Alva (1981), who found interlingual interference to be higher when the two languages shared the same script (Spanish–English) than when they had different scripts (Chinese–English and Japanese–English).

Furthermore, the degree of interlingual interference depends also upon the bilingual's proficiency in both languages. Magiste (1985) observed that, for Swedish–German bilinguals who had attained different degrees of dominance in one or the other language, the dominant language caused more interlingual interference than the weaker language; this is equally true for a Stroop task and for a bilingual dichotic listening[3] task (Magiste, 1986). This may be congruent with other results which found relatively more interlingual interference from the dominant language than from the weaker language. Ehri & Ryan (1980), for example, observed that in a picture–word interference task

Spanish–English bilinguals would display greater interlingual interference from Spanish than from English.

4.1.1.3 A two-switch model?

However, can we conclude on the basis of experiments done with single words that no input switch exists? Rather than rejecting the switch hypothesis Macnamara (1967b) proposed a two-switch model: one switch for the verbal input controlled by the environment and an independent output switch under the subject's control. This mechanism would allow the bilingual to encode in one language while decoding in the other. Thus the two languages would be simultaneously activated but independent from each other. In support of this approach Macnamara and his colleagues (Macnamara, 1967b; Macnamara, Krauthamer & Bolgar, 1968; Macnamara & Kushnir, 1971) cite results from studies using mixed-language reading. They found that, in reading a mixed-lingual text, bilingual subjects would take time for switching from one language to another; they estimated both the input and the output switch to be around 0.2 seconds.

Although this interpretation was supported by one other study (Kolers, 1966), Macnamara's two-switch model has been criticized by several authors. Dalrymple-Alford (1985) argues that no clear conclusion can be drawn from the fact that it takes time to switch languages in a mixed-lingual text. The estimate that the input switch is close to 0.2 seconds cannot be sustained, as there is a wide within- and between-experiments variation in the time observed. Furthermore, the time taken for switching can be accounted for in a different way: alternating languages within sentences in an artificial way must generate unfamiliar syntactically anomalous patterns and this could probably account for slower responding times. I. Taylor (1971), using a slightly modified version of the mixed-language reading task, demonstrated that when the subject controls the point of switching no time is taken up by changing languages. In a similar vein, Chan, Chau & Hoosain (1983) observed that, with two languages as different as Chinese and English, no time was taken for switching when the switch occurred at natural boundaries (as defined by bilinguals who code-switch in a natural setting). They conclude that natural code-switching does not take time for bilinguals familiar with code alternation and that there is no need to postulate the existence of an input switch.

Grosjean (1985a) and Grosjean & Soares (1986) recently attempted to identify some of the features in which bilingual speech modes might differ from monolingual ones. They observed that recognition of code-switched words depends on (1) general factors such as word properties (e.g. frequency of the word), preceding context and listener's pragmatic and cognitive knowledge; and (2) specific code-switching factors which are either psychosocial (speaker's habits and attitudes, listener's perception and situation) or linguistic (e.g.

density of code-switching in text or phonotactic characteristics) in nature. (For a further discussion of code-switching, see Chapter 6.2.3.)

If, as Macnamara suggested, an input switch really operates at a pre-attentive level, it does not account for the interlingual interference observable in the Stroop tasks. Further proof against the existence of an input switch comes from an experiment by Guttentag, Haith, Goodman & Hauch (1984). Using a cross-language flanker technique, they found that a different-language distractor has a similar effect to a same-language distractor. Goodman, Haith, Guttentag & Rao (1985) also argue against a voluntary input switch: they observed that the meaning of a distractor affects picture-naming in balanced bilingual children and in beginning-second-language learners as soon as they can read the distractor. Furthermore, several bilingual decoding tasks do not take more time than monolingual ones: responses to two-word signals are unaffected by language mixing (Dalrymple-Alford & Aamiry, 1967); reading mixed-language lists does not take more time than reading unilingual lists (Dalrymple-Alford, 1985); categorizations of words in one language are made equally fast in categories labelled in the same as in a different language (Caramazza & Brones, 1980) and mixing languages does not affect the judgement of comparisons (Desrochers & Petrusic, 1983).

The input-switch hypothesis is also disconfirmed by experiments in which a continuous text was used. In bilingual dichotic listening tasks[3] a subject is unable to attend to a message in one language received in one ear while ignoring a message in the other language, received in the other ear (Treisman, 1964; Moore, Macnamara & Tucker, 1970; Magiste, 1986). If a switch mechanism was operating at a pre-attentive level no interference from the distracting message would occur.

4.1.1.4 *The output-switch model*

Rather than postulating a switch mechanism, Treisman (1969) suggested that all characteristics of verbal input are analysed regardless of the language used. Treisman's approach has received empirical support from a number of studies. Looking at the errors produced in several Stroop-like interference tasks, Hamers & Lambert (1972, 1974) and Hamers (1973) concluded that the incorrect responses almost always corresponded to the stimulus word which was either read, repeated (in an auditory version) or translated; however, the language in which the response was expected was almost always correctly chosen. From these studies it was concluded that: (1) an output switch operating somewhere in the on-line output processing had to be responsible for the correct choice of the language in which to encode the response; (2) there was no evidence for a similar switch operating in the input processing; and (3) the major source of interference stemmed from semantic similarity between the stimulus word and a possible but incorrect response.

Further proof that bilinguals control their language of output but that they cannot avoid decoding in both languages comes from experiments using cross-language semantically ambiguous words (Hamers & Lambert, 1974). When bilinguals are presented with written words that can be part of both their languages but have different meanings in each language (e.g. the words *chat* and *pain* in French and English) they react to them as to homographs in one language: frequency and grammatical class are more powerful factors than language for identifying the meaning of the word. That is, when a bilingual was, for example, presented with the English words *chat* and *ail* in an English word list he would give the translation equivalents of the most common associations to the words *chat* and *ail* in French (e.g. DOG to the word *chat* in the English list). His language of response was however almost always correct. Professional translators trilingual in French–English–German would also often mistakenly translate these words in the list; for example, the word *chat* in the English list would often be translated into KATZE, that is, the German word for its French meaning. Hamers & Lambert interpret these results as proof that no switch mechanism is triggered off at the input level and that bilinguals decode all verbal material for meaning.

In summary, then, the experiments mentioned above show that there is a certain degree of independence between decoding and encoding mechanisms but fail to prove the existence of a switch mechanism in decoding at the semantic level. We cannot, however, exclude the possibility that a switch mechanism may occur at more surface levels of processing. One study (Caramazza, Yeni-Komshin & Zurif, 1974) tested the two-switch model at the phonological level: the authors concluded that, at the phonological level, a switch mechanism had to be postulated for the input as well as for the output process. However, we lack further empirical evidence on that point and the question remains: if there is an input switch, where along the on-line processing of language will it be activated? Altenberg & Cairns (1983) showed that in a lexical decision task both sets of phonotactic constraints are simultaneously active during processing by a bilingual, even though the task calls for one language only.

Mack (1986) argues that language interdependence is not limited to the semantic level but already exists at the syntactic level: she found that, in a laboratory setting where they were required to do rapid on-line processing, French–English bilinguals recognized grammatically incorrect English sentences that followed French word order as correct more often than did monolinguals. She concludes that there is no decoding switch mechanism operating but that bilinguals cannot avoid the interaction of their linguistic knowledge when decoding in one language and thus that keeping the languages functionally separated must occur further on in the on-line processing. She further suggests that a model for verbal decoding in the bilingual must include a mechanism of functional linguistic interdependence. Because the bilingual cannot suppress the automatic activation of one language in rapid on-line processing, he is more likely to use his two languages in active restructuring in either of his languages.

4.1.2 A model of the bilingual's information processing

If one of the bilingual's two languages cannot be switched off during the decoding of verbal information we may then wonder which type of mechanism enables the bilingual to function in one language without interference from the other in a natural setting. Hamers & Lambert (1974) demonstrated that context, especially linguistic context – for example, the presence of an article before a word – was a powerful factor in disambiguating cross-language ambiguous words. They interpret this as further proof that all perceptual input, verbal or not, is analysed; a bilingual processes all verbal information he receives and no input switch can account for his capacity to keep his two languages apart; this capacity seems to operate only at the output level; thus a bilingual must have developed some decision mechanism concerning the language of encoding. Indeed, in the Stroop-like tasks there were hardly any errors on the choice of the language of response, even when the task was to name the language of the stimulus in the other language (e.g. respond with the English word FRENCH to the French stimulus word *anglais* in a list where stimuli in both languages were mixed and the subject was constantly required to switch his response language) (Hamers & Bertrand, 1973). This is also consonant with Ben-Zeev's (1977a) assumption that bilinguals develop a greater sensitivity to perceptual clues and strategies which enables them to decide in which language to decode (discussed in Chapter 2.3.2).

Magiste (1982, 1985) observed that Spanish–English, English–German and Swedish–German bilinguals took more time than monolinguals to process verbal material in either language and that this was more pronounced with infrequent than with common words; Soares & Grosjean (1984) also assume that bilinguals search both their lexicons in monolingual processing. Magiste interprets her data as an indication that bilinguals have a central semantic system and have to take a greater number of decisions, that is, bilingual information processing requires more controlled processing and less automaticity than monolingual processing. Landry (1978) also suggested that bilingual information processing calls for a deeper semantic analysis than verbal processing in one language. This is also in line with Bialystok & Ryan's (1985a, b) hypothesis that early experience with two languages might demand a greater amount of analysed knowledge and exercise of control in linguistic processing (see Chapter 3.1.1).

Obler & Albert (1978) and Albert & Obler (1978) proposed an alternative to the input-switch model. It seems that a bilingual processes verbal input through a continuously operating monitor system which controls the input through an analysis-by-synthesis[4] device, that is, by constantly testing inputs

against their potential correctness. In a first stage all incoming stimuli are processed at the phonetic level and assigned to potential phonemes which are in
turn assigned to potential words; these are then interpreted syntactically; decisions on meaning would also take the linguistic and non-linguistic context
into consideration. The monitor assigns priorities in interpretation and is prepared to redirect decisions. Such a model takes into account the fact that all
verbal input is processed, that a subject can constrain output to a single
language, but allows borrowings and language switching when appropriate.
Even when the monitor is primed to decode in one language it can still process
the other language.

The approach presented by Albert & Obler has the merit of proposing a
model which accounts for the empirical evidence on the linguistic access
mechanisms in the bilingual, both for input and for output processing. However, from the above discussion it appears that the problem of interdependence
between the two languages occurs at a deeper level of processing than the
access mechanisms. At the same time we have to assume that there is a certain
degree of independence between the input and the output processes and that
somewhere in the on-line processing the subject is in control of the output
language. This is apparent from the preceding studies and also from the existence of simultaneous interpreters (see Chapter 10.1).

Green (1986) suggested that, in order to account for the data on bilingual
processing we must distinguish between three stages of a language system; a
selective stage, which plays a role in controlling speech output; an active stage,
in which language plays a role in ongoing processing; and a dormant stage, in
which language resides in long-term memory but with no role in ongoing processes. Green assumes that bilingual speech processing is the outcome of an
interplay between resource, activation and control. He proposes an inhibitory
control model which accounts for selection of one language of output and inhibition of the other; when speaking L_A, devices for recognizing L_A must be
activated and those for producing L_A must be selected; selection includes activation of L_A and suppression of L_B. In code-switching there is no suppression of
L_B, but regulation occurs in such a way that the syntactic rules of both
languages are observed (see Chapter 6.2.3); in translation (from L_A to L_B) internal suppression inhibits output in L_A. This approach is interesting in so far
as it explains bilingual behaviour in monolingual and bilingual speech modes
and abnormal bilingual behaviour as in polyglot aphasia. This model
attempts to explain how a monitor system can regulate bilingual behaviour.
We now turn to the question: how does the bilingual organize and store his
two languages?

4.2 Language representation in bilinguals

Any model of language processing must explain how physically different but functionally equivalent stimuli are interpreted, recognized and remembered as such. This is true for intramodality variations, such as differences in voice characteristics, accents and dialects, for differences between modalities as in speech and written language, and for differences between languages. Where in the on-line processing of language does this equation occur? Morton (1979a; 1980), for example, suggests that a superordinate cognitive structure, the *logogen*,[5] underlies different modalities which would have access to them via separate lexical stores. Is this also true for representations in two languages? How will bilingual experience influence the bilingual's organization of knowledge, storage and retrieval system? Whereas there is general agreement that the bilingual must have a representation common to both his languages, the controversial question to be addressed is: at what level of processing does this common representation occur? In the present section we will attempt to answer these questions, first by discussing how early bilingual experience might impinge on cognitive representations and secondly by discussing the different models of bilingual memory.

4.2.1 Coordinate versus compound bilinguals

When introducing the distinction between compound and coordinate bilinguality as a psychological concept, Ervin & Osgood (1954) suggested that for compound bilinguals a verbal label and its translation equivalent have one representation common to both languages, whereas for coordinate bilinguals there should be two distinct representations, one for each language. The compound–coordinate dimension has already been discussed in Chapter 1.2.1.3, where we insisted on the necessity of viewing this difference as two poles of a continuum on which bilinguals will vary. This distinction is relevant to the present discussion in so far as it implies that bilinguals do not all organize verbal material in the same way; coordinate bilinguals are expected to have a more independent organization than compound bilinguals, as is supported by a number of empirical studies.

Analysing the effect of language-acquisition context on bilingual organization, Lambert, Havelka & Crosby (1958) demonstrated that separate acquisition contexts for each language (as for example when one language is learned at home and the other at school as opposed to both languages being acquired in the family) will lead to more functional separation between the bilingual's two codes. More specifically, they assumed that, when compared with their compound counterparts, coordinate bilinguals (1) make more semantic distinctions between a word and its translation equivalent; (2) have two relatively independent association networks for translation equivalents; and (3) have greater difficulty with translation. Hypotheses (1) and (2) were confirmed, as their study indeed demonstrated that: (1) the semantic difference between translation equivalents, when measured with semantic-evaluation scales, is larger for coordinate bilinguals; and (2) repetition of translation equivalents will be of more help to the compound bilingual in a recall task, thereby pointing to a greater semantic interdependence. However, there was no difference in speed of translation; these results suggest that when required both types of bilinguals can switch equally fast from one language to the other (Lambert, 1969).

Semantic satiation and *semantic generalization* are two other techniques used in the study of bilingual organization. Semantic satiation controls the effect of continuous repetition of a word on its meaning. For example, a subject is exposed to the continuous repetition of the word *house*; the intensity of the connotative meaning, measured through the semantic differential technique,[6] is greatly diminished through its continuous repetition (Lambert & Jakobovits, 1960). In the bilingual form, one verifies if the semantic satiation obtained for a word in one language is extended to its translation equivalent. Semantic generalization controls if a conditioning to a word in one language (e.g. a key press to *glove* in English) is extended to its translation equivalent in another language (e.g. *gant* in French). Jakobovits & Lambert (1961; 1967) demonstrated that the degree of semantic satiation for translation equivalents is higher in compound than in coordinate bilinguals; they interpret this data as an indication that compound bilinguals have a common semantic store for both linguistic codes whereas coordinates would have more independent stores.

A large number of experiments call upon association techniques in order to assess the relation between the two linguistic codes in compound and coordinate bilinguals. Generally speaking these experiments demonstrate that compound bilinguals have a higher degree of interdependence in the organization of their two codes than coordinates. For example, compound bilinguals are more adept than coordinates at recognizing a core-concept (Lambert & Rawlings, 1969); in this experiment subjects were exposed to a bilingual word list in which were associates from a key word in both languages (e.g. from the French–English list including words such as *chaise, food, desk, bois, manger*, etc. they had to identify the word TABLE). The results indicated that it was easier for the compound bilinguals to identify the common concept, whereas coordinate bilinguals were more likely to recognize a frequent associate in one language only (e.g. the word *furniture*, a frequent associate of the English *table*).

However, this compound–coordinate distinction is not always evident. For example, in one study (Dillon, McCormack, Petrusic, Cook & Lafleur, 1973), where the compound–coordinate distinction would predict a lesser degree of interlingual interference in coordinates, no such differences were found. If subjects are constrained to follow an associative schema in a core-concept task this difference will also disappear (Arkwright & Viau, 1974). Compound bilinguals may possess dissimilar semantic networks for a word in one language and its translation equivalent (Lambert & Moore, 1966); for the same subject the degree of semantic overlap in two languages is not the same for concrete and abstract words (e.g. Kolers, 1963; Clark, 1978; Hammoud, 1982). Generally speaking a bilingual subject will have a more compound organization for concrete words and a more coordinate one for abstract words. If such a difference between compound and coordinate bilinguals has some psychological reality, as indeed appears from a number of studies, it must be kept in mind that these differences will vary not only according to the subjects but also according to the task and to the linguistic material involved.

From a study on association networks in compound and coordinate bilinguals, Gekoski (1980) concluded that there is only a weak difference between both types of bilingual. However, it must be noted that in this study subjects identified as compound bilinguals had learned their second language at the age of 15. Can we in this case speak of a real compound binguality? Or, as the author himself observed, are we not dealing rather with differences in degree on a compound–coordinate continuum? As we observed in Chapter 1, a real compound binguality can exist only when the language-acquisition histories are very similar for both languages, which cannot be the case when one of the two languages is learned after childhood. This might account for Gekoski's results, and in this sense his data might be viewed as supporting the distinction.

Another body of experimental data also supports the idea that language-acquisition history might play a crucial role in the way that bilingual language processing occurs. Bilinguals who learned their two languages in childhood display different association networks from equally fluent bilinguals who learned their second language later in life. Comparing the association networks of Swedish–Lettish childhood and adolescent/adult bilinguals, Ruke-Dravina (1971) observed that while all bilinguals gave associations in both their languages to a stimulus word, those who were dominant in their mother tongue, and had learned their L_2 as young adults, gave only associations which were either translations of the stimulus word or translations of associations already given in their L_1 when they switched languages in the association chain; in other words, when they switched languages they did not introduce a new concept at the same time. On the other hand, in addition to this type of association, childhood bilinguals also gave associations which were new concepts in the other language. Thus, compound bilinguals do not dissociate a semantic task from code-switching, whereas coordinate bilinguals proceed in two steps.

While it is reasonable to assume that all late bilinguals have a coordinate organization of their two languages, not all childhood bilinguals are compound. Opoku (1983) argues that in developing countries, children who are schooled through an official exogenous language which they use for very different purposes from their mother tongue start developing a compound form of binguality which will gradually evolve and become more coordinate. Comparing the Yoruba and English association networks given by Nigerian

Yoruba-speaking children schooled in English, from different age-groups and with different levels of competence in English, he observed that the older and more competent children gave more English associations which they could not translate into Yoruba; even though they were equally competent in Yoruba and more competent in English they had greater difficulty in translating words they had produced. Opoku concluded that the representational system of the bilingual is not stable over time, but evolves, particularly when the experiences with the two languages are different.

In conclusion, then, whereas there is some evidence in support of the compound–coordinate distinction, it must be viewed as distributed along a continuum, varying from one bilingual person to another, influenced by language-acquisition experience and by certain word characteristics. At present, this distinction is still questioned and its existence is not recognized by all scholars of bilingual language processing. From the above discussion it is clear that bilingual organization follows a relatively more interdependent pattern in compound than in coordinate bilinguals. We can conclude that the degree of interdependence is at least partially a function of the bilingual's language-acquisition history and language experience. As we saw in Chapter 2.2, early bilingual experience does impinge on neuropsychological organization and on cognitive functioning; it also determines a cognitive and semantic organization in which the two languages will be more or less interdependent. We can now turn to the next question: are the languages stored as separate entities which are language-tagged or does the bilingual have a common store for both his languages that will only become functionally separated at the speech-production end?

4.2.2 The bilingual's memory

The most analysed problem of bilingual memory is the degree to which a bilingual's representation of lexical information is common to both his languages. One view, the independence or separate-memories hypothesis, states that there are two independent language-specific memory stores that are in contact with each other via a translation mechanism. The other, the interdependence or common-store hypothesis, holds that bilingual memory is a single system in which information is stored as a complex set of attributes or tags which enables the bilingual to store non-semantic information, such as modality, frequency, spatial and temporal aspects, inclusion in a list and language. Language is then one of these tags through which the common store taps into two lexical systems via a switching mechanism. Both types of model postulate the existence of a mechanism which permits the bilingual to switch from one linguistic system to the other; they differ from each other as to where they locate this mechanism during on-line processing. In the common-store model this switch is situated before semantic memory, whereas in the separate-store model it

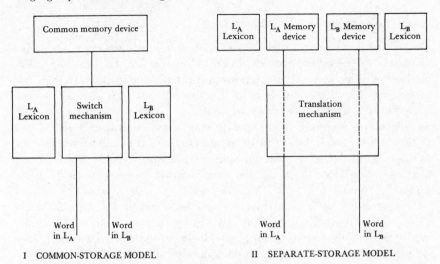

I   COMMON-STORAGE MODEL   II   SEPARATE-STORAGE MODEL

Figure 4.1 The two models of the bilingual's memory

occurs at a much deeper level, and two separate semantic memory devices are postulated. These two models are schematized in Figure 4.1.

If the independence hypothesis is correct, a balanced bilingual should react as a monolingual in both his languages, independently from what he learned in his other language; if, on the other hand, the interdependence hypothesis reflects the storage processes, then this would become evident in a variety of memory tasks. It must be observed that this assumption deals with semantic memory, which permits the storage of words and their meanings, and not with episodic memory[7] or with the different types of short-term memories relevant to the decoding and encoding processes. (For more details on memory processes in language behaviour we refer the reader to Underwood, 1969; Andersen & Bower, 1973; Morton, 1979b, 1980.)

Generally speaking the common-store model is supported by evidence indicating that intralingual behaviour does not differ from interlingual behaviour, whereas evidence for the separate-store model stems from studies in which bilinguals either respond differently in their two languages or fail to transfer from one language to the other. The controversy is still unresolved: McCormack (1977) claims that on the grounds of scientific parsimony and empirical evidence the common-store hypothesis is the more suitable one, whereas Kolers (1978) advocates the separate-store model on the grounds that empirical evidence using a variety of tasks cannot be explained by the common-storage model. Most of the evidence that sustains either approach comes from experiments with association tasks in the two languages, language-recognition tasks, free recall and recognition of monolingual and bilingual input and reaction times to bilingual stimuli.

4.2.2.1 *Evidence from association tasks*

One of the first studies to test this issue used a word-association technique (Kolers, 1963): English–Spanish, English–German and English–Thai bilinguals gave different word associations to translation equivalents in their two languages. (For example, a Spanish–English bilingual will give the associations WOOD, FURNITURE, CHAIR to the English word *table*, but associations such as COMER and CONSUMIR to its Spanish translation equivalent *mesa*.) Kolers (1968) interprets this data as proof for a separate storage and argues that if a bilingual person had a common storage then the response given in one language should be the translation equivalent of the response in the other language.

Similar results on association tasks were obtained by Lambert & Moore (1966) with French–English bilinguals and by Dalrymple-Alford & Aamiry (1970) with Arabic–English bilinguals. However, the authors attribute these differences to the fact that translation equivalents do not have identical referential and connotative meanings in both languages, and not to the existence of separate semantic memories. Translation equivalents are processed as synonyms in the same language. This latter interpretation has been questioned, as translation equivalents are processed neither as repetitions of the same word in one language (Kintsch, 1970) nor as synonyms; e.g. they are better than synonyms in facilitating recall (McLeod, 1976). Translation equivalents share the same supralinguistic semantic representation, whereas synonyms have distinct representations which share the same referent.

4.2.2.2 *Language tagging*

Another type of evidence used by Kolers to argue in favour of the separate-storage model is the fact that bilinguals recall the language of a verbal stimulus above chance level (Kolers, 1965; Lambert, Ignatov & Krauthamer, 1968; Saegert, Hamayan & Ahmar, 1975). According to a number of scholars (Goggin & Wickins, 1971; Rose, Rose, King & Perez, 1975; Paivio & Begg, 1981), this cannot, however, be used as proof for a separate-store model: an alternative explanation is equally valid. Verbal input can be stored in a common semantic or lexical memory with a language-tag attached to it. Evidence in favour of this interpretation comes from an experiment by Rose & Carroll (1974): when English–Spanish bilinguals were instructed to recall the language of a stimulus in addition to the word itself, they did this without errors. Light, Berger & Bardales (1975) demonstrated that several non-semantic attributes of a word can be stored if required by the task. However, phonology seems to act as a very powerful tag: Brown, Sharma & Kirsner (1984) observed that it was easy to remember the language of a written stimulus when there were important phonological differences between the two languages, as between English and Urdu, but difficult to remember the language when two stimuli differed in script only, as with Hindi and Urdu. They interpret their data as proof that modalities converge into a common lexical representation and that script is a 'weak' language attribute whereas phonology would be a 'strong' attribute.

4.2.2.3 Recall and recognition tasks

Support for the separate-storage model stems also from experiments on free recall. Tulving & Colotla (1970), because they observed that trilinguals recall unilingual word lists better than bi- or trilingual ones (French, English and Spanish), argue that memory is fairly well organized in one language, but deteriorates when language boundaries have to be crossed in order to form higher-order organizational units; thus, a bilingual would have difficulties in structuring coherent categories across his languages. Although she obtained opposite results on recall of bilingual prose (which is better recalled than monolingual prose), Hummel (1986) also argues for separate stores: a difference in performance results from separate underlying representations. However, this interpretation is not supported by other researchers: as no differences between learning of monolingual and bilingual lists are found, free-recall results in bilinguals are generally interpreted in support of the common-store hypothesis (Nott & Lambert, 1968). Furthermore, recalling a word list in one language (e.g. Spanish) is greatly facilitated if, prior to the recall, a list of translation equivalents (e.g. in English) has been learned (Young & Saegert, 1966; Lopez & Young, 1974).

Kolers & Gonzales (1980) found that word repetition and presentation of a translation equivalent have the same effect on improving recall, whereas this is not the case for a synonym in the same language. They attribute these results to the bilingual's ability to use translation equivalents in an interchangeable way, rather than to a common semantic memory. They argue that postulating two separate stores is more economical than postulating one common semantic store and one for the language-tag; however, they do not explain why it is more economical to postulate two semantic stores rather than a common semantic store and a linguistic-tag store. Their argumentation is therefore not very convincing and their results can be equally well interpreted in terms of the common store.

Young & Navar (1968) analysed retroactive inhibition[8] in lists of paired associations in the bilingual's two languages: a bilingual learns first a list of paired associates in one of his languages, e.g. the pair *gato–comer* in Spanish; he is then given a list of paired associates for which the first word of the pair is a translation equivalent but not the second word, in his second language, e.g. in the English list the word *cat* is associated with *house*. When asked to recall the pairs of the first list he will have great difficulty and will often give the translation equivalent of the second pair, e.g. *gato–casa*, instead of the correct response. The authors interpret these results as proof that bilinguals have a common store. These findings have been confirmed in a number of studies: by Kintsch & Kintsch (1969), using free recall of monolingual and bilingual lists with German–English bilinguals; by Lopez, Hicks & Young (1974), using paired-associates lists which differed either on the words only, the language only or on both, with Spanish–English bilinguals; by Liepmann & Saegert (1974), who tested Arabic–English bilinguals for their recall of the novelty of a word in monolingual and bilingual lists; and by Saegert, Kazarian & Young (1973), who used the part–whole transfer paradigm[9] in a bilingual Arabic–English version.

4.2.2.4 Processing time

Differences have been found between the processing time in monolingual and bilingual conditions. Kirsner, Brown, Abrul, Chadha & Sharma (1980) observed that Hindi–English bilinguals have longer reaction times in taking lexical decisions (about the novelty of the word) in intralingual than in interlingual conditions; they interpret these results as an indication that bilinguals have separate lexical stores. This interpretation is challenged by Magiste (1979, 1982, 1986), who observed that English–German and Swedish–German bilinguals take more time than monolinguals in monolingual verbal processing; according to her this is an indication that bilinguals have to choose between a larger number of alternatives, thus that they have a common semantic system to which words in different languages are linked by tags, and that in verbal processing they scan through the whole store.

4.2.2.5 Language dominance and memory

The degree of balance attained by a bilingual seems also to play a certain role in memory. Several studies with dominant bilinguals point to the fact that a higher proficiency in one language will influence bilingual memory. Whether this is due to different representations for both languages or to an influence on the retrieval process is not yet clear. Tulving & Colotla (1970) found that the dominant language was more impaired than the weaker language in recalling items from bi- and trilingual lists; they attribute these results to the difficulty of forming higher-level units and interpret them as an indication of independence between the different lexical storages.

Goggin & Wickins (1971) found that, when comparing the effect of a language switch versus a switch in semantic categories on recall (a semantic switch has a positive effect on recall) in balanced and dominant Spanish–English bilinguals, the balanced bilinguals evidenced more recovery under language change than did the dominant bilinguals; they concluded to a greater degree of independence in the balanced bilinguals. McCormack (1977), however, argues that an explanation in terms of a language-tag is equally consistent: according to Dillon *et al.* (1973) recovery could be attributable to a phonemic switch. This interpretation was confirmed by O'Neil & Huot (1984), who found that balanced bilinguals expressed a similar shift in responding to meaningless trigrams in French and English. Recovery effect observed as a consequence of language shift does not necessarily imply a separate semantic system but might just reflect separate phonological representations.

Berkovits, Abarbanel & Sitman (1984) found that in a sentence-recognition task of mixed-language passages, English-dominant and Hebrew-dominant bilinguals scored higher on the recognition task when the input was in their non-dominant language; furthermore, while they found that dominant bilinguals, proficient in their weaker language, scored higher on a recognition task in the weaker language than those less proficient in their weaker language, no evidence was found that either group of dominant bilinguals would use translation procedure. They interpret these results as an indication that dominant bilinguals do not store information via a translation process, but that they retain material in their weaker language better because processing in a weaker language calls for more controlled analysis and less automaticity.

In summary, then, although there appear to be some contradictions between the different research results, the sum of empirical evidence seems to favour the single-store model. As McCormack (1977) observes, the common-memory model makes most sense both in terms of parsimony and in terms of explanatory power. The one-store model is also consistent with cognitive theories that assume one single conceptual format for all knowledge (Paivio & Begg, 1981). However, it is not entirely satisfactory in the sense that it cannot account for all the empirical evidence.

4.2.3 The dual-coding model

In order to resolve the controversy between the one-store and the two-store model, Paivio & Begg (1981) proposed an alternative model. Several studies on paired associated show that recall is better if there is an interaction between the word-to-be-recalled and another word or an instruction that evokes imagery (Paivio, 1971; Paivio & Begg, 1981). Words are stored in two different ways: verbal representations (*logogens*) and non-verbal ones or imagery, *imagens*.[5] The two systems of representation are different from each other by the nature and the organization of their units, the way they process information and the function they perform in perception, language processing and cognition. Linguistic information is essentially stored as verbal representations, and non-linguistic information as imagery. The bilingual has verbal representations which correspond to words in each language; the two languages are organized in separate but interconnected associative structures resulting from the experience with the two languages. In addition, each subset also has connections with the imagery system (for example, the image *cat* will evoke the word CAT and vice versa). When a word is decoded, representations in each of the subsystems are activated and leave memory traces. Thus storage of a word is a direct function of the two codes: if the two codes are used in memorizing a word, its storage is facilitated (Paivio, 1971).

Pavio & Desrochers (1980) suggest that the bilingual has two verbal representations, one for each language, in addition to a representation in the imagery system. These three systems are independent and autonomous from each other but are interconnected at the referential level. Thus, the verbal representation in L_A is in relation with the verbal representation in L_B and a verbal unit (logogen) in L_A can activate a verbal unit in L_B. But a logogen in L_A can also activate an imagen in the imagery system, which can in turn activate a logogen in L_B. Translation equivalents will not necessarily activate the same imagen, but there is a degree of overlap between the imagery evoked by both logogens which is a function of the bilingual's experience with the two languages. This accounts for the compound–coordinate distinction discussed earlier (4.2.1). Winograd, Cohen & Baressi (1976) postulated the existence of *cultural imagery*, which implies that bilinguals would have slightly different images associated with translation equivalents. There is no one-to-one correspondence in the imagery system but rather a certain degree of overlap.

The two verbal–representational systems function independently from each other, but there is one memory in imagery which is in constant interaction with the two verbal systems. According to Paivio & Begg (1981) this model explains a larger number of findings on bilingual memory than would either the single-store or the separate-store model. In order to test the dual-coding model, Paivio & Lambert (1981) asked French–English bilinguals to respond to a list composed of either pictures, or French or English words, by either writing the name of the object in the picture in English, rewriting the English word or translating the French word into English; bilinguals were also asked either to copy an English word, to translate it into French, or to draw a picture of the object signified. A recall test for the English words was then given. The results demonstrate that recall improved from the unilingual (copying), to the bilingual (translating) and the dual-coding (naming a picture or drawing the referent of a word) conditions. The authors interpret these results as supporting the dual-coding model and as an indication that the verbal storages are relatively independent from each other.

That translation of concepts leads to better recall than simple repetition was also found by Glanzer & Duarte (1971). For Lambert & Paivio this would be due to the fact that, in translation, two verbal stores are put into play instead of one. The dual-coding model also explains Kolers's & Gonzales's (1980) findings that translation equivalents have similar effects to repetitions on recall, whereas this is not the case for synonyms. Further support for the dual-coding model comes from an experiment by Arnedt & Gentile (1986), who observed that picture-naming is a more powerful means of encoding than verbal means; in addition they found that the translation mode is influenced by language-acquisition history.

However, it must be noted that the dual-coding model concerns the access to representation rather than the organization of memory. A single semantic store could be reached through two verbal channels; the activation of more than one channel would facilitate recall and recognition. The higher scores obtained in the translation condition may be an indication of the existence of a unique semantic organization linked to more than one verbal channel. This interpretation is in agreement with Champagnol's (1978, 1979) work: he observed that a change of language between the stimulus and the response word in a recognition task, as, for example, recognizing the English word *horse* when the French word *cheval* had been presented, lowers the recognition level of an item. However, when the stimulus word was tagged as to the language of response that would be required (e.g. the French word *cheval* presented simultaneously with the letter E indicating that an English translation equivalent had to be recognized), then recognition would reach the same level as in the unilingual condition. Thus, the simple activation of one channel is enough to render information accessible.

Double verbal coding (translation condition) does not provoke as much recall as dual coding (language and picture); thus, one might assume that there is a store common to both languages different from the one accessible through imagery. Champagnol (1973) postulated the existence of super-ordinate semantic categories common to both languages in addition to language-specific semantic categories. In the same vein, Potter, So, von Eckhardt & Feldman (1984) suggest that in information processing the two languages are linked through a conceptual system; they asked several groups of Chinese–English and English–French dominant bilinguals, varying in their proficiency in the weaker language, to name pictures, read and translate words in both their languages. The findings indicate that dominant bilinguals take longer to translate a word from their dominant language into their weaker language than to name the referent of a picture in their weaker language. This outcome is interpreted as favouring a concept-mediation hypothesis rather than a word-association hypothesis suggested by the dual-coding model. The authors agree with Paivio & Desrochers (1980) that, if there is a single representation, it is shared by the image; they reject, however, the idea that translation equivalents in the two systems might be directly associated and share a linguistic representation which is not conceptual, as this would call for a faster response in L_2 to a word in the dominant language than to a picture.

Support for the dual-coding model comes also from experiments with concrete and abstract words. Saegert, Kazarian & Young (1973) analysed translation errors in recall of bilingual paired-associates lists in which Spanish and English translation equivalents had been paired with different words in the same list (e.g. *gato–casa* and *cat–food*); half of the pairs were concrete nouns and half abstract. They assumed that concrete items would be more likely than abstract terms to be stored in a non-verbal form and that this would result in more translation errors with the concrete pairs, which appeared to be the case. They concluded that concrete words are processed as images whereas abstract words are analysed through verbal representations; because the verbal channels are independent this will provoke fewer translation errors.

This independence of the verbal channels is, however, questioned by Magiste (1986): she observed not only that Swedish–English and German–English bilinguals are slower than monolinguals in decoding words in their two languages, but also that this difference is relatively more pronounced with infrequent than with frequent words (Magiste, 1982); she attributes the difference between access times for rare and common words to the degree of automaticity of the task and argues that the difference in time processing between bilinguals and monolinguals may be equally well explained by a separate-store model which calls for access time, or by a common-store where scanning time would be longer; the interaction between both has to be explained by a common-store model, as once the store is accessed it should not take the bilingual relatively more time to process rare words. From their findings that bilinguals take more time than monolinguals to process non-words Soares & Grosjean (1984) also conclude that bilinguals scan their whole lexicon in verbal processing, but that in decoding bilingual texts they scan the base-language lexicon first.

O'Neil & Dion (1983) found results similar to those of Saegert, Kazarian & Young (1973) with a recognition task for concrete and abstract sentences in the two languages; they suggest that the encoding of concrete verbal items shares more attributes common to both languages than that of abstract items and that, therefore, different-language encoding of abstract verbal information might lead to a greater variability in representation than concrete verbal encoding. Bilingual processing would be a double encoding of similar experiences and can be affected by different attributions and connotations peculiar to the context of encoding and to the particular languages. Bilingual memory organization then varies according to (1) the nature of the task, e.g. recognition relies more on perceptual, and recall more on semantic, characteristics (Champagnol, 1978); (2) the context of encoding (e.g. Champagnol, 1973; O'Neil & Dion, 1983); (3) the non-verbal and verbal characteristics of the stimulus (e.g. Saegert, Kazarian & Young, 1973); and (4) the presence of the two languages in the task (e.g. Magiste, 1986; Hummel, 1986). The degree to which storage is language-specific varies also with language-acquisition history and competence in both languages (e.g. Tulving & Colotla, 1970; Champagnol, 1973).

As suggested by Paivio & Desrochers (1980), there are several access channels to representations, namely imagery and two verbal channels. The two verbal channels join in a common semantic store and there is a referential link between imagery and the totality of the verbal representation structure. For each verbal channel there is a language-specific memory device which stores stimulus-specific features, such as phonology and perceptual aspects and possibly some limited lexical aspects: these are organized in language-specific logogens (in L_A and L_B). These logogens, linked via the referent, are further organized into higher-order semantic structures. This whole structure is related to the imagen through a referential link. We agree with Paivio & Desrochers that, in order to explain the functioning of bilingual memory, imagery is an important component of verbal memory; we disagree with them, however, that semantic memory is language-specific and suggest that postulating a common semantic memory fed by the two separate verbal channels, each one with a surface memory device, is a better explanation for the existing evidence. This model is depicted in Figure 4.2.

To sum up, then, the dual-coding model is a promising alternative to the unresolved issue of the common-store or the separate-store models. As we have mentioned before, however (Hamers & Blanc, 1983), besides a surface level on which two separate representations store specific characteristics, including tagging and perceptual aspects, there is a deeper level, that of semantic storage, which draws on both languages. This higher-order non-language-specific

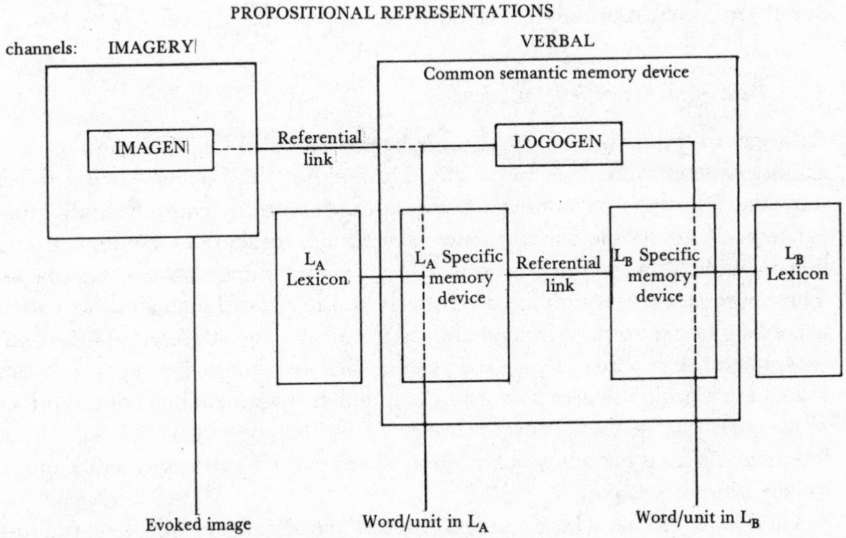

Figure 4.2 Double-coding model adapted to bilingual memory

organization, together with the imaging process, is then further organized into concepts and propositional representations. This approach is consistent with recent trends in psycholinguistics and information processing.

4.3 Non-verbal behaviour of the bilingual

Language processing is not an isolated phenomenon but is integrated in a complex pattern of human behaviour. The use of a language includes not only phonological, syntactic and semantic rules but also a repertoire of non-verbal behaviour. If we take an extreme view of the whorfian hypothesis (Whorf, 1956), that language moulds thought, then we have to assume that when a bilingual changes languages, he has to rely on a different set of representations. Birdwhistell (1970) suggested that the interaction between culture and language is such that each cultural group possesses a unique non-verbal behavioural repertoire inseparable from language. If this is the case then the bilingual's non-verbal behaviour must vary according to the language he uses. Bilingual experience will influence not only the paralinguistic behaviour and the gestural behaviour accompanying language but also the totality of the bilingual's behavioural repertoire including personality traits.

Research in these domains is, however, extremely scarce: there are just a few indications that bilinguals may react in different ways from monolinguals, but the amplitude of these differences is still unknown. More importantly, the whole field lacks theoretical underpinning. In this section we will briefly review some empirical data from which it is at present difficult to generalize but which may be an important addition to our knowledge on bilingual behaviour and therefore yield promises for further development.

4.3.1 Paralinguistic and gestural behaviour

Paralinguistic discourse features have been studied in English–German and English–French bilinguals by Wiens, Manuagh & Matarazzo (1976). They took the following paralinguistic measures: (1) mean length of individual expressions; (2) simple reaction times to verbal input and (3) the frequency of interruptions during conversations in each of the bilingual's two languages. These three measures remained relatively stable across languages but varied according to the content independently from the language used. These findings suggest that bilinguals do not process their two languages separately but that there is a high degree of overlap in linguistic organization. For a number of features, one memory structure selected by the content would serve both languages. This is further proof of the relevance of semantic representations in information processing.

Lacroix & Rioux (1978) videorecorded paralinguistic and gestural behaviour of francophone and anglophone monolinguals and of French–English bilinguals who spoke in either of their languages. Then, they asked franco-phone and anglophone judges to identify the language that was spoken from the visual clues only. Whereas it was easy for the judges to recognize the language spoken by monolinguals of both groups, they had great difficulty in guessing the language spoken by bilinguals. The authors concluded that gestural behaviour was not affected by the language spoken but that bilinguals develop a unique repertoire that they share across languages. It must however be observed that in this experiment the bilinguals were not balanced and that although they were highly proficient in their L_2, they could still be identified as anglophones and francophones. This invalidates Lacroix & Rioux's findings to a certain extent.

To what extent does a simultaneous infant bilingual develop two distinct sets of non-verbal behaviour and to what extent is he able to switch from one to the other when he switches languages? Although we lack empirical data to answer this question, anecdotal evidence, including our own experience, supports the notion that a balanced bilingual possesses two repertoires of non-verbal behaviour and switches between them when he switches languages. Indeed, a perfectly balanced bilingual can in all aspects behave as a native speaker of both his languages and will be perceived as such. We thus postulate an output switch for non-verbal behaviour, similar to the output switch for language discussed in 4.1.1.4.

4.3.2 Bilingual behaviour and stress

Non-verbal behaviour will affect linguistic behaviour. Stress, for example, will affect the bilingual's behaviour: Dornic (1978) reported that environmental noise and mental fatigue affect the bilingual's output, especially his weaker language. General language-processing mechanisms are affected by stress: semantic generalization, for example, is influenced by it in the sense that under stress conditions an individual will revert from semantic to phonemic generalization (Luria, 1981). Javier & Alpert (1986) analysed how stress conditions affect the balanced but coordinate bilingual's two languages. Measuring the shift from semantic to phonemic generalization under stress conditions, they concluded that the bilingual's behaviour in both his languages is equally affected by stress conditions, and that therefore both languages are involved in the representations relevant to linguistic generalizations.

4.3.3 The bilingual's personality

Does bilingual experience affect personality? One commonly heard stereotype about bilinguals is that they have 'split minds' (Adler, 1977). This stereotype is supported by anecdotal reports of introspection in which bilinguals affirm that they do not feel the same person when they speak in their different languages

(Grosjean, 1982). However, very little experimental evidence on the bilingual's personality is available. Only the studies by Ervin-Tripp are worth mentioning. She observed that bilinguals give different responses to personality measures presented in either of their languages: asking French–English bilinguals to respond to the TAT[10] in both their languages she found that responses, which are normally stable when repeated in the same language, vary with the language of response (Ervin-Tripp, 1964). Japanese–English bilinguals were found to give more emotional responses in Japanese than in English when responding to sentence completion (a current personality measure) in both languages (Ervin-Tripp, 1964) and to picture interpretation (Ervin-Tripp, 1973). She argues that this may be attributable to a difference in social roles and emotional attitudes linked with the use of each language. Thus, the use of one of his languages can make certain of the bilingual's personality traits more salient. What makes the bilingual unique is not some sort of personality split, but rather the fact that he has integrated behaviour patterns from two cultures in his personality and can apply them successfully to appropriate settings. We discuss this issue further in Chapter 5.2.

At the present time very little can be concluded from the bilingual's non-verbal behaviour or personality. The main and very broad conclusion is that bilingual experience impinges on all aspects of human behaviour and is not limited to language processing alone. Language processing is one of the most salient characteristics of human behaviour; if it is impaired, an individual's behaviour is drastically changed. Research on the interaction between language impairment and bilingual experience is scarce in some areas, such as in dyslexia, schizophrenia and mutism, and more intense in others, such as in stuttering and aphasia. Research on the bilingual nature of language processing in deaf people is developing fast since there is a justified claim that deaf people who have learned a natural language in addition to sign language develop a form of bilinguality (Kyle & Woll, 1985). Because we have limited our present analysis to natural languages we will not discuss this issue further. However, because of its relevance for bilingual processing in general, we will, before closing this chapter, review the state of the art in one area of language impairment, namely in those cases when language impairment results accidentally in bilinguals, that is in the cases of polyglot aphasics.

4.4 Polyglot aphasia

We are interested in the case-studies on aphasia in bilinguals (referred to in the clinical literature as polyglot aphasia) in so far as they shed some light on bilingual processing. Aphasia is a language disorder, associated in most cases with a localized lesion in the left hemisphere. Symptoms are numerous and vary according to the type of aphasia: for example, an aphasic may be capable of reading a word but incapable of identifying its referent; he may be incapable of reading a word but able to point to its referent; or he may be incapable of producing the word for a referent but will be able to recognize the written word. Some aphasics are not capable of naming referents, whereas others, who are, produce ungrammatical strings of words. It must also be observed that in most cases aphasics recover language, expecially if the loss was caused by a cranial trauma rather than by a chronic lesion. Recovery patterns also vary widely from one aphasic case to the other. We will not give a detailed description of all cases of polyglot aphasia (we refer to Paradis, 1977; 1983 and Albert & Obler, 1978 for reviews) but rather attempt to answer the following questions: (1) to what extent is recovery language-specific and able to occur in one language to the exclusion of the other? (2) to what extent are specific bilingual abilities, such as the ability to translate or code-switch, impaired? and (3) does the polyglot aphasic use forms of language mixing which did not occur premorbidly? Finally, we will briefly discuss the relevance of our knowledge on polyglot aphasia for bilingual processing in general.

4.4.1 Recovery in polyglot aphasia

Assumptions about recovery in aphasic polyglots date back to the last century. Ribot (1882) was the first to assess regularities in recovery; from his clinical observations he stated that *the first learned language is the less impaired and should recover first* (Ribot's law). Because this appears true for many, but not all, cases of polyglot aphasia, Pitrès (1895) formulated a second rule: *the most familiar or most used language is first recovered* (Pitrès's law). However, some cases of polyglot aphasia fit neither of these laws. Therefore, Albert & Obler (1978), reviewing 108 case-studies of polyglot aphasia, conclude that Ribot's law does not apply above chance level, whereas Pitrès's law is applicable in a number of cases when the patient is under the age of 60. These laws can be modified by a large number of factors determining the nature of the aphasia; Paradis (1977) identifies three sources of influence on selective recovery: psychosocial, modality (written language) and hemispheric laterality factors.

Language-acquisition history will determine the polyglot aphasic's behaviour. According to Lambert & Fillenbaum (1959) language-acquisition history, which is a determining factor in the degree of interdependence of the bilingual's representations, will play an important role in aphasia: they observed that polyglot aphasics, who had presumably developed a compound form of bilinguality, show more similar symptoms and recovery patterns in both languages than coordinate bilinguals who became aphasic. Although Whitaker (1978) criticizes the psychological reality of the compound–coordinate distinction, he admits that it is likely that the earlier a second language is acquired the more likely it is that a neural substrate will be shared by both languages. Recovery patterns are also influenced by the linguistic environment during recovery (Minkowski, 1963). However, Voinescu, Vish,

Sirian & Maretsis (1977) mention that even if the language of treatment is favoured in recovery, there is a transfer to the other languages known by the patient.

Emotional factors can also influence selective recovery. Critchley (1974) mentions the famous case of the French writer Pierre Loti who in a recovery phase conversed more easily in Turkish, a language to which he was emotionally attached, than in French, although the latter was his mother tongue, the language of his literary work and of his environment. It has also been postulated that differences in language structure affect selective recovery (Critchley, 1974): however, this is not strongly supported by empirical evidence, as the cases of polyglot aphasia where the two languages are structurally different are often those where the two languages were acquired under different circumstances. We lack empirical evidence on this point.

Mode of acquisition also affects selective recovery. Wechsler (1977) mentioned a case of polyglot aphasia in which the patient showed severe alexia (the incapacity to read) in his mother tongue (English), but only a mild form of alexia in French, a language he had learned in school during adolescence. Several cases of selective recovery mention the recovery of classical languages, learned essentially through the written mode, before aurally acquired languages (Whitaker, 1978). It is neuropsychologically sound to postulate that two languages may be affected differentially by brain damage, particularly when they involve visual and auditive modalities to different degrees (Albert & Obler, 1978). Wechsler (1977) postulated that later language acquisition would rely more heavily on both hemispheres and less heavily on the left hemisphere; therefore it would be easier to recover the later-learned language. However, no clinical evidence supports the assumption that becoming bilingual might lead to a transfer of dominance to the right hemisphere; most aphasic polyglots are left-brain damaged and there are no more right-brain damaged polyglot than monolingual aphasics.

The writing system may also play a role. Sasanuma (1975) observed that in Japanese aphasics the syllabic writing system, kana, was recovered differentially from the logographic system, kanji. Whitaker (1978) argues that this might result from different brain locations for phonetically and visually based languages; it has also been proposed that visual images of words may facilitate recovery (Minkowski, 1963). Because recovery is often reported to occur first for a language of literacy and later for a dialect or a language which is only spoken, it has been suggested that a language one reads and writes has a better chance of being recovered than a language which one only speaks (Grosjean, 1982). It might also be assumed that written language relies on a higher number of controlled processes which can facilitate recovery.

Paradis (1977) proposed a typology of recovery in aphasic polyglots: (1) parallel synergetic recovery, in which the two languages which are equally impaired progress simultaneously; (2) differential synergetic recovery, in which the two languages are unequally impaired but for which the degree of recovery is the same; (3) antagonistic recovery, in which one language recovers first, then begins to regress once the second language starts recovering; (4) success-ive recovery, in which one language recovers completely before the second one starts to recover; (5) selective recovery, in which one language is recovered while some others remain permanently impaired; and (6) mixed recovery, in which the patient mixes his languages in a way not present before the brain damage. The most common patterns of recovery are either the simultaneous recovery of both languages or a selective improvement in one language while the other language(s) remain impaired (Albert & Obler, 1978).

Selective recovery accounts for only 23% of the cases (Whitaker, 1978). Because aphasic polyglots might alternate between recovery in their two languages, being one day able to use one language fluently in spontaneous speech but not the other and conversely, it must be assumed that there is a functional dissociation between the languages, i.e. that one language becomes restrictively inaccessible for a period of time, under certain conditions (Paradis, Goldblum & Abidi, 1982). Because in polyglot aphasia languages are not destroyed, only inhibited (Green, 1986), this allows us to speculate about bilingual processing.

4.4.2 Bilingual specificity in recovery

How does brain damage affect specific bilingual abilities such as translation and code-switching? Several case studies report that polyglot aphasics retain the ability to translate both in simultaneous and selective recovery and, con-versely, the ability to translate or code-switch may be lost even in cases of mild impairment in each language; furthermore, a polyglot aphasic might be able to code-switch but totally unable to translate (Albert & Obler, 1978). He may be impaired in speaking one language but capable of producing a fluent trans-lation in his other language; or he may be incapable of speaking in one language but able to translate into that language; or he may not be able to translate in a language he speaks fluently (Paradis, 1980). Spontaneous trans-lating instead of responding to a verbal or non-verbal task (e.g. pointing) is frequently reported (Paradis, Goldblum & Abidi, 1982). Thus, code-switching ability and translation ability seem to be independent of speaking ability.

Surprisingly, aphasic polyglots rarely produce language mixing qualitat-ively different from the code-switching used premorbidly: interlanguage inter-ference is reported as a symptom in only 7% of polyglot aphasia cases, and most patients retain their switching ability (Albert & Obler, 1978). Fredman (1975) reported that aphasic mixing occurred more frequently in older patients; similar language structures (between Hebrew and Arabic) did not in-duce more mixing than different structures (as between Hebrew and French or Hungarian) but less; whether this relative absence of mixing between similar languages can be attributed to social factors (the study was conducted in Israel) or to the existence of a control mechanism to keep similar languages separated is open to speculation.

According to Perecman (1984), language mixing occurs at all levels of linguistic description, i.e. phonological, syntactic and lexical, in polyglot aphasia. She proposed that aphasic language mixing indicates a 'properly linguistic deficit' while spontaneous translation originates at the conceptual level. However, her interpretation is challenged by Grosjean (1985b), who argues that, because spontaneous translation and language mixing are common behaviours in the bilingual speech mode, it cannot be concluded that they are abnormal unless they have been compared with the patient's pre-morbid speech. The data on aphasic language mixing is still scarce and often we do not know how far aphasic mixing is different from normal code-mixing. We are just beginning to unravel the problem of code-switching and to describe the bilingual speech mode (Grosjean & Soares, 1986); before we can decide what is morbid about aphasic mixing we must be able to describe what is normal about normal bilingual speech-mode processing (see Chapters 6.2 and 7.3).

4.4.3 Polyglot aphasia and bilingualism

Summarizing the studies on polyglot aphasia, Albert & Obler (1978, 157–8) suggest that the following data might shed some light on bilingual processing: (1) sometimes there is apparent loss of one language and not the other; (2) there is parallel recovery in most cases but not all; (3) regression in the first re-covered language can be concurrent with recovery in the second; (4) affective factors influence recovery; (5) Pitrès's law is applicable above chance level; (6) there is a possible split between the recovery of formal/literacy and informal language; (7) there are possible differences between losses following chronic and traumatic lesions; (8) there is a possibility of right-hemisphere initiative in recovery and relearning language functions; (9) in some cases there is an apparent loss of switching ability; (10) there may be an apparent loss or im-pairment of translation; (11) lost childhood language can sometimes be re-covered through hypnosis; and (12) there are indications that multilingualism can have anatomical repercussions.

How far does this clinical data inform us on processing in bilinguals? From the data reviewed it appears that language-acquisition history is a determin-ing factor in polyglot aphasia. As Chernigovskaya, Balonov & Deglin (1983) point out, the method of appropriating the language is of prime importance. Drawing on a detailed analysis of recovery in Turkomen–Russian aphasics, they maintain that in the cases when the last learned language recovers first, this is so because the psychological mechanisms for processing semantic repres-entations and surface structures in the second language are located in the left (injured) hemisphere, while those for processing the semantic representations in the mother tongue are located in the right hemisphere with only the surface structures in the left hemisphere; early childhood bilinguality also follows the latter pattern with semantic representations for both languages in the right hemisphere. This model explains why a second language might be recovered first when it was learned at a later age: once recovery starts, both surface structure and semantic representations in L_2 are available; it also explains why, once L_1 recovery has started, it is recovered faster and more completely. This theoretical framework is tempting in so far as it explains a large body of polyglot aphasia data; unfortunately it is less convincing when it assumes right hemispheric involvement in semantic representations, an assumption not strongly supported in the literature (see Chapter 2.2).

Green (1986) recently attempted to propose a general model of bilingual processing which accommodates the performance of normal as well as brain-damaged bilinguals. Assuming that aphasic impairment reflects a problem in controlling intact language systems, he argues that the regulatory means, specifically the inhibitory resources, are responsible for the different types of impairment: each outcome is a direct consequence of the failure of a specific control system. This framework is interesting in so far as, without having to postulate specific mechanisms, it accounts for pathological as well as for normal behaviour; furthermore, it is congruent with more general models of speech production and skilled action. A number of assumptions in the model, however, have still to be verified.

To sum up, then, research on language processing in bilingual aphasics, although in many respects still in its infancy, is important for our understanding of bilingual processing. Whereas polyglot aphasia language impairment is so often no different from monolingual impairment and thus depends in the first place on the location of the brain damage, its specificity is essentially influenced by age and mode of acquisition of the two languages as well as by emotional factors. Specific bilingual behaviour in aphasics has to be explained in the larger framework of bilingual processing; therefore any model of bilingual processing has to account for language behaviour in aphasic bilinguals.

4.5 Conclusion

In this chapter we have attempted to review the research and theorizing on language processing in bilinguals. As we have mentioned all through this chapter, the bilingual's language processing is influenced by the history, context and mode of acquisition of his languages. We have discussed the extent to which the two languages are activated in the on-line processing and questioned the validity of the switch hypothesis. In the second section we addressed the issue of language representation in bilinguals: is there a psychological reality to the compound–coordinate distinction? We further discussed the controversy between the one-storage and the two-storage model of bilingual memory and ended this section with an assessment of the dual-coding model. We then briefly reported some non-verbal behaviour in the bilingual and ended this chapter by discussing the relevance of polyglot aphasic behaviour for bilingual processing.

From the above discussions it appears clearly that we are just beginning to understand how the bilingual processes languages and how he manages to keep his two languages separated. Whereas there is general agreement that he is able to keep his two languages functionally separated, the authors disagree as to how and at what level of processing this separation occurs. While being congruent with a general model of language processing, a model of bilingual processing must also account for both the functional separation in output and the activation of all language knowledge during processing. The controversy between the proponents of the common-store and the separate-store memory is still unresolved: it seems that, at the present time, all empirical evidence can be interpreted in favour of either model. However, the dual-coding approach is an interesting alternative even though it does not resolve the question of separate versus common storage.

One important methodological question arises in experimental studies on bilingual processing: because the age and mode of acquisition seem to play such a crucial role in processing by both normal and aphasic bilinguals, it is most important that studies on bilingual processing should be better documented in terms of language-acquisition history and should not treat bilinguals as a homogeneous group. Finally, any model of bilingual processing should account for the different levels of processing in both the monolingual and the bilingual speech mode, by normal and aphasic bilinguals, while being consistent with a general model of language processing.

5

Social psychological aspects of bilinguality: culture and identity

In the preceding chapters we have discussed the bilingual individual's language development and behaviour. In the present chapter we analyse, from a social psychological perspective, the relationships between the individual and the sociocultural group or groups around him when two or more languages are in contact. More specifically we focus on:

the relationship between language and culture;
the bilingual's cultural/ethnic identity;
the role of language(s) in the development of this identity;
culturation processes in their relations to language behaviour;
the perception of the bilingual individual by members of various ethnolinguistic groups;
attitudes, stereotypes and prejudices linked to different linguistic codes and their speakers.

The bilingual's development and behaviour cannot be envisaged independently from society, its structure and its cultural dimension. It must be borne in mind that the development of language and hence of bilinguality is part and parcel of the socialization process through which the child becomes a member of a given social group (see Chapter 3.2). The psychological mechanisms which result from this process should therefore be analysed within the framework of society and of the cultures in which they develop.

5.1 Language and culture

All definitions of culture agree that language is an important part of culture. There is a consensus that culture is a complex entity which comprises a set of symbolic systems, including knowledge, norms, values, beliefs, language, art and customs, as well as habits and skills learned by individuals as members of a given society. This definition, which was first put forward by Tylor (1873), has been elaborated upon by many scholars. Linton (1945), for example, insists that culture is a configuration of learned behaviour and the symbolic mean-

115

ings attached to it; moreover, the components of culture are transmitted by members of a society to other members and shared among them. According to Rohner (1984), however, the sharing of symbolic meanings and behaviour is only approximate in the sense that they are equivalent rather than identical for any two individuals and are unevenly distributed in the society.

Bruner (1965; 1973a), focussing on the dynamic, developmental aspects of human behaviour, defines culture as being among other things a system of techniques for giving shape and power to human capacities; the values, tools and ways of knowing of a culture equip members of a society with amplification systems. A culture is seen as a deviser, a repository and a transmitter of these amplification systems; their significance for the individual's cognitive, affective and social development is that they provide devices for the internal organization and shaping of experience. These 'amplifiers' will be crucial elements in the building up of an individual's social representations, that is representations of external reality shared with other members of the society.

Language is a component of culture along with other entities like, for example, values, beliefs and norms; language is a product of culture, transmitted from one generation to the next in the socialization process; it also moulds culture, that is to say, our cultural representations are shaped by language. But, unlike other components of culture, language interacts with it in specific ways: for language is a transmitter of culture; furthermore, it is the main tool for the internalization of culture by the individual. Although culture and language do not exist independently from each other, however, they are not homologous.

When more than one culture and/or more than one language are in contact in the same society, culture and language are not isomorphically distributed. To the extent that language is a component of culture, members of a society who do not share the same language do not share all meanings and behaviour of that society; however, there can exist a large degree of overlap between the cultural behaviour of members who do not speak the same language, as is for example the case in Luxemburg or in numerous societies of Africa and Asia, e.g. Nigeria and India. On the other hand, societies can be culturally very diverse and at the same time speak varieties of the same language, as, for example, English-speaking communities such as are found in Great Britain, the United States, Australia, the West Indies, Zimbabwe or India, or francophone communities, such as those in France, Belgium, French Canada or former French colonies in Africa.

5.2 Cultural identity and bilinguality

The integration of the complex configuration that is culture into the individual's personality constitutes his cultural identity. Cultural identity is part of, but not the same as, social identity. Whereas social identity exists within the same society and helps the individual to define himself in relation to the roles and the social groups in that society, one can only become aware of one's cultural identity to the extent that one becomes cognizant of the existence of other cultures in or outside one's own society. Because language is such an important component of culture it will be a salient feature of the individual's social cultural identity, while at the same time being a sociocultural marker of group membership in settings where cultures come into contact. Therefore the development of bilinguality has to be studied in relation to a more general approach to social perception and intergroup behaviour.

5.2.1 *The salience of cultural characteristics*

The salience of cultural characteristics will depend on a number of factors. From his analysis of the ethnic values of several groups Driedger (1975) concluded that although ethnic identity is determined by a multiplicity of factors such as language, religion and education, the relative importance of these factors varies from group to group. For example, in the pluralistic Canadian society in Manitoba Jewish people stress endogamy and relations of friendship, whereas Franco-Manitobans insist on language and parish education, and Scandinavians do not attach much importance to any of these characteristics. The last group therefore identify themselves less ethnically or culturally than the first.

In the same vein, Smolicz (1979) puts forward the idea that certain cultural values will be particularly salient in the construing of their cultural identity by members of one particular group, while these same values will be relatively irrelevant for the elaboration of cultural identity in another group. His model of *core values* suggests that each culture possesses a number of basic characteristics which are essential for the transmission and the maintenance of that culture; these core values identify a given culture. For example, in the Italian community in Australia, family, religion and language (dialect) appear to be three relevant core values, whereas for the Jewish community they are religion, cultural patrimony and historicity. If in a culturally plural society governed by consensus rather than coercion there exists a variety of power relations between the dominant group and subordinate groups, a set of values shared across cultures may evolve. These shared values are what Smolicz (1984) calls overarching core values; an individual can thus possess some values specific to his cultural community while at the same time adhering to wider societal values like, for instance, human rights (see Chapter 7.1.3).

When language is the core value of a cultural group, it may be an important factor in determining the members' cultural identity. In extreme cases it might even appear as the sole cultural core value, as is evidenced by the Flemings in Belgium or the Québécois in Canada, who built their national identity almost exclusively on the defence of their linguistic rights (see Chapter 7.1). The extent to which core values affect the bilingual's cultural identity will depend both on the pattern of core values resulting from a specific cultural contact and on the specific social and familial circumstances which shape the type of bilingual experience.

The situations in which languages and cultures are in contact comprise a variety of cases, e.g.:

(a) a person speaks one language in the home different from the language spoken in the community or society;

(b) a person speaks two languages in the home, one of which is the language of the community or society;

(c) a person speaks two languages in the home, which are both used in two communities in contact in the society;

(d) a person speaks two languages in the home, neither of which is used in the community or society.

These cases include children from bilingual homes as well as children from immigrant families who live in a society where two languages may or may not be in contact. When at least two languages are in contact in the society, power relations between the ethnolinguistic groups will influence the development of the child's cultural identity.

5.2.2 The development of cultural identity

How does a child develop the concept of cultural group membership? Group membership is one aspect of the concept of self and comes into existence through the development of social identity. According to Tajfel (1974), social identity results from the individual's knowledge of his membership of one or several social groups; it also includes all the values and affective meanings attached to this membership. A social group is defined by Tajfel as a psychological concept in the sense that it refers to a cognitive entity in the individual's mind. By a process of 'social categorization' the individual is able to construct his social environment according to certain criteria. He can recognize that others have common characteristics among themselves and between them and himself; he will then identify with the social groups with whom he shares these characteristics and distinguish himself from those who do not (social identity). Through a mechanism of 'social comparison', he can identify with all or only some of the group's characteristics, but it is necessary that the group recognizes him as a member. Similarly, at the collective level a group must perceive itself and be perceived by other groups as a distinctive entity. Thus an individual will perceive himself as similar to or different from others and act in such a way as to make his own group favourably and psychologically distinct from other groups with which he may compare it (psychological distinctiveness). In complex, multicultural societies, distinctiveness between social groups also includes linguistic, cultural and ethnic characteristics.[1]

Similarly Le Page (1968) and Le Page & Tabouret-Keller (1985) state that the individual behaves according to the behavioural patterns of groups he finds it desirable to identify with, to the extent that: '(i) he can identify the groups; (ii) he has adequate access to the groups and the ability to analyse their behavioural patterns; (iii) his motivation to join the groups is sufficiently powerful and is either reinforced or reversed by feedback from the groups; and (iv) he has the ability to modify his behaviour' (p. 182).

According to Commins & Lockwood (1979), the function of a social group is to provide a positive social identity for its members, who compare themselves with other groups and distinguish themselves from them along a number of salient dimensions. A group characteristic may become all the more salient as it is not possessed by other groups; for example, if a society consists only of white members, this ethnic trait is totally irrelevant for identifying social groups within the society. If, however, there are individuals of different skin colours, this feature may be used to characterize subgroups; if furthermore this feature is correlated with a social characteristic, such as socio-economic status, it may be perceived as a social characteristic and reacted to as such, as is the case in a racist society.

If in a given society certain groups can be identified in terms of ethnic, cultural or linguistic characteristics, these will become salient features, perceived as such by the individual and used by him for ethnic, cultural or linguistic categorization. In the social comparison process a member of a group will generally tend to favour his own salient group characteristics more than those of other groups on perceptual, attitudinal and behavioural dimensions (Turner, 1981). Furthermore, he will tend to use his own group characteristics as a standard by which to judge other groups (ethnocentrism).

Although little is known about the processes which bring cultural identity into being, some studies suggest that they start at an early age and that by the age of 6 children have developed some type of cultural identity. According to Lambert & Klineberg (1967) children of diverse ages and ethnic origins prefer to use such categories as sex, or being human, children or pupils, to describe themselves and only secondarily categories such as nationality, region or race. The latter will differ according to the child's ethnic origin. It would seem that 6-year-olds already possess the concept of ethnic identity which opposes the self to others, that is, to foreigners. It must be observed, however, that the child's concept of 'foreigner' differs from the adult's. Aboud & Skerry (1984) propose a three-stage model of development of ethnic attitudes. In a first stage, the child learns to identify and evaluate himself by comparison with other individuals who are different from himself. Then, he perceives himself as a group member and perceives others only as members of other groups; at this stage he accentuates within-group similarities and between-group differences; finally, he becomes capable of focussing on himself and others as individuals as well as group members.

If children are capable of developing cultural perceptions at an early age, do children who have an early bicultural experience develop specific cultural perceptions? Using a role-playing technique with 6- to 9-year-old children of Anglo-American and Canadian–Indian origins, Aboud & Mitchell (1977) concluded that in order for a child to identify positively with members of another ethnic group, he must first perceive this other group in a positive way. If language is a core value of ethnicity and there is incongruence between language and ethnicity the child will not be able to identify with another person, especially if this person is a member of his own group but speaks the language of another group. This is true of anglophone American children but not of Canadian–Indian children for whom language does not interfere with their perception of ethnic identity; for them a member of their family may speak both an Amerindian language and English. In other words, for these children speaking two languages is part of their sociocultural reality. Thus, the inclusion of two languages in one's ethnic identity may facilitate processes such as decentration and reciprocity, which are crucial for the development of the child's identity (Piaget & Weil, 1951).

Using a technique in which children expressed preferences for ethnic dolls, Genesee, Tucker & Lambert (1978) asked Anglo-Canadian children from different age groups and with different school experiences (English-medium, early immersion in French, and submersion in French) to express friendship preferences for the dolls; they also asked the children to imagine they were Franco-Canadians and in this case to identify which doll was most similar to them. Whereas all children from all groups preferred an Anglo-Canadian doll as their best friend and chose a Franco-Canadian doll as the best friend of a Franco-Canadian, children with some bilingual experience showed greater reciprocity in their choices. The younger children from the submersion group perceived all ethnic dolls as more similar to them than did the other children, who identified more clearly with the Anglo-Canadian dolls, but this difference disappeared with age, the English identity of all the children being well established by the age of 10. The authors conclude that, at least for children from a dominant group, the cultural orientation of the home and surrounding community prevails over the language of schooling in shaping the child's cultural identity. In other words, primary socialization appears to play a more important role in the process of cultural identification than secondary socialization.

In a different sociocultural environment, a francophone minority group in Ontario, Schneiderman (1976) observed that 5- to 12-year-old Franco-Ontarian children bilingual in French and English expressed a preference for the use of English while identifying with Franco-Canadian puppets. She concluded that preference for the majority language does not necessarily mean rejection of one's own cultural identity and that there is no one-to-one correspondence between linguistic assimilation and acculturation.

The relationships between bilinguality, language choice and cultural identity in the bilingual are very complex and depend on multiple factors. From the rare experimental evidence to date it appears that early bilingual experience influences the development of cultural identity, either because the child does not view language as an important identity characteristic or because he develops decentration and reciprocity earlier than the monolingual. Finally, bilingual preference does not necessarily coincide with cultural identification features. Thus, the development of cultural identity results from psychological as well as sociological factors. The relationship between bilinguality and cultural identity is reciprocal: bilinguality influences the development of cultural identity, which in turn influences the development of bilinguality. Differences in cultural identity are tolerated to a greater or lesser extent by different communities. Cultural identity, like language development, is a consequence of the socialization process the child undergoes. It is a dynamic mechanism developed by the child and it can be modified by social and psychological events throughout the individual's life. It is important to keep in mind that a bilingual child does not develop two cultural identities but integrates both his cultures into one unique identity.

5.2.3 Bicultural experience, affectivity and language proficiency

Because the development of bilinguality often co-occurs with socialization in a group minority situation, as is the case for an immigrant child, some developmental consequences of this situation have often been attributed to bilinguality. The best-known example is probably the attribution of personality disorders, such as emotional disorders, to an early bilingual experience (Diebold, 1968). However, the clinical cases cited by Diebold invariably concern bilingual children from socially disadvantaged backgrounds, a fact which is recognized by the author when he concludes that these cases are 'engendered by antagonistic acculturative pressures directed on a bicultural community by a sociologically dominant monolingual society within which the bicultural community is stigmatized as socially inferior and to which its bilingualism is itself an assimilative response' (p. 239).

Not only is there a dearth of convincing empirical evidence on a causal link between bilinguality and personality disorders, but such conclusions rest on controversial presuppositions, namely, that there exist fundamental psychological differences between cultural groups, that these differences are mutually exclusive and that they are necessarily reflected in the personality of the individual.

Another emotional disorder attributed to bilinguality is *anomie*, a complex psychological state implying feelings of alienation and isolation vis-à-vis the society one lives in, of disorientation and an absence of norms and values (McClosky & Schaar, 1965). Anomie is often associated with feelings of anxiety, a lack of cognitive and affective flexibility and a loss of identity. This state can be caused as much by sociological factors as by psychological ones.

From his study on second-generation Italians in the United States Child (1943) concluded that Italian adolescent males were faced with a dilemma: should they identify with the culture of their Italian community or should they assimilate into the American mainstream? Child found three typical modes of adjusting to this conflict: some rebelled against their Italian background and assimilated to the dominant culture; others rejected American ways, associating themselves with Italian culture; a third group displayed an apathetic withdrawal (anomie symptoms) and refused to think of themselves in ethnic terms, either by avoiding situations where the issue of cultural background might come up, or by denying that there were any differences between Italians and Americans. It seems that for Child the bilingual's identity can only be either monocultural or anomic. The possibility of a dual allegiance is never envisaged by him. This may be because in pre-Second World War America the values of the 'melting pot' prevailed and there was no room for cultural pluralism.

In their study of adolescents from the Franco-American minorities in Louisiana and New England, Gardner & Lambert (1972) observed similar phenomena. But, unlike Child, they also noticed a fourth subgroup who identified positively with both cultures, the American and the Franco-American. Moreover, (1) this group had acquired a balanced bilinguality and a native-like competence in both their languages, whereas the other groups were either (2) dominant in French, (3) dominant in English or (4) performed poorly in both languages. A high interest in one or the other culture as manifested by groups (2) and (3) was no guarantee of high proficiency in their dominant language, even though this proficiency was relatively higher than proficiency in their non-dominant language. Studying a group of Franco-American high-school students in Louisiana, Lambert, Just & Segalowitz (1970) found correlations between relative proficiency in the two languages and their cultural allegiance: those subjects who were more attached to American than to Franco-Louisianan values, and showed little interest in the French language, were more competent in English than in French and were relatively more motivated to improve their English; conversely, children who identified with the francophones had a relatively higher competence in French than in English. Those who had a cultural-identity conflict achieved poorly in both languages; those who identified strongly with both cultures also achieved above average in both languages.

Anomie, therefore, is not a necessary outcome of bicultural experience but results from the pattern of sociocultural conditions in which socialization takes place. If the child's twofold cultural heritage is not valorized, he may either align his identity on one culture at the expense of the other or he may refuse to align himself on either culture, in which case he is likely to develop anomie. If, however, the child's environment encourages the valorization of both cultures, then the child will be in a position to integrate elements of the two cultures into a harmonious bicultural identity. By harmonious we do not mean that such complex processes are free from tensions, contradictions and conflicts, but that the individual finds personal solutions without having to deny one of his cultures.

5.2.4 Enculturation, acculturation and deculturation

In order to understand the mechanisms by which a child accepts or rejects a culture, we must first take a closer look at what is meant by the internalization of a culture. According to Taft (1977), in order to become a member of society a child is 'enculturated to the particular ways and general style of life that constitutes its culture, and as a consequence becomes culturally competent' (p. 130); the child must acquire the means by which his behaviour may become meaningful to the other members of his society and by which he will attach meaning to the other members' behaviour; in other words, the child must learn how to mean and to communicate. Enculturation is part of the socialization process and begins with primary socialization. If a child is socialized in a bicultural environment enculturation will involve the two cultures. However, if a child lives in a monocultural home surrounded by another culture in the community, enculturation will start in his first culture, in which most of the primary socialization takes place, and he will have to cope with enculturation in a second culture, including the language of that culture. This will also happen to a child or an adult who immigrates to a country with a different culture.

When a child has already been through the enculturation process and comes into contact with a second culture, he will have to acculturate in order to adjust to the new culture. By acculturation we mean that in communicating with members of a new culture, the child must adjust his behaviour from the old culture to the new one. Acculturation includes 'a combination of acquisition of competence in performing culturally relevant behaviour and the adoption of culturally-defined roles and attitudes with respect to that behaviour' (Taft, 1977, 146). The more advanced the process of enculturation is, the more complex the process of cultural adjustment. In a harmonious acculturation process a person acquires the cultural rules and language skills of the new culture and integrates them appropriately with his primary culture. In other words, his identity becomes bicultural. In this process he also acquires the language of the new culture in addition to his mother tongue, which may be more or less maintained according to circumstances. On the other hand, the adult who has to adapt to a new culture must integrate new cultural elements, including language, in an already well-established identity. According to the requirements of his occupational status he must acquire more or less developed second-language skills (adulthood bilinguality). Although there is little reliable empirical evidence on adult acculturation (however, see Taft, 1977), from the existing data it may be argued that the older the individual the more difficult his cultural adaptation will be.

When an individual adapts to a new culture at the expense of his primary culture we speak of a process of deculturation. Extreme deculturation leads to assimilation, which may be accompanied by first-language loss (see Chapter 7.3.3). The type of bilinguality that will evolve is not independent of acculturation and deculturation processes. Learning a new language and becoming fluent in it, while at the same time maintaining or forgetting one's mother tongue, are an integral part of cultural adaptation. The processes of enculturation, acculturation and deculturation will play an important role in determining bilingual skills and the bilingual's cultural identity.

5.2.5 The bilingual's self-perception and cultural allegiance

A well-integrated cultural identity enriched by a bicultural situation is, at the affective level, the counterpart of Lambert's (1974) concept of 'additive' bilinguality at the cognitive level. The development of additive bilinguality is dependent on social factors that lead to the valorization of both languages and cultures. Similarly, the harmonious integration of two cultures into one's identity calls for a social setting that allows dual cultural or ethnic membership, as in the ideology of multiculturalism. For a child to develop a cultural identity which includes this dual membership, the society in which he lives must not present these two cultures as conflictual and mutually exclusive, as is the case with apartheid for example. The individual outcome of an early multilingual experience is dependent on the ideology of the society in which the person lives.

A number of empirical studies have addressed the issue of the bilingual's cultural identity. Aellen & Lambert (1969), using semantic differential techniques and social distance scales in order to measure ethnic identification, observed that Canadian adolescents of mixed-lingual French–English families identified harmoniously with both cultures; they displayed less extreme attitudes on authoritarianism and ethnocentrism scales than their monolingual peers. That children with a bilingual experience are capable of identifying positively with both cultures was also demonstrated by Lambert & Tucker (1972) in their longitudinal study of Anglo-Canadian children attending immersion programs in Montreal. This was confirmed in a survey of several immersion programs in Ontario (Swain & Lapkin, 1982). Employing a multi-dimensional scaling technique (MDS),[2] Cziko, Lambert & Gutter (1979) found that Anglo-Canadian children schooled in an immersion program attached less importance to language as a cultural marker than did their Anglophone peers in unilingual English-medium schools, that is, they defined themselves less in terms of antagonistic ethnolinguistic traits.

That bilinguality can be perceived as a cultural trait appears also from a study by Taylor, Bassili & Aboud (1973), who found that monolinguals from the two mainstream cultures in Canada perceived themselves as closer to monolinguals of both cultures than to bilinguals of both cultures. Cultural distance was measured by means of a MDS. In other words, a discrepancy between culture and language appears as a cultural distance for a monolingual who lacks experience in a second language and culture. Similar results were obtained by Hamers & Deshaies (1982), who also used a MDS; they concluded that monolingual anglophone and francophone elementary and secondary-school students in Quebec perceived language as an important cultural trait for themselves on which they differed not only from children of the other group but also from bilinguals of both groups. In the Quebec context, therefore, language is perceived as the most important cultural trait, and bilinguality as a cultural trait distinct from language. This cultural perception is already present in 10-year-old children.

How far can these differences between monolinguals and bilinguals be attributed to the child's own experience with language and how far to differences in parental cultural perceptions transmitted to the child? Using also a MDS technique, Frasure-Smith, Lambert & Taylor (1975) demonstrated that monolingual anglophone and francophone parents in the province of Quebec who chose to send their children to unilingual schools of their own culture identified more closely with the monocultural dimension of their group than did monolingual parents of both groups who opted for a school of the other language group for their children; these parents perceived themselves closer to bilingual Canadians of both groups than did the first group of parents. Thus it seems not only that the child's early experience with languages and cultures is relevant for shaping his cultural identity, but that parental cultural allegiance can play a role not only through the transmission of their own cultural attitudes but also in so far as they are able to decide to what extent their children will be exposed to other languages and cultures in formal education.

Empirical research on the bilingual's cultural identity is still scarce. Most of it has been conducted in North America, more specifically in the eastern part of Canada, thus making generalizations difficult. Despite these limitations one may conclude that a bilingual develops a cultural identity different from a monolingual's. Bilinguality and cultural identity are interrelated; the development of bilinguality influences the development of the child's cultural identity, which in turn is influenced by bilinguality. How does this developmental interrelation influence the degree of competence the bilingual will attain in his two languages?

5.2.6 Bicultural identity and language proficiency

What are the cultural identification characteristics which favour or impede the development of the bilingual's second-language competence? Among researchers who have attempted to address this question, Giles & Byrne (1982; see also Ball, Giles & Hewstone, 1984) formulated a number of propositions, based on a social psychological theory of intergroup behaviour, which claim to predict the development of L_2 proficiency in members of subordinate ethnolinguistic groups; these are most likely to acquire a native-like competence in L_2 provided that:

(1) ingroup identification is weak and/or L_1 is not a salient dimension of ethnic group membership;

(2) quiescent inter-ethnic comparisons exists (e.g. no awareness of cognitive alternatives to inferiority);

(3) perceived ingroup vitality is low;

(4(perceived ingroup boundaries are soft and open;

(5) strong identification exists with many other social categories, each of which provides adequate group identities and a satisfactory intragroup status (pp. 34–5).

In other words, a minority group member will approximate to a balanced bilingual competence if he identifies weakly with his own cultural group and does not consider his cultural identity to be dependent on language; if he perceives there are no alternatives to the inferiority social status of his cultural group; if he perceives the vitality of his own group as low compared with that of the dominant group whose language he is acquiring; if he perceives that social group mobility is easy, i.e. he can easily move from one social group to another; and if he identifies more strongly with social categories other than language and culture, e.g. profession.

If, on the other hand, those cultural-identity dimensions have opposite values (strong ingroup identification, L_1 a core value, etc.), Giles & Byrne predict that a person in a bilingual context will be more likely to develop a non-native competence in L_2. Although this model has the merit of stressing the role of intergroup relations in L_2 proficiency development, of adding an interesting perspective to models such as those of Gardner (1985) and Clément (1980, 1984) (see Chapter 9.8) and thus relating L_2 learning models to general social psychological theory, it has a number of shortcomings. Firstly, it is limited to the development of L_2 proficiency among members of minority groups; secondly, it proposes no explanation for the development of balanced bilinguality; and thirdly, it reduces all aspects of language competence to social psychological factors.

5.2.7 The bilingual's cultural identity

If it is true that such characteristics of cultural identity influence the degree of proficiency attained in L_2 in a bilingual setting, what then are the cultural-identity characteristics of the balanced bicultural bilingual? We suggest that: (1) he should identify positively with both his cultural/ethnic communities; (2) his two languages should be highly valorized; (3) he should perceive the relative status of both his cultural groups as dynamic; (4) he should perceive a minimum vitality for each of his reference groups; and (5) he should not perceive any unsurmountable contradiction in his membership of the two groups. Positive identification with one group must be matched by positive identification with the other group. Once again the issue of the interdependence between cultures and between languages is raised.

The cultural interdependence hypothesis

As we observed in Chapter 3.3.5 in respect of the development of bilinguality, it is necessary that the two languages be highly valorized if bilinguality is to evolve harmoniously. This valorization must also extend to the two ethnolinguistic communities in a bilingual setting. In other words, additive balanced bilinguality will develop only if the characteristics of the bilingual's cultural identity which are relevant for the development of the two languages are present without being conflictual for the individual and if society does not discourage dual membership. At the sociocultural level of analysis, the interdependence hypothesis suggests that a lack of identification with the L_1 culture would be correlated with a lack of identifiaction with the L_2 culture (Clément, 1984); in other words, in order to identify with the cultural group speaking the other language as L_1 (a condition necessary to attain native-like skills in L_2) a person must first identify with his L_1 group in a strong enough way.

Evidence supporting this sociocultural interdependence hypothesis is still scarce. Berry, Kalin & Taylor (1977) reported a positive correlation between attitudes of Canadians towards their own cultural group and attitudes towards other cultural groups in general: the more one perceives one's own group in a favourable light, the more attitudes towards other groups tend to be favourable. In a similar vein, Clément, Gardner & Smythe (1977a) observed that francophone Canadian adolescents who expressed positive attitudes towards French Canadians tended also to display positive attitudes towards anglophones.

Although to this day we have little empirical evidence for this hypothesis, it appears nonetheless as a plausible assumption because it fits with a more general approach to bilingual development. At the level of cognitive development, Cummins (1979) suggested that an adequate knowledge of L_1 will facilitate acquisition of a L_2 and that a deficit in the development of L_2 might be attributed to adverse social conditions for L_1 development. Lambert's (1974, 1977) theoretical approach suggests that the cognitive outcome of bilingual experience is a function of the relative valorization of the two languages. In their social psychological model of bilingual development Hamers & Blanc (1982, 1987) also suggest that underlying social psychological mechanisms, such as those relating to motivation and identity, are common to both languages and determine certain characteristics of the bilingual child's cultural identity as well as his competence in the two languages.

Affective dimensions of the bilingual's cultural identity

The affective dimensions underlying the bilingual's cultural identity have been analysed by Gardner & Lambert (1959, 1972) and by Clément (1980, 1984). Although these dimensions have essentially been studied in the context of L_2 acquisition (see Chapter 9.7), they are also applicable to the development of bilinguality. According to Clément several socio-affective mechanisms interact with each other and determine the level of competence in L_2 that a person will reach in a bicultural setting. A first affective mechanism enables the individual to develop certain affective relations with members of both cultural groups and languages; this mechanism determines the 'desire for integration'; a second, antagonistic force, 'fear of assimilation', interacts with the first one. If the resultant force is negative the primary process reflects fear of assimilation, and motivation to learn L_2 is relatively low. When the resultant force is positive the primary process reflects integrativeness and a high level of motivation. To these primary processes a secondary motivational process is added, which reflects self-confidence resulting from interaction with the members of the L_2 community. Thus, in a multicultural context, 'an individual's motivation is determined by both the primary and secondary motivational processes operating in sequence' (Clément, 1980, 151). It may be assumed that a similar process operates for the bilingual's cultural identity, i.e. his identity will be the result of a desire to integrate with the new culture and a fear of assimilation to the new culture.

For an additive balanced bilinguality to develop, the two languages and cultures must be favourably perceived and equally valorized. The models proposed by Lambert (1974) and Hamers & Blanc (1982) account for the socio-cultural factors which determine the bilingual child's cultural identity. How these factors come to play a crucial role depends on the characteristics of the child's social networks and his interpersonal contacts with members of both groups (Blanc & Hamers, 1987). Although these aspects of a child's bilingual development are still little understood, it seems that a harmonious bicultural identity has to rely on a state of equilibrium where possible conflicts between the two cultures have been resolved at the individual level.

5.3 Effects of bilinguality on perception and attitudes

How is a bilingual and bicultural individual perceived by others and how does he in turn perceive monolinguals and bilinguals? Before we address this question it is necessary to point out that cultural and ethnolinguistic perceptions are closely linked to the stereotypes and prejudices that a group forms towards another.[3] Speech is a powerful factor of identification, and social, cultural and ethnic categorizations and value judgements based upon them can be expressed about individuals and generalized to whole groups. Many studies have shown that individuals and groups may be positively or negatively evaluated according to the language or language variety they speak. It is usually the 'standard' or 'legitimate' variety, the 'imposed norm' or the majority language, which are valorized, the other languages or varieties being stigmatized.

Because of the wealth of research in the area of language attitudes we will not be able in this chapter to give an extensive review of the literature, but will only mention a few studies that are relevant to bilingualism (for a review of the field, see for example Giles & Powesland, 1975; Ryan & Giles, 1982; Giles, Hewstone & Ball, 1983). It is important to stress that, linguistically speaking, there is nothing intrinsic to a language or variety that makes it 'superior' or 'inferior'; it is merely a matter of social evaluation conferred upon a language or variety by social groups; we are dealing here with social stereotypes associated with ways of speaking. These value judgements express the attitudes, stereotypes and prejudices that members of a speech community have towards the speakers of another community and their language. These stereotyped judgements have important implications for intergroup relations, the life of individuals and the education of children.

5.3.1 *The measurement of language attitudes*

In order to measure the stereotypes attributed to languages, varieties, accents, dialects or styles, direct or indirect techniques have been employed. Among the former the most widely used is the attitude questionnaire; however, it fails to reveal unconsciously held or socially undesirable attitudes. To obviate these drawbacks, indirect techniques have been introduced, the most sophisticated being the 'matched guise', developed by W. E. Lambert and his team (Lambert, Hodgson, Gardner & Fillenbaum, 1960; Lambert, 1972). In this technique judges listen to tape-recordings of a number of bilingual speakers; they are asked to evaluate each speaker on a number of scales describing personality traits such as 'intelligent–stupid', 'interesting–uninteresting', 'good–bad'; the judges are however unaware that they hear the same speaker twice, in two different languages. As the matched recordings do not differ on voice characteristics but only in respect of the language used, differences in personality judgements can be safely attributed to value judgements on the languages. Since it was first used, the technique has been refined and widely applied in numerous studies on language attitudes.

The first study using a matched-guise technique in the context of languages in contact was that of Lambert *et al.* (1960). They asked French Canadian and English Canadian students in Montreal to judge voices of balanced French–English bilingual speakers on a number of personality traits. It was found that both the English and the French bilinguals judged the English guises more favourably than the French guises; furthermore, the Anglo-Canadian judges rated the French voices higher than did the Franco-Canadians. The authors interpreted these results as evidence of the existence of a negative stereotype about the French minority shared by both communities. This negative stereotype towards one's own cultural membership group was not found among 10-year-old French Canadian children in a subsequent study by Anisfeld & Lambert (1964): at the age of 10 both Franco- and Anglo-Canadian children rated their own group more favourably. However, Franco-Canadian girls had developed the negative stereotype by the age of 12 (Lambert, Franckel & Tucker, 1966). Moreover, in the Anisfeld & Lambert experiment the bilingual 10-year-old judges showed less cultural stereotyping than their monolingual peers and judged French and English guises as more similar. In their study of the attitudes of children in St Lambert in Montreal, Lambert & Tucker (1972) observed that anglophone children who had become bilingual through an immersion program displayed more favourable attitudes towards francophones than did monolingual controls in mainstream classes.

5.3.2 *The effect of bilingual experience on language attitudes*

The effect on cultural stereotypes of learning a L_2 has also been assessed in a different cultural setting. In a matched-guise study conducted in Wales, Bourhis, Giles & Tajfel (1973) observed that bilingual Welsh–English and monolingual English-speaking Welsh people who attended a course in Welsh language judged English spoken with a Welsh accent more favourably than did monolingual anglophone Welsh people who were not learning Welsh. Furthermore, the first two groups also rated their own competence in English more favourably than the monolinguals who did not learn Welsh rated their own English competence. Thus it would seem that being or becoming bilingual in English and Welsh would enhance their self-perception of both their Welsh accented English and their competence in English. A state of bilinguality seems to attenuate the stereotypes that people have developed about L_2 speakers.

It is important to distinguish between a foreign accent on the one hand and a regional, social or ethnic accent on the other hand. Most studies on evaluation of accented speech indicate that any accent different from the accepted norm is less positively evaluated than the norm itself (see, e.g., Giles, 1970; Giles & Powesland, 1975; Giles, Hewstone & Ball, 1983). Comparing the evaluative reactions given to RP English, social dialects (e.g. Cockney), regional (e.g. Irish, Yorkshire, Indian) and foreign (e.g. French, Italian) accents in Great Britain Giles (1970) observed that RP English was rated more favourably than any accented speech; the ratings given to regional and foreign accents would however vary according to their specificity; for example English spoken with an Indian accent was not evaluated more favourably than Cockney, whereas English spoken with a French foreign accent was rated in a very favourable way, as superior to any English regional accent and much superior to an Italian or German foreign accent. These findings have been confirmed for a variety of accents in different countries: Jewish accent in English (Anisfeld, Bogo & Lambert, 1962); Black versus White accent in the USA (Tucker & Lambert, 1969); Mexican American accent (Ryan & Carranza, 1975); Jamaican accent and Creole in the UK (V. K. Edwards, 1978a).

However, in a few studies it appears that accented speech is sometimes evaluated in a more favourable way than the standard variety. Bourhis, Giles & Tajfel (1973) found this to be the case for English spoken with a Welsh accent, which was perceived more favourably than RP English by Welsh–English bilinguals and Welsh people who were learning Welsh. These favourable ratings, obtained from bilingual adults, were not found in bilingual Welsh–English children living in a predominantly Welsh-speaking environment, who rated the standard variety of English higher than the Welsh-accented one (Price, Fluck & Giles, 1983). Ryan, Carranza & Moffie (1975) had Mexican American students rate Mexican American speakers, representing a wide range of accentedness. The results indicated that Mexican-born students rated the speakers more favourably as their accentedness increased, whereas American-born judges rated the least accented speakers more favourably. These apparently contradictory results might be attributed to the raters' self-image, as these results are found only when the evaluated accent is a marker of the judges' ethnic group membership.

According to Turner (1981, 1982), comparing oneself favourably with outgroups could be a means of maintaining self-esteem. In this sense, perceiving as positive the 'psycholinguistic distinctiveness' of a group, i.e. using linguistic markers in order to be identified as a member of a group, indicates a high appreciation of that group (see Chapter 6.1). Evaluative responses to perceived speech characteristics are the results of an interaction between these perceptions, the social value attributed to one's own speech and social knowledge about ethnic groups and ethnic relations. (For an attempt at a theoretical framework on the role of speech style evaluation, see Street & Hopper, 1982.)

5.3.3 The evaluation of non-native speech and ethnic clues

Although very few empirical studies have addressed the problem of foreign accents, i.e. a speech accented in such a way that it is evident that the speaker is not a member of the ethnolinguistic group, it might be assumed that the pattern of intervening social psychological mechanisms will be even more complicated than with regional or social accents. Segalowitz & Gadbonton (1977) studied evaluations of speech of non-balanced, but relatively fluent bilinguals by francophone judges in Quebec. A non-balanced fluent bilingual, while having reached a high level of competence in his second language, produces speech marked by a series of non-native features, e.g. accent. Judges would perceive certain markers as the expression of the speaker's ethnic allegiances: for example, a francophone Québécois who speaks English with a French accent is judged as having more nationalistic feelings than a francophone Québécois who speaks English without a French accent. The perception is independent of the speaker's real feelings: the authors found no correlation between the degree of nationalism expressed by the speakers and their competence in English. Furthermore, the judges' perceptions were not influenced by attitudes towards nationalism or by competence in English; however, their preferences were influenced by their attitudes in the sense that those who had nationalistic feelings preferred a marked accent, whereas those who expressed fewer nationalistic feelings preferred native-like English.

A balanced bilingual can be recognized as a native speaker in either one of his languages. However, this is not always the case in everyday ethnic interactions: certain non-linguistic, cultural or ethnic clues can influence the perception of the listener, who will categorize the speaker as a member of an ethnolinguistic group. Characteristics of a 'visible minority' will influence the listener's perception. The influence of non-linguistic clues will be all the greater as these group characteristics are more evident, as for example, sex or skin colour.

Using an adapted matched-guise, Williams, Whitehead & Miller (1971) presented video taped recordings of children speaking different varieties of accented English (Mexican American, Black American or Anglo-American) to trainee teachers. The films were dubbed with the voices either in a congruent way (e.g. the Black American child speaking Black English) or an incongruent way (e.g. the same child speaking Anglo-American English). The results indicated that non-linguistic ethnic clues influence the perception of linguistic clues, in the sense that when, for example, a Black American is shown speaking with an Anglo-American accent, this accent is perceived as closer to Black English than when the same accent is produced by an Anglo-American. Hopper (1977) investigated the effect of the interaction between race, accent and professional qualifications on employment interviewers' perception of candidates in the usa; although he found that race and accent were good predictors of employability, he nonetheless observed that when a positively perceived accent (i.e. Standard English) was combined with negatively perceived race characteristics (i.e. Black), e.g. a Black speaker with a Standard accent, the overall perception was highly favourable. Kalin (1982) interprets these results as an indication that language style is a powerful factor in social categorization. Thus, not only will accent be perceived as a marker of social and cultural distinctiveness but also this perception will be influenced by non-linguistic markers of ethnicity.

These findings have important implications for the way the bilingual is perceived. According to the ethnolinguistic relationships and sociocultural context of interaction it will be more or less difficult for the balanced bilingual to be identified as a member of either ethnolinguistic group. For example, it is relatively easy for a francophone or an anglophone Canadian bilingual in both languages to be perceived as either francophone or anglophone; on the other hand, it is relatively difficult if not impossible for a Black African who is a balanced bilingual in an African language and French, for example, to be identified as a member of the French community in Europe.

5.4 Conclusion

In the present chapter we have discussed the relationship between language and culture and its effect on the bilingual's identity development and behaviour. We first focussed on culture, cultural identity and its development in a language-contact situation. Cultural identity is an important aspect of personality. The bilingual develops a unique identity, different from that of the monolingual, but which can nonetheless be harmoniously adjusted if society allows it; contrary to the received opinion that bilinguality leads to a maladjusted personality, it should be stressed that anomie is not a necessary outcome of bilinguality but develops only when the individual has no possibility of resolving conflicts arising from his dual membership. While the bilingual's cultural identity is shaped by his bilingual experience, his bilinguality is in turn influenced by his cultural identity and its social psychological and affective correlates. A balanced bilinguality will develop only to the extent that the characteristics of cultural identity relevant to the acquisition of the two languages are salient for the child's identity without being conflictual. It is important to stress that a bilingual does not develop two parallel identities but integrates his two cultures into a unique identity in which aspects of both his cultures are closely interrelated (cultural interdependence hypothesis); this integration is the result of an interplay between enculturation, acculturation and deculturation processes.

Bilingual experience influences ethnic attitudes. Bilinguals focus less on language stereotypes than do monolinguals. Acquiring competence in a L_2 can modify ethnolinguistic attitudes and enhance positive perceptions of the other group. How the bilingual is perceived by members of his own and other communities is a function of the existing relations between the different communities. The level of language competence of a bilingual is also relevant in ethnic interactions. A perfectly balanced bilingual can be perceived as a member of either one of his ethnolinguistic groups provided that no non-linguistic ethnic clues interfere. A dominant bilingual, even if he is highly fluent in his L_2, will however be perceived as a member of his own ethnolinguistic group, since the 'foreign' language markers he uses in his speech are identified not only with ethnic group membership but also with ethnic allegiances. In summary, bilinguality is an important social–psychological dimension that influences interethnic relations, is shaped by social factors and will in turn condition the development of social psychological mechanisms relevant to the integration of the individual in society.

6

Social psychological aspects of bilinguality: intercultural communication

Whereas in Chapter 5 we focussed on the effects of a bilingual experience on social psychological mechanisms relevant to language behaviour, in the present chapter we shall discuss the interplay of these mechanisms with linguistic behaviour in interpersonal interaction situations. In order to understand interpersonal communication in an intercultural context one has to understand how meaning is negotiated when the interlocutors are members of different ethnolinguistic groups, how language interacts with social-cognition mediating processes, and thus how language may become a salient dimension of this interaction (Gudykunst, 1986). In intercultural communication people interact with each other both as individuals and as members of different social groups; social encounters are thus determined by interpersonal as well as by intergroup factors (Tajfel & Turner, 1979), and can be analysed along these two independent dimensions (Stephenson, 1981).

When two members from different cultural and ethnolinguistic groups communicate with each other, social categorization occurs in such a way that people will have a tendency to exaggerate differences on critical dimensions between categories and minimize differences within a social category (Tajfel, 1981). Social, cultural or ethnolinguistic groups are perceived as more distinct from each other if they differ on a large number of distinctive features such as language, race characteristics, religion and social status (as, for example, in an encounter between an Anglo-Celt and an Indian from South India) than if they differ on one or two characteristics only, as would be the case in an encounter between a Briton and an Anglo-Celtic Australian. Furthermore, social categorization produces ingroup bias which is based on ethnocentrism, that is, on the perception of one's own ethnic group as being superior to an outgroup.

If language is a salient aspect of group identity and an important distinctive feature for two members in a communication dyad, then either member will adopt strategies for positive linguistic distinctiveness when: (1) he identifies strongly with his own ethnolinguistic group; (2) he makes insecure intercultural comparisons with regard to his group status; (3) he perceives the other's ingroup as having high ethnolinguistic vitality (see Chapter 7.1.2) and closed and hard boundaries; (4) he does not identify strongly with other social categories, e.g. professional ones, perceives little overlap between himself and the other person in terms of social group membership and considers his social identity derived from other categories to be rather inadequate; and (5) he perceives intragroup status in his cultural group to be relatively higher than intragroup status in other social category groups (Giles & Johnson, 1981). In an intercultural communication these factors interact to determine the choice of language behaviour and the type of speech accommodation an individual will make. Furthermore, his evaluation of the other's language behaviour will be a function of his language attitudes, which are determined by two independent dimensions, one being 'person versus group-centred', the other 'solidarity versus status-stressing' (Giles & Ryan, 1982).

6.1 Speech accommodation

One of the most relevant characteristics of interpersonal communication is the adaptation of two speakers to each other's speech. Such adaptation can be observed in all types of verbal interaction, whether monolingual or bilingual, and at all linguistic levels (e.g. phonological, lexical, etc.). Among the many different types of accommodation those that come most readily to mind are motherese and fatherese, i.e. parental speech adjustment to children who are immature speakers (Snow & Ferguson, 1977), and 'foreigner talk', i.e. the simplification of one's language when addressing a non-fluent foreign speaker (Clyne, 1981; see 6.2.2). It seems that in the course of a conversation between two individuals the most common behaviour for the speakers is to converge towards each other in the speech they use; this has been shown for such features as speech rate, pauses, accent, etc.

6.1.1 Foundations of speech accommodation theory

In order to explain this tendency to adapt, Giles (1973) and Giles & Powesland (1975) proposed a model of speech accommodation which focusses on the underlying social cognitive processes mediating between the individual's perception of the communication situation and his communicative behaviour. Briefly, speech accommodation theory is based on the following social psychological processes: (i) similarity attraction, (ii) social exchange, (iii) causal attribution and (iv) intergroup distinctiveness. Through similarity-attraction mechanisms an individual is the more attracted to others as his attitudes and beliefs are similar to theirs (Byrne, 1969). By attenuating linguistic differences between himself and his interlocutor the speaker increases social attraction, since he is perceived as more similar by the listener; this process is called 'convergent accommodation'. Accommodation is also the outcome of another social psychological mechanism, that of 'social exchange' through which, prior to acting, one attempts to assess the rewards and costs of alternative courses of action (Homans, 1961). A speaker will accommodate provided he perceives that the cost of accommodation, e.g. a threat to his ethnic identity, is less than the reward gained from an increased social attraction. According to Thakerar, Giles & Cheshire (1982) speakers are motivated to adapt their speech style in order to gain the listener's social approval, increase the efficacy of the communication and maintain a positive social, cultural or ethnic identity.

In an interaction the listener interprets the speaker's behaviour in terms of the motives and intentions that he attributes to this behaviour. This process of causal attribution (Heider, 1958; Jones & Davies, 1965; Kelly, 1973) explains how convergent accommodation is perceived as an intention to reduce social distance; speech convergence is perceived more favourably if it is attributed to the speaker's desires to bridge a social gap than if it is attributed to external pressures on the speaker's behaviour, such as the lack of competence of the interlocutor or sociolinguistic norms which impose a specific code. Finally, intergroup distinctiveness also influences speech accommodation (Giles & Smith, 1979). Tajfel (1974) suggested that when two members of different groups interact they compare themselves on relevant dimensions and this leads them to identify those dimensions which make them distinct from each other.

If language is a salient dimension of the speaker's identity, he can use distinctive linguistic markers of his own group to assert his cultural identity and to distinguish himself from his interlocutor. Divergent accommodation, i.e. when a speaker's speech becomes more dissimilar from his interlocutor's, is a communication strategy which enables the speaker to distinguish himself psychologically from his interlocutor as a member of a distinct ethnolinguistic group. This 'psycholinguistic distinctiveness' (Giles, Bourhis & Taylor, 1977) enables an individual to express ethnolinguistic group allegiances in intercultural interpersonal communication.

6.1.2 *Empirical support for speech accommodation theory*

The validity of the speech accommodation model has been verified in a number of empirical studies in multilingual contexts. How is speech convergence expressed? Studying speech accommodation between Anglo-Canadian and Franco-Canadian bilinguals Giles, Taylor & Bourhis (1973) demonstrated that Anglo-Canadians perceived Franco-Canadian bilingual speakers in a more favourable light when they also perceived accommodation to be high; in turn, they tended to accommodate the more if they attributed a high accommodation intention to the speaker. Simard, Taylor & Giles (1976) observed that lack of accommodation by a speaker is perceived in a different way if it is perceived as resulting from either (i) a lack of speaker's competence in the listener's language; or (ii) external pressures on the speech style of the interaction; or (iii) a lack of effort on the part of the speaker to attenuate dissimilarities and diminish social distance. The listener reacts more favourably to a lack of accommodation if he perceives it as resulting from a lack of competence rather than from a lack of effort on the part of the speaker.

Because status and solidarity dimensions are among the most salient characteristics of social interactions they influence speech accommodation in a dyad (Brown & Gilman, 1960). Sociolinguistic stereotypes, i.e. stereotypes about how members of certain social groups are supposed to speak and how one should address members of given social groups, are powerful mediating social cognitive processes for speech accommodation (Hewstone & Giles, 1986). In a socially unequal interaction accommodation generally implies that the speaker with the lower social status accommodates relatively more to his interlocutor rather than the reverse, although in most interactions some form of mutual accommodation can be observed. This is equally true for individual (Thakerar, Giles & Cheshire, 1982) and for ethnolinguistic group status (Taylor, Simard & Papineau, 1978). In an intercultural encounter cultural group status will interplay with social group status to determine the power relations and hence the type of speech accommodation.

Deshaies & Hamers (1982) analysed speech accommodation in a role play between bilingual workers, foremen and managers from different ethnolinguistic backgrounds (francophone, anglophone and other) in firms in Montreal. They observed that, whereas the main goal was to maintain good working relations in the first place (and thus all employees would accommodate linguistically), there was relatively more upward than downward convergence in all interactions, the type of linguistic accommodation being tempered, however, by the speaker's linguistic competence. In a different context Valdes-Fallis (1977) showed that bilingual Mexican American women tend to accommodate to male speech by imitating their code alternation when addressing Mexican American men, whereas they use little code alternation when speaking among themselves. Thus, bilinguals' speech accommodation is influenced as much by social as by linguistic factors.

Children's speech accommodation strategies are also influenced by the relative status of the speakers' ethnolinguistic groups. Aboud (1976) observed that when explaining the rules of a game, 6-year-old Spanish–English bilingual Chicanos converged more frequently to anglophone than to hispanophone interlocutors. Non-verbal characteristics of the intercultural encounter can also influence speech accommodation: Beebe (1981) found that Chinese–Thaï bilingual children used Chinese phonological variants in their Thaï speech when interviewed by a speaker of Standard Thaï who looked ethnically Chinese.

Many experiments on speech accommodation study only short interactions; however, in real life interpersonal interactions often extend over a period of time. As verbal interaction is a dynamic phenomenon little is known about speech accommodation changes during the course of the interaction. Analysing intercultural speech accommodation, Belair Lockhead (1987) demonstrated that in half-hour-long conversations between francophone and anglophone college students in Ottawa, members of a dyad change the way they adjust in the sense that, after a while, interpersonal aspects of the communication overrule intergroup considerations and that content rather than language would become the most important issue.

Linguistic convergence is not always a one-way strategy but is effected by both members of a communication dyad, if not by each of them to the same extent. In experiments with same-sex and mixed-sex dyads Mulac, Wiemann, Yoerks & Gibson (1983) observed that mixed-dyad participants both converged and met mid-way, whereas in same-sex dyads one member was mainly responsible for convergence. Mutual convergence was also found in a multicultural setting in commercial transactions in Taïwan; in the market place customers converged downwardly to sales-persons and the latter converged upwardly in return, while in banks it was the customer who converged upwardly to the clerk who converged downwardly to him. Sometimes upward and downward convergence may miscarry, as in the cases studied by Platt & Weber (1984) in Singapore and Australia, where natives or immigrants tried to match upwardly the speech of native English speakers, and native English speakers mismanaged their downward convergent attempts towards what they believed the other group sounded like.

Linguistic divergence occurs when a speaker is in an intercultural situation in which he has to affirm his cultural identity. In an experiment carried out in Wales it was found that when an anglophone speaker expressed a verbal threat against Welsh cultural identity, an anglophone Welsh interlocutor learning Welsh would reply in English, but in a style diverging strongly from the speaker's and characterized by a high number of Welsh markers (Bourhis & Giles, 1977). The expression of psycholinguistic distinctiveness under cultural threat has also been observed in a study of intercultural contacts in Belgium by Bourhis, Giles, Leyens & Tajfel (1979): they found that Flemish-speaking Belgians diverged linguistically from their French-speaking interlocutors when they felt their ethnolinguistic group membership threatened; furthermore, this divergence could go as far as a change of language. According to Sandilands & Fleury (1979), a divergent strategy used by an outgroup speaker will often be perceived as impolite, hostile, and insulting. Thakerar, Giles & Cheshire (1982) suggest that there is a hierarchy of strategies to express psycholinguistic distinctiveness: some of these strategies would act more as symbols of social dissociation than others. Maintenance of a speech style or switching to an ingroup code in front of an outgroup interlocutor would be among the most powerful ways of expressing psycholinguistic distinctiveness.

Ethnolinguistic identity is affirmed all the more strongly as the cross-cultural characteristic of an interaction situation is stressed. In experiments with Chinese students bilingual in Cantonese and English from the Chinese university of Hong Kong, Yang & Bond (1980) observed that these students affirmed their Chinese identity more strongly when responding to a questionnaire presented in English than when responding to the same questionnaire presented in Chinese. Similarly, in a second experiment Bond & Yang (1982) found that students expressed their Chinese identity less strongly in interaction with a Chinese interviewer than with an English interviewer; moreover, they responded to culturally threatening questions by expressing their cultural allegiance but accommodated to Western culture when the questions were neutral. The authors interpret these results as proof that interlocutors feel the need to affirm their cultural identity less in a situation which is culturally congruent with their own cultural background than in a cross-cultural situation.

Overconvergence occurs when the speaker's degree of convergence is perceived by the listener as inappropriate for a given situation, as when for example handicapped, sick or elderly people are talked down to by medical personnel (Caporael, Lukaszewsky & Culbertson, 1983). Presenting different messages in which an Anglo-Canadian speaker converged towards a British English listener on three linguistic dimensions (pronunciation, speech rate, and message content), Giles & Smith (1979) found that whereas convergence on each of the dimensions separately was perceived positively, simultaneous convergence on all three dimensions was perceived as negative and patronizing. The authors suggest that in a situation of interethnic contact there exists a level of optimal convergence beyond which it is perceived as irritating. In their investigation of market-place interaction Platt & Weber (1984) suggested that overconvergence might be attributed to a wrong stereotyped perception about the 'other' 's speech style. Overconvergence, then, can occur because accommodation is a scripted behaviour (see Chapter 3.1.5), the speaker applying a convergence script to what he thinks is his interlocutor's speech style. This is also the case in foreigner talk (see below, 6.2.2) when the speaker simplifies his mother tongue in the belief that his interlocutor, perceived as relatively incompetent in that language, will understand better.

6.1.3 Psychological reality of speech accommodation

Linguistic accommodation must not be confused with psychological accommodation, which can be expressed in a variety of ways including linguistic convergence and linguistic divergence (Deshaies, 1981; Deshaies & Hamers, 1982; Thakerar, Giles & Cheshire, 1982). From their study of intercultural interactions in different multilingual working settings in firms in Montreal, Deshaies & Hamers (1982) concluded that in hierarchical interactions, psychological convergence is a speaker's main concern and that content convergence generally overrides linguistic convergence.

Studying the reactions of bilingual Cantonese–English Chinese, dominant in Cantonese but highly fluent in English, to American interviewers who used either English or Cantonese, a language in which they were not very fluent, Pierson & Bond (1982) obtained the following results: social psychologically the interviewees converged upwards towards their higher-status interviewer, but linguistically they adjusted their Cantonese speech style to their interlocutor's lower level of linguistic competence in Cantonese and did not switch to the use of English. The authors interpret these results as showing that in the power relations existing in the interview situation, the interviewee would perceive that the language to be used was the interviewer's decision. Thakerar, Giles & Cheshire (1982) have suggested that objective linguistic and subjective psychological accommodation are in fact two independent dimensions; for example, linguistic convergence can be the manifestation of a psychological divergence, and conversely; in addition, the relation between objective linguistic accommodation and subjective psychological accommodation does not have the same meaning in socially upward as in socially downward convergence.

Accommodation behaviour does not necessarily imply a high level of awareness. From an experiment on accommodation to speech rate and response latency Street (1982) concluded that while subjects were highly conscious of using divergent behaviours, they were unaware of their convergent speech accommodation. In an experimental intercultural interaction between francophones and anglophones in Montreal, Taylor & Royer (1980) demonstrated that subjects appeared to be aware not only of their accommodation behaviour but also of the motives for such behaviour; awareness was especially high for ethnically divergent behaviour. The lower level of awareness observed for convergent behaviour might be attributed to the fact that we are dealing with a highly automatized scripted behaviour, the subject applying action schemata (see Chapter 3.1.5) to his behaviour (C.R. Berger, 1986).

Evaluative speech-accommodation processes interact, however, with the speaker's perception of the listener's linguistic competence (Deshaies & Hamers, 1982) and with the presence of constraining sociolinguistic norms. Ball, Giles, Byrne & Berechree (1984) have observed that speech convergence is evaluated negatively when the convergent act violates the situational norms and that divergence is viewed positively when it adheres to the prevailing situational norms.

6.1.4 *Towards a model of speech accommodation*

Giles and his colleagues have summarized the theory of speech accommodation in the form of propositions (see, for example, Thakerar, Giles & Cheshire, 1982; Street & Giles, 1982):

(1) Speakers will attempt to converge linguistically towards the speech patterns believed to be characteristic of their interlocutors when (a) they desire their social approval and the perceived costs of so acting are lower than the

rewards anticipated; and/or (b) they desire a high level of communicational efficiency and (c) social norms and/or linguistic competence are not perceived to dictate alternative speech strategies.

(2) The degree of linguistic convergence will be a function of (a) the extent of the speakers' repertoires, and (b) factors (individual differences and situation) that may increase the need for social approval and/or communicational efficiency.

(3) Speech convergence will be positively evaluated by listeners when the resultant behaviour is (a) perceived as such psychologically, (b) perceived to be an optimal sociolinguistic distance from them, and (c) credited with positive intent.

(4) Speakers will attempt to maintain their speech patterns or even diverge linguistically away from characteristics they believe their interlocutors possess when they (a) define the encounter in intergroup terms and desire a positive ingroup identity, or (b) wish to dissociate personally from another in an interpersonal encounter, or (c) wish to bring another's speech behaviours to a personally acceptable level.

(5) The degree of divergence will be a function of (a) the extent of speakers' repertoires, and (b) individual differences and situational factors increasing the salience of the cognitive or affective functions in proposition (4).

(6) Speech maintenance and divergence will be negatively evaluated by listeners when the acts are perceived as psychologically divergent, but favourably reacted to by observers of the encounter who define the interaction in intergroup terms and who share a common positively valued group membership with the speaker.

Recently, Giles, Mulac, Bradac & Johnson (1986) reformulated speech-accommodation theory and refined some of the propositions. They reformulated Tajfel & Turner's (1979) interpersonal–intergroup dialectic by focussing on the concept of 'presentation of self' (Goffman, 1959). According to the model of self-presentation, in an interaction an individual wishes to create a positive impression along the dimensions desired by socially influential others. The latest formulation of the speech-accommodation model stresses the relevance not only of self- and group-presentation but also of relational identities arising from the 'couple comparisons' present in an interpersonal interaction.

Furthermore, linguistic convergence and divergence may be motivated by the desire to extend one's social influence through individual self-presentations. Convergence strategies will be positively evaluated by the listener provided that: they match the listener's communication style; they match the listener's ethnolinguistic stereotype; they are produced as being optimal in terms of linguistic traits; the speaker's style conforms to a valued norm; the speaker's effort is perceived as high, his language choice as appropriate and his intent as positive. Divergence will be negatively rated by listeners when they perceive: a mismatch between the speaker's communication style and their own; a mismatch with their linguistic group stereotype; the speaker's divergence to be excessively distant and frequent; the speaker's style to depart from a valued norm; the speaker's effort to diverge as being great and the speaker as intentionally selfish and malevolent (Giles *et al.*, 1986).

Speech-accommodation theory has the merit of proposing a valid theoretical framework which can explain how and why people modify their language behaviour in different interaction situations. It has been found to be helpful in linking speech style and its modifications to social psychological processes, like cultural identity, attitudes and social perceptions, and to intercultural relations. It stresses the role of language and language variation in these relations, both at the interpersonal and at the intergroup level. It enables us to make predictions with regard to the monolingual's and the bilingual's behaviour in interethnic contacts. However, because of the complexity of the theory, it may prove difficult to verify it as a whole. It is useful as a series of conceptual constructs, but its empirical assessment might prove too difficult (Bourhis, personal communication).

6.2 Communication strategies in intercultural interaction

In so far as intercultural interpersonal communications are concerned, we are interested in interactions between bilingual speakers and between a bilingual and a monolingual speaker, as well as between monolinguals from different ethnolinguistic backgrounds. The distinction between monolinguals and bilinguals is not as clear-cut as might by suggested by this dichotomy: often individuals vary on a continuum from total monolinguality to balanced bilinguality, and multilingual communities also vary on a similar continuum (see Chapter 7.3.1). However, for the sake of clarity we will consider that in a situation of languages in contact the following interactions may occur (note that for ease of demonstration we ignore the social context of the interactions, in particular the power relations between the interlocutors):

(1) The speakers (X and Y) share at least some linguistic competence in common:
  a. both X and Y are bilingual in A and B;
  b. X is bilingual in A and B and Y is monolingual in either A or B;
  c. X is bilingual in A and B, but with only a receptive competence in B, and Y is bilingual in A and B, but with a receptive competence in A;
  d. both X and Y are bilingual but share only one language, C, in common; i.e. X is bilingual in A and C and Y in B and C.

In all four cases X and Y can communicate without mediators.

(2) Speakers X and Y do not share a common linguistic competence:
   a. X speaks A and Y speaks B. They make use of either non-verbal communication strategies such as gestures, mimic, etc., or verbal communication strategies like 'foreigner talk', 'broken language', 'pidgin' etc.;
   b. X and Y call on the services of a third speaker, Z, who is bilingual in A and B and acts as interpreter. In this case communication is possible but only through relay. This is typically the case of the professional interpreter (see Chapter 10);
   c. X and Y have no linguistic competence in common and call on two interpreters, Z and W, who share language C, Z being bilingual in A and C and W in B and C; this is the case of double relay, commonly found in multilingual countries.

Before examining bilinguals' communication strategies in intercultural interactions it must be borne in mind that there are relatively few rigorous empirical studies on these strategies and that there is a great deal of confusion over the use of such terms as 'code choice', 'code-switching', 'code-mixing', etc. We will attempt to define them as they are introduced.

6.2.1 Code selection

On the basis of the model of speech accommodation presented in the first half of the chapter we can say that the strategies used to maximize the efficiency of communication in interpersonal interethnic interactions are governed by the following principles:

(1) *Linguistic competence principle* The code selected in the interaction will be that in which the sum of the individual communicative competences of the interlocutors is maximum. Code selection or choice is defined here as the speaker's decision, in a given communication interaction situation, to use one code rather than another; by code we mean a separate language, a language variety, a creole or certain types of mixed or switched language. The application of the competence principle may be counteracted by the following factors:

(2) *Ethnolinguistic affirmation principle* If the gain of choosing a code well within the competence of the speaker is perceived by him to be less than the cost (e.g. threat) to his ethnic identity, the competence principle may not be applied and a code-divergence strategy may even be chosen.

(3) *Interlocutor-perceived intention* Other things being equal, if the speaker perceives hostile intentions on the part of the interlocutor, whether at the interpersonal or at the intergroup level, he may refuse to converge towards the interlocutor by choosing a code other than the most effective one.

(4) *Personal, situational and social factors*, such as, for example, the roles of the interactants, the topic of the communication, the social norms or the status of the languages, may also influence the application of the competence principle.

It should be stressed that a bilingual's communication strategies vary within an interaction situation and therefore a code that is optimal at one point may cease to be so later as a result of changes in the situation, the topic, role relations, etc. One should add that speakers are not necessarily conscious of using these strategies.

In any interethnic interpersonal encounter the first speaker selects a code on the basis of the four principles enunciated above. In response to the speaker's initial choice his interlocutor in turn will have to choose a code; he may choose the same code, or the same code with modifications, or he may change codes. How are the speaker's and the interlocutor's code choices to be explained? Examining the selection of lingue franche in the context of multilingual–polyglossic Singapore (see Chapter 7.3.1), Platt (1980) asks the question: why do speakers choose a particular lingua franca for particular situations? He found that in addition to the appropriateness of the code and the verbal repertoire of speaker and addressee, other factors were relevant, like the ethnicity, education, sex, age and socio-economic background of both speaker and addressee. If the speaker knows the various characteristics of his addressee, a selection is relatively easy; in many cases, however, e.g. in transactions with strangers, no prior information is available to the speaker and he has to rely first on his direct perception of the physical and social appearance of his interlocutor, secondly on his appreciation of the domain and situation of interaction.

In the interlocutors' perception of a bilingual interaction situation Genesee & Bourhis (1982) analysed the role played by social norms, sociocultural status of the languages, ingroup favouritism and interpersonal speech accommodation in determining code choice. English and French Canadians gave evaluative reactions to code selection by English- and French-speaking Canadian actors who were heard interacting in a simulated salesman–customer situation. Four different patterns of code choice, consisting of three or four speaker turns each, were played in each study and subjects' reactions elicited after each turn. The authors found that (1) in the initial stages of a cross-cultural encounter constrained by clearly defined situational norms, interpretations of the interlocutors' language behaviour will be significantly influenced by situational norms; (2) in bilingual contexts characterized by intergroup conflict (the setting is Montreal in the late 1970s), closely adhering to situational norms ('the customer is always right') is a safe way of behaving in tense interactions with outgroup members; (3) language choices at this point in the encounter which clash with situational norms can signal that one or both interlocutors want to redefine the status relationship associated with the roles in question. For example, a French Canadian salesman's use of French with an English Canadian customer may signify his desire to upgrade his status by not giving in to the traditional dominance of English. It is noteworthy that the bilingual English–French subjects who had followed French immersion programs were more sensitive to sociolinguistic rules than monolingual French- or English-speaking judges.

Scotton (1980) provides a sociological framework for interpreting and predicting code choice which is based on a theory of markedness. For her code choices, although always in situation, are not a function of the situation *per se* but of negotiations of rights and obligations between participants. As such, choices are both given and new: they are given in the sense that speakers have social representations of the norms of interaction by which they have an expectation of how their choices will be interpreted and how they may interpret the choices of others; they are also original because speakers make their own choices to the extent that they construe the speech event. A lot depends on how conventionalized the exchange is. If the role relationship between participants is well defined there is usually agreement as to the unmarked code choice for both interlocutors. If speakers choose the unmarked code they are identifying with the status associated with their given role relationship; if, however, the speakers choose the marked variety they are clearly rejecting that role. If the situation is weakly defined a series of exploratory choices will be made to try and identify the type of role relationship and the speakers' identities.

Scotton proposes two main hypotheses:

(1) In well-defined role relationships in which a power differential is a factor in status identification, unmarked choices predominate. Code selection can then best be predicted in terms of the salient group identities of the participants and other situational factors. For example, Black British speakers interviewed by white British researchers will choose British English as the unmarked code; if they use creole/patois they are making a marked choice and rejecting the inferior status of creole/patois within the role relationship; they are making statements about both the immediate situation and their attitudes to the dominant society.

(2) In weakly defined role relationships the unmarked choice is more difficult to identify and individual personality characteristics will be better predictors of language choices than group identities or situational factors. Such an approach is complementary to the social psychological theory of speech accommodation. (See, for example, the Genesee & Bourhis (1982) experiment detailed earlier and Bourhis *et al.*, 1979, mentioned in 6.1.2.)

It would seem that perception of physical and social indices as clues for selecting the right code in intercultural interactions begins very early in the bilingual child. At first, of course, the most important variable is the significant interactant (McClure, 1981) but soon other clues are used. Fantini (1978) observed that young Spanish–English children use certain physical clues like hair and skin colour to make decisions about their unknown interlocutors' language. Soon the child is able to detect fluency (or absence of it) in his interlocutors. Bilingual children develop typical strategies for dealing with bilingual situations, learning how to adapt their language to the situation, the roles and the interlocutors, to the extent of playing the role of interpreters between monolingual speakers of different languages (Swain, 1972).

6.2.2 Speech modification strategies

Once the code has been chosen the speaker must adapt to his addressee by selecting from a range of alteration or modification strategies. The repertoire at his disposal will of course be a function of his bilingual communicative competence (First Principle). If the speaker is monolingual or, though bilingual, does not share a common language with his interlocutor, he can adapt only by modifying his $L_1(s)$ (we exclude other types of adaptation which call upon non-verbal strategies). One such strategy is 'foreigner talk', which has been studied in connection with the development of pidgins (Ferguson & DeBose, 1977; Mühlhäusler, 1986); in foreigner talk the speaker simplifies his L_1 to make himself understood by an interlocutor who has little knowledge of the former's language (Clyne, 1981).

Empirical evidence on foreigner talk is hard to come by, but more recently it has appeared in the form of elicitation experiments, observation and archival research. One of the problems is the number of inconsistencies in the production of speakers. Typical features of foreigner talk include variable omission of verb inflections, deletion of the copula and the article, reduction of personal pronoun to one form (e.g. *me, him*), utilization of lexical words as in telegraphic style, short juxtaposed sentences, slowing down of delivery, voice amplification, and the use of expressive devices, etc., some of which are typical of pidgins also and reflect natural intuitions on language simplification (Ferguson & DeBose, 1977; Hinnenkamp, 1982). It is interesting to note with Clyne (1981) that in Australia some immigrant children make use of foreigner talk with their parents and grand-parents, sometimes instead of the ethnic language, sometimes in alternation with it; it is modelled on their parents' non-fluent English. It is even used by both children and parents with whoever has difficulty with English, whatever their ethnic origin.

Another adaptive strategy is 'broken language', in which the speaker tries to speak the interlocutor's L_1 although he has little proficiency in it (Ferguson & DeBose, 1977; Kendall, 1980). It is a kind of 'interlanguage' (see Chapter 9.2.2). This strategy uses such devices as simplification, reduction, overgeneralization, transfer and formulaic language ('prefabricated routines'). It is not an uncommon practice among speakers of different ethnolinguistic backgrounds for one to use foreigner talk in his L_1 while the other tries to speak it in broken language (Clyne, 1981).

Between the choice of one language or the other there exists for the bilingual speaker a whole range of intermediary strategies which include the modification of either code and the relative use of both. Thus, the bilingual speaker possesses a far wider repertoire of adaptive and modification devices than the monolingual speaker (Grosjean, 1985a). Giles, Taylor & Bourhis (1973) have identified some 14 different accommodation strategies. These vary from maximum accommodation, which consists in the exclusive use of the interlocutor's language, to minimal accommodation where the speaker apologizes in his L_1 for not speaking his interlocutor's language.

6.2.3 Code alternation

One of the most common and original strategies used by bilingual speakers among themselves is code-switching. A general definition is 'the alternate use of two or more languages in the same utterance or conversation' (Grosjean, 1982, 145). We will first analyse this phenomenon from a linguistic point of view, distinguishing it from other language contact phenomena like borrowing and code-mixing.

6.2.3.1 The nature of code-switching

Code-switching differs from those other phenomena because the latter involve deformation or replacement of parts of the grammar or lexicon of the languages concerned, whereas code-switching leaves both intact; furthermore, unlike the other phenomena, which refer to specialized functions, code-switching in our sense is used for a wider range of functions and situations and obeys socially determined norms prevalent in certain multilingual communities. In code-switching two languages are present in the discourse, chunks from one language alternating with chunks from the other. Chunk /x/ belongs only to language L_X, chunk /y/ solely to L_Y. A chunk can vary in length from a morpheme to an utterance. There are two main categories of code-switching: intersentential, and intrasentential in which the alternate chunks are constituents of the sentence. Poplack (1980) further distinguishes what she calls 'extrasentential' code-switching, such as tags, fillers, etc. which the speaker introduces in his discourse. This code-switching of the third kind requires minimal competence in the second language; next in order of difficulty comes intersentential code-switching which makes more demands on the speaker's competence but less than intrasentential code-switching, which demands a near-balanced bilinguality. In her study of code-switching among bilingual Spanish–English speakers in an old Puerto Rican speech community of New York, Poplack (1980) found that bilinguals dominant in Spanish make use of intersentential alternation while balanced bilinguals use significantly more intrasentential switches. She suggests that this last type of switching might be a good test of balanced bilinguality.

One should not confuse code-switching with code-mixing. Code-mixing, like code-switching, is a language-contact communication strategy, but the speaker of L_X transfers elements or rules of L_Y to L_X at all linguistic levels of L_X, otherwise they would be considered as loans (in other words, code-mixing is a phenomenon of *parole*, not *langue*). In code-mixing there is necessarily a base language and it is possible to distinguish in an utterance monolingual chunks in the base language which alternate with chunks calling upon the rules of both languages. For example, in Chiac (a mixed French-English vernacular of New Brunswick) 'je vais back venir' is a French sentence comprising a French phrasal verb 'je vais venir' and an English morpheme 'back', which is prepositioned to the verb according to a French rule unacceptable in English. Typical utterances of code-mixing and code-switching might be schematized as in Figure 6.1. It is of course possible to observe these two phenomena within a single utterance, in which case code-mixing can be embedded in code-switching, but not the reverse. Note that the distinction between the two is not absolute and there are utterances which can be classified in either category. Note also that code-mixing can trigger off code-switching (Clyne, 1967; Kachru, 1982).

CODE-MIXING $/L_X/(L_X\ L_Y)/L_X/(L_Y\ L_X)/L_X/$ etc.

CODE-SWITCHING $/L_X/L_Y/L_X/L_Y/$ etc.

Figure 6.1 Schematic representation of code-mixing and code-switching

A further distinction should be made between code-switching which results from the bilingual's competence and code-switching resulting from a speaker's lack of competence in L_2. We call the former *bilingual code-switching* and the latter *incompetence code-switching*. An example of the former is the use of two languages by children of mixed-lingual families; the latter is typical of certain immigrant populations who have acquired a limited functional competence in L_2 but have to resort to their L_1 to compensate for their lack of knowledge of L_2. There is the opposite case of immigrants who have lost some of their competence in L_1 and call upon resources of their newly acquired L_2 to communicate with the ingroup and thus resort to code-switching. Note that it can be a code of transitional competence or interlanguage along the language-shift continuum. However, this type of code-switching is different from bilingual code-switching as it does not follow the same linguistic and sociolinguistic rules (Gumperz, 1982).

6.2.3.2 Bilingual code-switching

Intersentential code-switching does not raise any linguistic problem. Intrasentential switching does. Are there grammatical constraints on intrasentential switching? In the case of bilingual code-switching the switch from one language to the other does not appear to violate the grammatical rules of either language. Poplack (1980) and Sankoff & Poplack (1981) have postulated two general linguistic constraints operating on this kind of codeswitching: (1) The *free morpheme constraint*: a switch may not occur between a bound morpheme and a lexical form unless the latter has been phonologically integrated into the language of the bound morpheme (borrowing); for example, in the Spanish–English code-switched language *flipeando* is a wellformed Spanish form, whereas *run-eando* is not, because the phonology of *run* is unambiguously English and that of *eando* Spanish. (2) The *equivalence constraint*: the order of sentence constituents immediately adjacent to and on both sides of the switch must be grammatical with respect to both languages simultaneously. The equivalence constraint is illustrated in Figure 6.2, where the dotted lines indicate permissible switch points, and the arrows indicate the surface relationship of the two languages. Switches may occur at, but not between, the dotted lines.

Linguistic performance constrained in this way must be based on simultaneous access to the grammatical rules of both languages. This raises the question of the existence and nature of a bilingual code-switching grammar. Sankoff & Poplack (1981) argue that intrasentential code-switching involves the juxtaposition of constituents from two codes which are too closely connected to be generated by rules from two distinct grammars; an additional argument is that switching takes place without any pauses or hesitations. The authors postulate the existence of two monolingual grammars and one codeswitching grammar. This grammar is made up of the combined lexicons of the two languages as well as the grammatical categories of the two monolingual grammars, limited by the free morpheme constraint and the equivalence constraint.

The hypothesis of a grammar specific to code-switching has been challenged by a number of linguists and psycholinguists. Woolford (1983), for example, proposes an overlap for the two monolingual grammars at the level of phrase-

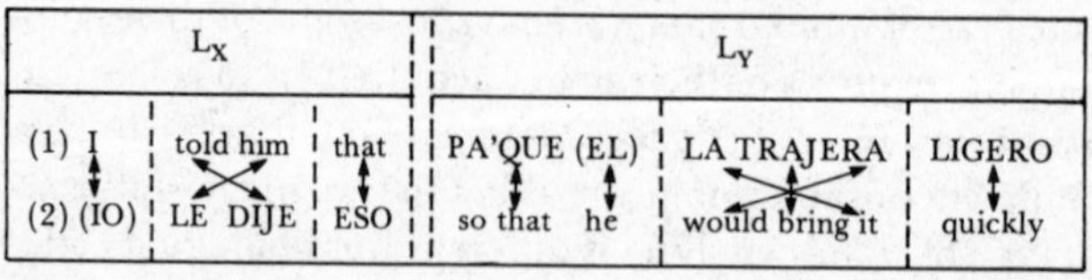

Figure 6.2 Equivalence constraint rule in bilingual code-switching (from Sankoff and Poplack, 1981)

structure rules. When constructing a phrase-structure tree the speaker draws from the phrase-structure rules of either language; when the rules are the same in both languages, then the categories (NP, VP, etc.) may be filled freely from either lexicon. However, when the categories are created by a rule that exists in only one language, they must be filled from the lexicon of that language. The two lexicons remain separate, as do the word-formation components, thus accounting for the free morpheme constraint. Other criticisms of the code-switching grammar are based on different language dyads from those used by Sankoff & Poplack or Woolford. For example, Bentahila & Davies (1983) and Berk-Seligson (1986) analysed, the former Arabic–French, the latter Spanish–Hebrew conversations and found that their subjects switched freely and did not seem to judge switches that broke the equivalence constraint as deviant; the free morpheme constraint, however, seemed to hold. They conclude from their evidence that although code-switching is clearly rule-governed, the equivalence rule is not universal. Moreover, they find it is difficult to accept that intrasentential code-switching is proof of balanced bilinguality.

The main problem with this debate is the comparability of the findings. Are the cases reported by the different researchers similar? Are the Spanish–Hebrew speakers and situations of Berk-Seligson and the Arabic–French speakers and situations of Bentahila & Davies really comparable with the stable norm-governed bilingual community described by Poplack (1980)? Until code-switching situations are more clearly defined and a greater variety of contexts have been studied, the universality of the two constraint rules and the validity of a bilingual code-switching grammar cannot be demonstrated.

Many situational variables seem to affect the type and frequency of code-switching: the topic of conversation, the participants, the setting, the affective aspect of the message, and so on. It also seems that 'because of its reliance on unverbalized shared understanding, code-switching is typical of the communicative conventions of closed network situations' (Gumperz, 1982, 71–2). Is code-switching a learned behaviour, and, if so, how is it learned and when? The alternate use of two languages in the same utterance begins early in childhood, but it is different from adult code alternation in a number of ways. McClure (1981) reports that Mexican American children use different ways depending on their age. Younger bilinguals produce more examples of code-mixing than code-switching; children over the age of nine switch languages for at least a phrase or a sentence as often as they code-mix. In time code-switching is used as a communicative strategy and a marker of ethnic group membership and identity.

Studying intergenerational variation in the use of English and Spanish in the same Puerto Rican community in New York, Poplack (1983) observed that both English and Spanish are used increasingly in conjunction without any functional separation, i.e. without diglossia (see Chapter 7.3.2). There seems to be no trend towards a convergence of English and Spanish; English loan words are regularly being integrated into Spanish and code-switching is a distinctive communicative resource for the community of skilled bilinguals. But the younger generation diverges markedly from the older in its use of code-switching. As in the cases studied by McClure (1981), children switch or mix mostly single nouns, which suggests a lack of lexical availability; learning to code-switch intrasententially is a maturational social process similar to the development of stylistic and repertoire usage, and children learn it later since it requires full development of syntactic rules for both languages. It is interesting to note that bilingual community norms are transmitted down the generations regardless of whether children are taught bilingually or in English only. It looks as though code-switching in this situation has become an institutionalized code, which is the expression of a particular ethnic identity, but, as far as its use in the speech community is concerned, it is an unmarked choice (see Scotton, 1986).

The sociolinguistic context in which code-switching takes place is paramount in determining the type of code and the speakers' relations to it. In the case richly documented by Poplack (1980) we appear to have a stable, closely knit speech community with focussed norms; its speakers, renewed by fresh immigration, have between then a variable repertoire ranging from Spanish-dominant to balanced Spanish–English bilinguals. Code-switching in this context is not a stage in a language shift from Spanish to English, as is often the case in the acculturation process. Code-switching as a communicative strategy is a stage in the linguistic and cultural assimilation of, for example, children who are recent immigrants in a foreign country. (See Auer, 1987 on the interlanguages of guestworkers and their children.)

6.2.4 Code-mixing

Code-mixing, as we have already explained, is a process characterized by the transfer of elements from a language L_Y to the base language L_X; in the mixed utterance which results we can distinguish monolingual chunks of L_X alternating with chunks of L_Y which refer to the rules of two codes. Unlike borrowing, which is generally limited to lexical units which are more or less well assimilated, code-mixing transfers elements of all linguistic levels and units ranging from a lexical item to a sentence, so that it is not always easy to distinguish code-mixing from code-switching. Like code-switching, code-mixing is a strategy of the bilingual speaker, whereas borrowing is not, in the sense that monolinguals can practise it in language-contact situations. Code-mixing can of course express a lack of competence in the base language, such as, e.g., lexical items, and in this case code-mixing can compensate for this lack. But, as for code-switching, code-mixing can be a bilingual's specific code which enables him to express attitudes, intentions, roles, and to identify with a particular group.

A fascinating example of the latter kind of code-mixing is that given
Kachru (1978), who has studied it in the multilingual and multicultural cont
of India. He defines three main varieties of code-mixing. The base langua̧
can be any one of the languages of India; three languages may be mixed with
it, English, Sanskrit, or Persian. In the first case, called Englishization, the
English language (which is one of the two official languages and has great
prestige) is mixed to a large number of regional languages in a wide variety of
contexts. The resulting mixed code is a marker of high social status and
membership of an educated elite; it expresses power and prestige and is characteristic of the Indian middle class. For example, the speech repertoire (see
Chapter 7.3.1) of an educated Indian woman includes a strongly Englishized
Hindi, which she speaks with members of her family, and a non-Englishized
Hindi, which she reserves for a servant. The same woman will also use English
and alternate English and Hindi. This Englishized code is used in political,
administrative, and scientific and technological discourse. It is noteworthy
that a bilingual speaker will use a strongly Englishized code in order to hide his
social, regional, religious or ethnic identity (neutralization). One may also
wonder if attempts at Englishization are made by lower middle-class Indians
who have upward social aspiration, and if so, whether hypercorrect forms can
be expected.

A second mixed variety results from the mixing of Sanskrit or High Hindi
with an Indian language (Sanskritization). It can be a marker of caste or religious identity. It is used in philosophical, literary or religious (Hindu) discourse. In some contexts Sanskritized speech is a sign of pedantry or political
conservatism. Persianization is the third kind of code-mixing and is associated
with Muslim culture. The language of the law courts borrows its vocabulary
from Persian, and in some parts of India Persianized code-mixing is a marker
of Muslim religious identity and of professional status.

6.3 Conclusion

The interplay between social psychological mechanisms and linguistic behaviour in intercultural interactions has been discussed in this chapter. Accentuating the speech markers of ethnic identity can become an important
strategy in intergroup relations as it enables individuals to affirm their group
membership. This psychological differentiation is an important component of
speech accommodation in interpersonal intercultural relations. First we analysed some theoretical foundations of speech-accommodation theory and the
empirical evidence in its support. We then discussed the psychological reality
of convergent and divergent linguistic accommodation through which the
speaker expresses his intention to be more similar to, or differentiate himself
from, his interlocutor as an individual and as a member of an ethnolinguistic

community. We ended this first section by reviewing the current state of the art in speech-accommodation theory.

The second half of this chapter addressed the question of communication strategies in intercultural interaction. We attempted to understand the principle governing code selection, speech modification and code alternation. Code-switching, the most striking communication strategy characteristic of bilinguals in monolingual and multicultural communities, may follow language-specific rules and code-switching rules simultaneously. Bilingual code-switching can become an autonomous code which develops in closed social settings and identifies an ethnolinguistic group. This type of rule-governed code raises important questions for linguistic description and theory.

Whereas in the first part of the chapter we addressed the psychological processes of communication strategies, in the second part we looked essentially at the linguistic outcome. Communication strategies specific to languages in contact arise from the need to continuously accommodate to the intercultural encounter; for the monolingual in that situation strategies are limited to non-linguistic accommodation and L_1 speech modifications; the bilingual, on the other hand, can also call upon mixed-lingual strategies which can evolve into autonomous codes. Although we have been concerned with the bilingual individual in interaction with others, we have analysed his behaviour primarily as a member of an ethnolinguistic group. It is to language behaviour between ethnolinguistic groups and their interrelations that we turn in the next chapter.

7

Multilingualism and intergroup relations

So far, we have been concerned mainly with the bilingual individual, from a number of different points of view and scientific disciplines: language and development (Chapters 2 and 3), information processing (Chapter 4), cultural identity (Chapter 5), and interpersonal communication interaction (Chapter 6). If in the two preceding chapters intergroup relations were also mentioned, it was as an interpersonal process in which individuals interact with each other as members of different ethnolinguistic groups. In the present chapter we shall examine the role of language in intergroup relations at the societal level when different languages and cultures are in contact.

This chapter differs from the earlier chapters in a number of respects. After addressing the problems of the bilingual speaker as an individual and in his interpersonal relations, we now consider relations between ethnolinguistic groups. Thus we move from a micrological to a macrological level of analysis and to disciplines which are concerned with sociostructural factors, like sociology, sociolinguistics and the sociology of language. Because these disciplines deal with a multiplicity of factors and multidimensional phenomena, it is difficult to control all these factors. As a result, theories are thin on the ground and what pass for models are often mere typologies and taxonomies which are more descriptive than predictive; their methodologies include the measures of societal bilingualism reviewed in Chapter 1.2.3. But social and cultural phenomena have also a psychological reality, and the intergroup and interpersonal levels are only the two poles of a social-interaction continuum. This chapter therefore also considers intergroup relations from the point of view of the individual as member of a group and calls upon disciplines like the social psychology of language and the ethnography of speaking. Our problem is how to integrate these different levels of analysis into a unified interdisciplinary framework. In view of the vast domain encompassed here we have limited our analysis to a few fundamental questions and cases and considered only soundly based theories and well-documented evidence.

7.1 The role of language in intergroup relations

To the extent that language is a salient dimension of ethnic identity it will play an important role in intergroup relations when languages and cultures are in contact, not only as a symbol but also as an instrument for upholding or promoting the groups' ethnic identities.[1] The role of language will therefore vary according to its importance as a symbol of group identity and as a function of the power relations holding between the different ethnolinguistic groups. A number of social scientists have investigated the role of language in ethnic group relations from a variety of theoretical and methodological standpoints and it is to their views and to the empirical evidence that we now turn.

First, it is important to stress that an ethnic group is not an objective, rigidly defined, homogeneous category. It can cut across other social categories, such as class, race, caste and religious or political group. Its boundaries are not closed but more or less permeable, since groups do not develop in isolation from one another and individuals can have multiple group membership, as is the case for the bicultural individual. Boundaries are not fixed but change, since the cultures within them change; conversely, group boundaries may be maintained across generations in spite of social and cultural changes. One cannot assume a one-to-one correspondence between ethnic group and cultural characteristics: some dimensions, e.g. language, may be regarded as significant symbols while others are not. A group may respond differently on different dimensions, and subgroups within a group may react in various, sometimes conflicting, ways.

If there is one point on which most social scientists seem to agree, it is on the subjective definition of ethnic groups. Only those dimensions which members themselves perceive as significant are defining characteristics of the group (Barth, 1970). Weber (1968) writes: 'We shall call ethnic groups those human groups that entertain a subjective belief in their common descent ... ethnic membership [is] a presumed identity' (p. 389). Similarly, for Tajfel (1978), who does not deny the importance of objective factors, a social or ethnic group is defined as one which perceives itself and is perceived by other groups as a distinctive entity (see Chapter 5.2.2). Thus, the criteria for group membership are defined both externally by objective standards (e.g. skin colour) and internally by members themselves. External criteria may be imposed from outside by a dominant group which thereby defines the minority group; but individual members may then refuse to identify with that group.

Secondly, according to Tajfel's (1978) dynamic theory of intergroup relations, a group aims to differentiate itself from other groups in order to achieve or maintain superiority on some relevant dimension of comparison. Positive group identity therefore occurs not in isolation but through mutual comparisons and differentiations between groups. Social relationships between groups are seldom static, and since any changes in power relations will have consequences for the outcome of intergroup comparisons, social identity, which is maintained by such comparisons, also changes; in turn, variations in social identity may alter existing intergroup relations. These changes in identity are explained in Tajfel's theory by 'insecurity', which arises whenever an alternative in the status quo is perceived as possible, either because of instability in the positions of the groups, or because power and status are perceived as having been acquired illegitimately. The consequences of an insecure identity are a renewed search for positive distinctiveness, either through direct competition on the relevant dimensions of comparison or by redefining or altering the elements of the comparative situation ('social creativity'). Success in imposing a new positive distinctiveness will depend partly on some recognition by the other groups; if that recognition is not forthcoming renewed and more vigorous attempts at differentiation can be expected.

Thirdly, language itself is dynamic and refers to a very complex objective and subjective reality. Linguistic descriptions, even when they take into account intra- and interlanguage variations, do not necessarily correspond to the speakers' own perceptions of what constitutes their language(s), precisely because language can be a marker of group ethnic identity; thus, what is defined by linguists as one and the same language or as a linguistic continuum may in fact be perceived as different languages by different speakers of that language. For example, Hindustani is perceived as Hindi, Urdu or Punjabi according to the cultural, religious or political allegiances of its speakers (Brass, 1974). This might help to explain why the definition of 'speech community' has proved so intractable (Hudson, 1980). Languages, like groups, have more or less permeable boundaries. 'Who are the Lue?' asks Moerman (1965), who provides different views both from outsiders (neighbours of those whom some call Lue) and by insiders (those who sometimes call themselves Lue); those views show variation in the ethnic designation, the language label and the link between the two.

A language may be the defining characteristic of an ethnic group, in which case it is necessary to understand and speak it in order to belong to the group; but it is not always a condition of group membership. Trudgill & Tzavaras (1977) have shown that it is not essential for the Albanian Arvanites in Greece to speak Arvanitika in order to be considered 'good' Arvanites. An individual or a group can abandon their language for another without necessarily losing their original sense of identity. For ethnicity is sometimes related more to the symbol of a language than to its actual use by members of a group (de Vos & Romanucci-Ross, 1975; Gans, 1979). The nineteenth-century notion of one group (nation) = one language does not match reality either, since some groups (or nations) speak more than one language, and the same language can be spoken by more than one group (or nation). As with the notion of ethnic group identity, language identity is very much a function of the interlocutors' perceptions.

7.1.1 Language as symbol and instrument of group identity

Before we examine in detail the role of language in interethnic group relations it is useful to define the possible forms that ethnic relations may take in multi-cultural and multilingual societies. Berry (1980) distinguishes five possible forms of acculturation (see also Chapter 5.2.4) by individuals or groups: assimilation, integration, segregation, separation and deculturation (these categories are not discrete but continuous); he further discriminates between cultural acculturation, in which the behaviour of one group becomes more similar to that of another, and structural acculturation, in which one group participates in the economic and social systems of the larger society without losing its cultural distinctiveness. Assimilation for the subordinate group means the surrender of its cultural identity and its absorption into the larger society. Assimilation is complete when the members of the group see them-selves as belonging to another group and when that other group accepts them as full members. In the case of integration a group becomes an integral part of the society while retaining its cultural distinctiveness to varying degrees. In the case of segregation the dominant group imposes its solution (e.g. apartheid in South Africa); in the case of separation it is the subordinate group that decides to assert its distinctiveness and leave the society. In deculturation a group loses its cultural identity without gaining another: this happens when the sub-ordinate group is marginalized. These five possibilities are at the collective level more or less the equivalent of Gardner & Lambert's (1972) distinctions at an individual level (see Chapter 5.2.3). Berry's model, it must be admitted, is rather static and rests on an ideology of liberal pluralism more applicable to individuals than to groups (Gordon, 1981) and to Western types of society than to Third World societies. Its merit lies in providing us with a useful typology. But it can and should be integrated into a social theory of ethnic group rela-tions, such as Schermerhorn's (1970), which we will also use in Chapter 8.3.

The relationship between language and group ethnic identity is not static but varies as a function of the type of power relations obtaining between the groups and the level of economic and social development reached by the groups. From a sociohistorical perspective Ross (1979) has proposed a model of group identity development in four stages, which are successively the com-munal, minority, ethnic and national group identity modes. Note that a group can remain at a particular stage, that the four stages overlap, and that it is pos-sible for a group to miss a stage and accelerate its development. Building on this taxonomy, Taylor & Giles (1979) have put forward a tentative social psychological theoretical framework for research in intergroup relations, which also posits four stages but ignores the communal.

In the communal mode typical of isolated traditional societies group iden-tity is not an issue: group and self-identity are taken for granted, since com-parison with other groups is non-existent. Language is the repository of the culture. Communal groups often coexist on a same territory, keep their speech repertoires distinct and do not learn each other's language, with the exception of bilingual intermediaries (Fishman, 1972). Successful territorial bilingualism may be the modern equivalent of the communal mode; in this case Switzerland would be an example of ethnolinguistic coexistence (McRae, 1983). It is when traditional communal groups come into contact with the modern world that problems arise: few resist this impact and most are destroyed or assimilated into the new society (examples from developing countries abound). Language shift and language death are significant aspects of this assimilation. Ross's view of communal groups is limited and fails to take into account communal groups in such cultures as are found in South Asia, for example, where intercommunal contacts and conflicts are much greater.

A communal group may not wish, or be allowed, to assimilate; it will then become a minority group. The existence of a minority suggests that of a majority which dominates the society through its ability to impose unequal terms on minority groups rather than through its numerical strength. A minority group, therefore, is characterized by its powerlessness to define the nature of its relationship with the majority, and therefore its own identity. Its status is defined by the majority and this is mirrored in the minority's negative self-image. This may extend to the language itself, which comes to reflect the subordinate position of the group. The survival or loss of the minority language will be dependent upon the interests of the majority.

Sometimes the dominant group decides to maintain minority languages in order to divide and rule. It may do this through segregation or apartheid, as in South Africa, or as in (for example) the case of a high-status group of Brahmins in Karnataka, India, who never used their caste dialect with non-Brahmins (Ullrich, 1971). Or it may try to achieve the same result by keeping minority groups apart and preserving linguistic differences to prevent inter-ethnic communication (e.g. Arabic and Berber speakers in North Africa under French rule, or negro slaves from different ethnolinguistic backgrounds on the plantations). In modern industrialized societies there is often an 'ethnolinguistic division of labour', where cultural and linguistic boundaries are also class boundaries and upward mobility is denied to minority members (Hughes, 1970; Hechter, 1975).

More frequently the majority imposes its own language upon the minorities as the only legitimate one and pursues a policy of assimilation. In this case the minority language is devalorized, stigmatized and sometimes even eradicated; in order to survive as individuals minority group members have to learn the legitimate language. But not all necessarily develop native competence in L_2, nor even acculturate, let alone assimilate; nor do they always lose their L_1; these members then run the risk of marginalization. However great their desire to assimilate, some minority groups are unable to do so because of some external characteristic, like race, which makes them 'visible'.

This may lead to a kind of reactive ethnicity, when the visible minority, or at least some of its members, become aware of the impossibility of complete assimilation.

Minorization, or the imposition of minority status on subordinate groups by the majority, produces negative group identity, and some members will strive to achieve a more positive identity by 'passing' into the majority. Passing of course includes speaking the legitimate language and these individuals will acculturate linguistically, i.e. they will converge upwardly in their speech patterns towards the dominant group, even if for a time some remain bilingual. But many members are not able or not allowed to pass because of certain individual characteristics or impermeable group boundaries or both. Some come to realize that status enhancement lies in the redefinition of the minority status of the whole group by raising the group consciousness of its members, persuading them that their status is illegitimate and that only concerted collective action can improve their position. This redefinition is achieved by the transformation of the minority into an ethnic group. Ross (1979) defines an ethnic group as 'a politically mobilized collectivity whose members share a perceived distinctive self-identity' (p. 9). If language is one of the salient features of the ethnic group, it is around the language issue that the group will mobilize; language may of course interact with other factors.

The dominant group will usually resist such demands for the recognition of collective rights, including language rights, and if it makes concessions, as in the case of the liberal pluralist ideology, it will only concede individual rights; equality is understood in terms of equal opportunity for individuals only, regardless of ethnic or other characteristics, never in terms of equality of outcome for groups considered collectively (Gordon, 1981). If a compromise is not reached between ethnic groups and the majority, the conflict can escalate, with calls for autonomy, separation or national self-determination if a homeland exists within the boundaries of the society, or for emigration if it exists outside it. A nationalist solution is reached when an ethnic group acquires a state of its own. With nationhood, however, the issue of a national language and its relation to other dialects and languages, where they exist, at once arises. Contemporary history abounds in examples of nationalist movements based essentially, though not exclusively, on language demands. (For examples see C. H. Williams, 1984, on ethnolinguistic separatist movements in the West, and Brass, 1974 and Das Gupta, 1975 on the relationship between ethnicity, language demands and national developments in India.)

When it is a salient dimension of group identity language can play many roles in ethnic mobilization. First, an ethnic group can revive an ancestral language, as happened when Hebrew, which replaced Yiddish (perceived by Zionists as a symbol of negative self-identity), became once again the expression of, and vehicle for, a revived Jewish state (on the relation between

Hebrew and Yiddish see Fishman, 1985). The ancestral language may be a myth which the group creates for itself as a symbol: in the 1960s many Black Americans took up the study of Swahili in an attempt to promote their new ethnic identity, regardless of the fact that their West African ancestors had never spoken that language. As a symbol of ethnicity a language need not be used for communication, as the case of Irish testifies (J. Edwards, 1982).

Ethnic mobilization can unite a group around the defence of its culture from a perceived language threat, especially if the language has a territorial base. Two contemporary examples come to mind, francophone Quebec and the Flemish-speaking half of Belgium. In Quebec the defence of the French language has been directly linked to the demands by the French-speaking population for economic and political power within their province; while polarizing the struggle on cultural and linguistic issues the people of Quebec gained control of the economic and social 'capital', until then predominantly in the hands of the English-speaking community. The francization of the province also enabled the Québécois to lessen their sense of insecurity and partly remove the stigma of inferiority which had attached to them and their language for two centuries, and to build a positive ethnic identity (Bourhis, 1984). In Belgium the Flemish-speaking population reversed the power relationship which had favoured the dominant French-speaking group, not only by taking over the control of their economy but also by imposing Flemish unilingualism on their French-speaking middle-class elites (Witte & Baetens Beardsmore, 1987). In both cases a territorial form of bilingualism ensures two unilingualisms, with bilingual intermediaries.

A third mode of ethnolinguistic mobilization is, paradoxically, the use of the dominant language by ethnic groups to voice their demands and rally support: for instance, nationalist elites in India effectively used English in their struggle for independence, while Amerindians in the USA have found English a powerful lingua franca for expressing their ethnic identity.

Finally, when the status of a hitherto stigmatized language is revalorized, the language is usually standardized, modernized and even 'purified' as a symbol of the newly found or reborn ethnic identity, in an effort to mark it off from lower-status varieties. This happened in Quebec in the 1960s with the setting up of a number of boards, like the *Conseil de la Langue Française*, with the aim of monitoring and implementing the use and 'quality' of the French language (Bourhis, 1984). Similarly, the 1979 campaign for the promotion of Mandarin in Singapore was based on the claim that dialects are incapable of expressing educated thoughts and refined feelings (Kuo, 1984).

Conversely, ethnolinguistic groups can redefine a vernacular by valorizing it as the symbol of their distinctiveness, despite wider social stigmatization. Black Americans in the USA (Labov, 1972) and adolescent British blacks of Afro-Caribbean parentage in Britain (Hewitt, 1986) have emphasized their salient ethnic characteristics, like colour ('black is beautiful') and language

(Black English Vernacular, creole, patois). Black British youngsters speak, in addition to a local urban variety of English, a dialect closely related to one of the Caribbean creoles, such as British Jamaican Creole, and code-switch between these different varieties (V. K. Edwards, 1986). Prestige black speech forms of West Indian adolescents are even appropriated and used by some of their white working-class adolescent peers, both unconsciously and consciously, in interracial communication interactions and friendship networks, as the expression of their desire to identify with black youth culture (Hewitt, 1986). Thus, class and race interact and their boundaries are bridged, albeit temporarily.

For all its dynamic qualities Ross's (1979) model of the interaction between intergroup relations, group ethnic identity, and language has three main limitations. Firstly, its macro-categories are too general for precise operationalization to be possible; secondly, it tends to underestimate individuals' subjective perceptions of the objective societal reality; thirdly, it is 'Western-centric' and predicated on a 'dominant majority-dominated minorities' paradigm; but not all societies are neatly divided into hierarchical social classes with an economically, socially, politically and culturally powerful majority group and a number of ethnolinguistic minority groups which are under pressure to assimilate. Many developing countries in the Third World have multicultural and multilingual communities with different social structures, where for example communal groups have evolved in a different way. In the next sections we will be looking at these different situations and considering other theoretical constructs and methodologies which attempt to account for the role of language in intergroup relations. The first of these is the model of ethnolinguistic vitality, to which we now turn.

7.1.2 *Ethnolinguistic vitality*

In order to link social psychological processes underlying inter-ethnolinguistic group behaviour to their proper sociocultural settings and identify the socio-structural factors which promote or impede the maintenance of an ethnic minority language, Giles, Bourhis & Taylor (1977) developed the concept of *ethnolinguistic vitality*, which has since been extended and applied in a variety of contexts. They define the vitality of an ethnolinguistic group as 'that which makes a group behave as a distinctive and active collective entity in intergroup situations' (p. 308). Ethnolinguistic vitality can be evaluated by three classes of objective factors, namely status, demography and institutional support. Briefly, the status factors include those variables which reflect a group's economic and political power, its social status, its socio-historical standing and the status of the ethnic language(s), relative to the various outgroups. The demographic factors refer to the total population of the group, and its concentration and distribution over a territory; the number of mixed marriages, birth rate and patterns of immigration and emigration are relevant variables here. Institutional support factors refer to the degree of support the group and its language(s) enjoy in the various informal and formal institutions of the society, such as for example in the home, the mass media and education.

Giles, Bourhis & Taylor (1977) hypothesized that each of these factors would affect in a positive or negative way the vitality of an ethnolinguistic group. They further proposed that ethnolinguistic communities could be meaningfully grouped according to the above three factors on the basis of the available historical, sociological, demographic and other data. Using such a framework, ethnolinguistic groups could be classified as possessing high, medium or low vitality, which would help define and compare ethnolinguistic groups across cultures. It is argued that the higher the vitality the more likely a group and its language(s) are to survive as a distinctive entity. So far, the discussion has focussed on 'objective' assessments of ethnolinguistic vitality. But do ethnolinguistic group members perceive their situation subjectively along the same lines as the objective analysis? Their subjective assessment may be just as important in determining interethnic group behaviour; members may underestimate or exaggerate the ethnolinguistic vitality of the ingroup or of the outgroup, and so on. A combination of objective and subjective measures would provide a better understanding of relations between groups in terms of their ethnolinguistic vitality.

The concept of *perceived ethnolinguistic vitality* takes into account individual members' cognitive representations of the social conditions in which they live and mediates their intergroup behaviour. This concept provides a theoretical and empirical starting-point for bridging the conceptual gap between sociological and social psychological approaches to inter-ethnolinguistic group relations. To try and measure perceived ethnolinguistic vitality a 'Subjective Vitality Questionnaire' was designed by Bourhis, Giles & Rosenthal (1981). On this questionnaire members rate their own group relative to one or more outgroups on the three main vitality dimensions. The relationships between objective and subjective vitality have been explored in a number of empirical investigations. We will review only two of them because they come up with very different conclusions as to the validity of the construct of perceived ethnolinguistic vitality.

In a detailed study of ethnolinguistic vitality in Melbourne, Giles, Rosenthal & Young (1985) elicited vitality perceptions from adolescent members of dominant majority (Anglo-Australian) and ethnic minority (Greek Australian) groups with the threefold aim of determining (1) whether the subjects construed their own and the outgroup's vitalities in the same way as more objective assessments; (2) whether majority and minority groups differed in their cognitive representations of their own and each other's sociostructural positions; and (3) to what extent these cognitive representations correspond with the three factors of status, demography and institutional support. Objectively, the Greeks in Melbourne have a high vitality, but compared with the Anglo-Australian majority, they have only medium vitality. In terms of perceived vitality the two groups agreed that Anglo-Australians had more vitality on certain status and institutional-support variables, while Greeks had more vitality on certain demographic items; they disagreed frequently about each other's sociostructural positions, however, both groups tending to downgrade the vitality of the outgroup and correspondingly to upgrade the positions of their ingroup. Lastly, the factored structure of status, demography and institutional support received some confirmation. The factors received relative cognitive weight (in terms of percentage of variance accounted for) in the following descending order: institutional support, demography, status. According to the authors, these results seem to provide empirical support for the social psychological reality of the construct of perceived ethnolinguistic vitality.

Investigating the perceived ethnolinguistic vitality of 13- to 16-year-old francophone schoolchildren in the bilingual city of Moncton, New Brunswick, Labrie (1984) found no correlation between vitality and attitudes towards the majority anglophone outgroup on the one hand and fear of assimilation on the other. He concludes from these negative results that the questionnaire developed by Bourhis, Giles & Rosenthal fails to take account of affective factors relevant to second-language acquisition and use; he suggests that the ethnolinguistic vitality construct is based not on the intergroup relations as they are perceived and lived by the individual in his immediate environment, but on his knowledge of these relations as they are relayed to him by the media and education. The influence of sociostructural factors is thus further mediated by the individual's social networks, through which he develops social representations of his own and other ethnolinguistic groups (see Chapter 3.2). This might explain why, in the Giles, Rosenthal & Young (1985) study, the Greek Australians had an exaggerated perception of their business influence: they perceived that their group was a sizeable community in the particular suburb of Melbourne where they lived. (See also how the localized conditions of an ethnolinguistic community can affect its perceptions of the ingroup's position as a whole in the wider society in Bourhis & Sachdev, 1984.)

Another critique of the concept of perceived ethnolinguistic vitality comes from Allard & Landry (1986), who reinterpret it in terms of the beliefs that underlie social identity; they analyse these beliefs from a cognitive-orientation theory perspective (Kreitler & Kreitler, 1976). Accordingly, they take into consideration not only the group members' perceptions of what exists now or may exist in the future (the general beliefs tapped by the subjective ethnolinguistic vitality questionnaire) but also their beliefs about what should exist (norms and rules), about their own desires (self-beliefs) and about goals. In order to predict inter-ethnolinguistic group behaviour they devised and administered a questionnaire to assess individual beliefs about the ethnolinguistic vitality of the francophone minority in Moncton. The results suggested that general beliefs, i.e. perceptions of factual situations, contributed minimally to the prediction of language behaviour, but that all the types of beliefs in combination best predicted that behaviour: the stronger the beliefs of francophone subjects about their own ethnolinguistic vitality, the less they tended to communicate in the majority language, in this case English. The authors compare their findings with those of Bourhis & Sachdev (1984) who concluded from their study of language attitudes and reported behaviour among Italian and English schoolchildren in Hamilton, Ontario, that group members who perceive that they have high ethnolinguistic vitality are likely to use their mother tongue more frequently and in a wider range of domains than those who have a low perceived vitality.

The construct of ethnolinguistic vitality can be criticized on theoretical grounds from other perspectives. The first objection concerns the status of the sociostructural variables; these form a purely descriptive taxonomy which lacks theoretical justification. For this reason, the factors and their variables have little predictive value: indeed, any one of them can have diametrically opposed consequences. For example, in his study of factors influencing the maintenance or loss of ethnic minority languages in the USA, Kloss (1966) has shown how the same factor can either enhance or depress the ethnolinguistic vitality of a group. Take the demographic factor, for example. While there may be safety in numbers and large groups have a greater chance of survival than small ones, this is not always the case: a numerous minority group, unless it is territorially circumscribed, is exposed to multiple contacts with the dominant group and experiences internal divisions and a dilution of its strength; for example, the German-speaking communities in North America were by far the largest and most powerful immigrant groups in the nineteenth century, yet they have gradually been assimilated. Conversely, numerical weakness can lead to greater group solidarity and cohesion; perceptions of inferiority do not necessarily lead to the demise of an ethnic group and its language but can be a spur to the revitalization of its self-identity and its language, as can the dominant group's policy of enforced assimilation (Glazer, 1966). In all this, group self-awareness and ethnic mobilization are essential to the survival of a group and its language.

Another critique is directed against the macro (objective)–micro (subjective) dichotomy of the (perceived) ethnolinguistic vitality construct. Husband & Saifullah Khan (1982) maintain that this dichotomy disappears if one analyses intergroup interaction processes at different levels of social organization, such as primary groups, social networks, interest groups and social classes. They argue that the relationship between, for example, (Pakistani) Punjabi–English speakers and English monolingual speakers in Britain can only be understood by looking at the respective historical, economic and political processes which have led to the present imbalance of power and perceived cultural differences between the two populations. Perceived from within, many Pakistani Punjabis would rate their language rather low relatively to the wider context of Britain and Pakistan; however, for its members this language (or variety, since most speak the Mirpuri dialect) is valued as a fundamental part of regional culture and symbol of group membership and loyalty. The authors criticize the very concept of 'ethnolinguistic group' which, like that of language, refers to too high a level of abstraction; they propose instead that of 'speech community', defined in terms of shared norms and values and language interactions. Language, as a salient symbol of ethnic identity, is a multidimensional concept varying in space and time. The younger generation of Pakistani Punjabis belongs at the same time both to the Pakistani–Punjabi– Mirpuri community and to the anglophone community.

Their view is supported by, among others, a study of linguistic and cultural affiliations amongst first-generation Asian (Gujarati) adolescents in Britain by Mercer, Mercer & Mears (1977). These researchers treat the relation between ethnic identity and language loyalty as problematic, since the main identifying trait of this group is not language but their physical appearance, more specifically their skin colour, and since a common expression of their self-identity in encounters with whites is their Indianness (an ethnic, not an ethnolinguistic label, as Indians speak a variety of Indian languages). Attitudes to language seem to be associated with the individual's conception of the most desirable future for himself and his group within British society. Those who opt for British identity seem to favour assimilation; those who choose Indian identity favour a pluralistic cultural development in which their ethnic identity is maintained. Thus, the wide range of attitudes to the Gujarati language and to the traditional Indian culture should warn us against assuming that members of ethnolinguistic minority groups share, by virtue of their common background, a similar set of attitudes to their ethnic language and a similar conception of their place in the new society. Ethnicity is essentially a form of interaction between cultural groups within common social contexts, and different social contexts will generate different ethnic identities. The ethnolinguistic vitality construct fails to some extent to account for the dynamics of ethnic groups in multilingual communities.

7.1.3 Language and ethnicity in multicultural settings

We have seen that language may be a salient characteristic of a group's ethnic identity. Smolicz (1979) has developed the concept of *core values* to refer to those values that are regarded by the group as forming the most fundamental components of its culture; they act as identifying characteristics which are symbolic of the group and its membership. It is through them that groups can be identified as distinctive cultural entities. Rejection of core values carries with it the threat of exclusion from the group. Now cultural groups differ in the extent to which they emphasize certain core values, e.g. language, and there are variations between and within groups over time and in space in the way groups define core values (Smolicz, 1981). For example, there are in many countries of the world people with a strongly developed sense of Jewish identity who speak neither Hebrew nor Yiddish; on the other hand, in Israel today there is no doubt that Hebrew is one of the chief core values of the country and the culture (see Chapter 5.2.1).

There are groups which stress language as the main carrier of their culture and the expression of their identity, and have used it as the main defence mechanism against assimilation. An index of the strength of language as a core value for an immigrant group, for example, can be inferred from the host country's population census data (where such data include language questions); moreover, cross-national comparisons can be made to see if members of the same groups immigrating to different countries have consistent ethnolinguistic behaviour patterns over generations. A comparison between Australia and Canada, for instance, suggests that in both countries immigrant Chinese, Italians and Greeks exhibit the smallest language shift and the Dutch and Germans the largest, while Poles and Serbo-Croats occupy an intermediate position (Clyne, 1982; Blanc, 1986). In different contexts the 'same' original group may develop totally differently (Patterson, 1975).

In pluralist countries like Australia, Canada and the USA groups, or members of those groups, who do not assimilate, integrate both their culture and language, but a strong linguistic core value does not prevent them from developing a 'hyphenated' Australian, Canadian or American identity. This is because the different ethnic groups, while representing different cultures, share with minority and majority alike a set of what Smolicz (1984) calls 'overarching core values', such as acceptance of, for example, capitalism, liberal democracy, and the English language as an indispensable medium for national cross-cultural communication and economic and social success. But groups and individuals may be forced to adopt the core values of the majority and surrender their own; the loss of core values reduces the culture to mere residues, which represent only superficial manifestations of that culture. When ethnic cultures have been degraded to residues through the loss of their valued language, we have what Smolicz (1984) calls the phenomenon of 'residual multiculturalism'.

So far we have been concerned mainly with situations in which languages and cultures are frequently defined as the distinctive characteristics of separate ethnic groups in competition, conflict or open confrontation with each other. But in many parts of the Third World, especially in those countries which have recently freed themselves from colonial rule, the ethnolinguistic situation can be very different. One such situation has been called 'emergent multilingualism' by Parkin (1977); it usually involves an indigenous, pre-colonial, lingua franca and an exogenous colonial lingua franca which are both used alongside different regional and local vernaculars in ethnically mixed speech communities of recent creation. Unlike the ethnic vernaculars, however, the two lingue franche are not unambiguously regarded as the property of any one ethnic group, nor even of a distinct class or status group (examples are English and Swahili in Eastern Africa and French and Wolof in Western Africa). The multilingual situation is emergent in the sense that these ethnically and socioculturally unattached lingue franche have the potential for becoming identified with a particular ethnic or sociocultural group (e.g. English of an elite or of an ethnic group that has become dominant, and Swahili of an urban proletariat in Kenya). So, though still emergent, the use of one or the other of these lingue franche already carries with it social symbols of identity and connotations as High or Low speech varieties.

In the Kenyan case described by Parkin (1977), adolescents from the same ethnolinguistic backgrounds vehemently claim to be either 'Swahili speakers' or 'English speakers', but this distinction does not reflect their actual use of either language: rather, it reflects their perceptions of a socio-economic and educational cleavage between disadvantaged adolescents, expressed as Swahili-speaking, and privileged youths, expressed as English-speaking. This putative difference between Swahili and English usage cuts across the bonds of everyday vernacular usage, which, for each ethnic group, continues to have great practical and symbolic significance. Parkin compares and contrasts this emergent multilingualism with a more stabilized form of bilingualism where there is an unambiguous association between educational norms, standard speech style, and dominant ethnic group or class. In this kind of situation ethnic/class polarization is usually reflected in a polarization between speech styles or languages. Research to test Parkin's model of emergent multilingualism to other Third World multicultural settings still awaits execution.

To conclude on this section, it has become clear in the course of the discussion that, partly because of the variety and complexity of inter-ethnolinguistic group relations in the world, partly because of the difficulty of bridging the gap between objective macro-sociostructural phenomena and their perception by individuals at a subjective micro-social psychological level, there exists as yet no adequate theory for the study of language, ethnic identity and intergroup relations. We have, however, tried to raise some of the fundamental issues and problems, and have, we hope, suggested in our analysis some fruitful lines of inquiry. In the next section we look at the implications of multilingual situations and ethnolinguistic group relations for language planning at the national and the international level.

7.2 Language planning

Confronted with many different languages within its boundaries, how does a country solve its communication problems, given the complexities of ethnolinguistic group relations, some of which have been described in the preceding pages? There are a number of alternative solutions. First, a state can impose one official, national language, usually the dominant legitimized language, upon the population as a whole by devalorizing, ignoring or eliminating the other languages. This solution has often been adopted in the history of the world, leading to the extinction of minority and regional languages. France is a case in point. In the pursuit of national unity, the French State, using a variety of methods, succeeded, from the 1539 Ordonnance de Villers-Coterêts onwards, in imposing the Parisian dialect of the ruling elites upon the whole French population and most of its overseas colonies (Calvet, 1974; Bourhis, 1982).

Today, however, the state will use the subtler instrument of language planning, which is a particular form of economic and social planning. Indeed, language can be considered as a human resource, and society, or a group claiming to speak on its behalf, takes upon itself the task of organizing language communication in interethnic group language relations. It is therefore in the context of the economic, social and cultural conditions in which it is applied that language planning should be studied. Too many works on the subject fail to examine the assumptions upon which language planners base their practices, namely the legitimizing philosophy of the dominant group(s) in society (for a critique see G. Williams, 1986). Language planning can be a tool for domination and control by the majority; but it can also be used as a potentially revolutionary force by minorities.

Two main aspects of language planning can be distinguished, an internal and an external aspect:

(1) Internal planning, or language engineering (Wurm, 1977), or language corpus planning (Kloss, 1969) constitutes a systematic interference with the internal dynamic processes to which languages are subject. Such interference can be restrictive or creative. The former includes standardization through artificial neutralization of geographical and social variations or the 'purification' of the language from foreign influences; among the latter are the reduction to writing of an unwritten language, the standardization of its alphabet or orthography, the expansion and modernization of the lexicon through terminology and neology, etc. The reasons for this interference are implicit in the cases listed above; but the reasons are not only internal to the language, they are matters of policy decision and implementation, as the language reform in China demonstrates (de Francis, 1984).

Confronted with the problems posed by the many mutually unintelligible dialects (languages), Chinese language planners had to standardize the spoken language (Pǔtōnghàa, or common speech), taking Northern speech as the basic regional dialect, Beijing pronunciation as the phonetic standard, and modern vernacular works as the grammatical norm; the vocabulary was based on modern popular literature; characters were simplified and a new phonetic alphabet, Pīnyīn, created (but its use to date remains limited). The reasons put forward for the reform are demographic (70% of Chinese speak the Northern dialect), geographic (this dialect is spoken from Manchuria to Yunnan), communicative–linguistic (the dialects are mutually unintelligible), political (the country's diversity is an obstacle to political unity and economic development), educational (the rural masses were illiterate) and ideological (cf. the Marxist–Leninist position on the national language question). China is caught in a dilemma: if it maintains the traditional system of characters as the exclusive means of writing, most Chinese will be condemned to illiteracy and the country's modernization program will be impeded; if it makes Pīnyīn a proper phonetic alphabet to meet the needs of modern society, it risks a breakdown in communication through the written word.

(2) External language planning (Wurm, 1977), or language-status planning (Kloss, 1969), is concerned with artificially interfering with the existing status relations between the languages in contact. Now, as we saw in the preceding section, that status is a function of the relative economic, demographic, social and political power of the linguistic groups that speak those languages and of their subjective perceptions of the power relations in the wider society. Two main approaches confront each other, nationalism and nationism (Fishman, 1968). Briefly stated, in the case of nationalism language acts as a powerful symbol of ethnic identification for groups who, resisting fusion into the larger nationality, develop a national consciousness of their own. In nationism, on the other hand, a language is selected for reasons of national efficiency. The requirements of nationalism and nationism can of course be in conflict where language is concerned; but the two notions are not dichotomous, rather they stand on a continuum. The Chinese language reform is typical of nationism. The cases of Quebec and Flanders, cited earlier, exemplify a nationalist solution. But most cases fall somewhere between the two, especially in multinational states, where the solution adopted may be variable: either one or more indigenous languages are used for all circumstances; or one or more regional languages are given national status together with an international language; or an international language is used exclusively as an official language. All three solutions have their advantages and drawbacks (Le Page, 1964). A comparative study of Singapore and Malaysia is relevant in this respect.

Both Singapore and Malaysia are multicultural, multi-ethnic, multireligious and multilingual societies. It is noteworthy that while these countries have evolved along similar historical lines and are composed of the same ethnic communities – though in different proportions – they have chosen radically different approaches to language planning. Malaysia seems to have chosen the solution of nationism (or 'depluralization'): divided along political, linguistic, ethnic, religious and economic lines, it has followed a cultural assimilation path with the adoption of Malay (Bahasa Malaysia) as the sole official language of the country. In Singapore, by contrast, the traditional values of each major ethnic group have been fostered, promoting multiculturalism and pluralism; a policy of cultural integration has been pursued, with the four main languages (English, Malay, Mandarin and Tamil) having been declared official. But this policy is not strictly speaking one of nationalism: while encouraging the ethnic languages as a cultural foundation for the retention of traditional values, it has also emphasized the utilitarian nature of English as the basis for a supra-ethnic Singaporean identity. (See Ward & Hewstone, 1985, who have also made cross-cultural comparisons of the two situations in terms of ethnic identity and intergroup relations.)

It is beyond the scope of this chapter to propose a typology of language planning solutions throughout the world. (For a recent anthology on language planning see Cobarrubias & Fishman, 1983; for detailed case studies see Bourhis, 1984, for Quebec, and Wurm, 1977, on the choice of an extended pidgin as lingua franca for Papua New Guinea.) We will end this section by examining the presumed link between multilingualism and national underdevelopment. Does the fact that a country is culturally and linguistically diverse and heterogeneous cause that country to be economically disadvantaged? Are nation-states more likely to be stable than multinational states? Given the importance of language for ethnicity and nationalism, is a sense of nation more difficult to develop for a multilingual state than for a unilingual one? Choosing (1) gross domestic product (GDP) per capita as a measure of economic development and (2) the size of the largest native speech community relative to the total population as a measure of linguistic diversity, Pool (1969) calculated these two values and the correlations between them for 133 countries. He concluded that a country can have any degree of linguistic uniformity or fragmentation and still be underdeveloped; and a wholly unilingual country can be anywhere from very rich to very poor. But a country that is linguistically highly heterogeneous is always under- or semi-developed, whereas a country that is highly developed always has considerable language uniformity.

Both Pool's evidence and his methodology have been challenged. First, are the measures valid and reliable? The operationalization of the concepts is problematic and the data on which the correlations are based are at best unreliable. In any case, correlation does not mean causality: in order to demonstrate causality it would be necessary to use longitudinal data to show that reduction in diversity resulted in increased development and vice versa. Lieberson & Hansen (1974) correlated the Greenberg–Lieberson measure of linguistic diversity (see Chapter 1.2.3.1) with three measures of development (GNP per capita, urbanization, literacy) between 1930 and 1960 and found only a small tendency for low-language-diversity (i.e. unilingual) nations to have a high per capita GNP; diversity was not related to either lack of urbanization or illiteracy; and increasing the time difference to 100 years also failed to produce any connection between development and diversity. A crucial factor seems to be the fact that less developed nations are former colonies whose language diversity was artificially produced by the imperial powers who carved up countries (e.g. Africa) without the slightest concern for ethnic and linguistic boundaries.

In reviewing language-planning policies we saw that languages that were adopted as national languages often had what Kuo (1979) calls high communicativity (e.g. China's Putonghua or Malaysia's Bahasa Malaysia; other examples are Tanzania's Swahili and Indonesia's Bahasa Indonesia). Moreover, today some of the most dynamic cities in the world are among the most ethnically and linguistically heterogeneous: Hong Kong, New York, Singapore, Sydney and Toronto, to name but a few. But we must let Weinreich (1953) have the final word: he rightly points out that the higher the linguistic diversity of a country the higher the degree of bilingualism; where there are many people who speak different languages people will learn each other's languages. In other words, bilingualism compensates for diversity.

7.3 Sociolinguistic variations in language contact situations

In a situation of language contact the status of each language varies on the one hand as a function of the nature of intergroup relations, in particular power relations and the values and norms attached to these, and on the other hand as a function of the perceptions that speakers form of these relations, their values and norms. It follows that language attitudes and uses vary in social, geographical and historical space as a function of these relations and perceptions. When relations change, status relationships, and therefore perceptions, attitudes and uses, change. It is worth stressing that it is not so much the languages that vary as their speakers, who select from a variety of possible models which are socially marked; as Le Page points out, change only takes place when the social values of the models change and the behaviour of the speech community also changes (Le Page & Tabouret-Keller, 1985). It is to such sociolinguistic variations that we turn in this section.

7.3.1 Speech repertoires in bilingual communities

In a multilingual speech community a whole range of languages, or repertoire, is available to speakers, who use some of them in their linguistic interaction to perform particular social roles. The term 'repertoire' is also used to refer to the range of dialects, registers and styles typical of a unilingual community of speakers where the choice of one variety over another can have the same social significance as code selection in a multilingual community (Gumperz, 1968). Repertoire applies at two different levels to both the community and the individual. A speaker does not usually control the whole range of the codes that constitute a community's repertoire continuum but only a number of these. Now does the idea of a continuum exist in the minds of the speakers, or is it a mere artefact of the sociolinguist? Willemyns (1987) shows convincingly that, while being aware of which code to use when, speakers do not actually experience a continuum but consider their own utterances to be, for example, either dialect or standard language, never something in between. This leaves no room for an intermediate variant.

An illustration of a complex multilingual speech repertoire at both the community and the individual level is given by Platt (1977), who describes English-educated Chinese communities in Singapore and Malaysia. The verbal repertoires of both communities consist of various Chinese languages, of which one is regionally dominant; formal and colloquial varieties of English; and standard and 'bazaar' varieties of Malay. For a typical English-educated Chinese in Malaysia, a common speech repertoire might include: his mother tongue, one of the Chinese languages; some formal Malaysian English; some colloquial Malaysian English; some Bahasa Malaysia (see above 7.2); and Bazaar Malay, a low-prestige lingua franca (each language or variety being arranged in a 'linear polyglossic distribution', see below 7.3.2). An example of how a multilingual speaker might use the different codes in his repertoire is given by Pandit (1979), who describes an Indian businessman living in a suburb of Bombay. His mother tongue and home language is Kathiawari, a dialect of Gujarati (his daily newspaper is printed in the standard Gujarati variety); in the market he uses a familiar variety of Marathi, the state language; at the railway station, where he catches his train for Bombay, he speaks the pan-Indian lingua franca, Hindustani; the language of work is Kachchi, the code of the spice trade; in the evening he will watch a film in Hindi or in English and listen to a cricket-match commentary on the radio in English. Kachru (1982) has put forward a typology of speech repertoires to which the reader is referred. What role(s) does each of these different languages and varieties perform in the community and the individual?

7.3.2 Bilingualism and diglossia

The various codes in a multilingual speech community, as in a bilingual individual, are neither used nor valued in similar ways; if they were, all but one would become redundant. They usually fulfil complementary functions in the twofold sense that they are used differentially according to interlocutor, domain, topic and role, and that the choice of one rather than the other involves an 'act of identity' (Le Page & Tabouret-Keller, 1985) on the part of the speaker. When different varieties or languages co-occur throughout a speech community, each with a distinct range of social functions in complementary distribution, we have a situation of diglossia.

The concept of diglossia was originally developed by Ferguson (1959)[2] to describe two functional varieties within one language, one of which, called the High (H) variety, is reserved for formal functions and is formally learned, the other, the Low (L) variety, is used in informal situations (e.g. Greek katharévusa and dhimotiki, Classical and Colloquial Arabic, Standard German and Swiss German, Standard French and Haitian French). H is the language of status, L the speech of solidarity. The notion of diglossia was extended by Gumperz (1971) to multilingual situations, and by Fishman (1967), who distinguished between diglossia and bilingualism, the former referring to the social functional distribution, the latter to an individual's ability to use more than one code (bilinguality in our sense). Whatever the applications of the concept, the defining criterion is that of functional distribution, whether the language forms are separate languages, subsystems of the same language, or stylistic varieties. (For a full discussion of the issues see Fasold, 1984, Chapter 2.)

Examples of multilingual diglossia range from simple binary contexts, e.g. Guaraní (L) and Spanish (H) in Paraguay (Rubin, 1968), to double-overlapping diglossia, e.g. African vernacular (L), Swahili (H and L), English (H) in Tanzania (Abdulaziz Mkilifi, 1978) or double-nested diglossia, with L and H having both a Low and a High, e.g. Khalapur in Northern India (Gumperz, 1964b), to the linear polyglossic situation in Singapore and Malaysia quoted above (Platt, 1977). A full discussion of these types of diglossia will be found in Fasold (1984). An equally complex situation is that of Brussels (de Vriendt & Willemyns, 1987), where six groups of speakers are distinguished: monolinguals in Dutch or French, and bilinguals in the two languages but with varying degrees of dominance, each with a High and a Low variety; if one adds to these the increasing number of foreign immigrants, some of whom are bi- or trilingual, the language configuration of the city is complex indeed. Instead of the High–Low dichotomy of diglossia with bilingualism, a triglossic situation is proposed, with an L (dialect), an H (regional standard) and a 'supreme language' or super-superposed variety which has a higher status than H (T'Sou, 1980); in the multilingual situation of Brussels, the supreme languages are the Standard French of France and the Standard Dutch of the Netherlands, over and above the regional high languages, Standard Belgian French and Standard Belgian Dutch (Baetens Beardsmore, 1982). The 'supreme language' concept is not unlike Platt's (1977) notion of 'Dummy High', which refers to a speech variety of which some members of the community have a certain knowledge, and which is given prestige by the speakers, but which is not in fact much used.

Perhaps one of the most complex polyglossic situations is that of Northern India (Khubchandani, 1979). At the local level dialects vary considerably from village to village to the extent of becoming mutually incomprehensible; when a villager visits the bazaar of a neighbouring town he must speak a less localized variety in order to be understood. This is how local trade languages developed and became regional dialects and the mother tongues of town dwellers. Above regional dialects are the state languages recognized as official by the Indian Constitution. Each state language in turn comprises a colloquial and a literary standard form, the latter being mastered only by literate people, who also speak the vernacular. Over and above these are the two 'supreme languages', Hindi and English, both official national languages; Hindi is also a regional language covering several states and diversified into a number of dialects, of which Khari Boli, the New Delhi standard, is the basis for the official language. In Northern India the Hindi–Urdu–Punjabi linguistic–geographic area, comprising 46% of the total Indian population, is a vast polyglossic continuum where languages and dialects complement, merge or compete with each other according to functions, domains and group affiliations.

Stable diglossia (called 'broad' by Fasold, 1984) evolves and changes. It is said to 'leak' when one variety takes over the functions formerly reserved for the other and this is a sign of the incipient breakdown of the diglossic relationship, reflecting changes in the power relations between the groups. The outcome will be either a new variety which is a mixture of the former High and Low varieties (especially when the two languages are structurally similar) or the replacement of one language by another (especially if they are structurally dissimilar). An example of the latter is the receding of the Low German variety spoken in the deprived German-speaking area of Belgium before the relatively High French variety (Verdoodt, 1972). The shift from German to French is preceded by widespread bilingualism in which either language may be used almost indiscriminately (see Chapter 6.2.3 on this type of code-switching as a sign of language shift). Along the way to complete shift the language of the subordinate group comes under the influence of the dominant language and undergoes important changes, some of which were considered in Chapter 6.2 at the interpersonal-interaction level. In turn, the dominant language will be affected by the other.

7.3.3 Language shift

In stable diglossia a multilingual community maintains its different languages by reserving each of them for certain domains, roles and functions with little encroachment of one language upon the domains, roles and functions of another. This maintenance is dependent upon relatively stable relations between the groups of the community. When these relations change, however, and one group begins to assimilate to another, language maintenance starts to break down. Members of that group begin to use the language of another group for domains, roles and functions hitherto reserved for the first language.

Its own language is affected by the dominant group's language. When the group gives up its mother tongue the process of language shift is complete. A similar phenomenon occurs when an indigenous monolingual minority group is absorbed into the dominant majority or an exogenous ethnic group moves to a new society where the dominant language is different from its own and is assimilated. When the group's language ceases to be spoken by its members we have a case of 'language death', even though the language may continue to be spoken somewhere else and the ethnic identity of the group survives because the language is not one of its core values.

The various forms of intergroup relations and dependency analysed in 7.1.1 mean that when the subordinate groups' internal cohesion if affected, the dominant language spreads and gradually invades the domains, functions, and forms of the subordinate language, or rather speakers of the latter gradually adopt the forms of the dominant language in more and more roles, functions and domains. When the family domain is invaded language shift is almost complete. As groups are not homogeneous, this spread and shift takes place to varying degrees, in different ways and at different rates of development. Taking the group as a whole, with its different generations and social categories, we can represent the process on a continuum ranging from unilingualism in the minority language at the one end to unilingualism in the majority language at the other. In between we have different levels of bilinguality and bilingualism, from dominant in L_1 to dominant in L_2, with a stage of relative balance between the languages half way along.[3] This multidimensional process may be schematized on the unidimensional model in Figure 7.1.

Language shift typically takes place over three generations, the first being monolingual or dominant in L_1, the second differentially bilingual, and the third dominant or monolingual in L_2. The variable of ethnicity may of course intervene and slow down or prevent the shift to total assimilation (see 7.1). According to Reitz (1974), who studied the rate of language shift amongst three generations of immigrants to Canada, the most important factors impeding the progress of shift are, in descending order of importance, maintenance of close ties with the ethnic group, identification with the ingroup, endogamy, and religious affiliation. In other words, keeping close links with the ethnic social network is the most important factor of language maintenance in Canada. For Fishman (1964) three main classes of factors account for language shift: (1) changes in the way of life of a group that weaken the strength of its social networks; (2) changes in the power relationships between

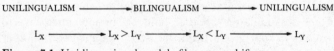

UNILINGUALISM ⟶ BILINGUALISM ⟶ UNILINGUALISM

L_X ⟶ $L_X > L_Y$ ⟶ $L_X < L_Y$ ⟶ L_Y

Figure 7.1 Unidimensional model of language shift

the groups; (3) stigmatized attitudes towards the minority group values and language, shared by minority and majority alike; or various combinations of all three.

Criticizing Fishman's (1964) model as ambiguous and static, MacKinnon (1984) has put forward a three-dimensional model capable of accommodating the dynamics of societal language shift. In this model the three independent dimensions of power, social variation and linguistic variation can produce eight possible configurations. The first two dimensions define four types of speech communities, with two subdivisions in each type: (1) truly diglossic societies subdivided into 'internal colonies' of the Celtic type (Hechter, 1975) and the 'incorporated satellites' of the 'Swiss German' type; (2) schizoglossic societies in which distinctive language variants are conserved by different social groups in terms of different languages in the multi-ethnic colonial case (Singapore), and in terms of different social dialects in developed industrial class societies; (3) a-glossic smaller-scale folk-societies with little internal language variation and mobilizing ethnic groups and developing nationalities, with geographical rather than social dialect variation; and (4) monoglossic societies comprising national or colonial elites on the one hand, and the highly homogenized cores of developed or post-industrial societies. Such a model requires further elaboration and empirical verification before its validity can be proven.

From a macro-sociological perspective Tabouret-Keller (1968, 1972) has attempted to explain language-shift-pattern phenomena from bilingualism to monolingualism in Western and Third World countries by reference to socio-economic, demographic and geographical infrastructures. Using methods of correlational statistics she defined the factors that determined shift in Western European and West African countries, in both rural and urban contexts, and compared nineteenth-century Europe with contemporary Africa. *Mutatis mutandis*, she found that shift or maintenance can be attributed to the same fundamental economic, technological and social factors, and in particular to urbanization and schooling. Comparing the evolution of dialects and minority languages within France itself she found a correlation between industrialization/urbanization and language shift: social mobility, migration into cities, development of communications and media are factors that accelerate assimilation to the standard. Alsace, where the German dialect survives (Tabouret-Keller & Luckel, 1981), seems to be an exception to the rule because of the following factors: economic (modern intensive farming), historical (recent integration of the province), and social geographical (vicinity of Germany with movements of population across the border). No such favourable factors were found in Southern France, where the dialects and languages have been losing ground before the invasion of Standard French.

Sociostructural approaches, however useful for defining macro-factors of change, fail to account for the influence of intervening variables such as the importance of social networks, individual perceptions of the relative ethno-linguistic vitality of groups in contact, and the communication interactions of participants. These are better apprehended with speech-ethnographic methods. Using participant-observation techniques to study language choice and shift in a rural Hungarian–German speech community on the border between Austria and Hungary (Oberwart in German, Felsöör in Hungarian), Gal (1979) found that from an original unilingual Hungarian situation Oberwart had shifted to a German-dominant bilingual community. The local Hungarian dialect is associated with rural values, Austrian German with urban ones; while most peasant children are still growing up bilingual and their religion is identified with the Hungarian language, exogamous marriages, urban employment and education favour German, which has the higher status. At the same time the Hungarian dialect is being devalued by comparison with the standard spoken in Hungary, which is, however, not acceptable because of its different ethnic affiliation. Code-switching occurs in asymmetrical communication interaction varying according to differences in age, ethnic identity, and social status and role between interlocutors. Gal predicts that the whole community will be more or less assimilated to an Austrian–German culture within a few generations.

Another case of language-shift continuum is that documented by Dorian (1981) in the Gaelic-speaking fishing community of East Sutherland in the Highlands of Scotland. The shift here is from unilingual Gaelic to unilingual Scottish English (which has higher status), but of greater interest is the lag between this community and the other communities in the area: when the former was unilingual Gaelic-speaking the latter were already Gaelic–English bilingual; when it became bilingual the other communities had assimilated to English. In this way the shift itself can be a marker of ethnolinguistic distinct-iveness. The continuum ranges from fully fluent speakers (subdivided into old and young) to imperfect 'semi-speakers' dominant in English but still making some use of Gaelic though with an aberrant phonology and grammar; another significant subgroup in the community are the 'passive bilinguals' who do not speak Gaelic but understand it sufficiently to be accepted as members of the community: acceptance of group values and knowledge of social norms are more important than active mastery of the language and are sufficient con-ditions of group membership.

The area of 'language death', at both macro- and micro-levels, is still under-researched. Yet this subject affects the state of bilingualism in the world, that is, the fate of ethnolinguistic groups, and research is needed to determine the circumstances under which particular languages come under threat or dis-appear. Do languages suddenly cease to have speakers, and if so, under what circumstances? If the process is gradual, what linguistic changes occur during the last stages of the 'life' of a language? What are the identifying features of a dying language? Under what conditions should collective corrective measures be taken? What are these measures? (For a discussion of these issues see Pan & Gleason, 1986.)

Bilingual diglossia is a relatively stable phenomenon in which a speech community maintains its different languages functionally separate; when diglossia breaks down speakers of subordinate languages shift to the dominant language and ultimately give up their mother tongue. A language can actually die. There is, however, another situation of languages in contact in which a new language is born out of the contact: this happens in the case of pidginization.

7.3.4 Pidginization, creolization and decreolization[4]

Of the three processes of pidginization, creolization and decreolization only the first and the last arise out of language-contact phenomena, whereas creoles are the outcome of a language shift; in this section we will therefore focus on pidginization and decreolization in general and on the relations between the groups that engage in these processes. Linguistic descriptions of pidgins and post-creole continua, which have been studied extensively, will receive only scanty treatment here.

7.3.4.1 Pidginization

Basically, most theories of pidginization assume that pidgins develop through the need for restricted communication between groups which do not share a common language; the starting-point is therefore a situation of plurilingualism without bilinguality. Typically, a pidgin evolves out of low-status 'substrate' languages (L_1s, e.g. the African languages of slaves), which are the principal source of semantic structures, in contact with a high-status 'superstrate' or 'base' language (L_2s, e.g. English or French, which provide the lexical source), linguistic universals being the main source of syntactic development (Mühlhäusler, 1986). Pidgins result from an incomplete learning of the superstrate L_2 owing to a quantitatively and qualitatively restricted input. Pidgins are much simpler than the languages to which they are related in that they are more systematic, having got rid of morphological and syntactic irregularities, but without sacrificing the ability to communicate the needs of their speakers effectively. They have a less extensive vocabulary than either L_1 or L_2, but they make use of polysemy, metaphors, and the extralinguistic context of situation. It must be borne in mind that speakers of a pidgin already have a L_1 and acquire the pidgin as an auxiliary code which does not need to serve all the domains, roles and functions of the L_1. Within those limits, however, pidgins are adequate for the domains, roles and functions for which they have been developed, and if necessary they can be expanded to take on further functions.

Pidgins have sometimes evolved from trade languages, that is, they are codes used only for limited exchange, like trade or administration. A possible

example of a pidgin that developed in this way is Neo-Melanesian Pidgin or
Tok Pisin, an English-based pidgin used in Papua New Guinea, which evolved
this century as a lingua franca between English administrators and the indigenous people, who speak a large number of mutually unintelligible
languages, and between these people themselves. So effective did this pidgin
become that it has been adopted as the standard language of Papua New
Guinea (Todd, 1984). Another origin of pidgins is when people from different
language backgrounds are thrown together and have to communicate with
one another and with members of a dominant group in order to survive. This
is the situation in which Africans taken as slaves to the plantations of the New
World, and separated from each other to prevent intragroup communication
and possible rebellion, found themselves. The only way they could communicate with each other and with their slavers was through a pidgin which they
learned from the latter, and which remained their only means of intergroup
communication. Yet, at the same time, the pidgin was also a way for the
dominant group to maintain distance and non-solidarity with the slaves.
When pidgins came to be used in an increasingly wide range of situations for a
larger number of functions and acquired native speakers, they became creoles.
A creole is thus the outcome of a pidgin that extends its functions, stabilizes
and is nativized.

7.3.4.2 Decreolization

If creoles are allowed to develop in isolation from the superstrate languages,
then they become distinct languages. But the majority of them have coexisted
with their base languages and this coexistence has brought about a post-creole
continuum, often described as decreolization, the process by which the creole
is modified at all linguistic levels in the direction of the standard variety of the
superstrate. This modification varies as a function of speakers' attempts to
identify with the speakers of the high-status base language. According to Bickerton (1975), the post-creole continuum links a series of 'lects' or varieties,
each arising from a minimal restructuring of the preceding one, ranging from
the most archaic and socially low lect (or basilect) to the least creolized and
closest to the regional standard (or acrolect). But since speakers are differentially affected by decreolization and, according to Bickerton, can even understand and speak different lects, it is not the language that is changing but
speakers who use different varieties in different situations as so many acts of
identity (Le Page & Tabouret-Keller, 1985); and one question is whether the
continuum has psychological reality (Willemyns, 1987).

We may have given the impression that the threefold process of pidginization, creolization and decreolization is unidirectional and inevitable. This is
not so. We are dealing here with dynamic and changing systems of communication which develop from languages in contact; but creolization will not

follow pidginization if the speech community has no need for it; and decreolization will not occur if the creole remains outside the influence of the base language. Some creoles have disappeared, like Negerhollands in the Virgin Islands; others have developed independently from the superstrate, like the creoles of Surinam, St Lucia or Curaçao; in a diglossic situation, like that of Haiti, the creole not only survives but invades domains and functions hitherto reserved for the High language, French. There is some evidence that the Creole English of slaves who were released from slavery and returned to West Africa was repidginized by the peoples among whom the ex-slaves settled, and became the Pidgin English of countries like Cameroon (Todd, 1984). We saw in 7.1.1 how West Indian adolescents in Britain actually recreolize their speech as a symbol of their redefined identity.

Thus, speakers of mutually unintelligible languages in unequal and asymmetrical intergroup relations, like slaves in relation to their slavers, develop a new language for limited communication purposes; when this limited language extends its domains of use and its range of communicative and other functions, it becomes more complex and expands linguistically, begins to stabilize and, if it is learned as a mother tongue, evolves into a creole. Decreolization occurs in a multilingual situation in contact with the base language and changes in its direction because of social and economic pressures to use the standard. Pidgins and creoles are therefore real languages, suited to the uses for which they are developed. Furthermore, their study enables us to witness and try to understand how languages evolve; their variety and speed of transformation give us insights into language and language behaviour. In the last section of this chapter we bring together some of the language-contact phenomena examined in this and the preceding chapter and look at the implications of these phenomena for language behaviour and linguistic theory.

7.4 Implications for language behaviour and linguistic theory

The study of languages in contact has confirmed us in the view that variation and change in language and language behaviour at the group as well as the individual and the interpersonal level are the norm. This is because language, in addition to being a tool for communication and a cognitive organizer (see Chapter 3.1), is also a symbol and an instrument of individual and group identity and norms and of intergroup power relations. And as these relations, identities and norms change, so do language and language behaviour. But variation and change are not uniform; individuals and groups behave differently and change at different rates on differential dimensions. As a result, language contact will have differential and at times opposite consequences for language and language behaviour. These opposites, however, are not dichotomies but continua, or rather they are the results of dynamic tensions. We will look at examples, some of which have been discussed in this and earlier chapters (e.g. 6.2), and re-examine them in terms of variation and change.

When individuals and groups come into contact their languages come into contact. They may either converge or diverge, or converge and diverge at one and the same time. This is because the degree of variation in intralingual and interlingual uses depends on the relative strength of two tendencies in society: the tendency to reduce intergroup and interpersonal differences (convergence) and the tendency to accentuate these differences (divergence). The former, convergence, which Le Page (1978) calls 'focussing', is found where speakers are in close and constant contact and there is consensus on the norms of language behaviour; it characterizes small communities with dense and multiplex social networks, or else societies where a written standard language is imposed as the legitimate norm on a nation or a linguistic 'commonwealth' (e.g. International French on 'le monde de la francophonie' or Koranic Arabic on the Islamic world). The latter, divergence, which Le Page calls 'diffusion', prevails in situations where there are no imposed or self-imposed norms, where social network links are loose and multiplex, leading to wide variations in usage. Language creativity is then at its highest, as in pidginization. In one case we have stability, in the other variability. Sometimes both tendencies are at work. A few examples will make our point clear.

The 3,000 inhabitants of Kupwar, a small border village in South India, between them speak four languages: Marathi, Urdu (both Indo-European), Kannada and Telugu (both Dravidian). The village is divided into clearly distinct groups or castes, each identified by its language. As they need to communicate, they, especially the men, learn each other's languages. These languages have coexisted for centuries and they have converged, at least as far as the syntax is concerned, and have become much more similar than they are elsewhere (the convergence is essentially towards Marathi, the state language). However, they are still totally distinct in their vocabulary, which serves as a powerful symbol of each group's ethnic identity and distinctiveness (Gumperz & Wilson, 1971).

To explain the Kupwar case Hudson (1980) has put forward a tentative hypothesis regarding the relations of the different linguistic levels to intergroup interactions. Syntax is the marker of cohesion; in contrast, vocabulary is a marker of caste and religion; pronunciation reflects the permanent group with which the speaker identifies. 'This results in a tendency for individuals to suppress alternatives, but in contrast to the tendency with syntax, different groups suppress different alternatives in order to distinguish themselves from each other, and some individuals keep some alternatives "alive" in order to be able to identify their origins even more precisely, by using them in a particular and distinctive proportion relative to other alternatives' (p. 48). This explanation is completely in line with Le Page (1968) on the one hand and with Tajfel's theory of social-psychological distinctiveness on the other (Chapter 5.2.2).

Or take another example, that of emergent multilingualism in Nairobi, documented in Parkin (1977) and discussed in 7.1.3. At a time of great social change and in the space of two generations, children from four different ethnic and language backgrounds, who mix in the streets (where they communicate in Swahili) will, as adolescents, divide into two ethnolinguistic camps, each one identifying with one or the other ritual lingua franca: the indigenous Swahili or the exogenous English, each symbolizing their different relations to the social structure; later, as adults, they return to their original ethnic and language background through endogamy and universally use Swahili, while a large minority of men and a small minority of women are also capable of speaking English. We have here successively acts of convergence and divergence subtly expressed by allegiance to groups and languages. This situation contrasts sharply with that of stabilized diglossic bilingualism where there is polarization of ethnic groups and languages.

If we now take the examples of code-switching and code-mixing discussed in Chapter 6.2 we find very different types of situation. On the one hand, we have those cases where code-switching appears to be random (though the free morpheme constraint seems to hold for all types of code-switching) which may signal that processes of shift are at work in a language or in the relationship between two languages; the situation is a diffuse one, interactants not seemingly engaging in acts of identity, and presumably this type of code-switching will not be transmitted, as circumstances are changing all the time. On the other hand, we have a rule-governed type of code-switching, with constraint rules that do not suggest any convergence of the codes, used as a variety for communicating between members of a close community and symbolizing their membership; not all members, however, have the same communicative competence in the type which is acquired through a process of syntactic maturation. In this case we have focussed behaviour converging on a code-switching norm, though it would appear that it is already diversifying through the differential competence of its speakers.

We will borrow our final example from a hybrid vernacular which is not unlike a pidgin. In Moncton, New Brunswick, two speech communities, a dominant English-speaking and a subordinate but ethnically mobilized French-speaking group, interact. The language of the minority used to be a rural dialect of France transplanted to New France (Acadian), but at the turn of this century many of its speakers had migrated to the towns in search of employment with the Canadian Pacific Railway. Exposed to the overwhelming influence of English some assimilated, others hung on to their dialects. But adolescents, caught between the dialect as a sign of the past, an alien French standard norm imposed by the school system, and the English of the dominant majority, have evolved an original vernacular, called Chiac, which is characterized by code-mixing and code-switching between French and English. It seems to us that Chiac is the symbol and instrument of a group's allegiance:

these adolescents could identify neither with the language of the older generations (because it represented a depressed past) nor with the language of the
dominant group without losing their own sense of identity. The hybrid
vernacular is a way of resolving their conflict. Basically French in its structure,
Chiac expresses their roots in a community which is fighting for survival;
mixed and switched with English, it looks to the other community and the
modern world of employment, the media and the North American culture
(Blanc & Hamers, 1982).

Thus, variation and change are the essence of language because the latter is
at once the expression, symbol and instrument of a group's ethnic identity and
of its dynamic relations to other groups in a society. As group boundaries are
not static but change so identity changes and language with it. And so do
speakers' relations to language. Languages are not homogeneous entities; the
same language, depending on whether its speakers are converging on a stable
norm or diverging and causing the language to diffuse, will change little or
fragment into different varieties. But different levels of language will change
differentially to express varying group identities. From the semantics of one
language, the lexis of another and the universal rules of language acquisition, a
pidgin will evolve to allow its speakers to communicate and express definite relationships between two groups who could not communicate otherwise. A
switched code can both borrow and assimilate nouns from one language and
be used in alternation with it intrasententially, and yet the two languages do
not appear to converge. Language varies along multidimensional continua
and its speakers will identify with some of the varieties and their verbal repertoire will be an expression of these identities. But where does all this leave
language? Where is the ideal speaker–hearer in a homogeneous speech community? Where is the variable rule which deals with community grammars
and alternative ways of saying the same thing? How can one identify, describe
and compare every lect on a creole continuum? One tends to forget that when
one says 'language' one means its user(s). Only a social and psychological
linguistics of the future may be able to tackle these questions. All we can hope
to achieve now is to ask some of the right ones.

7.5 Conclusion

This chapter has dealt with languages in contact at the level of intergroup
relations. In a first part we looked at language as a symbol of a group's identity; we saw that language is not only a reflection of intergroup and intragroup
relations, it can also be a powerful factor in the definition, creation, maintenance and transformation of these relations; to the social *symbolic function* of
language should be added a social *instrumental function*. Next we examined the
construct of *ethnolinguistic vitality* as one attempt to explain the role of sociostructural factors in interethnic group relations and the perception of these fac-

tors by individuals in the maintenance or loss of the language(s) of a group. We concluded that the relationship between language and ethnicity is not a simple one: not only is it not a necessary relation, but language and ethnicity do not stand in a one-to-one correspondence. For language to be a salient characteristic of group identity it must be perceived by members of a group as a *core value* of their culture. We went on to stress the fact that a group is no more homogeneous in its perception of the role and value of its language(s) than it is in its language behaviour. We surveyed a number of multicultural and multi-lingual situations in which the relations of ethnolinguistic groups to the different languages in contact are highly complex and vary in geographical and social space as well as over time. In the second part of the chapter we analysed ethnolinguistic group relations at the national level and discussed some of the social, political, linguistic and educational problems raised by *language planning*.

In a third part three sociolinguistic phenomena relating to languages in contact at the intergroup level were examined. These are: (i) *diglossia*, a rela-tively stable situation in which two different languages co-occur throughout the speech community, each with a distinct range of social functions; (ii) *language shift*, a situation in which over a period of time a social group gives up the use of its first language and replaces it by another spoken in the society; and (iii) *pidginization*, or the development of a new code resulting from the need of different groups speaking mutually unintelligible languages to communi-cate with one another over a limited range of social functions; we followed the evolution of pidgins through the processes of creolization and decreolization.

In a final section we briefly discussed the implications of language-contact phenomena for linguistic and sociolinguistic theory. In particular, we argued that the study of speech repertoires, code-switching, pidginization and de-creolization calls into question certain current views on the nature of language and verbal communication.

One of the main concerns of this chapter has been the necessity of bringing together objective group factors and their subjective perceptions and interpre-tations by group members and of bridging the conceptual gap between macro-social phenomena and micro-psychological processes. We are conscious that the gap is as wide as ever. To end with, we would like to draw attention to a tentative project planned by the authors in cooperation with a team of researchers from a wide range of disciplines to study the factors which in-fluence variation in language behaviour when two languages are in contact. In this project variation in language behaviour is viewed as the resultant force of complex mechanisms involving collective aspects linked to levels of social structure and to the power relations within that structure as well as the indi-vidual characteristics of the speakers, such as their linguistic and communica-tive competence, their attitudes towards the speech communities and their languages, their perceptions of the relationships between the groups and languages in contact, and their motivation to learn and use the other languages. The individual and the societal meet in communication interactions, and it is through his social network that the individual learns the social rules of language and develops his own rules of individual and interpersonal language behaviour. We can only refer the reader to Prujiner, Deshaies, Hamers, Blanc, Clément & Landry (1984); for a summary of the project see Hamers & Blanc (1983).

8

Bilingual education

This chapter and the next two address the question of the application of theories of bilinguality and bilingualism in three different domains: (1) bilingual education (Chapter 8); (2) second-language acquisition (Chapter 9); and (3) interpretation and translation (Chapter 10). In the present chapter we first review a number of definitions and discuss some typologies of bilingual education; then we analyse two types of bilingual education; one developed for children of the dominant group in society, the other for ethnolinguistic minorities, and discuss their outcome in the light of our knowledge about bilingual development.

In Chapters 2 and 3 we hypothesized that simultaneous bilinguality as well as consecutive early bilinguality, in which the two languages were highly valorized and used for all functions with the child, both lead to an additive form, whereas consecutive childhood bilinguality, in which the mother tongue is devalorized and language is not used in all its functions, may lead to a subtractive form. We insisted on the importance for the child of developing the appropriate social representations of language, especially when he is introduced to formal schooling and literacy through a highly valorized L_2 (see Chapter 3.3.1).

8.1 Literacy and language planning in education

Education, defined as an 'organized and sustained communication designed to bring about learning' (UNESCO, 1976), aims at developing the organization of knowledge and skilled abilities. In modern societies these goals are attained through the development of literacy skills in a school environment. In an educational perspective literacy can be viewed as a communication skill which involves a written mode of verbal transmission (reading and writing) employed by literate societies for effective functioning in a changing socio-ecological setting (Srivastava, 1984a). The importance attached to the development of literacy is based on a world-wide conviction that literacy is an instrument for changing the individual's perception and organization of cognition, which leads to economic improvement, and is a prerequisite for all functional education. The choice of the medium through which literacy is achieved is an important issue in a multicultural setting.

Two opposite claims are made by planners concerning the achievement of literacy: (1) literacy is most effectively achieved in the mother tongue; (2) it is most effectively achieved in a language of wider communication which possesses a written culture and economic power. The first claim is based on pedagogical concerns, whereas the second claim relies more on economic preoccupations. These two claims result in two different planning choices with regard to the language of education. The first claim, in its extreme form, leads to a curriculum exclusively in the mother tongue; this is the case in many developed countries, for majority groups whose mother tongue is also a language of wider communication with an extended written tradition (e.g. the anglophones in the United States and the French in France who can follow the entire curriculum from nursery school to university degrees in one language).

The second claim, in its most extreme form, leads to a monolingual curriculum in an official language which is not the child's mother tongue, as, for example, in some of the former French colonies in Africa where the one and only language of instruction is the exogenous language left by the colonizers (e.g. Bénin and Togo, where education starts in French from nursery school onwards). Education exclusively through a L_2 often occurs for minority groups, all over the world, because either language planning is such that it does not recognize the right to be educated in a non-official language (e.g. France, Belgium, Zaïre); or the community size is too small to justify mother-tongue education (e.g. the case of many minorities in African and Asian countries, where a limited number of the numerically important national languages are used in education, e.g. Mali, India); or the cost of writing down a non-written language, creating teaching materials and teacher training in the mother tongue is too high.

Between these two extreme cases we find a variety of solutions which combine mother tongue and second languages to various extents in the curriculum. Most of these programs are based on the 'linguistic mismatch hypothesis', endorsed by UNESCO (1953), according to which a mismatch between home language and school language is the major cause of poor academic achievement of minority children. Srivastava (1984a), for example, advocates a literacy model for minority children in India, in which literacy is first introduced in the child's mother tongue; once the basic literacy skills are attained, the curriculum transfers to a formal language of education. Many varieties of these Vernacular-cum-Transfer literacy models are to be found all over the world (e.g. the numerous African countries where part or whole of elementary school is taught through the child's mother tongue and then education is continued through the exogenous official language, English or

French). However, this switch is often not planned through a bilingual education program and children are not prepared for it.

8.2 *Definition and typologies of bilingual education*

In the literature on 'bilingual education' the term is used to describe a variety of educational programs involving two or more languages to varying degrees. In this chapter we limit our definition to describe *any system of school education in which, at a given moment in time and for a varying amount of time, simultaneously or consecutively, instruction is planned and given in at least two languages!* [1]

This definition insists on the use of the two languages as media of instruction; it does not include curricula in which a second or foreign language is taught as a subject, with no other use in academic activities, although L_2 teaching may be part of a bilingual education program. We also exclude from our definition the cases in which a switch in the medium of instruction occurs at a given moment with no further planning of the two languages in the curriculum, as it happens for instance in Burundi, and, of course, the numerous examples of 'submersion' in which an individual child attends a program taught in the mother tongue of a different ethnolinguistic group and where the curriculum ignores this child's mother tongue: this is usually the case with immigrant children in mainstream education. However, we will refer to some of these cases in so far as they tell us something about bilingual development in education.

Considering our definition, most programs of bilingual education fit into one of three categories:

(1) Instruction is given in both languages simultaneously;
(2) Instruction is given first in L_1 and the pupil is taught until such time when he is able to use L_2 as a means of learning;
(3) The largest part of instruction is given through L_2, and L_1 is introduced at a later stage, first as a subject and later as a medium of instruction.

This is a far cry from Mackey's (1970, 1976) typology in which he distinguishes 90 different types of bilingual education. He proposes a typology based on language use and distributed in space and time in four domains: home, school, environment and nation. However detailed this typology may be, it lacks a theoretical base and fails to distinguish wider categories of bilingual education. More satisfactory is the taxonomy developed by Fishman & Lovas (1970) in a sociolinguistic perspective. This taxonomy comprises three large categories defined by three sets of variables: *intensity*, *goal* and *status*. Within the first category (intensity) four types of bilingual programs are identified:

(1) *transitional bilingualism*, in which L_1 is only used to facilitate the transition to an unmarked language (an assimilationist perspective);

(2) *mono-literate bilingualism*, in which the school uses two languages in all its activities, but only one (L_2) to initiate the child into literacy skills;
(3) *partial bi-literate bilingualism*, in which both languages are used orally and for writing, but academic subjects are divided in such a way that L_1 is used for so-called 'cultural subjects', i.e. history, arts and folklore, and L_2 for science, technology and economics (here we are dealing with a case of school diglossia);
(4) *total bi-literate bilingualism*, in which all abilities are developed in the two languages for all domains.

According to its goal bilingual education can be divided into:

(1) *compensatory programs*, in which the child is first schooled in his mother tongue in order to be better integrated into the mainstream education;
(2) *enrichment programs*, normally designed for majority children, which aim at developing an additive form of bilinguality;
(3) *group-maintenance programs*, in which the language and culture of the minority child are preserved and enhanced; the argument against these programs is that they lead to sociopolitical disruption, while the programs are defended on ideological grounds, in the name of linguistic and cultural pluralism.

The third set of variables, status, etc. comprises four dimensions:

(1) language of primary importance versus language of secondary importance in education;
(2) home language versus school language;
(3) major world language versus minor language and;
(4) institutionalized versus non-institutionalized language in the community.

Some of these combinations are more predictive of success of bilingual education than others (Fishman, 1977a)
    Although these typologies attempt to classify bilingual education, they lack theoretical foundations and tend to ignore the determining factors in bilingual education. These factors are social, historical, social structural, cultural, ideological and social psychological in nature. Therefore, only an interdisciplinary approach which takes all these factors simultaneously into account will enable us to understand the problems and sort out the confusion existing in the field of bilingual education (Paulston, 1975). In the next pages we attempt to examine these factors in detail.

8.3 Factors conditioning bilingual education

8.3.1 Social historical and ideological factors

In the last four decades the problems of bilingual education have increasingly taken on a world-wide importance because of a number of political, economic, ideological and educational events. Politically former colonies became independent: most of these countries are multilingual as a consequence of the arbitrary divisions by colonial powers; furthermore, they are countries facing serious problems of development. As economic development demands the use of a language of wider communication, the language of the colonizer is still used and often remains the official or one of the official languages as, for example, in many African countries or in India (Calvet, 1974). Furthermore, these countries must cope with problems of language planning and choice of the language of education: often there is a lack of teachers and teaching materials for teaching in national languages (Calvet, 1981; Siguan & Mackey, 1987).

From a demographic perspective we have often witnessed massive movements of populations for different reasons: internal migration due to the exodus towards rapidly industrializing urban centres; external migrations as a consequence of revolutions (e.g. Cuba), wars (e.g. Vietnam), and decolonization (e.g. the end of colonial empires); or migration of labour from undeveloped regions towards highly industrialized countries in Europe, Canada and Australia. In addition, more and more individuals and their families stay abroad for a lengthy period of time. All these population movements have important consequences for languages in contact and bilingual education (Lewis, 1978, 1981).

The period following the Second World War witnessed an *ethnic revolution* (Fishman, 1976b) in which numerous minorized ethnic groups (whose status was defined by a dominant group) became conscious of their ethnic identity and mobilized around language as a symbol (see Chapter 7.1.1). This happened simultaneously for indigenous minorities living in underdeveloped regions of Europe, such as the Welsh in Great Britain, the Bretons and Basques in France, the Basques and Catalans in Spain and the Frisians in Holland; for the American and Canadian Indians and Inuit in North America; for more recently established ethnic minorities in countries like the United States, Canada and Australia (in the USA, for example, ethnic minorities which were thought to be assimilated into the American melting pot started claiming their right to their language, their culture and bilingual education for their children: Glazer & Moynihan, 1963); and for 'guestworkers' all over Europe (see J. Edwards, 1984, 1985).

The diversity and expansion of bilingual education programs are also determined by other social historical factors: the expansion and democratization of education throughout the world, and more particularly in developing countries; economic, social, political and technical development; the universalization of mass media; and recent ideological trends which confer positive values on cultural pluralism. Developing countries have to plan nationwide education, sometimes for numerous ethnolinguistic groups, some of which speak an unwritten language; developed countries where education was traditionally monolingual have started planning programs which should answer some of the demands of their ethnic minorities.

✗   In which language should a child be schooled? UNESCO (UNESCO, 1953), stressing the relevance of the mother tongue for children's development, recognized for every child the right to be educated through his own vernacular. In a number of countries, where for many children the mainstream education language is different from the mother tongue, legislation has recognized the right to bilingual education. In the United States of America, for example, the passage of the *Bilingual Education Act* (Title VII) in 1968 recognized the right of minority children with limited English-speaking abilities to receive education in their early school years through their mother tongue while they become proficient in English (for further details, see Thernstrom, 1980; J. Edwards, 1985). In 1977, an EEC Council Directive asked its members to take appropriate measures to guarantee that education provide guestworkers' children with the opportunity to learn the host language while maintaining the heritage language and culture, in accordance with the legislation of each country. In the United Kingdom, where the legal responsibility for school curricula lay with local education authorities, several mother-tongue teaching programs were developed in areas with high concentrations of ethnic minorities (V. K. Edwards, 1984).

However, the movement in favour of bilingual education in industrialized countries seems to have peaked in the late seventies. In the eighties funding for bilingual education programs in the United States has been constantly diminishing (Gray, 1982); special bilingual education programs are still being cancelled and resources diverted into ESL programs intended to assimilate children in the mainstream programs (Kirp, 1983). In the United Kingdom, an 800-page government report (*Education for all*, 1985, known as the 'Swann Report') completely misinterpreted research data on mother-tongue teaching and bilingual education and concluded that education should provide better ESL programs, but that mother-tongue education should be the responsibility of ethnolinguistic minorities. These conclusions, both in the United States and the United Kingdom, were reached on exclusively ideological grounds: they completely disregard the existing empirical evidence on bilingual education, and in particular the consequences for minority children of teaching exclusively through the mainstream language.

Among the minorities we must distinguish those with a particular territorial status, such as the Basques and the Catalans in Spain, and those who constitute a province or state within a larger political structure such as the Québécois in Canada and several states in India, from those who, without territorial status, coexist with the dominant group. In the case of minorities with territorial status either the national language(s) are used as language(s) of instruction in addition to the official language, or else the latter is taught only as a second language. But language planning in education depends a great deal on the ethnolinguistic vitality of the group. In Catalonia, for example, where Castilian is not only the official language but is spoken by a majority of immigrant workers while Catalan, the regional language with official territorial status and a literary tradition, is used by the middle classes, intellectuals and peasants, the autonomous government has made the 'catalanization' of the Generalità one of its main objectives. By 1985 it was estimated that half the children received their education through both Catalan and Castilian, while the other half studied Catalan at the rate of five hours a week (Siguan & Mackey, 1987). In Euskadi, by contrast, the Euskarian (Basque) language, which is also promoted by the autonomous Basque government, is encountering difficulties because it is spoken only by a minority, is little used as a literary and scientific medium, is unrelated to Spanish and is thus isolated (Siguan & Mackey, 1987).

In India, where every state has the right to choose regional languages as official languages (Constitution, art. 345), there exists a trilingual education system which develops throughout the curriculum (Khubchandani, 1978). This trilingualism can be schematized as in Table 8.1.

However, this schema is not always followed and many contradictions can be observed. It is not unusual to come across schools where teachers and students communicate in one language, teaching is conducted in another, school materials are in a third language and homework is done in a fourth (Khubchandani, 1978). Furthermore, only a few of the most important ethnolinguistic groups have a territorial status in India and most communities are minorities inside a State. There are no experimental studies or assessment of the bilingual education programs in India. The same holds for the USSR, which also has a complicated pattern of bilingual education (we refer the reader to Lewis, 1972, 1981).

For the second type of minorities, those without territorial status, who are even more subordinate in the sense that the gap between them and the dominant group is wider, we have to distinguish between: indigenous minorities, e.g. the Indians and Inuit in North America, the Aboriginals in Australia and the

Table 8.1 Trilingual education pattern in India (Khubchandani, 1978)

Pupil's L_1	Levels of education			
	Elementary Language 1	Secondary 1 Language 2	Secondary 2	Higher
Hindi Non-Hindi	Hindi L_1	Regional L_2 Hindi	English English	English English

Blacks in South Africa; minorities who arrived after the dominant group, either through forced immigration (e.g. the African slaves) or free immigration, e.g. the Mexican Americans and Italo-Americans in the United States; and more recent immigrations such as the West Indians, Indians and Pakistanis in the United Kingdom and the guestworkers in several European countries. We must also distinguish the indigenous ethnolinguistic minorities who are granted no territorial status in multilingual countries. India, for example, must plan education for 450 tribes with no less than 294 mother tongues of which some are not written (Srivastava, 1984b). For all these minorities to survive, some or all of their members must become bilingual and acquire some functional knowledge of an official language.

The UNESCO statement (UNESCO, 1953) that every child has a rightful claim to mother-tongue education is not applied to many minority children. The claim itself has been criticized on the grounds that the economic burden is too big for developing countries: there is a plethora of different vernaculars, some without written forms, and a lack of teaching materials and trained teachers (Bull, 1964). Furthermore, it is not proven that it is better to introduce literacy through the mother tongue *per se*; Le Page (1964) argues that in multilingual Third World countries children are already multilingual before starting school and the term 'mother tongue' does not have the same meaning as in the West: more relevant are the attitudes of the family and the community who desire social promotion.

Most of the Third World countries, however, advocate literacy initiation in the vernacular. Srivastava (1984b) proposes that in a country like India: (1) literacy should be initiated 'in the language style in which the child has oral competence and then transfer, if necessary, to the language recognized as the medium of instruction in the formal educational system of the region' (Vernacular-cum-Transfer Model) (p. 46); and (2) if the vernacular has no written system, it should 'select the script of the regional language rather than devise a new script' (*ibid.*); however, if attitudes are strongly negative towards the regional language, the Devanagari script recognized by the Constitution as the official form should be chosen; a tribal language with a written tradition should not be forced to discontinue the use of its own script. Bamgbose (1984) holds similar views for Nigeria. In the first phase of literacy the local language should be used; therefore core materials must be developed in all the main Nigerian languages; for those minorities where this is not possible, either literacy should be initiated through a L_2 in which they have some proficiency or a transitional period during which they acquire the basic skills must be planned.

To sum up, there is a world-wide claim that literacy for minorities should be initiated through the vernacular; however, whether, once the basic skills have been acquired, education is continued in the vernacular depends essentially on the degree of subordinateness of the minority: a territorially well-established minority generally has the means and the power to ensure mother-tongue education, at least up to a certain level; a small minority with no territorial claims has neither the means nor the power to demand anything but a transition program in its mother tongue.

8.3.2 Intergroup power-relation factors

According to Schermerhorn (1970), when two ethnolinguistic groups with a different cultural and linguistic history establish lasting contacts, one of the groups tends to dominate the other. The nature of these contacts determines interethnic relations. The degree of integration of both groups in the society depends on a number of factors of which the most important is the power relation. There are several possibilities: (1) the dominant group assimilates the subordinate group through persuasion or force, in which case the subordinate group gives up its cultural distinctiveness and adopts the dominant group's values, including language; (2) the dominant group allows the subordinate group to maintain cultural distinctiveness, including language; (3) the minority chooses to remain segregated and ghettoized; (4) the subordinate group attempts to gain control over the dominant group and becomes in turn dominant; (5) the dominant group imposes segregation and ghettoization upon the subordinate group (apartheid); and (6) the subordinate group takes control of its own destiny and decides to separate from the dominant group (see Chapter 7.1.1).

If we apply Schermerhorn's model to bilingual education, a number of questions arise. Of which group is the child a member? What are the power relations between the dominant and the subordinate group? Who decides about bilingual education and for whom? What are the goals of bilingual education: assimilation, pluralism or segregation? What is the collective outcome? Which group is going to gain by the chosen solution? What are the individual outcomes of bilingual education? Will the child develop an additive or a subtractive form of bilinguality through education? A subtractive form is a negative asset not only for the individual but also for the group, and indeed for society, since having members who have not developed their full cognitive potential leads to lower economic success. What are the consequences for a group if a member loses his mother tongue? No group wants to lose its members through assimilation, neither do they want to see subtractive bilinguality develop. For these reasons, the minority group tends to minimize the risks of assimilation and subtraction in education. Power relations therefore determine the direction of language planning in education.

Social historical, ideological and power-relation factors are not the only ones to influence bilingual education. Social psychological factors also influence bilingual development and must be taken into consideration in bilingual education.

8.3.3 Social psychological factors

From our discussion of bilingual development (see Chapters 2.4 and 3.3) we make a number of hypotheses concerning the consequences of bilingual education. The outcome of bilingual education depends upon a number of pre-school factors as well as upon the way the two languages are planned in education. Two factors are of relevance in education; (1) to what extent is the child proficient in the school language? and (2) to what extent has he developed the cognitive function in one or both of his languages before starting school? Considering the interplay of educational factors with the following factors: social psychological and cognitive developmental factors, such as onset of, and proficiency in, both languages; functions developed for language; valorization of one or both languages for all or a limited number of functions; and the social representations which the child developed as a consequence, we make the following hypotheses:

(1) If both languages are acquired simultaneously or if the child is fully proficient in both languages before entering school, he does not have the double learning burden of acquiring new language skills and literacy skills simultaneously; if, in addition, the child has already developed language as a cognitive tool, the acquisition of literacy skills will be facilitated; and, if the child has also developed an analysed representation of language in which both languages are perceived as interchangeable, thus amplifying cognitive functioning, the acquisition of literacy skills will further amplify this functioning and the child is more likely to develop an additive form of bilinguality. This is the case of the child in an educated mixed-lingual family.

(2) If the child is only proficient in his L_1 when starting school in L_2, he will have to acquire the primary communicative skills in L_2 at the same time as the literacy skills in L_2. If he has already developed an analysed representation of language through his L_1, he can transfer it to the acquisition of literacy skills; the two languages will become interchangeable for cognitive operations, thus amplifying cognitive functioning. Because both languages are valorized in their cognitive function, this transfer will be relatively easy. The degree to which his analysed representation of language includes both languages as interchangeable tools will determine the degree of additivity. This is the case of immersion-school children and of some advantaged submersion children.

(3) If a child proficient in his L_1 only or with a limited knowledge of L_2 at the onset of schooling in a relatively more prestigious L_2 has not developed the cognitive functions of language in his L_1, he also faces the double burden of acquiring the primary communicative skills in L_2 simultaneously with the literacy skills. Because he does not possess the analytic representation of language the task of acquiring literacy skills is harder (as is the case for some

monolingual children schooled in L_1. If, in addition, his L_1 is devalorized and stigmatized, he will not transfer the newly acquired skills to his L_1 but limit them to a L_2 in which he is not proficient. In the worst case, because he does not use his full language potential as does a monolingual child coping with the problem of acquiring literacy, the development of the analysed representation of language might be slowed down. Further devalorization of L_1 by society and the school, where it is not used for the development of literacy skills, will lead to a perception that his two languages are not interchangeable as cognitive tools and that only L_2 can be used in that function. This might ultimately lead to a subtractive form of bilinguality.

In the next section we discuss some of the bilingual education programs developed for dominant- and subordinate-group children and analyse the possible outcomes of these language-planning models in education.

8.4 Bilingual education for children of the dominant group

In all cultures and at all times elites have provided their children with bilingual education when they considered it necessary, either by employing a private teacher or by sending the child to an elite school, often in the country where the second language was spoken. In the last decades, certain dominant groups have adopted a more democratic way of ensuring bilingual education, namely through immersion programs.

8.4.1 The multilingual international schools

Multilingual international schools are found in various parts of the world, from Mexico and New York to Brussels and Berlin. In Europe alone there are nine international schools under EEC jurisdiction: Karlsruhe, Munich, Luxemburg, Culham, Bergen, Varese, Mol-Geel and two in Brussels (Baetens Beardsmore, 1980; Baetens Beardsmore & Swain, 1985). In addition, there are numerous private multilingual schools in North America and Europe, as, for example, the American School in Paris and the Lycée Français in London. These schools have slightly different approaches and combine two, three or four languages to a different extent. For example, the International School in Brussels is primarily meant for children of European civil servants from different EEC countries; the school is divided into several linguistic groups; children start elementary education in their mother tongue if it is one of the four working languages of the EEC (French, English, German and Italian), otherwise they choose one of these linguistic groups. In the second year a L_2 is introduced which is either French, English or German. At a later stage 'European classes' are organized in which the four working languages are used interchangeably.

Very little research has been conducted on the consequences of bilingual education in multilingual international schools and their reputation is essentially based on anecdotal evidence and parental attitudes. The one exception is a comparative study between the Brussels International School and an immersion program in Toronto (Baetens Beardsmore & Swain, 1985) which we discuss in the next section. At present we cannot conclude that the success of these schools is attributable to their multilingual and not to their elitist character.

8.4.2 *Immersion programs*

It is no accident that immersion programs started developing in Quebec. Because the political evolution of Canada's French Province, which expressed itself in the 'Révolution Tranquille' and the subsequent separatist movement in the sixties and seventies, transformed Quebec into a unilingual French Province (Charte de la Langue Française, known as Bill 101, already mentioned in Chapter 7.1.1), the Anglo-Québécois minority, which was essentially monolingual in English, had to adjust and become proficient enough in French to use it as a working language. This prompted the anglophone minority to provide their children with a better proficiency in French than the one they attained through traditional second-language teaching methods. Different approaches for improving their working knowledge of French have been developed; amongst these *immersion* stands out as the most successful venture. Immersion simply means that a group of L_1-speaking children receive all or part of their schooling through a L_2 as medium of instruction. The immersion approach is based on two assumptions: (1) that a L_2 is learned in a similar way to a L_1; and (2) that a language is best learned in a stimulating context which enhances the language functions and exposes the child to the natural forms of language.

In the mid-sixties research in experimental and social psychology started indicating that early bilingual experience might enhance cognitive development and lead to an additive form of bilinguality (Chapter 2.4). It is in this political and social psychological context that the first immersion program for anglophone children was initiated by parents in St-Lambert, a middle-class neighbourhood of Montreal, in collaboration with a team of psychologists from McGill University (Lambert & Tucker, 1972).

8.4.2.1 *Types of immersion*

The term 'immersion' refers to a program in which teaching is planned through the means of a L_2; however, since the St-Lambert program was initiated, many forms of immersion have been developed. Because immersion was first developed in Canada we will refer to French immersion for anglophones; however it must be kept in mind that immersion programs can be applied to all majority groups schooled in a subordinate language.

Early Total Immersion. This program was first developed for anglophone children in the St-Lambert pilot-school which serves as the prototype for all early immersion programs. Education through French starts in kindergarten and is given by francophone or fluently bilingual teachers. During the first two years of elementary school instruction is given exclusively through the medium of French; children acquire literacy skills in their L_2; English is introduced in the third year (that is, after three years in French if we include kindergarten), taught as a first language for daily periods of thirty-five minutes. The amount of time taught in French drops gradually and reaches 50% by the end of elementary. In the early stages children tend to communicate among themselves and with the teachers through the medium of English; however, very soon French is used as a means of communication in the classroom. After the introduction of English there is a bilingual stage in which some subjects are taught in French and others in English; finally, during a consolidation stage, the pupil can choose to take certain subjects in French or English. No particular L_2 methodology is followed.

Early partial immersion. It differs from total immersion in that both languages are used as means of instruction from the onset of schooling. The relative use of both language varies widely from one program to another.

Late immersion. These programs have been designed for high-school students and aim at developing French language skills in students who have so far received a traditional L_2 instruction in French; the goal of the program is to enable the students to attain a functional bilinguality by the time they finish high school. For example, during the first year, 85% of the curriculum is taught through French while in the remaining 15% English is taught as a first language; during the following years the student has a choice and can attend 40% of the classes in French (see Genesee, 1979; Swain & Lapkin, 1982).

8.4.2.2 *Assessment of immersion programs*

Numerous immersion programs have been evaluated over the last twenty years. Whereas the St-Lambert project (Lambert & Tucker, 1972) is the prototype of immersion assessment, other large-scale evaluations have also been conducted for different immersion programs in several Canadian cities: among the most important are those by Genesee (1979, 1984) for Greater Montreal, and by Swain & Lapkin (1982) for Carleton in the Ottawa suburbs and for Toronto. In these follow-up studies, assessments of immersion children were compared with those of monolingual English-speaking children in traditional

English programs (English Control Groups) and with those of French-speaking children in French schools (French Control Groups). Three general issues are addressed by the assessment studies: (1) the effect of receiving instruction through French on English-language skills; (2) the effect of immersion on academic achievement; and (3) the effectiveness of immersion for the development of L_2 skills (Genesee, 1984). A variety of assessment tests have been used in these evaluations: standardized tests in English-L_1 and French-L_1 language skills, speaking, listening comprehension and writing tests in both languages and academic achievement tests. The results of assessment of immersion programs have so far been relatively stable across Canada (Swain, 1982) and can be summarized as follows:

(1) *Mother-tongue proficiency.* Generally speaking there is no lag in the comprehension and expression skills; the immersion children lag behind the English controls in literacy skills during the first two years, but this difference disappears once the English literacy skills are introduced. Children in partial immersion do not score better on literacy tests in English than total-immersion children once literacy skills in English have been introduced. In late immersion, the students do not lag behind the English controls after their one year's instruction in French. Thus, there is no deficit of mother-tongue skills.

(2) *Proficiency in L_2.* The results in L_2 are far superior to those obtained by English controls who receive traditional L_2 instruction, to the extent that the tests used with the immersion children are too difficult for the children of the control group. When compared with the French controls, the children in the immersion programs score comparably for oral and written comprehension and on vocabulary tests, but their written and particularly oral expression skills are not native-like and they will rarely initiate a conversation in French. They perceive themselves and are perceived by francophones as having superior French-language skills to English children in a traditional program. Children in partial immersion do not score as highly on French skills as those in total immersion while they do not score higher on English skills; thus the reduction of the time spent teaching through French reduces the L_2 skills but does not enhance the L_1 skills. The assessment of children in late immersion follows the same pattern: they achieve higher levels than the English controls but do not reach native-like command of French in expression skills.

(3) *Academic achievement.* Total immersion children score as highly as their English-schools counterparts on tests of mathematics and science, despite the fact that they received their instruction in French. Children in late immersion are not impeded by the use of their L_2 as a medium of instruction and score as highly as the controls in traditional English programs. They also score above the average provincial norms on a number of subjects in French; this last result

must be interpreted in a careful way as there was a socio-economic bias in favour of the immersion students (Genesee, 1984).

(4) *Other assessments.* Some studies report other measures taken with immersion children. There are some indications that immersion might lead to cognitive enhancement; IQ measures seem to increase more over the years for immersion students than for children in traditional English programs (Barik & Swain, 1978); immersion children in Grades 5 and 6 score higher on creativity tests (Edwards, Doutriaux, McCarrey & Fu, 1976) and on divergent thinking measures (Scott, 1973). Comparing below-average, average and above-average students in early immersion programs, Genesee (1981a) observed that below-average students scored significantly lower than average and above-average students on literacy tests in French, but that the three groups did not differ from each other on interpersonal communication tests. This was not the case with late-immersion below-average students, who scored lower than above-average students on interpersonal communication skills in French.

To sum up, then, with regard to the assessment of immersion programs it seems that: (1) immersion programs are superior to traditional FSL programs, with students attaining a high level of proficiency, especially for receptive skills in L_2; (2) students are not handicapped in mother-tongue skills nor in academic achievement; (3) when differences occur between results in different immersion programs, they favour the early total immersion over partial immersion (Genesee, 1981b) and over late immersion (Morrison, 1981); (4) there are some indications that early immersion programs might favour the child's overall cognitive development.

8.4.2.3 A critique of immersion

Immersion programs have received a number of criticisms from different perspectives: experimental, linguistic, pedagogical and social. From an experimental perspective it has often been remarked that the immersion groups were not comparable with the controls, because immersion was favoured by the parents; or that the results might be attributed to a 'Hawthorne effect'. It has been argued that immersion programs favour gifted children; Genesee (1976) concluded that they are suitable for all children, since below-average children in early immersion develop the same proficiency in communicative skills in L_2 as above-average children. Bruck (1982) argues that children with learning difficulties and slow learners benefit from an immersion program to the extent that they do not lag behind other children with learning difficulties, and in addition learn French, which is not the case in regular programs. Trites (1981), on the basis of a follow-up study, suggests that children with learning difficulties should be removed from immersion programs; Genesee (1984) argues, however, that unless it can be demonstrated that these children would not experience similar difficulties in traditional programs, Trites's argument does not hold. Immersion programs have often been judged to be suitable for middle-class children only. Assessing working-class children in immersion programs, Bruck, Jakimik & Tucker (1975) found that they were not different from their English counterparts in traditional programs for English skills, but superior to them in French skills; unfortunately they did not follow up their study.

A few studies address the question of the communicative and linguistic output of immersion children. Harley & Swain (1977, 1978) compared the use of verbal tenses by immersion children with that by monolingual and infant bilingual children: they observed that immersion children use a reduced tense system; they do not use conditional and modalities. The authors concluded that immersion children develop a competence which permits them to interact with their peers and teachers, but lack the necessary social motivation to develop native-like competence. According to Blanc (1980) and Dodson (1981), teaching methods are partly responsible for this lack of expressive abilities: teaching is too directive, pupils too passive, and texts are not exploited at the linguistic level; furthermore it might be a mistake to postulate that a L_2 is learned in a similar way to an L_1. Cziko, Lambert, Sidoti & Tucker (1978) observed that although students schooled through immersion are capable of functioning in French and motivated to do so, they hardly come into contact with members of the francophone community. The relevance of social contacts with members of the ethnolinguistic community has been demonstrated by Chun (1979), who compared the oral expression skills of English children in immersion with English children who spent one year in France; the latter were far superior to the former in oral skills.

8.4.2.4 Comparison of immersion with other programs

The Culver City Bilingual Program. This early total immersion program is a duplication of the St-Lambert project with Anglo-American children schooled through Spanish (Cohen, 1976). In addition to the St-Lambert program, a small group of Spanish speakers were introduced in Grade 1 to serve as models and to stimulate communication in Spanish. The assessment results are comparable to the Canadian immersion evaluations: children compared favourably with monolingual English-speaking controls for English skills and for academic achievement and with Spanish-speaking controls for their Spanish skills, although they did not reach native-like competence. Their attitudes towards Hispanics and the Spanish culture were extremely favourable. However, it must be observed that in the American context Spanish has no 'official' status unlike French in Canada, and if it is spoken by a large number of Americans it is also highly devalorized., The children who participated probably had favourable attitudes before they started the program.

The Welsh Bilingual Project. Beaudouin, Cummins, Dunlop, Genesee & Obadia (1981) compared immersion in Welsh for anglophones with the Canadian results. The Schools Council Bilingual Project (SCBP) aimed at making monolingual English-speaking children fluent bilinguals by the age of eleven. Half the school day was conducted in Welsh and the other half in English from nursery to the end of primary school. The SCBP has been very successful at the infant level: listening comprehension and speaking skills are established by the age of seven. Teaching Welsh at the junior level, however, was less successful and in some instances skills in Welsh regressed; but there was no evidence that academic subjects had suffered as a result. In the experimental group only the children with high socio-economic status scored significantly better than the control group.

The difference in performance between the infant and junior school children in the project has been attributed by Dodson (1981) essentially to differences in teaching methods, the infant schools being far more flexible and dynamic in their approach than the junior schools. Furthermore Dodson has put forward an interesting hypothesis to account for some deficiencies in immersion bilingual programs. He starts from two premises, namely that learning a second language through immersion is not comparable to the acquisition of the first and that, in the immersion bilingual experience, the child does not have a first and a second language but, rather, a 'preferred' and another language, neither being always the same one (the bilingual may be more at ease in one for a set of functions or activities, and more at ease in the other for another set of functions or activities). In the course of evaluating the Welsh program Dodson found that those schools which followed a 'total' immersion program, in the sense of placing the focus on the message and not the medium, were achieving lower results than those which applied phased methodological sequencing from 'medium-oriented' to 'message-oriented' communication in a continuous cycle. He further advocates the use of both languages, the preferred and the other language, within the same lesson, claiming that the two languages reinforce each other.

Comparison between immersion and international schools. Baetens Beardsmore & Swain (1985) compared achievement in the L_2 obtained in two different models of bilingual education: a French immersion program in Toronto and the International School in Brussels. They observed that, although the students in the International School received only part of their schooling through French and had thus received much less exposure to the language, both groups of students had a relatively high proficiency in French and achieved equally well. They attribute these results to contextual conditions: the children in the

International School used French more as a lingua franca in the school; were more exposed to French in the community at large and at home with the parents; and they had a larger experience of living in countries where their mother tongue was not spoken. For the children in the immersion program, on the other hand, the L_2 often lacks relevance beyond the classroom. This suggests that classroom activities should be combined with social activities in order to attain native-like command of L_2.

Introducing the majority child to a valorized second language used as medium of instruction at the age of five not only does not delay the child's acquisition of linguistic and academic skills, but it gives him a competence in the other language far superior to what he might have achieved by traditional methods and it may even enhance his cognitive skills and produce an additive balanced bilinguality. However, what has proved valid for the advantaged child of majority groups, whose culture and first language are valorized in his community and who has already reached a sufficient level of analysed language by the time he goes to school, does not necessarily apply in the case of the minority child. It is to him that we now turn.

8.5 Bilingual education for ethnic minority children

When discussing bilingual education for minority children two important contextual aspects of their development must be underlined: (1) they come from a little-valorized mother-tongue background and (2) because they often come from socially deprived communities their literacy-oriented skills are less well developed.

8.5.1 The myth of the bilingual handicap

A major problem with education for ethnolinguistic minority children is the so-called 'cognitive handicap' attributed to their bilinguality, or what Cummins (1981, 1984a) calls the *myth of bilingual handicap*. According to this myth the academic failure of minority children is attributed to their state of bilinguality; the solution, therefore, is seen as learning the dominant L_2 and using it for education. Cummins's views are schematized in Table 8.2.

In this myth the overt goal of L_2 education is to teach L_2 to the minority child in order to give him equal chances, the covert goal being to assimilate him; therefore, L_1 is devalorized and children are forbidden to use it in the school, because it could interfere with L_2 acquisition; as a result the child becomes ashamed of his own culture and language, substitutes L_2 for L_1 and obtains poor academic results; these are in turn attributed to the state of bilinguality and to a cognitive deficit; hence, education insists even more on eliminating the 'cause' of the deficit, i.e. the L_1, and reinforces the myth. If this circle can be broken, then the poor academic achievement of the minority child can

Table 8.2 The myth of the bilingual handicap (adapted from Cummins, 1981)

A. Overt aim	Covert aim	D. Outcomes	
Teach English to minority children in order to create a harmonious society with equal opportunity for all.	Anglicize minority children because linguistic and cultural diversity are seen as a threat to social cohesion.	Even more intense efforts by the school to eradicate the deficiencies inherent in minority children.	The failure of these efforts only serves to reinforce the myth of minority group deficiencies.
B. Method	Justification	C. Results	'Scientific' explanation
Prohibit use of L_1 in schools and make children reject their own culture and language in order to identify with majority English group.	1. L_1 should be eradicated because it will interfere with the learning of English. 2. Identification with L_1 culture will reduce child's ability to identify with English-speaking culture.	1. Shame in L_1 language and culture. 2. Replacement of L_1 by L_2. 3. School failure among many children.	1. Bilingualism causes confusion in thinking, emotional insecurity, and school failures. 2. Minority group children are 'culturally deprived' by definition since they are not Anglos. 3. Some minority language groups are genetically inferior (common theory in the United States in the 1920s and 1930s).

This table reflects the assumptions of North American school systems in the first half of this century. However, similar assumptions have been made about minority language children in the school systems of many other countries.

be improved. To achieve this, however, one must accept that the school system rather than the child's bilinguality is the main factor responsible for poor achievement. As we argued in Chapter 2.3, it is not the state of bilinguality, but sociostructural, sociocultural and sociopsychological factors which are responsible for poor academic achievement.

The debate on 'semilingualism', although ill-founded, has had a considerable impact on designing education programs for minorities. When 'semilingualism' was introduced as a concept, it was interpreted as an inherent characteristic of the minority child, even though Skutnabb-Kangas (1981) made it clear later that the principal cause was social structural and ideological. Several solutions have been proposed. In order to avoid academic failure, Skutnabb-Kangas & Toukomaa (1976), for example, advocated L_1 shelter-programs in which Finnish immigrant children in Sweden would receive an elementary education exclusively through the medium of Finnish. This solution has been criticized by Ekstrand (1978) on the ground that it might not only shelter the minority child but also ghettoize him to the extent that he is completely isolated from the larger community; he suggests that when a child lives in a bicultural and bilingual environment, this should be reflected in the school, which should also be bicultural and bilingual.

Cummins (1984a) gives an excellent review of the use made of academic assessment tests to 'demonstrate' the bilingual deficit of minority children. He suggests that language planning in education should opt neither for a 'linguistic mismatch' nor for a 'maximum exposure to L_1' solution. Because there is strong evidence that promoting L_1 literacy skills enhances overall academic achievement, this should always be considered in planning minority education. The school should further employ every means to valorize the child's mother tongue and encourage its use. The factors operating in determining scholastic success for minority children vary from one minority community to another; therefore, no single solution can be proposed but each case should be assessed separately. Needs analysis, the definition of specific objectives, the training of community or heritage language teachers, the design of valid and reliable tests for children of ethnolinguistic minorities are an urgent task everywhere.

8.5.2 Examples of bilingual education programs for minority children

Numerous experiments have been conducted on bilingual education programs for minority children and a certain number of them demonstrate that a subtractive form of bilinguality is not a necessary outcome. We have chosen to describe some of these because they each represent a solution to somewhat different situations.

The bilingual program for Finnish immigrant children in Sweden (Hanson, 1979). This program uses Finnish as the main language of instruction; Swedish becomes an important means of instruction from Grade 3 onwards. At the end of the elementary school children obtain results comparable with Swedish and Finnish control groups. This is an improvement compared with the monolingual and the shelter-programs.

Reading programs for Chiapas children (Modiano, 1973). This program initiates Chiapas children, who are normally schooled exclusively through Spanish, into reading skills in their mother tongue, which is a highly devalorized language in Mexico. Compared with Chiapas children who learned to read in

Spanish only, the experimental group scored higher on written comprehension tests in Spanish after a three-year program. *Mutatis mutandis*, these results are comparable with those obtained with Navajo children in the United States.

The Rock Point Experiment with Navajo children (Rosier & Farella, 1976). Before the start of this Navajo/English bilingual education program the Navajo children were two years behind the American norms for reading skills in English at the end of Grade 6, despite an extensive teaching program of ESL. The bilingual program used Navajo as the main language of instruction throughout elementary education. The introduction of English was delayed until the reading skills in Navajo were well acquired. At the end of elementary school Navajo children in the program scored slightly higher than the American norms, although they had been less exposed to English than the children in the ESL program.

The Redwood City Project (Cohen, 1975). In this 'mixed' four-year-long project Mexican American and Anglo-American children were mixed together in a proportion of two to one. Teachers used both Spanish and English in the same class and translated freely from one language to the other. Results were different for both groups. Anglo-American did not acquire much Spanish, as they could use English when they wanted to and were afraid of speaking Spanish. However, the Mexican Americans learned English as well as a control group who received exclusively English-language instruction, and scored equally well on mathematics tests and on English-language measures, except in vocabulary. Furthermore their attitudes towards, and their use of, Spanish were positively affected: use of Spanish did not diminish to the same extent as it did in the control group (Hernandez-Chavez, 1978).

The California experiment (Legaretta, 1979). The author compared three types of bilingual kindergarten programs for Mexican Americans with two unilingual English programs. The three bilingual education programs were significantly more efficient in developing communicative skills than the English-only programs. The most efficient program shared equal time between Spanish and English.

The Franco-Manitoban experiment (Hébert, 1976). Franco-Manitoban children in Grades 3, 6 and 9 who received bilingual education in French and English made similar progress in English, regardless of the amount of time spent on English; those who had 20% English and 80% French schooling were as good in English and had superior results in French skills than those children who received 80% of their instruction in English and 20% in French. In other words mother-tongue skills benefited from a bigger exposure time without any loss in L_2 skills.

The St-John's Valley bilingual education program (Dubé & Herbert, 1975). The sub-tractive situation of Franco-American children was improved when one third of the elementary program was taught through French. After five years these chil-dren obtained better scores in academic achievement and English-language skills than control groups in English-only programs; furthermore, they were flu-ent in French reading and writing skills (Lambert, Giles & Picard, 1975).

The 'MOTET' Project (Mother Tongue & English Teaching Project, 1981). Two groups of Mirpuri (a Punjabi dialect) mother-tongue children attended a bi-lingual 50% Mirpuri–50% English nursery school program in Bradford (UK). The results indicated that one experimental group obtained superior results in English comprehension skills to the control group, but the reverse was true for the other group; both groups scored higher on English-expression measures and on all Punjabi tests. These results were confirmed in a follow-up study (Fitzpatrick, 1987): the children continued to improve their English and Pun-jabi skills to a greater extent than Mirpuri children who had not attended a bilingual program; however, large differences were observed between the chil-dren who were dispersed in different schools; if the school did not keep up with the Punjabi language the improvement trends faded out.

The Carpinteria Spanish-language pre-school program (Carpinteria Unified School District, 1982). The goal of this pre-school Spanish-only program is to bring Spanish-speaking children entering kindergarten to the level of school readi-ness attained by the English-speaking children. Children who had attended the program scored higher than Spanish-speaking controls, both on Spanish and on English measures.

8.5.3 *Features of bilingual education programs for minority children*

What can be concluded from this variety of experiments on bilingual education for minority children? They all deal with potentially highly subtractive contexts; all make use of the mother tongue for formal education, either simultaneously with the dominant language, or before instruction is given in the dominant language. In all cases, academic and linguistic proficiency results in both languages are superior to those obtained by control groups where instruction is in L_2 only. In all cases, the program valorizes the mother tongue and culture, motivates the child to learn through his L_1, and develops his linguistic–concep-tual capacities to the extent that he will make better progress in a L_2 than his peers schooled exclusively through L_2. These studies provide strong support for the view that for minority children, the acquisition of literacy skills should be dissociated from the acquisition of L_2 skills and that formal instruction should valorize the mother tongue. This is exactly what Tizard, Schofield & Hewison (1982) showed with their reading experiments in London (see Chapter 3.3.1).

The large majority of bilingual programs for minority children are transition programs which do not aim at functional bilinguality as do immersion programs. For most programs language planning has been decided by the dominant group; their ultimate goal is assimilation of the subordinate group. Even if they aim at developing a certain degree of bilinguality, it is likely that in the long run the students will become dominant in L_2 and acculturate. If bilingual education appears to be a necessary condition for ethnolinguistic minority children, it is however not a sufficient one. For example, the existence of bilingual education for the Franco-Ontarian minority in Canada is not sufficient to impede assimilation (Mougeon & Canale, 1978). It is the ethnolinguistic vitality of the group (see Chapter 7.1.2), the use of the mother tongue in the home and in the community, and the allegiance to the cultural group that will ensure cultural survival.

Far from representing a handicap, the use of the mother tongue in the home is an important factor in helping to attain academic achievement. In a longitudinal study Chesarek (1981) demonstrated that among elementary-school children from a Crow Indian reservation, those who had one Crow-speaking parent and who spoke exclusively English at home scored significantly lower on non-verbal intelligence tests than Crow children who spoke Crow as their first language, or English-speaking Crow children whose parents were both anglophones. Moreover, after three years of education in Crow, these children scored better than those educated in English only.

In a similar vein, Bhatnagar (1980), studying the adjustment of Italian immigrant children in Montreal, concluded that mother-tongue maintenance in the home leads to superior academic achievement, better proficiency in their second language, French, and improved social relations. Dolson (1985) obtained similar results with Hispanic children in California; those who came from homes where Spanish was spoken scored consistently better than Hispanic children from homes that had shifted to English. The relevance of the home in language maintenance has already been discussed in Chapter 7.3.3; of all domains it is the family network that most resists the penetration of the dominant language. If the minority language invades the family network the survival chances of the subordinate language are extremely small. (See Lieberson, 1970; Fishman, Cooper & Ma, 1971; Gal, 1979 and Mougeon, Brent-Palmer, Bélanger & Cichocki, 1982, among others.)

8.6 Bidialectal education

Similar educational problems arise when the child's mother tongue is a non-standard variety of the language, as for example Black English Vernacular (BEV) and creoles. There is another myth about the 'linguistic deficit' of Black Americans and West Indians who speak an English-based creole. Bereiter & Englemann (1966), for example, inferred the existence of an intellectual deficit in lower-class Black Americans, on the grounds that they were 'linguistically deficient': they were supposedly incapable of producing complete sentences and answered all questions by yes or no; their utterances lacked the copula *be* and therefore could not represent reality. Because of this linguistic deficit compensatory education, in which Black children performed structural exercises in English, was promoted.

Labov (1972), in his studies on Black English, demonstrated the ill-foundedness of Bereiter & Engelmann's theory: first the Black child belongs to a different culture; second, the tests used put him in a totally artificial situation; given a natural communication setting, he will express himself on all subjects, using the language of his own culture. Inner-city Black children have been described as non-verbal because the school setting does not allow them to express themselves in the ways they are accustomed to. Black English has its own rules, including the optional use of the copula *be* and the double negation. To attempt to eradicate these rules can only lead to confusion. The Black child does not speak 'improper English', he speaks a different language, stigmatized and devalorized by the school where the standard variety is the only language of instruction.

Three types of solution to bi-dialectalism have been proposed:

(1) the creation of *compensatory programs*, which we have already mentioned and which are based on the notion of a linguistic deficit; these programs aim at changing the linguistic habits of the child and re-educate him into speaking the 'proper' language;

(2) *bidialectal* programs in which the child learns to use the standard variety at school but is also encouraged by the school to use his vernacular in his own environment (Fasold & Shuy, 1970; Cheshire, 1987);

(3) attempts to reduce the attitudes and prejudices of standard speakers of the dominant group, rather than modify the child's behaviour.

In a number of studies on West Indian children in Great Britain V. K. Edwards (1978a, 1978b) demonstrated that linguistic factors (differences between creole and Standard) and non-linguistic factors (attitudes of peers, teacher and community members) affect the West Indian child's comprehension of the Standard as well as his motivation to learn it. The low academic achievement of West Indian children was first attributed to temporary problems of adjustment, then to a negative self-conception and racist teaching. There has thus been a shift in the perception of the causes of low achievement: from blaming it on factors intrinsic to the community and the child, including his 'improper' language use, it has moved to attributing it to structural forces in the host society (V. K. Edwards, 1986).

Bidialectal education is facing extremely complex problems which are socioeconomic, sociocultural, social psychological, pedagogical and linguistic in nature. The communities concerned are generally socio-economically and culturally deprived and are often visible minorities (for which race markers are easily perceived). Bidialectal education has to face attitudes and prejudices developed in the dominant group and often shared by the subordinate group itself: dialect is often perceived as a stigma to be got rid of. Several experiments and solutions have been proposed (e.g. Dillard, 1978 for the United States; Le Page, 1981 for the West Indies and Great Britain), but too often the problem is ignored and submersion in the mainstream is the solution. The results obtained with the bilingual programs discussed earlier could be used as guidelines for bidialectal education. Teacher training and re-education should help to change attitudes and the expectations of the school, and the integration of community teachers should help the child to valorize his vernacular and to use it in literacy-oriented activities. Such an approach is now being experimented with in several programs.

Bilingual education for immigrant children also faces a bidialectal problem. Many immigrants do not speak a standard variety of their home language. When the L_1 is taught in the host country, should it be the standard variety, or the dialect which is the child's real mother tongue? Tosi (1984) stresses the difficulties originating from the dichotomy between Standard Italian and Sicilian dialect in teaching Standard Italian in bilingual programs for Italian immigrants in Great Britain. For bidialectal teaching to become efficient, the dialect must first be valorized. A dominant language may be threatening, not only for students but also for teachers: Bentolila & Gani (1981) mention the case of Haiti where the school system pretended that Standard French was used in the school, whereas neither pupils nor teachers were capable of communicating in French. The end result was the use of a mesolect in which French stereotypes and French words took on a symbolic function. Since 1975 Haiti has been experimenting with bidialectal programs and creole is used in the first years of elementary schooling; however, Haitians are now coping with the problem of a written standard for creole. The relative status of both Standard French and creole in the Haitian society will determine the future of bidialectal education in Haiti.

8.7 Community bilingual education

In an idealized model of bilingual education the different groups of a community decide jointly the languages in which instruction will be given. They not only have pluralist views of education but aim at a 'multicultural synthesis' (Robinson, 1981). Not only the minority children but also the majority children are instructed in both the dominant and the subordinate languages. The choice of the subordinate language varies according to the presence and the size of the minority groups; the school attempts to reflect the linguistic and cultural pattern of the community; hence the name 'community languages' given to this type of bilingual education. Lambert & Taylor (1981) have suggested a model of community education for American schools: the goals of education and the languages used to attain these goals should be decided by the three main groups, the Anglo-Americans, the Black Americans and the other ethnic minorities. This model implies teaching in at least three codes for all children: Standard English, BEV and one heritage language chosen according to the ethnic concentration in the community (e.g. Spanish in California). Smolicz (1979) and Robinson (1981) advocate bilingual education in which majority and minority children are both taught together in each other's languages; for example, where the Greek Australian group is numerous, Anglo-Australian children and Greek Australian children would be taught the same curriculum in both English and modern Greek (see also Blanc, 1987b).

Interesting though this model may be, nothing allows us to conclude that, if it was applied, it would lead to a multilingual and multicultural synthesis. The model overlooks power relations existing in the community as well as the ethnolinguistic vitality of each of the groups involved. For example, in his analysis of Franco-Manitoban schools, Hébert (1976) has demonstrated that it is sufficient to introduce one English-speaking pupil into a francophone class in order for all the francophone students to switch to English. Fishman (1980) has warned that in a language-contact situation the subordinate language will survive only in a diglossic relation with the dominant language (see Chapter 7.3.2). Community bilingual education aims at destroying this diglossia by conferring equal status on all languages: will this not make one of the languages superfluous (Quinn, 1981)? And this can only mean the minority language. Although community bilingual education might, at first view, appear a very tempting solution, we wonder whether it can be put into practice. The question is still unanswered.

8.8 Conclusion

This chapter has dealt with the issues of language planning in bilingual education and their consequences for the child. We first discussed the relation between the development of literacy and languages of instruction. Bilingual education is determined by social historical, ideological, power-relation and social psychological factors which interact with each other and have to be taken into consideration when deciding on the language or languages of instruction. We then looked at bilingual education programs designed for majority children, namely in international schools and in immersion, and discussed the consequences of immersion programs for the child's linguistic skills and academic achievement. Whereas immersion appears as an applicable solution for majority children, the reverse is true for minority children. We further discussed the myth of the bilingual handicap of the minority child and showed how it leads to wrong pedagogical decisions. Some examples of bilingual programs for minority children and their results in terms of academic achievement were described; finally we attempted to explain the underlying principles of bilingual education.

For the child to benefit from a bilingual experience both languages must be valorized around him. How this is done must be assessed by those who plan language in education. What are the goals of education and how are they to be reached? Does education aim at developing functional bilinguality in the majority child, assimilation of the minority child into the mainstream culture, integration of the immigrant child in a pluralistic society or functional bilinguality for all children? When the child's home language is the dominant language in the society, and when it is valorized by the family environment as well, especially for literacy skills, then an immersion program is the solution for reaching functional bilinguality; if the immersion program is planned at an early age, the child can develop an additive form of bilinguality in addition to becoming functionally bilingual. Similar results are probably obtained by the programs in international schools; however, we lack the experimental evidence for it.

The picture is different for the minority child. Whereas there are many indications that the minority child benefits from being introduced to literacy in his mother tongue, this is too often ignored, either because the covert goal is assimilation of the minority child into the mainstream culture; or because the means are unattainable or economically too costly (as for example when the language is not written, or when there are no teaching materials or trained teachers available); or because those who plan education are still ignorant of research results, believe in the myth of bilingual handicap and are convinced that the earlier the child is introduced to a prestigious L_2 the better he will develop academically. Bilingual education programs and mother-tongue teaching in the early school years have been shown to benefit minority children and improve their academic achievement. Time spent on teaching the mother tongue does not slow down their proficiency in L_2 and increases their language skills in the mother tongue. Issues of bidialectal education are similar to those of bilingual education.

In contrast with the bilingual education for majority children, bilingual programs designed for minority children do not aim at functional bilinguality; they are rather a way of ensuring a better preparation for further education in a dominant L_2. This is achieved neither by total submersion in the L_2 nor by ghettoization in a shelter program. Transition programs in which instruction is given entirely or partially in the L_1 enable the minority child to catch up on academic achievement; they do not, however, provide him with the benefits of bilingual education that a majority child can gain from early bilingual experience or immersion programs.

The linguistic mismatch hypothesis which led UNESCO (1953) to declare the right of all children to mother-tongue education is an over-simplification

(Cummins, 1981). It is gospel to many educators who do not see the complexity of the problem. That a child can develop an additive form of bilinguality while literacy is taught via a L_2 has been proved by the positive results of immersion programs. The state of the art in the theories of bilingual development suggests a certain degree of interlanguage interdependence in the development of cognitive skills (see Chapters 2.3 and 3.3); they also justify the assumption that positive consequences of bilingual education can be obtained for all children, provided that the context of development of bilinguality is adequate (Hamers & Blanc, 1982). There is no simple universal solution in bilingual education, but each program must be planned as a function of the many sociocultural, sociostructural and sociopsychological factors relevant to a particular situation (Hamers, 1979).

One of the major differences between bilingual programs for majority and minority children lies in their final goals: functional bilinguality versus mainstream assimilation. When functional bilinguality is promoted in the minority child, as, for example, when the family valorizes the mother tongue sufficiently so as to maintain it, academic achievement is improved. Community bilingual education aims at promoting functional bilinguality for all children. However, at present we have no empirical evidence that community bilingual education promotes additive bilinguality in minority children. It is not enough to bring majority and minority children together in a community bilingual education program in order to ensure its success. Too many important factors, such as the existing power relations, have been overlooked. Only a better understanding of bilingual development and its relation to cognitive development and social conditions will help transform community bilingual education from utopia to reality.

9

Bilinguality and second language acquisition

Since the aim of learning a second language is to reach a state of bilinguality, a better understanding of the mechanisms involved in the development of bilinguality should help us to understand second language acquisition.[1] L_2 acquisition covers all cases of acquisition of a second language after the basic forms and functions of L_1 have been mastered. This includes consecutive childhood bilinguality as well as adolescent and adult bilinguality, whether acquired through informal or formal learning. In the present chapter we raise the following questions: (1) Does L_2 acquisition follow a universal order and can stages be identified? (2) To what extent is L_2 acquisition similar to L_1 acquisition and influenced by L_1? (3) What are the psychological mechanisms that are relevant for L_2 acquisition? Although we are interested in the theoretical foundations on which second language teaching rests, we will not discuss second language teaching methodology; rather, we will analyse the psycholinguistic and psychological processes upon which sound teaching methodology should be based.

9.1 L_2 acquisition

When we speak of L_2 acquisition, the first question that comes to mind is, 'to what extent is it similar to L_1 acquisition?' In analysing this phenomenon two major aspects should be considered: (1) L_2 acquisition, whether by children, adolescents or adults, takes place at a more advanced developmental stage than that attained by children at the onset of language acquisition; (2) L_2 learners already possess linguistic knowledge in their L_1. How far, therefore, is this twofold cognitive and linguistic knowledge responsible for different acquisition mechanisms? There are many theoretical approaches to this issue, which range on a continuum: at one extreme we find the view that this knowledge has no influence on L_2 acquisition, which calls on similar mechanisms as mother-tongue acquisition; at the other extreme, L_2 acquisition is considered to be completely determined by previous cognitive and linguistic knowledge.

Most researchers would agree that L_2 learners, regardless of their age, do not come up against the same problems of semantic-concept acquisition as children developing their first language. For example, a 6–7-year-old child no longer needs to acquire concepts such as time, space or possession. It may be assumed that the cognitive complexity underlying a linguistic form already acquired in L_1 will not be the main factor in determining the acquisition of its translation equivalent in L_2. For example, if the development of the cognitive concept 'possession' is the main determining factor in the order of acquisition of the possessive in L_1, we may expect that this will not be the case in the acquisition of the possessive in L_2, as the child has already acquired the concept of the possessor–possessed relationship. This does not mean that the acquisition of the rules of the possessive in L_2 is a simple task. However, considering the acquisition of L_2 as different from that of L_1 on the grounds of cognitive developmental differences does not help us to understand the role that a particular L_1 can play in the acquisition of a L_2.

This brings us to a second question: To what extent do characteristics unique to the mother tongue influence L_2 acquisition? This question is at the origin of two major trends in L_2 acquisition research: on the one hand, there are those who stress the universal developmental aspect of language learning, and on the other, those who privilege the relative importance of L_1 in L_2 acquisition. The former trend has led to such approaches as *error analysis, interlanguage, transitional competence* and *approximate systems*, in which L_2 acquisition is analysed in terms of developmental stages while the role of L_1 is minimized; the latter emphasizes the role and relevance of L_1 characteristics for L_2 acquisition, as in the study of *interference* and *contrastive analysis*. In order to answer these two questions we will first review current knowledge on L_2 acquisition by young children who have already mastered one linguistic system.

9.1.1 Developmental aspects of L_2 acquisition

The first detailed description of a L_2 acquisition by a young child was given by Kenyeres (1938), who observed her 6-year-old daughter whose mother tongue was Hungarian and who was learning French in a school in Geneva. The author concluded from her observations that L_2 acquisition, while being achieved in a harmonious fashion, does not follow the same route as L_1 acquisition, and that the majority of errors in L_2 can be attributed to mother-tongue interference. Tits (1948), on the other hand, concluded from his observations of a 7-year-old Spanish-speaking girl acquiring French in Brussels that her L_2 acquisition followed the same stages of development as L_1 acquisition, though at a faster pace. These studies, like the biographies of bilingual children by Ronjat (1913) and Leopold (1939–49), were carried out at a time when no language-acquisition theory was available; for this reason these descriptions, however detailed, tell us very little about the mechanisms involved in L_2 acquisition.

In a number of more recent studies on L_2 acquisition scholars have attempted to describe the evolution of certain specific features in L_2 acquisition over a period of time. Because of the large number of studies in this area we will only be able to discuss a few; for detailed reviews see Hatch (1978a, 1983) and McLaughlin (1984, 1987). Wode (1976) summarizes the questions raised in these studies as follows: (1) Does L_2 acquisition follow developmental stages? (2) Are these stages the same for L_1 and L_2? (3) What are the main variables that determine these developmental sequences? For example, do children rely on previously acquired L_1 knowledge? Do target-language structures influence the order of acquisition? On what processes and strategies does the learner rely? To what extent are these processes similar to those used in mastering L_1? Are those processes and strategies universal and similar for all learners? We must point out that the mass of empirical data does not yield clear and unambiguous answers on these issues and that often we are dealing with apparently contradictory evidence. Moreover, many of these studies are longitudinal observations of one or two children and it is difficult to generalize from so few cases; researchers do not always focus on the same linguistic aspects; and observational methodologies are not always comparable across studies. Cross-sectional research, on the other hand, while neglecting to some extent the developmental aspects of L_2 acquisition, enables one to obtain a larger body of data from larger samples of learners on specific features of acquisition.

9.1.2 Developmental stages of L_2 acquisition

A majority of studies agree on the existence of developmental sequences. According to Ellis (1985) there is evidence for the universality of the sequences, although minor differences are reported in the order in which specific features are acquired. Among the most studied features is the acquisition of the AUX system,[2] which includes negatives and interrogatives. Synthesizing the data from some forty cases of learners of English as L_2, Hatch (1983) concludes that the development of, for example, *wh-questions* is similar for all subjects. The following sequence can be observed for ESL: (1) The *wh-word* appears at the beginning of the question followed by declarative word order (e.g. *What you want?*); (2) Inversion of BE appears (e.g. *Who are you?*); (3) BE is used correctly in *wh-questions*; *do-support* appears in *yes–no questions* and emerges shortly afterwards in *wh-questions*.

The universality of developmental stages has also been observed for other features of L_2 acquisition, such as negation, phrase structure, word order, plurality, tense and aspect, determiners and possessive (for a review of these studies see e.g. Dulay, Burt & Krashen, 1982; Hatch, 1983; McLaughlin, 1984). Hatch (1974) examined data from fifteen observational studies of a total of forty children learning L_2 in a natural setting for evidence of L_2 acquisition universals. Generally speaking, she found the following developmental pattern: two-word noun phrases without verb appear first; next come NP + VP, but the verb is unmarked and no AUX is used; then polysemic 'dummy verbs' are used (e.g. *get*); BE follows in the form of *is*; later, aspect appears first in the suffix -ING, but the verb stands alone without AUX, etc. She points out, however, that the order and rate of acquisition of forms in the AUX system vary from learner to learner.

Is the order of acquisition of grammatical features invariant for all L_2 learners? A number of studies, generally referred to as *morpheme studies*, focus on analysing the accuracy of grammatical morphemes in L_2 learners (for a review see, for example, McLaughlin, 1984). Studying the acquisition of a number of English grammatical morphemes (the same as some of the functors[3] used by R. Brown, 1973) by Spanish- and Chinese-speaking children, Dulay & Burt (1973, 1974a, 1975a) concluded that children of different language backgrounds learning English in a variety of host-country environments acquire grammatical morphemes in a similar order. They pointed out, however, that groups of features are acquired rather than one feature at a time and that acquisitions of different features may overlap.

A major difficulty with morpheme studies is that they measure acquisition by the degree to which the morphemes are accurately produced by learners; they therefore measure accuracy of production rather than sequence of acquisition, which is what studies taking a longitudinal approach do. The principal determinant of accuracy order of morphemes in L_2 learners seems to be the frequency of occurrence of these morphemes in L_2 input (McLaughlin, 1984). Furthermore, morphemes might be used in both correct and incorrect contexts and the production of an accurate morpheme may imply that the learner has acquired the form but not necessarily the rule or the function (Hatch, 1983). Wode, Bahns, Bedey & Frank (1978) define L_2 acquisition as a process of decomposing complex structures and rebuilding them step by step; such a process cannot be understood by focussing on discrete morphemes alone.

Adult learners seem to show similar acquisition sequences to those of younger learners. Bailey, Madden & Krashen (1974), studying the acquisition sequence of English morphemes by 73 adults from 12 different language backgrounds, showed that these followed the same stages observed in young learners. Larsen-Freeman (1976) found, however, that in adult learners the order of accuracy varies according to the elicitation instruments employed. Thus, L_2 acquisition sequences seem to be independent of learners' age and mother tongue, but not necessarily of L_2 input.

Ellis (1985) summarizes the developmental aspect of L_2 acquisition observed in the preceding studies by identifying four broad stages of development. The first is characterized by a standard word order and propositionally reduced utterances; in the second stage the learner expands his propositions to include more sentence constituents, and varies word order on the model of L_2;

in the third stage morphemes are used systematically and meaningfully; the final stage consists of complex sentence structures. Throughout the four stages the learner also uses prefabricated routines, as for example, *You shut up!* and *la ferme!*. Frequent use of formulaic speech (Wong Fillmore, 1976) or prefabricated routines (Hakuta, 1976) is a particularity of L_2 acquisition. Formulaic speech consists of expressions learned as unanalysable wholes; it has been suggested in L_1 as well as L_2 research that it is the basis for creative speech when the learner starts analysing these formulae. According to Lightbown (1985) there are predictable sequences in L_2 acquisition in the sense that certain structures have to be acquired before others can be integrated.

Lightbown (1978) remarks that most studies on the development of structures in L_2 have neglected the analysis of the functions in favour of that of the forms. Wagner-Gough (1978) also drew attention to the fact that a L_2 learner, because his cognitive development is relatively more advanced than his linguistic development in L_2, must be content with a small number of linguistic forms to express a large number of semantic and pragmatic functions. In a study of the development of wh-questions in two 6–7-year-old English-speaking children learning French, Lightbown (1978) observed that not only is the sequential development of wh-questions similar to that in L_1, but that the learners use these questions for a larger number of questions than the linguistic forms permit. The most frequently used strategies are: (1) Substitution of known for unknown wh-morphemes; (2) incorrect use of embedded questions; and (3) circumlocution, a strategy in which a grammatical form different from the wh-morpheme is used in its place. She concludes that these strategies are more frequently used by a L_2 learner than by a child developing L_1 because they permit the expression of a degree of cognitive complexity for which the learner does not possess the necessary linguistic forms. Such strategies, therefore, are assumed to be typical of L_2 learning.

9.1.3 L_2 and L_1 acquisition

Because similar order and stages are observed among children and adults of different mother-tongue backgrounds, most authors generally conclude that L_2 acquisition is in the first place controlled by developmental sequences of L_2 and not by the learner's knowledge of L_1. Are these sequences similar to the sequences observed in mother-tongue acquisition? The similarity between L_2 and L_1 development is supported by a number of empirical studies. Comparing the observations made by Hatch (1974) on the acquisition of English as L_2 with that of English as L_1, Wagner-Gough (1975) concludes that the development of questions is identical in L_2 and L_1. These conclusions have been confirmed by other studies as, for example, by Raven (1974) for a Norwegian child acquiring the rules of English and by Milon (1974) for the development of negation in a Japanese child acquiring English. Dato (1971) found evidence with English-speaking children learning Spanish that L_2 syntactic development in general follows the same sequence of rules as L_1 syntactic development: base structures are acquired before transformations. This would suggest that order of L_2, like L_1, acquisition is characterized by an increasing complexity.

However, some authors point out that L_2 developmental sequences may vary as a function of L_1. Hakuta (1976), for example, observed that the order of acquisition of certain grammatical morphemes of English is not the same for all Japanese children learning English but varies from one child to the other. A number of observations point to differences between L_1 and L_2 acquisition. Wode (1978, 1983) concludes from the study of English L_2 acquisition by his four German-speaking children that neither negation nor interrogation is acquired in a similar way in L_2 as in L_1, but that L_2 acquisition is a function of L_1. Similarly, Cancino, Rosansky & Schumann (1974, 1975) concluded that L_2 acquisition is different from that of L_1 by native speakers: for example, for L_2 learners of English the inversion of yes-no questions does not systematically precede the inversion of wh-questions, as is the case for native L_1 learners. Dulay & Burt (1974b) have suggested that the L_2 learner relies on a *creative construction process* just like the child acquiring L_1, that is, he extracts more or less complex rules from the linguistic input. This process is shown by the presence of regularities in L_2 acquisition. The authors' assumption does not necessarily imply that L_2 acquisition relies on L_1 but rather that both call upon a similar process.

How far is the development of L_2 independent of L_1? The evidence on this is contradictory: on the one hand, some points to a minimal dependence, whereas other evidence (e.g. Wode, 1976, 1978; Keller-Cohen, 1979) suggests a relatively important interdependency. As Politzer (1974) noted, the degree of interdependence will vary according to the developmental approach adopted: from a cognitive–developmental point of view the acquisitions of L_1 and L_2 might seem rather different, whereas if the focus is on processes and strategies, there might be a greater interdependence between the acquisitions of L_1 and L_2. Does a L_2 learner rely on his elementary knowledge of L_1 when he is learning L_2 (*regression hypothesis*) or does he recapitulate the learning process of a native L_2 speaker (*recapitulation hypothesis*) (McLaughlin, 1984)? Although most of the evidence (e.g. Wagner-Gough, 1975; Raven, 1974; Milon, 1974) is in support of the regression hypothesis, it is probable that both types of strategies are used to different degrees by different learners.

More recent research on L_2 acquisition processes tends to support the idea that there is an interaction between learning strategies relying on knowledge of L_1, and strategies recapitulating a native speaker's acquisition of L_2. Evidence for L_1 influence on L_2 acquisition comes from a number of studies: Schumann (1982), for example, found that *no + verb form* is more difficult to eradicate for Spanish-speaking learners of English than for other learner groups because the structure exists in Spanish. Similarly, Zobl (1982) observed that Chinese- and

Spanish-speaking children followed different learning strategies in English as L_2 probably because they relied on knowledge of different rules in their respective L_1's.

Zobl (1980) suggests that structural transfer from L_1 is selective along a developmental and a formal axis; the learner will rely in the first place on developmental strategies for learning L_2 while he takes into account the constraints of language universals and of the target language; the formal axis is defined in terms of systems and structures of L_2 that differ from L_1. The developmental process of L_2 acquisition is therefore influenced by formal features of L_2 controlling the relevant aspects of its acquisition, including the activation of L_1 knowledge. In other words, L_1 knowledge can influence L_2 acquisition only after L_2 developmental prerequisites have been met. A crucial prerequisite is a certain degree of similarity between L_1 and L_2 structures and the recognition of this structural similarity by the learner (Gass, 1984). Zobl (1984) proposes that transfer from L_1 occurs when the learner perceives the L_2 rules as fuzzy or ill-defined (for further discussion of transfer, see 9.2.1). L_2 learning strategy may thus be viewed as an interaction between transfer from L_1 and developmental processes; strategies will however also depend on individual differences.

The problem of individual differences in learning a L_2 has been stressed by a number of authors (e.g. Hatch, 1974; Dulay & Burt, 1974b; Hakuta, 1976; McLaughlin, 1984; Ellis, 1985). Interindividual variation is observed regardless of L_1 background and learner's age. These differences seem however to be larger for some structures than for others. Individual differences have been explained chiefly by variations in the learner's cognitive characteristics (aptitude, cognitive style, etc.) and his effective characteristics (attitude, motivation, etc.). Studying five Spanish-speaking children learning English Wong Fillmore (1979) observed important variations in sequence and rate of acquisition of L_2; she attributes these differences to the patterns of interactions between cognitive and social strategies, the nature of the learning task, and personal characteristics.

9.1.4 The social context of L_2 acquisition

Wong Fillmore's (1976, 1979) research stresses the relevance of social factors in L_2 acquisition; according to her the L_2 learner's first task is to establish social relations with his interlocutor. Because he will rely on social cognitive strategies to attain this end, he will be able to learn L_2; by interpreting cues from the communication setting the child begins to guess and understand the other speaker's language and to respond to it. The child will develop the L_2 syntax from this social-interaction situation. The author attributes differences in rate of acquisition mainly to individual differences in social skills. This interpretation is in line with the research on the role of attitudes and motivation in L_2

learning essentially conducted with adolescent and adult learners (discussed in 9.8).

The conversational context of L_2 also plays an important role in L_2 acquisition. Native speakers of L_2, when in interaction with a non-native speaker, simplify the language and make use of foreigner talk (see Chapter 6.2.2). Keller-Cohen (1979) analysed this conversational aspect, and in particular turn-taking. Studying the development of English as L_2 in 4–6-year-old Japanese, Finnish and German-speaking children in interaction with native English speaking adults, she observed that the number of turn-takings under the child's control more than doubled over a period of eight months. The child uses two types of strategies for turn-allocation, either questions or attention-directing utterances, e.g. *look!*. She infers from this that the child must first learn that speaking is turn-taking and turn-allocation for both the child and his interlocutor. She views this aspect as central to L_2 learning.

Peck (1978) also insists on the relevance of social interaction in L_2 acquisition, namely on the role of the child–child discourse, particularly of play involving language. She argues that the child learns the rules of L_2 through discourse produced in social interaction with other children and adults. In the same vein, Hatch (1978b) proposes that discourse analysis of L_2 learning might explain the order of acquisition: there is strong evidence that children develop syntactic forms (*horizontal construction*) out of building conversations with interlocutors (*vertical construction*). The relevance of social interaction has also been stressed by Ervin-Tripp (1974) who found that L_1 interference in L_2 learning was maximum when L_2 was not the language of the social milieu. Although Ervin-Tripp noticed that L_2 learning strategies were similar for all ages, nonetheless older children seemed to have some advantages: they are better at storing longer verbal units, combining new elements of vocabulary, identifying these elements with previously acquired knowledge, and discovering new symbolic relations. These observations raise the question of the optimal age for acquiring L_2.

9.1.5 Optimal age and sensitive period

Another controversial area in L_2 acquisition is that of the optimal age of the learner. It is important to distinguish between studies of L_2 learning in a formal classroom situation, and those of informal L_2 acquisition in natural settings. The former indicate that adolescents and adults learn certain aspects of L_2 faster and with greater ease than children (Burstall, 1975; Snow & Hoefnagel-Hohle, 1978), whereas the latter report the opposite (Penfield & Roberts, 1959). The relative ease with which a young child masters more than one language as compared with the effort expended by an adult in learning a L_2 prompted Penfield & Roberts (1959) to assume that this facility might be attributed to the relatively greater cerebral plasticity of the child. Neuropsychological evidence confirms that hemispheric lateralization for language is not present at birth but will develop during childhood, and that bilingual experience influences this lateralization and its behavioural correlates (for a discussion see Chapter 2.2.5). The relevant questions here are: (1) how far will learning a L_2 influence this neuropsychological development in L_2 childhood acquisition? and (2) how far is L_2 acquisition after neuropsychological maturity different from L_2 acquisition during this period?

Lenneberg (1967) hypothesized the existence of a *critical period* for language acquisition which terminates with neuropsychological maturity, that is, at around puberty. This hypothesis implies that all language acquisition, be it L_1 or L_2, beyond the critical period will be qualitatively different from childhood language acquisition. However, this hypothesis is supported by little empirical evidence, most of it stemming from clinical data. If such a critical period exists, it is not absolute and there are indications that linguistic competence can be acquired and improved after puberty (see, for example, Curtiss, 1977). For this reason Oyama (1979) prefers to refer to a *sensitive* rather than a critical period, that is, a developmental period during which there should be a greater receptivity for language.

The existence of a sensitive period for L_2 acquisition has also been questioned. Positive evidence varies according to the linguistic skill focussed on. There is general agreement that younger children acquire a more native-like pronunciation than older learners (Fathman, 1975; Seliger, Krashen & Ladefoged, 1975). For other skills the evidence is contradictory: older children seem to acquire L_2 morphology and syntax faster than younger ones (Ervin-Tripp, 1974; Fathman, 1975; Krashen, Long & Scarcella, 1979) and are better at auditory comprehension (Asher & Price, 1967). Generally, older learners are faster at acquiring academic-related skills in L_2 (for a review see Harley, 1986). Note, however, that all these studies were conducted in classroom settings and that the L_2 input varies widely across the studies. On the other hand, there is strong evidence that shows that in natural settings early L_2 acquisition is more likely to lead in the long run to native-like competence in all language skills (Seliger, Krashen & Ladefoged, 1975; Oyama, 1976). According to Genesee (1980) younger learners in early immersion programs in French develop a better competence than students in late immersion. Studying the integration of Italian immigrants in an English-speaking environment, Oyama (1976) concludes that the sensitive period extends from 18 months to puberty, a period after which a native-like pronunciation is highly unlikely. Patkowski (1980), however, suggests that the ability to reach native-like syntactic skills may extend as late as the age of 15.

Summarizing some forty studies on the sensitive period for L_2 acquisition, Ekstrand (1981) concludes that there is no clear evidence for a sensitive period and a biologically determined optimal age for L_2 acquisition. According to him the greatest advantage arising from the introduction of a L_2 at an early age rests on the fact that it allows a longer period of learning, starting at a time when the learner has to acquire a smaller linguistic baggage in order to attain native-like competence; therefore, this acquisition is faster. The young child does not have a greater facility for learning, but a less complex task for which he has more time.

For these reasons it is not the assumption about a facilitating sensitive period, but rather the cognitive (see Chapter 2.3) and linguistic advantages linked to early bilinguality, that should enable us to draw conclusions about the optimal age for introducing a L_2. Relatively few children have the opportunity to develop a simultaneous bilinguality; most bilinguals have acquired a L_2 after their L_1, more often than not through educational programs introduced at different age-levels, which will not necessarily lead to a balanced bilinguality. In this case their linguistic output will be different from the native speaker's. In the next section we will review the different approaches to the study of non-native language production.

9.2 Contrastive analysis, error analysis and interlanguages

In the preceding section we discussed the role of L_1 knowledge in L_2 acquisition and asked the question how far the learner's L_2 production might be affected by transfer from L_1. Traditionally, difficulties and errors in L_2 learning were attributed to a transfer of L_1 habits (Lado, 1957). Negative transfer or interference was conceived as essentially interlingual in nature (Corder, 1975). This approach relied heavily on *contrastive analysis* which allegedly enabled errors to be predicted, and therefore, prevented (James, 1980).

9.2.1 Contrastive analysis, transfer, interference and error analysis

Based on a behaviourist model, contrastive analysis is founded on a number of assumptions on language learning: (1) language learning is a set of habit formation, that is, a response is automatically associated with a given stimulus; and (2) an established set of habits (in L_1) either facilitates or impedes the establishment of a new set (in L_2). This last assumption prompts the notions of transfer and interference. In its most extreme form contrastive analysis claims to predict all errors in L_2 from a comparison between L_1 and L_2; in its weak form it only makes a claim to explain a limited number of errors without predicting them (Wardhaugh, 1970) and thus attributes a limited role to the influence of L_1 (Ellis, 1985).

The reliance on contrastive analysis in L_2 teaching methodology has been criticized by a number of scholars because it can only predict a limited number of errors (Richards & Sampson, 1974); it makes false predictions (Nickel, 1971); furthermore, there are serious theoretical difficulties in comparing the grammatical structures of two different languages (Hamp, 1965; van Buren,

1974). As a result of these criticisms contrastive analysis has been neglected as a predictive device for L_2 errors. More recently, however, it has been re-evaluated. As Sridhar (1981) points out, interference may be a learner's strategy and L_1 knowledge can serve as input to L_2 learning; for instance, when a learner experiences difficulties in L_2 because of a lack of resources he may borrow from L_1. Corder (1981) suggests replacing 'interference' by 'intercession', thereby focussing on a communication strategy rather than on a learning feature. The use of L_1 knowledge in L_2 learning strategies might be the manifestation of a general psychological process, that is, the reliance on previous knowledge to facilitate new learning (McLaughlin, 1984).

Transfer and L_1 interference will not be used to the same extent by all learners. While it has been suggested by Zobl (1980) that knowledge of L_1 can be transferred to L_2, the extent to which this strategy is used will vary from learner to learner and from situation to situation. It tends to be maximized when the learner has little contact with L_2 speakers in natural settings (Ervin-Tripp, 1974); this is particularly the case in foreign-language teaching in the classroom. Under certain conditions the learner's L_1 will determine the kind of errors made in L_2 learning; transfer from L_1 will occur particularly when the L_2 rules are unclear (Zobl, 1984). Because of this evidence L_1 transfer cannot be excluded in the processes involved in L_2 acquisition. As Ellis (1985) points out, in understanding L_2 learning 'contrastive analysis needs to work hand in hand with error analysis' (p. 24).

Advances in developmental psycholinguistics, in particular studies of L_1 and L_2 acquisition, have drawn attention to a type of errors that cannot be attributed to L_1 interference, but seem rather to stem from the acquisition process itself. They are called *developmental errors* or *intralingual interference* (Richards, 1971). Analysing L_2 learners' errors, Richards (1974) concludes that they are caused by overgeneralization, ignorance of rule restrictions, incomplete application of the rules, or by developing false concepts about L_2. Because the same errors are committed by L_2 learners from different L_1 backgrounds (Buteau, 1970; Richards, 1971), they cannot be attributed to L_1 interference. This approach assumes that L_2 acquisition is a creative process, similar if not identical to L_1 acquisition, but relatively independent from the latter (Corder, 1967). In this case L_1 cannot be the cause of the majority of difficulties and error analysis must be approached from a developmental angle.

9.2.2 *Interlanguages*

The merit of this approach is to have drawn attention to the psychological processes underlying L_2 learning and their linguistic manifestations, i.e. *interlanguages*. Selinker (1972) suggested that an interlanguage is a separate linguistic system resulting from the learner's attempt to produce the target language. For him interlanguage is an intermediate system composed of rules built on different strategies, e.g. simplification, overgeneralization and transfer. At any given time, an interlanguage is a complex of different types of rules. In this sense, L_2 acquisition is a cognitive learning process, and proficiency in L_2 is the expression of a competence rather than the ability to answer a given stimulus with a set of responses (Corder, 1975). Interlanguage is a series of approximative systems which evolve and resemble more and more the system used by native speakers.

9.2.2.1 *Interlanguage, fossilization and pidginization*

However, stable varieties of approximate systems can be identified, as for example in the case of a L_2 spoken by certain immigrants who seem to have reached a threshold in their L_2 proficiency. Selinker (1972) calls this phenomenon *fossilization*. This fossilized system is intermediate between L_1 and the target language. The rules used in this interlanguage stem from three different sources: mother tongue, acquired knowledge of target language, and cognitive processes of L_2 learning (Selinker, 1971). Therefore, the errors produced are caused partly by developmental processes, partly by an incomplete knowledge of L_2 rules, and partly by L_1 transfers. Fossilization does not occur in L_1 acquisition; it exists when the learner's interlanguage ceases to evolve towards native-like norms, regardless of the L_2 input. Although fossilization occurs essentially with adult learners, Selinker, Swain & Dumas (1975) extended this to younger learners as well; it develops primarily when native speakers of the target language are absent, as for example in French immersion schools in anglophone Canada.

Early L_2 acquisition which fossilizes has been described as analogous to the process of pidginization. By pidginization authors like Schumann (1978a) and Andersen (1981) refer to an interlanguage with several features characteristic of pidgins, i.e. simplification and reduction. As in the case of pidgin formation (see Chapter 7.3.4), L_2 learners have a limited access to native input. Late L_2 acquisition is seen as analogous to the process of depidginization to the extent that learner output tends to approximate more and more to the target-language norms. According to this approach L_2 acquisition occurs on a pidginization–depidginization continuum. The merit of these analogies is to stress the dynamics of interlanguage. In our view, however, an interlanguage is an approximate system which shares certain features with pidgins but not all of them: a pidgin is a relatively stable system of verbal communication developed by a group of people who do not share a language in common, whereas an interlanguage is a changing language, acquired by an individual trying to approximate to a target language in order to interact with native speakers. Even in the case of an ethnolinguistically homogeneous group of people learning a L_2, e.g. migrant workers in Western Europe (see Meisel, 1977; Klein & Dittmar, 1979), their interlanguage cannot be labelled a pidgin because the group shares a common L_1, there is a L_2 target and there is no extreme isolation from native speakers of L_2. For these reasons we prefer the terms 'interlanguage' and 'fossilization' to 'pidginization–depidginization'.

9.2.2.2 *Interlanguages and universals*

Because fossilization does not occur in L_1 acquisition, this does not mean that interlanguage is different from natural languages; on the contrary, the basic assumption underlying interlanguage is that the linguistic system of L_2 learners is that of natural languages and is constrained by linguistic universals. Ellis (1985) specified two hypotheses concerning the role of linguistic universals in interlanguages: (1) implicational universals predict the order of appearance of L_2 features in interlanguage, and therefore (2) L_2 learners acquire unmarked properties before marked properties. A small number of studies seem to support these assumptions. Schmidt (1980), analysing deletion in English coordinate structures produced by L_2 learners from different language backgrounds, concluded that L_2 acquisition obeys natural language universals and that the unmarked items are acquired before marked ones. In a study of the acquisition of relative clauses in English by adult L_2 learners from various L_1 backgrounds, Gass (1979) concluded that the implicational ordering of rules predicts accuracy order.

Empirical evidence, however, is still scarce on this issue, and what little there is is controversial. The concept of markedness is ill-defined: it is not clear whether it is a linguistic or a psychological concept, nor whether it has psycholinguistic reality. It can be assumed that the role of universals is more complex in L_2 than in L_1 acquisition; L_2 acquisition involves linguistic knowledge stemming from two sources, the target language and the learner's mother tongue. A number of questions remain unanswered. Which aspects of interlanguage are constrained by universals, which by the specificity of L_1 and L_2 and which by the context of learning? Which universals are specific to characteristics of L_2 acquisition, such as transfer? How do language universals interact with the learning processes?

9.2.2.3 *Psychological processes and context in interlanguage*

It has been suggested that two different types of cognitive structures are used in the internalization of grammatical rules; in one type they are automatic and spontaneous, without conscious awareness of the rules, in the other there is a conscious effort on the part of the learner to internalize the rules (Lambert, 1966; Lawler & Selinker, 1971). Although both psychological processes come into play in L_2 learning, they will do so to different extents; this prompted d'Anglejan (1978) to make a distinction between formal and informal learning contexts. Krashen (1981) further introduced a systematic distinction between *acquisition* and *learning*. For him it is no longer the setting *per se*, but the conscious attention paid to linguistic rules, that separates acquisition from learning. He defines acquisition as a subconscious process with implicit rule internalization in which attention is paid to meaning rather than to form, similar to mother-tongue acquisition; learning, on the other hand, is conscious, with explicit internalization of rules and attention to forms, typical of classroom instruction.

Tarone (1979, 1982) defines interlanguage as a set of rule-governed styles ranging along a continuum which varies according to the degree of attention given to speech forms by the learner: at one end there is a standard variety which corresponds to the L_2 used in the classroom; at the other end is the vernacular in which the speaker does not focus attention on language forms. From the empirical evidence the author argues that interlanguage output varies systematically with context and task. Felix (1981) observed that there was less L_1 interference in the spontaneous speech of L_2 learners than in their more formal speech; some structures occurred only in spontaneous speech, in which the order of acquisition was different from that of the speech produced in the classroom; in experimental settings L_2 learners produced grammatical structures which never occurred in their more spontaneous speech. Felix interpreted this evidence as proof that the classroom situation compels the learner to go beyond his competence, thereby encouraging the production of errors and the reliance on his knowledge of L_1. Interlanguage and error analysis studies should therefore concentrate on both formal- and informal-learner language behaviour.

9.2.2.4 Acquisition versus learning?

The acquisition–learning distinction led Krashen (1981) to postulate the existence of a *monitor*, that is, a control system which can modify or correct spontaneous output and relies essentially on learning. For Krashen 'the fundamental claim of monitor theory is that conscious learning is available to the performer only as a monitor' (p. 2); L_2 output is initiated by acquisition and learned components serve only as a monitor which alters the output, given enough time, and focus on form. The use of the monitor is optimal when it acts as a complement to unconscious internalization of rules (acquisition) and when it does not interfere with spontaneous output. An excessive use of the monitor will lead to a L_2 output closer to the standard, but will impede spontaneous communication in a natural setting. A limited use of the monitor, while not preventing communication, will result in a fossilized interlanguage.

The monitor is part of a more general model proposed by Dulay & Burt (1975b) in which L_2 learning is viewed as a creative construction. This model proposes that linguistic input is processed through three internal mechanisms: the filter, the organizer and the monitor. The first two are subconscious while the third one is conscious. The filter refers to the affective factors which first select elements from the linguistic input; selected elements are then processed by the organizer, a language-specific unit which gradually builds up the rules of the new language system and permits the organization necessary for the linguistic output; finally, the monitor, an internal system responsible for conscious linguistic processing, can modify the L_2 output. These three mechanisms are also influenced by personality and L_1 knowledge factors (Dulay, Burt & Krashen, 1982).

The monitor model has been criticized on a number of points. For McLaughlin (1978, 1987) the main difficulty with this model stems from the acquisition–learning distinction. The distinction between conscious and subconscious processes has never been clearly defined and is not testable. The claim of the monitor model that acquisition and learning are entirely separate and that learning does not become acquisition has been challenged by a number of authors. Gregg (1984), for example, remarks that when learned knowledge becomes automatized it is available for spontaneous speech. Skehan (1984) points out that the monitor model ignores what we know of skill formation in psychology, which stresses the role of conscious learning mechanisms in the early establishment of complex skills; he further suggests that chunks of linguistic input, such as idioms and formulae, play a major role in L_2 acquisition which is completely ignored by the model. A criticism of the general theoretical approach comes from McLaughlin (1978, 1987), who claims that a L_2 learning model should focus on behavioural acts and should be empirically falsifiable. Generally speaking, the supporting evidence for the monitor model is weak and not easily obtainable. Given the present state of theorization we think it premature to attempt to construct a L_2 acquisition model on discrete psychological concepts as vaguely defined as acquisition and learning.

9.3 Communicative competence

Whatever the nature of the internal mechanisms relevant to L_2 acquisition, their relevance will be partly determined by the linguistic input, and it may be assumed that formal and informal learning will not rely to the same extent on the different mechanisms (d'Anglejan, 1978). For example, knowledge of grammatical rules might help the learner with his production in a classroom situation, thereby improving his formal language output, but will not necessarily be helpful in a situation of communication with native speakers, where he will lack the discourse and non-verbal communication rules and the knowledge of the idiosyncratic peculiarities of the target group. This prompted several researchers to pay greater attention to the development of *communicative competence* in L_2 acquisition.

Communicative competence includes a variety of competences: *grammatical competence*, that is, knowledge of the linguistic code; *sociolinguistic competence*, which refers to the socially appropriate use of the linguistic code; and *strategic competence*, made up of verbal and non-verbal communication strategies that may be called into action when communication breaks down because of deficiencies in the other two (Canale & Swain, 1980). Communicative competence is a concept borrowed from Hymes (1971), who defined it as the native speaker's ability to use and interpret language in a manner appropriate to the social context; it challenges Chomsky's (1965) view of linguistic competence as the knowledge of rules of grammar by an idealized speaker–hearer independent from social context. The merit of the communicative approach is to have maximized informal L_2 input, which seems to be a prerequisite for a native-like acquisition of L_2. It has been criticized for failing to take advantage of the knowledge and skills which language learners bring with them (Swan, 1985). Furthermore, communicative competence should also include the competence involved in communicating cognitively sophisticated knowledge (see Chapter 3.1).

The relative importance of the L_2 learner's individual factors have been stressed in a number of correlational studies. For example, Naiman, Frohlich, Stern & Todesco (1978) attempted to identify the characteristics of 'the good language learner' by correlating a large number of individual factors with achievement in L_2. From this study it appears that individual variables likely to influence L_2 learning are affective and cognitive in nature; they are factors such as intelligence, aptitude, cognitive styles, attitudes and motivations, and certain personality factors. In the following sections we will analyse the role of some of these factors.

9.4 Aptitude and memory in L_2 acquisition

9.4.1 L_2 aptitude

The first individual variables relevant to L_2 acquisition are aptitude variables, that is, variables involved in the cognitive organization necessary for the internalization of L_2. They include general cognitive processes, such as generalization, imitation, analogy, memory, etc. These cognitive mechanisms are relatively well documented and their identification has led to the elaboration of L_2 aptitude tests (e.g. Carroll & Sapon, 1959; Pimsleur, 1966). Language aptitude has been defined as a set of skills similar to intelligence but more specifically related to L_2 competence. Carroll (1965, 1973) identified four major components of L_2 aptitude: phonemic encoding, grammatical sensitivity, inductive language-learning ability, and memory.

Phonemic encoding is the ability to associate sound and symbol and to discriminate and encode foreign sounds so that they can be recalled later. Jakobovits (1970) observed that the main component of this ability is not auditory discrimination *per se*, but rather the brain's capacity to encode and store auditory information. Grammatical sensitivity is the ability to recognize linguistic functions, to manipulate, organize and produce linguistic forms. Inductive language-learning ability enables the learner to infer from the linguistic input the forms, grammatical rules and patterns specific to a given language. Finally, memory refers to the capacity to learn a large number of associations in a short time. Language aptitude tests are better than verbal intelligence tests at predicting language-learning success. While aptitude is known to be the best predictor of L_2 proficiency, it is fixed at a very young age, it varies from learner to learner, and it is not easily trainable. But if aptitude cannot be modified in the classroom, nevertheless a greater awareness of its role in the learning process enables us to maximize the use of strategies which call on existing aptitude.

Where does L_2 aptitude come from? It has been proposed that aptitude tests draw on skills used in decontextualized language (Skehan, 1986). From the latest research on literacy it seems that skills used in decontextualized language, which are predictive of academic success (Wells, 1985a), are developed in early childhood from the verbal interaction between a child and the adults around him (see Chapter 3.1.7). In the follow-up study of 53 adolescents who at the ages of 15–60 months had participated in a research project on L_1 development (Bristol Study, see Wells, 1985b), Skehan demonstrated that foreign-language aptitude and achievement correlated with certain patterns of relations between variables relevant to L_1 development. L_2 aptitude measures correlate significantly with syntactic L_1 measures (e.g. MLU)[4] taken in early childhood; L_1 comprehension and vocabulary measures are powerful predictors of L_2 aptitude; thirdly, family background indices, such as parental education, quantity of adult reading to the child, and literacy-oriented behaviour at home seem to play an important role in the development of aptitude; finally, a different pattern of childhood L_1 indices correlates with L_2 proficiency tests. The author concludes that L_2 aptitude is a hybrid combining a language-processing ability with a capacity to handle decontextualized language. Thus, L_2 aptitude can be traced to general language experience at an early age (this has already been discussed in Chapter 3.3 in relation to early bilinguality).

9.4.2 Memory variables

Another important psychological mechanism relevant to L_2 acquisition is memory, in particular the verbal storage necessary for L_2 behaviour. This is a well-documented psychological field for which we have adequate operational models (see Chapter 4.2.2). The application of a model of bilingual memory to L_2 learning and teaching, and the results of such an application, are the object of this section. In Chapter 4.2.3 we presented the bilingual form of the dual-coding model, developed by Paivio & Desrochers (1980); in this model access to semantic storage is achieved by a twofold channel, namely through imagery and verbal coding. In the bilingual-memory there are two verbal codes. In Paivio & Desrochers's (1979, 1980) perspective, access to a double coding in L_2 vocabulary learning facilitates the storage and enables a better acquisition of the target-language vocabulary. Within this theoretical framework the two authors have developed a mnemotechnic which maximizes the access to double coding by using both verbal coding and imagery.

Although mnemotechnics have been known and used since ancient times, it is only recently that they have been systematically experimented with in L_2 acquisition research. In order for a verbal-mnemonic technique to be efficient two steps are required: (1) the overlearning of the code to be used and (2) the establishment of a link between the mental image evoked by the code and that evoked by the trigger word. The mental image as a support for L_2 vocabulary learning has been used in several techniques such as the *key-word* technique (Atkinson & Raugh, 1975; Atkinson, 1975; Raugh & Atkinson, 1975) and the *hook-word* technique[5] (Paivio, 1978; Paivio & Begg, 1981; Paivio & Desrochers, 1980). Whereas in the key-word technique a L_1 word is used to create an acoustic and imagery link with the translation equivalent in L_2, the hook-word technique, on the other hand, relies on overlearned L_2 hook-words which can easily evoke images; they permit the establishment of a link between acoustic or graphemic units and imagery. Paivio & Desrochers (1980) demonstrated the superiority of this technique over others in vocabulary acquisition and concluded that imagery increases comprehension and recall of words in L_2.

However, these mnemonic techniques have their own limitations. Hammoud (1982) comments that they present translation equivalents as synonyms; they help to memorize items in L_2 but not to understand the cultural context of these items nor their meaning in the target language. This is particularly important for abstract words and for learning the L_2 of a very different culture where translation equivalents often denote very different realities. Hammoud has elaborated an association-field technique in which she asks learners to create images for themselves from associations in both target and mother tongues. Like the hook-word method, this technique (designed for francophones learning Arabic) calls upon mental imagery and aims at the enrichment of the imagery and verbal-associations process; it also stresses the cultural differences between the meanings of translation equivalents.

Hammoud (1983) compared her association-field with traditional rote-learning and hook-word technique (with francophones learning Arabic in a classroom situation in Quebec), and found a highly significant superiority of this technique over the other two. In this technique the learner receives first the verbal associations of the L_1 translation equivalent of the L_2 target word; next, the learner is invited to create a mental image and discover the L_1 word;

then, he receives the L_2 translation equivalent (target word) and is asked to repeat it and to associate it with the mental image he has created; finally, he receives the most frequent verbal associations in the target language and is asked to enrich his mental image by creating new images resulting from both associative networks. It has been observed that the more extensive the associative field of a word, the higher the imagery and the easier the learning of that word (Paivio, Yuille & Madigan, 1968). The technique is valid for abstract as well as for concrete words, since abstract words can be concretized through their associations and the images evoked by these. One important advantage of the method is that the target vocabulary is set in its cultural context.

Both the hook and the association-field techniques rely on the double-coding theory and show how theorizing in experimental psychology can be applied to L_2 acquisition. But they also point to the complexities of such an application. They illustrate how L_2 teaching methodology can successfully make use of our knowledge of a well-documented psychological process like memory for a specific linguistic level. This is a good example of how psychological science can be helpful in L_2 learning, provided it is used in designing specific techniques for developing specific skills. The complexity and variety of psychological mechanisms involved in L_2 learning suggest that no single psychological theory will embrace all aspects of second-language acquisition.

9.5 Communication modes

The advantage of relying on information processing in L_1 and in L_2 for L_2 acquisition has also been demonstrated in a study of modes of communication. Testing how use of L_1 scripts and dialogues in audiovisual media might improve L_2 processing, Lambert (1986) showed that bimodal input (dialogue with subscript) is superior to unimodal input (either dialogue or script), provided that the bimodal input is bilingual. A unilingual bimodal input in L_2 does not help the L_2 learner in comprehension of contextual meaning but rather seems to be an overload for his information-processing capacity; a standard bilingual input (dialogue in L_2, script in L_1) is not superior to a unilingual L_1 input, suggesting that in this case L_2 learners rely exclusively on their L_1 decoding; the most interesting finding is that in the reversed bilingual condition (dialogue in L_1, script in L_2) comprehension is superior to all other conditions for advanced students as well as for beginners. The author interprets these findings as evidence that L_2 learners process L_1 and L_2 differently and that dual-access processing can be helpful in developing L_2 teaching methods. Therefore, L_2 methodology should not rely on one mode of communication to the exclusion of the other but should make the most of bimodal bilingual L_2 processing.

9.6 Cognitive styles

It has been suggested that learning strategies of L_2 learners will be influenced by cognitive styles (Richards, 1972; Selinker, 1972). Cognitive style is a choice of, or preference for, particular cognitive strategies; it seems to be a combination of cognitive and affective factors. Its affective dimension stems from the fact that a given cognitive style will always co-vary with personality factors: for example, cognitive styles in L_2 acquisition will vary on an impulsivity–reflexivity scale (H. D. Brown, 1973). Impulsivity is a tendency to respond quickly to a problem while taking the risk of giving the wrong response, while reflexivity is the response style which corresponds to a slow but precise response. Examining the relations between cognitive style and achievement in L_2 reading Doron (1973) demonstrated that reflexive L_2 learners were slower at reading in L_2 but produced fewer errors than impulsive learners.

Another relevant cognitive style dimension is that of field dependency–independency: the independent learner is capable of extracting abstract structures from given information whereas a dependent learner is more influenced by the immediate context. Naiman *et al.* (1978) showed that an independent style is positively correlated with oral comprehension and imitation in L_2; however, this difference has little effect on reading comprehension (Bialystok & Frohlich, 1977). As these results were not replicated at different age-levels the authors concluded that cognitive style is age-related. From a study with university beginners in Spanish as L_2 Hansen & Stansfield (1981) concluded that cognitive style plays only a minor role in overall L_2 acquisition. It has also been suggested that cognitive style may interact with other factors, as for example the source culture of the learner. Wong & Fillmore (1980) showed that L_2 learners from Mexican and from Chinese backgrounds called upon different cognitive styles. The evidence on the role of cognitive styles on L_2 learning is still scarce; furthermore, it is not evident that the relation between cognitive styles and L_2 learning is unidirectional: for example, Scott's (1973) data on divergent thinking in bilingual children (discussed in Chapter 2.3.2) suggest that bilingual experience might help to shape cognitive style. It is premature to conclude in the current state of our knowledge either that cognitive style is an important factor in L_2 acquisition or that differences such as reflexive–intuitive, field dependent–independent or analytical–global will correspond to differences in L_2 acquisition.

9.7 Affective dimensions

Correlational studies, such as for example Naiman *et al.* (1978), have shown that a large number of individual variables influence L_2 acquisition. Schumann (1978b) proposed a typology of 49 factors affecting L_2 acquisition: he distinguishes between social, affective, personality, cognitive, biological, aptitude, personal, input and instructional factors. Whereas the evidence on the role of personality variables is still scarce and the theorization fuzzy (see, for example, the notion of *linguistic ego* developed by Guiora, 1972), the role of other affective variables is better understood; this understanding ranges from attempts at building a theory on the basis of a typology to the designing of social psychological models of the affective processes involved in L_2 acquisition.

One attempt at theorizing on the basis of a typology is Schumann's (1978c) *acculturation model*; for him all the factors mentioned in the typology above determine the degree of *social* and *psychological distance* between the learner and the target language, which in turn determine the degree of *acculturation*. The greater the social and psychological distance between the L_2 learner and the target-language group, the lower the degree of acculturation, and the less the degree of success in L_2 acquisition: in other words, in the case of maximum social distance, the learner will receive minimal L_2 input, while in the case of maximum psychological distance he will fail to exploit whatever input is available. 'Pidginization', or what we prefer to call interlanguage, is the result of persisting social and psychological distance. Schumann's model has been further elaborated by Andersen (1983), who perceives L_2 acquisition as a result of two antagonistic forces, *nativization* and *denativization*: in nativization the learner assimilates the L_2 input to his own L_2 system, whereas in denativization he accommodates his internalized L_2 system to the L_2 input.

Both these models are interesting in so far as they explain why L_2 learners succeed or fail to achieve native-like L_2 competence. They have, however, a number of shortcomings: they do not explain how L_2 is internalized; they lack a social psychological construct and do not account for the interaction between the relevant factors. An unstructured typology of factors cannot be used as a basis for explaining behaviour and we have to turn to theoretical constructs of psychological processes involved in L_2 acquisition in order to understand how a L_2 learner internalizes the target language.

9.8 Affective processes

The most-studied affective dimension of L_2 acquisition is probably 'motivation', including correlated factors such as attitudes, anxiety, ethnocentrism, etc. The focus on this dimension is justified by the fact that it is the second most important set of variables for predicting achievement in L_2, after aptitude (Carroll, 1962). The advantage of motivational variables is that, unlike aptitude, they can easily be manipulated and modified in order to achieve better results in L_2. A first detailed analysis of these variables was conducted by Gardner & Lambert (1959), who suggested that the learner's motivation to learn a L_2 is influenced by his attitudes towards the target group and by his orientation towards the learning task itself. Motivation is defined as the effort that the learner is prepared to make in order to attain competence in L_2, and his desire to achieve this goal. It is essentially a product of the environment and can for this reason be easily influenced by the latter. The influence of the environment on L_2 achievement is mediated through a complex psychological mechanism which we will refer to as the motivational process. Only a better understanding of mediational processes will allow an accurate identification of environmental variables, whose manipulation can lead to greater linguistic, paralinguistic and communicative competence in L_2.

The first mediational model proposed by Gardner & Lambert (1972) is a linear one: attitudes influence motivation which in turn influences competence in L_2. The authors identify two orientations towards the learning task: at one extreme, an integrative orientation reflects the learner's desire to resemble members of the L_2 target group; at the other, an instrumental orientation refers to a set of practical reasons for learning L_2. The first studies on orientations indicated the integrative motive as the more important in the motivational process. Besides the empirical evidence gathered by Gardner & Lambert in support of their model it was also demonstrated that for anglophones learning French in a classroom situation in Western Ontario, integrative orientation was correlated with learners' determination to persist with L_2 learning tasks (Gardner & Smythe, 1975; Clément, Smythe & Gardner, 1978) and with level of activity in the L_2 class (Gliksman & Gardner, 1976).

If integrative orientation appears to be the main determinant of motivation for Anglo-Canadians learning French, this is not necessarily the case for other L_2 learners in other communities. Several studies stress the role of instrumental orientation: it was demonstrated that for francophones learning English in Montreal, instrumental and pragmatic reasons would orientate the learners rather than integrative ones (Gagnon, 1970, 1974; Maréchal, Bourdon & Lapierre, 1973). Lukmani (1972) found similar orientations in Marathi high-school learners of English in Bombay. However, these results are not found for all communities: Clément, Gardner & Smythe (1977b) found integrative and instrumental orientation to be equally important for francophone L_2 learners of English in Quebec; Gardner & Lambert (1972) found similar orientations for Franco-American learners of English in New England.

The existence of a positive link between motivational orientations and achievement in L_2 has not been confirmed experimentally by Oller and his associates (Oller, Hudson & Liu, 1977; Oller, Baca & Vigil, 1977; Chihara & Oller, 1978). Oller & Perkins (1978) conclude that the link between motivational orientations and L_2 proficiency is weak if it exists at all. This criticism has been refuted by Gardner (1980) on the basis of methodological weaknesses on the part of Oller and his associates. Clément & Kruidenier (1983) attribute the disparity between Oller's research and most other studies on motivational orientation to two main sources: (1) the ambiguity of definitions and concepts such as integrative and instrumental orientation in some of the studies and (2) the influence of the language environment on the individual's orientations. As far as ambiguities are concerned, the definitions of integrative and instrumental orientations used by Oller are different from those used by Gardner and colleagues to the extent that the same item used to measure integrative orientation in one set of studies is used to measure instrumental orientation in the other. As far as the cultural and linguistic environment is concerned Gardner & Lambert (1972) remark that in 'settings where there is an urgency about mastering a second language – as there is in the Philippines and in North America for members of linguistic minority groups – the instrumental approach to language study is extremely effective' (p. 114). From the great number of studies supporting the existence of a relationship between orientations and L_2 proficiency it appears that this relationship varies according to the context of acquisition which must be taken into account by a theoretical model of L_2 acquisition (Clément & Hamers, 1979; Gardner, 1980; Clément & Kruidenier, 1983).

In their study of orientations Clément & Kruidenier (1983) identified three aspects of learning context which are relevant to orientation: learners' ethnic group membership, the presence of other ethnolinguistic groups in the community and L_2 status. Group membership influences orientations in so far as integration with a majority group might equal assimilation, whereas integration with a minority group might be a way of maintaining dominance. For these reasons it might be expected that in Canada, for example, the orientations of francophones learning English, and of anglophones learning French, would not be the same. The ethnic composition of the community also plays a role: the learners' orientations will not be the same according to whether they live in a unicultural L_1 environment or in a multicultural setting where the relative status of L_1 and the target language is more visible. Finally, the sociopolitical status of the target language is relevant: in a multilingual country learning the official language as a L_2 is not done for the same reasons as learning a foreign language.

Studying the orientation of francophone high-school learners of English in communities varying in their degree of cultural homogeneity (in the francophone city of Quebec, in the anglophone town of London, Ontario, and in the bilingual community of Ottawa), learning either an official language (French or English) or a foreign language (Spanish), Clément & Kruidenier (1985) identified nine different types of orientation, of which four were common to all groups studied. Generally speaking, L_2 is learned for pragmatic reasons, those included in instrumental orientation, such as better job prospects, but also in order to travel, to create new friendships or to acquire additional knowledge. Other orientations, such as the desire to meet other groups, the recognition of the relevance of a minority, an influence-seeking orientation, an interest in the sociocultural dimensions of the target group, and specific academic interest, were present in certain groups, though not in all. Whereas instrumental orientation was common to all groups, this was not the case for integrative orientation, which was present only in the francophones and anglophones who were learning a foreign language (i.e. Spanish) in a multicultural environment, Integrative orientation, in its purest form, was present only in the anglophone group. The authors conclude that the desire to learn a L_2 in order to identify with members of the target group is found only among individuals who do not feel that their language and culture are threatened and who have experienced close contacts with other ethnolinguistic groups. They further observed that only certain orientations seem to be universal, when L_2 learning occurs in a context of ethnic group relations. For these reasons, it is important to determine which orientations relevant to L_2 can be considered as universal, and which are context-specific.

If, since the first study by Gardner & Lambert (1959), it is evident that motivational orientations are closely linked to attitudes, later research stresses also the relevance of other affective factors. For example, Gardner & Smythe (1975) showed that the motivation of Anglo-Canadian learners of French L_2 is not only a function of instrumental and integrative orientations, but is also associated with more general predispositions, such as ethnocentrism and authoritarianism, as well as L_2 course-specific variables, such as attitude towards the teacher and anxiety over the course. Gardner (1979) demonstrated that in bilingual environments, such as Ottawa, Montreal and Moncton, anxiety is the most important affective factor to predict anglophone learners' proficiency in French, whereas in unilingual environments, such as London, Ontario, motivation is the best predictor of L_2 proficiency. These results confirm the idea developed by Clément & Kruidenier (1983) that social context of learning will at least partly determine the affective dimension of L_2 learning and that anxiety, attitudes and motivation form a complex pattern of interaction which will influence the motivation mechanism. This state of the art has led both Gardner (1985) and Clément (1980) to propose a social psychological model of L_2 learning.

Gardner (1985) proposed a socio-educational model of L_2 acquisition which accounts for most of the empirical research evidence on motivational processes in L_2. The author also makes use of recent developments in causal modelling (Joreskog & Sorbom, 1978) in order to assess the validity of his construct and test the hypothesized causal link. The model (depicted in Figure 9.1) is composed of four classes of variables: social milieu, individual differences, language-acquisition context, and outcomes. The L_2 acquisition process results from a particular causal interplay of these four types of variables. One important feature of the model is that L_2 acquisition occurs in a particular context; it further proposes that attitudes and beliefs of the community concerning language learning, expectations about the nature of L_2 skill development and individual differences will all influence L_2 acquisition. For example, the model predicts that if it is expected that most individuals will learn a L_2,

SOCIAL   LANGUAGE
MILIEU   INDIVIDUAL DIFFERENCES   ACQUISITION   OUTCOMES
                                                                 CONTEXTS

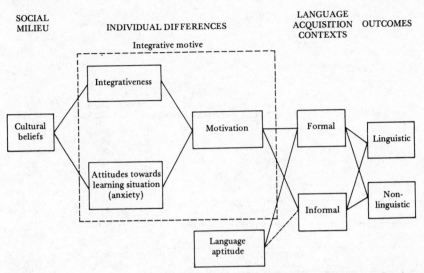

Figure 9.1 Social psychological model of L_2 acquisition (adapted from Gardner, 1985)

then the general level of achievement will be high and individual differences in achievement will be more related to aptitude and intelligence than to other variables. Gardner's approach is conceptually similar to other theoretical social psychological models, but is unique in the sense that it draws heavily on empirical evidence and on the latest statistical techniques.

A slightly different model has been proposed by Clément (1980). It is based on the assumption that there is a close relationship between socio-affective mechanisms in L_1 and L_2. This model is depicted in Figure 9.2. Clément distinguishes between a primary and a secondary motivational process. The primary motivational process, including integrativeness, i.e. the affective predisposition towards the target group, is checked by fear of assimilation, i.e. the fear that learning L_2 may lead to a loss of first culture and language. If the result of these two contrary forces is negative, then motivation to learn L_2 will be low and the learner will not seek contact with the members of the target group. The existence of the primary motivational process has been demonstrated by a number of studies (Gardner & Smythe, 1975; Taylor, Meynard & Rhéault, 1977; Clément, 1978) in which negative correlations were found between fear of assimilation and self-evaluation in L_2, and between fear of assimilation and integrative orientation.

However, in a multicultural setting a secondary motivational process might operate. Gardner (1979) found that in bilingual settings in Canada anxiety to use a L_2 is the best predictor for attitudes and motivation. The resulting force between the desire to integrate and the fear of assimilation will interact with

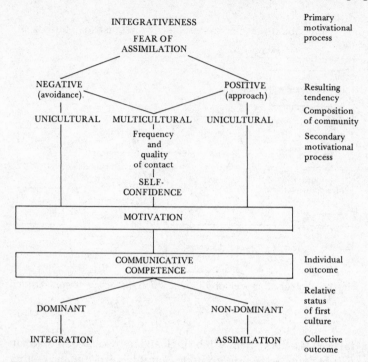

Figure 9.2 Schematic representation of individual motivational processes (from Clément, 1980)

confidence in self to communicate in L_2. This self-confidence is a result of real interethnic contacts. The frequency of these contacts, however, is not sufficient to increase self-confidence, but their quality is overriding (Amir, 1969; Wrightsman, 1972). Frequent and agreeable contacts tend to improve confidence in self to use L_2. According to Clément (1980) the motivation to acquire communicative competence in L_2 is a function of self-confidence and/or the tendency resulting from the primary motivational process, depending on the context. The extent to which each of these variables will be important varies according to the relative status of L_1 and L_2.

This model has recently been tested with 1,180 francophone students of different age-groups learning English in Quebec (Clément & Kruidenier, 1985). The authors made use of a causal-modelling technique in order to verify the causal relationships between the different theoretical constructs utilized. Generally speaking, the results indicated that: (1) integrativeness was inversely related to fear of assimilation; (2) integrativeness and fear of assimilation have an opposite effect on the secondary motivational process; (3) the existence of the secondary motivational process and the causal sequence of contact and self-confidence was supported; (4) the secondary motivational process mediated the effect of the primary motivational process; and (5) self-confidence is defined by language-use anxiety and self-evaluation in L_2 proficiency. Thus, the results support the key psychological processes postulated by Clément and their contextual dependency.

For many years now interethnic contacts have been part of L_2 teaching methodology. What was once an elitist privilege has become more widespread: in several countries exchange programs have been established so that L_2 learners may come into contact with L_2 native speakers in order to improve their proficiency in the second language. As already mentioned, the mere occurrence of contacts is not sufficient to modify attitudes; the contacts have to be positive and agreeable in nature. The central question concerning contacts is the following: 'How can intergroup contacts influence and improve L_2 achievement?' In a number of studies Hamers & Deshaies (1981a, b) evaluated the relevance of interethnic exchange programs on the motivational mechanisms in francophone and anglophone pupils in Quebec. From their studies it appears that even short, one-off visits have a favourable impact on pupils of all ages, even if the type of impact varies with age. For example, for young children interethnic contacts with the target group do not impinge directly on the motivation to learn L_2 but rather on attitudes towards ethnic contacts, whereas for adolescents the exchange has a direct impact on motivation. Identifying the characteristics of relevant contacts Hamers & Deshaies demonstrated that this relevance is a function of the learners' age, their ethnic group membership, their geographical provenance and that of the target group members, as well as their share in the decision-making process. They conclude that interethnic exchanges can be a useful aid to language-teaching methodology, provided that they take into account the specificity of the learning situation and the existing intergroup relations.

When interethnic contacts are not positive, as in the case of many migrant workers' communities in Western Europe, L_2 acquisition may be impeded by these negative contacts. From the *Heidelberg Projekt* in West Germany (Heidelberger Forschungsprojekt 'Pidgin-Deutsch', 1976) it appears that leisure contacts have the highest correlation with syntactic development in L_2. In another German research project with migrant workers (Meisel, 1980) it was suggested that the learners' achievements in the target language (German) depended on two variables: development stage and social psychological orientation. The author proposes that learners vary on a segregative–integrative orientation continuum. The segregative learner is more likely to fossilize than the integrative learner. In this sense, fossilization of the learner's L_2 occurs because of a combination of social and psychological factors.

9.9 Conclusion

In the present chapter we have analysed several theoretical approaches to the psychological processes involved in L_2 acquisition and their possble consequences for L_2 teaching. After discussing the developmental aspects of L_2 acquisition, the existence of developmental stages and the comparison between L_1 and L_2 acquisition, we stressed the relevance of the social context of L_2 acquisition. We further raised the question of the existence of a sensitive period for L_2 acquisition. In a second part we discussed some of the models developed as prerequisites for L_2 teaching methodology, namely contrastive analysis, error analysis and interlanguages. The later part of the chapter addressed the question of some psychological mechanisms of second language acquisition, such as aptitude and memory, cognitive styles, and affective dimensions and processes.

To summarize the present state of the art in theoretical issues in second language acquisition, the following generalizations may be made:

(1) whereas the empirical evidence is somewhat contradictory as to whether L_2 acquisition parallels or differs from L_1 acquisition, most authors agree that there are developmental stages in L_2 acquisition;

(2) recent development in theorizing about L_2 acquisition stresses the relevance of cognitive and social interaction strategies which interact with each other;

(3) there is no general agreement on the existence of a sensitive period for L_2 acquisition; neither is there strong empirical support for it;

(4) errors in L_2 can be attributed either to transfer from L_1 or to different development stages reached by the learner who creates a systematic interlanguage;

(5) universals of language seem to predict the order of appearance of L_2 features in interlanguage;

(6) aptitude for L_2 depends on a general language experience at an early age and a language-processing ability;

(7) psychological processes such as memory, communication modes and cognitive styles all play an important role in L_2 acquisition and should be taken into consideration in teaching;

(8) affective processes are crucial in determining the level reached in L_2 acquisition; while some orientations are universal, others seem to be context-bound; L_2 teaching should not therefore be conducted in isolation from ethnic contacts with L_2 speakers.

In this survey of the different theoretical models of L_2 acquisition we have attempted to identify the most relevant factors while trying to understand how new knowledge on psychological mechanisms can point to new directions in language teaching. We have insisted more especially on the relevance of the affective dimensions in a L_2 acquisition model and its implications for L_2 teaching. We have also emphasized the need for an operational model which takes into account all the relevant factors and the inadequacy of a mere typology of these factors. Finally, we have demonstrated how one theoretical model, i.e. of memory and vocabulary learning, can be operationalized and applied to the language classroom.

In spite of the theoretical progress accomplished in the last decade in L_2 acquisition processes our understanding of how one acquires a second language is still limited. One reason is the degree of complexity of the problem and the large number of psychological, social and linguistic factors involved; a second reason is the difficulty of operationalizing existing theoretical models in a classroom situation; a third reason is the lack of precision and prediction of the models themselves; and, finally, there is an absence of more general theoretical constructs which might link the different relevant factors into a coherent model. Lightbown (1984) suggests that theoretical constructs of L_2 learning should be interdisciplinary and draw on at least five disciplines, that is, linguistics, sociolinguistics, social psychology, neurolinguistics and cognitive psychology.

To conclude, we would like to stress the fact that there is no simple and easy application of theories of L_2 acquisition to L_2 teaching. A pedagogical approach cannot be reduced to a single method but must, on the contrary, combine a large number of different techniques each corresponding to specific aspects of the learning process. Affective and cognitive factors, the influence of L_1, information processing, social context and social interaction, must all be taken into consideration and put to use in L_2 teaching methodology.

10

Interpretation, translation and bilinguality

Translation and interpretation are two tasks which require decoding of a message in one language and its encoding in a different language. This is another field in which bilingual processing mechanisms are relevant; fluent bilinguality is indeed a prerequisite for both professions. Both tasks call for language processing in a source language, that has to be transformed into an output in a target language, while the content of the message is kept intact. Although their goals are similar, the modes of processing are different in translation and in consecutive and simultaneous interpretation. Simultaneous interpretation into and from sign language also achieve the same goals, with the difference that, as Ingram (1985) claims, it is not conversion from an aural message into another aural message, but from a natural spoken language into a natural sign language and vice versa; however, as we limit ourselves to processing of spoken and written language, we will not discuss this issue further.

In translation a source message written in L_A has to be transformed into a written form in the target language L_B. As, in normal circumstances, it does not have to be done under severe time constraints, the translator can rely on a number of supporting techniques such as the use of dictionaries, specialized reference works and a computerized data bank, in order to produce a precise text in the target language which resembles as closely as possible the message in the source language. In interpretation, on the other hand, a spoken message in source language L_A must be communicated orally in target language L_B. In consecutive interpretation , the interpreter listens to the speaker in the source language and awaits a pause or the end of the talk to transmit the message in the target language to the listener; he can call on supporting techniques such as note-taking, thus relying on a written mode to organize his output in L_B, or on computer assistance. In simultaneous translation the interpreter listens to the speaker in L_A, processes the message and produces the output in L_B simultaneously; in other words, he speaks one part of the message in the target language while listening simultaneously to the next part of the message in the source language.

Translation and interpretation differ from each other in more ways than one. The obvious difference is the use of the written versus the spoken mode. In the written mode linguistic forms are different, as the language is entirely decontextualized and the whole message is contained in the text, whereas spoken language relies on non-verbal contextual clues. A written text has been constructed, reread and reconstructed before it reaches the translator, who in turn has time to construct and reorganize the text in the target language. A spoken text, on the other hand, although it is generally more or less planned, displays many characteristics of spontaneous speech: greater use of contextualized language, hesitations, pauses and unfinished sentences produced by the speaker. Time constraints are also important: while decoding the speaker's spontaneous language, the interpreter must simultaneously produce an oral text reflecting the spontaneous characteristics of the source message. Unlike the translator, the interpreter cannot rely on revision, and errors can only be corrected within time limits; there are also a number of phonological and idiosyncratic constraints stemming from each particular speaker. Furthermore, the storage processes, i.e. short-term memory, play an important role in interpretation (Stenzl, 1983). The two activities share a general mechanism of bilingual processing and can only be performed by bilinguals who process the two languages in such a way that the message remains intact while the code is changed. But, because of the constraints imposed by each task, different psychological mechanisms are also called into play. Keeping in mind that research is extremely scarce in the field, we will briefly discuss some of the relevant problems which might lead to a better understanding of language processing in interpretation and translation: (1) simultaneous speaking and listening; (2) memory for text and note-taking; and (3) the link between linguistic skills, bilingual competence and interpretation and translation.

10.1 Simultaneous speaking and listening

Almost all features of information processing are relevant to interpretation. The interpreter is expected to listen to the speaker, dwell on what is being said and implied, extract meaning from talk and gestures, search for deep meaning, store this information so as to relay it to a listener, with as much fidelity as possible, through another language (W. E. Lambert, 1978). What is characteristic of an interpreter is not his bilinguality, which often includes native-like competence in several languages, as much as his capacity to decode a message in the source language while simultaneously re-encoding it in the target language. Because one of the features of language behaviour is turn-taking which implies consecutive alternation between speaking and listening, it is rather exceptional to produce a message while simultaneously listening to another (Miller, 1963).

10.1.1 The role of pauses in simultaneous speaking and listening

Goldman-Eisler's (1968) assumption that interpreters use the pauses in the speaker's discourse in order to minimize the time they have to spend listening and speaking simultaneously has been tested by Barik (1973), who demonstrated that simultaneous interpreters do indeed make a greater use of the speaker's pauses than predicted by chance. Commenting on his study, Stenzl (1982) points out that, as he failed to obtain correlations between the use of pauses and the quality of the interpretation, it cannot be concluded that the pauses are used to make up for the simultaneous processing. She further comments that the use of the pauses forces the interpreter to continuously adjust his output to the speaker's rhythm, and suggests that this adjustment might constrain the interpreter more than simultaneous processing does. However, she did not test this assumption and the question remains unanswered.

Analysing 804 speaker pauses in French and English texts produced as the source language in interpretation, Gerver (1972a) found that 96% of the pauses are shorter than two seconds and almost half of them (48%) last only between 0.25 and 0.50 seconds. He further observed that interpreters spend between 64% and 75% of the total time listening and speaking simultaneously (Gerver, 1972b). Because very little speech can be produced during pauses shorter than two seconds (Gerver, 1976), he concludes that the largest part of the interpreter's task calls for simultaneous processing.

10.1.2 Simultaneous processing and selective attention

As we mentioned earlier simultaneous speaking and listening occurs rarely in everyday life. *Shadowing* is a task commonly used in experimental psychology to explore simultaneous processing of input and output language. In shadowing the subject is required to repeat an incoming message aloud, as he hears it and as accurately as possible (Cherry, 1953); the task is relatively easy and can be performed without errors provided that the incoming message is not too fast and unpredictable (Neisser, 1966). Shadowing is frequently used in studies on selective attention (e.g. Broadbent, 1958; Treisman, 1964), in particular to analyse human capacity to ignore an interfering message or to divide attention between two sources.

Simultaneous interpretation has often been described as shadowing in another language (Neisser, 1966; S. Lambert, 1983). As in all tasks of divided attention, there are two sources of messages in shadowing and interpretation; in both tasks the second source to be attended to is internally generated. As errors in shadowing and in simultaneous interpretation are corrected it can be argued that the output language is attended to (Gerver, 1971). Experiments with shadowing shed some light on the interpretation processes in so far as they permit us to analyse the difficulties of dividing attention between an external source of spoken language and an internally generated message.

Whereas simultaneous processing is not impossible, it is not very frequent in everyday life either; furthermore, the difficulty is increased when both tasks call on the same processing mechanisms. Because simultaneous processing is possible, every information-processing model must provide either a way to store simultaneous information or a device for parallel processing. Neisser (1966) suggested that parallel processing occurs at a pre-attentive level where information which cannot be processed immediately is either stored for later use or rejected. A response can be processed at this pre-attentive level, in which case it becomes an automatism. Welford (1968), for example, describes the interpreter's acquired capacity to ignore his own feedback as an automatism. Automatisms in interpretation are developed through learning and training: Pintner (1969) compared skilled simultaneous interpreters, advanced and beginning student interpreters, with bilinguals with no professional experience in interpreting, for sentence repetition and for responses to spoken questions presented simultaneously with another aural message. She observed that skilled interpreters and advanced students were better at answering cognitively demanding questions than the two groups who did not have training in simultaneous processing. She interpreted these results as proof that the interpreters learned to automatize part of the simultaneous processing and could therefore attend better to the cognitive task.

Simultaneity of information processing, rather than the need to draw on two languages, is the major source of difficulty in interpreting. S. Lambert (1983) compared the effect of four listening conditions on comprehension and information retention: silent listening, listening while shadowing, simultaneous and consecutive interpretation. In a first experiment the messages heard were in French and the retention and comprehension questions had to be answered in English (bilingual condition). Retention was worst in the two conditions calling for simultaneous processing, i.e. shadowing and simultaneous translation, and best in the silent listening condition. However, these results were not confirmed when the responses had to be given in the same language as the listening task (monolingual condition); in this case silent listening was not superior to shadowing. From these results S. Lambert concluded that listening to a language while preparing oneself to respond in a different language calls for a deeper level of analysis than when both tasks are performed in the same language. She further argues that recall of verbal material is facilitated if processing the verbal input calls on a translation task, as is the case in silent listening in the bilingual condition or in consecutive interpretation. On the other hand, recognition, which calls for verbatim encoding, seems to be complicated by a translation activity.

10.1.3 Chunking in simultaneous processing

A typical behaviour observed in interpreters is the segmentation, chunking or parsing of the source language in units-to-be-encoded in the target language. Analysing skilled interpreters who interpreted from English into German or French, Goldman-Eisler (1972) identified three types of chunking of the source language: (1) *identity*, when the interpreter awaits a pause in the speaker's source language in order to encode a complete chunk in the target language; (2) *fission*, when the interpreter starts encoding a chunk before the end of its production by the speaker; and (3) *fusion*, when two or more chunks are fused into one single output unit. These two last types represent 89% of the interpreter's output.

Another important feature of simultaneous interpretation is the ear–voice span (EVS), that is the time between the moment a message unit reaches the ear and the moment it is reproduced in the target language; the length of the EVS equals about four to five words. Goldman-Eisler (1972) identified seven categories of chunks which fit in the time of the EVS: adverbial expressions; NP–VP (noun phrase–verb phrase) without object; NP; VP with an object, adverb, etc.; NP–VP and certain elements of the next phrase; end of a proposition; end of a proposition followed by the beginning of the next one. The majority of the EVS segments consist of at least one predicate and are of the last three types; that is, in chunking the interpreter still produces part of the source-language chunk that preceded the chunk produced by the speaker at the time the interpreter translates. Goldman-Eisler concludes that the interpreter makes use of his own chunking as well as the chunks produced by the speaker; thus segmentation is an active processing which is a function of both languages involved in interpretation.

10.2 Memory for text and note-taking

If simultaneous interpretation is characterized by the co-occurrence of decoding in the source language while encoding in the target language, and therefore calls essentially on the ability to divide attention, the main characteristic of consecutive interpretation is its reliance on memory processes and on the ability to reconstruct a text after a certain delay. Attempting to identify what distinguished the successful student interpreters from those who failed the final examination, Gerver, Longley, Long & Lambert (1980) identified two discriminating factors: (1) a general verbal factor which includes linguistic fluency in terms of speed as well as precision; and (2) a memory factor dealing more specifically with memory for text. The latter is predictive for consecutive interpretation, which relies on memory processes for reconstructing a text, whereas the former is more characteristic of simultaneous interpreters, who have to rely on speed of verbal response and on precision in order to perform their task.

Short-term memory is an important process in simultaneous interpretation because speech production is constantly lagging behind listening (EVS) by four to five words, whereas long-term memory plays a rather minor role. In support of this, Gerver (1976) confirmed that simultaneous interpreters are rarely aware of the interpreted message, once they have completed their task. Long-term memory is, however, not totally irrelevant to simultaneous translation. Speed of translation is facilitated by certain word characteristics stored in semantic memory, such as frequency, familiarity and the similarity between translation equivalents, but not by word characteristics stored in episodic memory, such as emotionality and imagery, which do not affect speed of translation (Murray, 1986). One possible explanation postulated by the author is that when the former variables are high, translation is relatively unmediated and has become automatized.

On the other hand, long-term memory plays an important role in consecutive interpretation, particularly concerning the content of the message. The average delay between source message and target message is around five minutes. Both the delay and the quantity of information that has to be processed during that time call upon memory processes which are different from those called into play by simultaneous interpretation. In consecutive interpretation, speed of translation of words and chunks is less relevant than memory for text.

Memory for prose is not a simple passive reactivation from memory traces but calls on an active reconstruction process from units stored in a conceptual form. This view of memory, put forward by Bartlett (1932), has been further developed by a number of scholars. Kintsch & Van Dijk (1978), for example, propose a memory model of discourse comprehension and production. Their model implies that semantic units are stored after being transformed and organized and are reorganized and transformed when used to reproduce the text. Therefore, the latter can be reproduced in such a way that the semantic content is respected but in a totally different textual form.

In consecutive interpretation, the interpreter listens to five-minute discourse chunks; during that time, while processing the source language, he takes notes, normally in the target language. After listening to the five-minute chunk, the interpreter must reconstitute the text from his own processing and storing and from the notes taken during listening. S. Lambert (1983) analysed the notes taken by final-year student interpreters and observed that these notes vary greatly from one interpreter to the other; each interpreter develops his own system of symbols and individual abbreviations. While translating the notes, the interpreter selects about one third of the information given; some perfectly balanced bilinguals, however, take their notes in the source language. On the whole, it seems that the translation process occurs during note-taking rather than during the production of the reconstituted message in the target language.

Note-taking seems to fulfil a double function in consecutive interpretation. First, it serves as an external storing device; and, second and more important, it contains essential indices for the organization and reconstitution of the text in the target language (di Vesta & Gray, 1972). S. Lambert (1983) compared recognition and recall of text under three listening conditions: one without note-taking; one with note-taking that could be used in the text reconstruction as is normally done in consecutive interpretation; and one with note-taking that could not be used while the interpreter reconstructed the text, and thus served exclusively as an external storage. She observed that when the notes can actively be used in the text reconstitution this will significantly help the recall of a text, whereas when notes can only be used as an external storage device, this will rather hinder recall. This confirms the role of note-taking in the text reconstruction: notes would act as an external tool in active information processing.

Summarizing and recalling a text call upon important cognitive operations in addition to language processing. Long & Harding-Esch (1978) demonstrated that bilinguals, rather fluent in their L_2 but not balanced, produce lower-quality summaries and do not recall texts in their second language as accurately as in their mother tongue: the quantity of information reproduced is smaller, the information is less correct and less relevant; but the amount of irrelevant information is the same. The authors conclude that non-balanced bilinguals are less selective in the choice of the information to be reproduced from a message in their L_2. A limited competence in the source language would limit the choice of information to be retained and thus lead to a lesser quality in organization and restructuring of the message. A high competence in L_2 is a prerequisite for ensuring a high quality in processing L_2; it is a necessary but not sufficient condition to ensure that the relevant information will be selected, organized and stored.

If the application of cognitive processes is likely to be influenced by the competence in the languages which plays an important role in accessing the information, the cognitive operations involved in interpretation are themselves dependent on the earlier development of general processes for the selection and organization of information. Summary and recall tasks, both of them important aspects of interpretation, have a cognitive as well as a language component. Considering language competence as a prerequisite for interpretation, the cognitive dimension of the task should be considered as the crucial factor for information processing by interpreters and translators.

10.3 Information processing in translation and interpretation

It is beyond the scope of this book to present detailed descriptions of models of information processing and their application to translation and interpretation. We refer the reader to general models of information processing such as the ones developed by Massaro (1975, 1978) and Kintsch & Van Dijk (1978) which have been applied to interpretation and translation. Specific models of information processing in interpretation have been developed in recent years: by Chernov (1973), Gerver (1976), Moser (1978), who bases her model for simultaneous interpretation on Massaro's model, and Mackintosh (1985), who proposes a model for consecutive interpretation based on Kintsch & Van Dijk (1978) and Van Dijk's (1980) model of semantic processing and macro-structures.

Adaptation of a general model of information processing implies assumptions about how the message is reproduced in the target language. Moser (1978), for example, using Schank's (1972) semantic-organization model, postulates that the phonological input is first chunked into information segments, which lose their verbal characteristics and are further processed at a semantic–conceptual level. Semantic organization takes the form of a conceptual base that is interlingual and on which linguistic structures in a given language are mapped during understanding. The conceptual basis consists of concepts and the relations between them; a concept is neither a word nor a definition of a word, but rather everything known about it; concepts not only contain language-independent semantic information, but also sensory, phonetic and syntactic information which is language-dependent. Therefore, source- and target-language equivalents may be regarded as stored within the same concept, interconnected by relations. In understanding the source language, the interpreter connects words with conceptual constructions in memory which, in turn, activate the connection with the target language. The more intra- and interlanguage connections exist, the easier the activation process, or, in other words, the more the interpreter knows about the concept the easier the interpretation. However, as Mackintosh (1985) points out, Moser does not address the question whether there is an additional processing load stemming from operating in two languages.

Mackintosh (1985) applied Kintsch & Van Dijk's (1978) and Van Dijk's (1980) model to interpretation processes. In this semantic processing model for comprehension and production three sets of operations are postulated: (1) organization of the text into a coherent whole; (2) condensing the full meaning of the text into its gist; and (3) generating a new text from the memory traces of the comprehension process. The model assumes that the surface structure of a discourse is interpreted as a set of propositions, some of which are present in the surface structure and others inferred from prior knowledge and from the context. Macro-rules of processing are applied in order to transform the micro-structures into macro-structures. Note-taking in consecutive interpretation corresponds to 'a schematic notation of the semantic features of the discourse resulting from the application of macrorules to the micropropositions of the original message' (p. 40); the notes then reproduce the resultant macro-propositions. In reconstructing the message in the target language, the interpreter applies the macro-rules in inverse direction. In simultaneous interpretation completely processed chunks are produced while incoming segments are being processed; in consecutive interpretation these processes are separated in time. Although, as Mackintosh observes, the model accounts fairly well for consecutive interpretation, it tells us very little about a possible additional load stemming from the language-switching operation required by translation; there are some indications that the two-language load increases the complexity of the task (Mackintosh, 1983) but further empirical evidence is needed to determine the nature of this complexity.

From this discussion it appears that translation and interpretation must be viewed in terms of general information processing and text comprehension. This view is also taken in recent linguistic theories on translation. De Beaugrande (1987) views meaning as a control process, that is it limits indeterminacy: 'to understand a thing is to control it in the sense of placing limits upon the set of things it can be or can be related to' (p. 10). Translation is also viewed as a control process more complicated than understanding; however, this complexity is not additive and translation cannot be viewed as twice as complex because two languages are involved. Translation involves control sharing between two sets of language categories. It is this control-sharing ability that makes translators and interpreters different from other fluent bilinguals.

10.4 The interpreter's linguistic skills and bilingual competence

If most professional interpreters and translators are highly proficient in several languages, rare are those who are perfectly balanced in two, let alone in three or four languages. This will generally happen when the interpreter is also an infant bilingual, which is not the case for the vast majority. Generally speaking, an interpreter masters one, sometimes two, active languages and several passive ones, i.e. languages which he understands perfectly but in which his production is not native-like (Longley, 1978). Traditionally, training in European and American translators' and interpreters' programs teaches to translate from a passive to an active language. However, as we mentioned in the preceding section, decoding from a passive language in which one is not highly fluent might impair the organizing processes required for reconstructing the text in the target language. How 'passive' a passive language can be is a question that remains to be explored. Highly developed language skills in each of their languages is an important prerequisite for translators and interpreters, even though translation requires verbal and cognitive skills which are totally unrelated to proficiency in specific languages.

Carroll (1978) attempted to identify the verbal factors relevant to translation and interpretation. In addition to cognitive factors, a verbal intelligence factor and a general culture factor, he identified four verbal-fluency factors: word fluency, i.e. the ability to manipulate orthographic materials such as prefixes; ideational fluency, i.e. the facility to call up ideas; expressional fluency, i.e. the ability to think rapidly of appropriate wording of ideas; and associational fluency, i.e. the ability to produce words from a restricted area of meaning. Carroll further observed that these fluency factors are independent of verbal intelligence and relate to an ability to store, retrieve and manipulate elements of information. This fluency should be linked to personality traits such as extraversion and exuberance (Cattell, 1971).

If most scholars agree that a certain level of bilinguality is a prerequisite for translation and interpretation, no conclusions can yet be drawn concerning the fact that one type of bilingual might be more suitable to perform these tasks. Only a few speculations have been expressed but there is an evident lack of empirical evidence to support any of them. Andersen (1976), for example, argued that a coordinate bilingual would make a better interpreter than a compound one, on the grounds that a coordinate bilingual possesses two cognitive units, one for each translation equivalent. This argument is, however, weak: if the compound bilingual possesses only one cognitive unit corresponding to two translation equivalents, he can still be aware of the degree of overlap between the two translation equivalents. To date, there is no evidence which permits us to conclude that coordinate bilinguals might make better translators than compound ones, and vice versa. More interesting perhaps is the type of experimental evidence stemming from studies on information processing in bilinguals. For example, if, as was discussed (see Chapter 2.2.3), infant bilinguals tend to prefer semantic processing to phonetic processing when the task allows it, as compared with adolescent and adulthood bilinguals, this might help them to perform the cognitive tasks required by translation and interpretation. This, however, is still speculative and more empirical evidence is required before we can reach more positive conclusions.

It is frequently stated that infant bilinguals make good translators. However, no empirical evidence supports this assumption. Harris & Sherwood (1978) observed that infant bilinguals develop very early the capacity to translate from one language into the other while retaining the meaning of the message. How far this capacity can be used in the information processing required by interpretation and translation is not yet known. Are the abilties of the social bilingual comparable with those of the professional bilingual? They both share a bilingual competence, but, as we have already observed, translation and interpretation call for special cognitive operations; so far, we can only be sure that what social bilinguals bring to interpretation is their flawless bilinguality. Whether the social bilingual has developed other abilities likely to help the translation task remains an open question.

10.5 Conclusion

In this chapter we have briefly discussed some of the issues concerning a specific form of bilingual behaviour, namely translation and interpretation. We

first reviewed the most salient features of interpretation, namely the simultaneity required between two processing mechanisms and its consequences for
language processing, such as the use of pauses and chunking. We further discussed the importance of memory processes in interpretation and analysed the
role of note-taking in consecutive interpretation. We then looked at the
attempts to develop models of processing in interpreters, consistent with more
general models of information and text processing. The issues of the interpreters' linguistic skills have been touched upon and we ended this chapter by
raising the question of what makes the interpreter different from the fluent bilingual.

Many issues have not been discussed in these few pages, either because we
lack the required information and the necessary evidence or because they call
for too detailed analysis which is beyond our scope. For example, we did not
discuss personality variables in interpreters because too little is known about
the subject. The 'interpreter's personality' is at present more a myth than a
psychological reality, even though there are some indications about a link
between certain personality traits and the ability to translate. Gerver (1976)
demonstrated, for example, that the ability to interpret under stress conditions
co-occurs with anxiety factors; however, we have no indications as yet whether
anxiety promotes or is promoted by the ability to translate. The link between
personality traits and the ability to translate remains to be explored.

Artificial intelligence and computer translation are also domains where
studies of interpretation have some relevance: a model for parsing a natural
language developed in artificial intelligence work might shed some light on
chunking by interpreters, and vice versa; translation computers have benefit-
ted from ideas such as frames and schemata, or from concepts that view comprehension as mapped by a general knowledge-based procedure which
imposes a top-down coherence on verbal input (Wilks, 1975, 1981). In turn,
translation theories have benefited from recent developments in theories on
natural-language processing.

A psycholinguistic theory of translation and interpretation must be consistent with a larger framework of information processing in general and with
models of bilingual processing; it must also explain all forms of translation,
including sign language interpretation. The task required by interpretation is
in the first place a complex cognitive activity of information processing which
also calls into play high competences in two or more languages. What makes
the translator or the interpreter distinct from other bilinguals is neither his
fluency in several languages, nor his bilingual competence, but his ability to
use them in complex information-processing activities.

In conclusion

This book has attempted to present the state of the art in our present knowledge about bilinguality and bilingualism. Throughout our discussion it has been apparent that the issues and the problems raised by these phenomena are of a degree of complexity such that we are only beginning to appreciate the magnitude of the task. All along we have stressed the need to approach the study of languages in contact from multiple and complementary perspectives. We had hoped that an interdisciplinary approach might be possible; unfortunately, we have been compelled to admit that all we had was, at best, a series of different disciplinary approaches which we might attempt to integrate, without however pretending that this could pass for interdisciplinarity. But there are definite areas of the field which can already benefit from such an integration and in this conclusion we will attempt to give an overview of the book in terms of the different levels of analysis and multiple perspectives which we need to consider in order to understand the varied and complex phenomena of bilinguality and bilingualism.

We have examined the phenomenon of language in contact at three different levels of analysis: individual, interpersonal and intergroup. Because we are interested in language behaviour, the linguistic aspect is present at all levels though differently focussed at each level. We first examined the different facets of bilingual development. At this level of analysis it was found necessary to integrate developmental, neuropsychological and social cognitive approaches. Whenever some explanation attempted to integrate two or more levels, this led to some improvement in our theorizing: for example, when Lambert (1974) integrated the social cultural and the cognitive dimensions in his model of bilingual development, this accounted for the contradictory results on the consequences of early bilingual experience. In our own social cognitive model of bilingual development we attempted to integrate a social cognitive model of linguistic development with a social psychological model of representation and a social-network approach. We viewed the social representations and the social networks as the interface between the individual and the social vari-

255

ables, thereby trying to integrate a micrological level of analysis with a macro-logical one.

A different perspective is taken when bilinguality is analysed at an inter-personal level. The development of the bilingual's cultural identity was ana-lysed in terms of its salient characteristics and the cultural features of the society. We attempted to bring together social psychological views with socio-logical constructs, like ethnolinguistic vitality and social networks, to explain behaviours such as attitudes, enculturation and deculturation, cultural per-ceptions and speech accommodation. We consider the linguistic behaviour of the bilingual as the result of social and psychological factors. Code-switching, for example, is a linguistic phenomenon which can be understood only if we consider and integrate neuropsychological, individual, interpersonal, inter-group and societal factors. Behaviour in interpersonal interaction can be accounted for along a continuum varying from being fully determined by interindividual relationships to being fully determined by the individual's re-spective membership of ethnolinguistic groups. This approach calls for an integration of a social psychological level of analysis with a social level of inter-group behaviour.

In the contacts between ethnolinguistic groups we saw how group member-ship was defined not objectively but subjectively, from inside by ingroup mem-bers and from outside by outgroup members. In an attempt to bridge the cenceptual gap between social structural factors and the individuals' percep-tions of these factors social psychologists of language have developed the con-struct of subjective ethnolinguistic vitality. But beliefs about society, its social structure and dynamics were shown to be just as important as knowledge about social reality. According to the type of group power relations different linguistic relations will develop, such as diglossia, language shift, pidginiza-tion or decreolization, and changes in the social structure will bring about changes in the relations between languages and in speakers' responses to these changes.

While it is possible up to a point to isolate any one aspect of bilinguality or bilingualism in order to analyse the phenomenon, any field of application, be it bilingual education, second language acquisition or interpreting, must con-sider the totality of the phenomenon. For example, bilingual education must take in developmental, cognitive, social structural, cultural, pedagogical and linguistic factors. Similarly, second language methodology must take into account the various dimensions of second language acquisition, from the social affective processes to the relevant information-processing mechanisms and representations. In interpretation, while the specificity of information process-ing, such as simultaneous speaking and listening, is the most distinguishing characteristic of this activity, other aspects such as the social cultural group membership of the participants, discourse, linguistic skills and bilingual com-petence, all play an important role in the execution of the task.

Students of languages in contact, whether at the individual, interpersonal or intergroup levels, commonly address the issues from one narrow disciplinary perspective, using either a micrological or a macrological type of analysis. In order to capture the totality of this complex phenomenon it is essential not only to examine it from different disciplinary viewpoints but also to integrate these various viewpoints both at the theoretical and the methodological level in order to design interdisciplinary models. Because of the magnitude of the task no interdisciplinary team has yet made the attempt and succeeded. Studies of binguality and bilingualism are unidisciplinary, at best multi-disciplinary, hardly ever interdisciplinary.

At the present time there is a lack of theorizing in the field of research in languages in contact. There is a glut of data gathering on the subject which is not productive because, as with all observed facts, they are ambiguous unless they can be organized in an interpretative framework. As Clément (1987) rightly comments, 'results are only interpretable in the context of the rationale justifying the choice of the chosen observational paradigm' (p. 4). Examples of uninterpreted data are innumerable in studies on bilingualism, from recording bilingual child biographies to amassing statistical data on speech communities; these only become useful once they can be interpreted in terms of a theoretical model. Typologies should not be confused with an interpretative framework: putting the data into boxes helps only if the boxes have been assigned a function within a theoretical construct with predictive power. For example, gathering data on 'who speaks what language to whom and when' is useless unless it is collected in answer to particular hypotheses. Untheoretical typologies of bilingualism can always be invented and reinvented; they tell us nothing about bilinguals except that they are different but not why they are different, nor how these differences have come about.

We therefore need to develop theoretical constructs which can be verified empirically. Such constructs should be interdisciplinary and fit the epistemology of all the different disciplines involved. Information technology has eliminated the problem of treating masses of data; however, data banks will only be of use if the right questions can be asked. One of the problems with interdisciplinary team research is precisely that not all the disciplines involved have reached a similar level of hypothesis generating. In recent years, however, some theorizing has been achieved for specific features of bilingual behaviour. For example, we know a lot more about information processing in bilinguals than when Weinreich (1953) wrote his classic study on languages in contact. From the conception of the bilingual as someone whose speech shows interferences and who is at worst cognitively deficient and at best the sum of two monolinguals, we have moved to the conception of an integrated person, 'a unique and specific speaker–hearer, a communicator of a different sort' (Grosjean, 1985a, p. 476), for whom bilingual experience may enhance cognitive functioning.

In future research, bilinguality will be studied as a whole, in all its aspects, and more attention will be paid to its specificity. Bilingualism at the societal level will no longer be viewed as a stigma but as a resource worth developing, since it can produce individuals with a unique set of languages, cultures and experiences that should be of value to a multicultural world.

NOTES

1. Dimensions and measurement of bilinguality and bilingualism

1 On the different meanings of *language* see Introduction.
2 Translated by the authors.
3 A cloze test consists of a spoken or written text in which single words have been deleted at regular intervals, e.g. every fifth, sixth or seventh word. The ability to fill in the missing words is a valid measure of the testee's comprehension of the text and of his expectancy grammar (Oller, 1979).
4 By macrosociological approach we mean the type of analysis which examines large amounts of data to draw broad conclusions about group relationships; a microsociological approach, on the other hand, focusses on the distribution of specific items along social dimensions.

2. The ontogenesis of bilinguality

1 These authors used the Visual Reinforced Infant Speech Discrimination technique (VRISD) in which the infant is first conditioned to turn his head in response to a change in a continuous auditory stimulation. Once the infant is conditioned this technique can be used to assess other discriminations he is capable of.
2 Brown (1973) describes the language of the child in terms of five successive stages. Each stage is mainly defined by a measure of the Mean Length of Utterance (MLU). Brown's study suggests that child language acquisition is a continuous process of cumulative complexity: before acceding to the next stage the child must master the structures of the previous stage. The author shows that the stages are invariant even if children do not acquire language at the same pace.
3 These morphemes are characteristic of Canadian English and Canadian French respectively.
4 Aphasia is a loss of ability to use or to understand speech as a result of brain injury; see further Chapter 4.
5 Functional asymmetry refers to the fact that, although the two hemispheres of the human brain are anatomically similar, each takes charge of a specific range of behaviour and therefore they differ in the functions each controls.
6 The terms 'propositional' and 'appositional' refer both to typological differences between languages and to differences in modes of thinking related to languages.

259

Thus, for example, Amerindian languages are polysynthetic and allegedly appositional while English or Chinese are analytic and allegedly propositional.

7 In the dichotic listening technique the subject receives two messages simultaneously,
one in the left ear, the other in the right. Because in simultaneous auditory stimulation ipsi-lateral neural connections are suppressed in favour of the contra-lateral
ones, each stimulus will only reach the contra-lateral hemisphere. With this technique it is therefore possible to check whether one hemisphere dominates the other
in information processing.

8 An auditory stimulus is semantically incongruent when its auditory characteristic,
e.g., its pitch frequency, conflicts with the meaning of the word, as for example,
when the word 'low' is pronounced in a high-pitched voice.

9 See Chapter 3.1.4.

10 Bruner distinguishes three stages of cognitive growth: the echoic, the iconic and the
symbolic. The last stage is moulded by the cultural environment. Therefore, one
has to take into consideration the role of the cultural setting in which the development of the symbolic stage takes place.

3. The social and psychological foundations of bilinguality

1 For example, the construction of the image of a physical object of which one has
some early perceptual or motor experience, e.g. a fruit, depends in the first place on
the interaction with the object itself; whereas the image of a more social object, such
as a book, relies essentially on the three-way interaction between the child, the
object and the adult who transmits the social function and meaning of the object to
the child.

2 By decontextualized language is meant the appropriate use of language to refer to
objects and events in their absence or to express abstract ideas (see 3.1.7).

3 A text is a sequence of words, either spoken or written, which has a definable communicative function and is characterized by cohesion and coherence.

4 Socialization is defined as a complex set of learning processes which evolves into a
number of social psychological mechanisms, such as internalization of social values,
social representations, social, cultural and ethnic identity, and motivational processes involved in learning. In our view, as with all rule-governed behaviour, this
complex set of processes includes different levels of learning, from stimulus–response
to more elaborate processes such as perceptual learning, observational learning,
immediate and delayed imitation, abstract modelling, motivation and feedback
(Hebb, Lambert & Tucker, 1971; Bandura, 1977). These processes apply to the
overall socialization of the child, which includes the more specific task of learning
the rules of language behaviour (Hamers & Blanc, 1982).

4. Information processing in the bilingual

1 Among theoretical approaches we include the models of language behaviour originating from experimental psychology and psycholinguistics such as those by Broadbent (1958), Deutsch & Deutsch (1963), Treisman (1969), Morton (1964, 1980) or
by Osgood (1963, 1971) as well as those stemming from transformational grammar

such as Chomsky (1965), Fillmore (1968), Lakoff (1971) or McCawley (1972). Although it is beyond our scope to discuss the relevance of these models in the present book, it must be understood that any model of bilingual processing must be consistent with a more general model of language behaviour.

2 A pre-attentive level of processing postulates a device capable of attending to certain clues which determine the perceptual features on which attention focusses; only these features are then further analysed (see Neisser, 1966, 91).

3 See Chapter 2, Note 7.

4 Analysis-by-synthesis is a theoretical construct which assumes that in a first phase of information processing relevant elements are extracted from the available information and synthesized in configurations which are then compared with the real input (See Neisser, 1966, 189–190).

5 Morton (1979b; 1980) uses the word '*logogen*' to describe a unit of verbal representation which is not the word but rather the process by which the word becomes accessible in the presence of a given stimulus. For Paivio & Begg (1981) a logogen is a cognitive process which generates a word, while an *imagen* generates an evoked image.

6 The semantic differential is a technique developed by Osgood, Suci & Tannenbaum (1957) for measuring emotional reactions to words. Subjects are asked to rate each of many words, such as those for a language and its speakers, on twenty bipolar adjective scales, e.g. 'happy–sad', 'hard–soft', 'slow–fast'. Three dominant factors consistently appear across all the cultures and languages, namely *evaluation*, *potency* and *activity*, which can thus serve as reference points for comparing otherwise culture-bound concepts.

7 The distinction between semantic and episodic memory was introduced by Tulving (1972): semantic memory refers to the storage of representations of the outside world and includes conceptual mechanisms such as categorization and superordination (e.g. a cat is an animal); episodic memory refers to the storage of single events (e.g. my cat ate my neighbour's goldfish).

8 In retroactive inhibition (or interference) a new learning inhibits an older established learning; for example, if the association *cat–crazy* has been well established in a previous learning, the subsequent learning of the association *cat–stubborn* will interfere with the previous learning, and the recall of the first paired associate deteriorates when no second learning occurs.

9 In the part–whole transfer paradigm one learns first a partial list, then a whole list which includes the partial list in addition to new words; the subject is required to recognize if a word is part of the whole list or of the partial list.

10 The TAT (Thematic Aperception Test) is a projective technique consisting of one blank card and 19 cards with black and white pictures; the pictures represent persons alone or in interaction with others and the subject is asked to tell a story about each picture and to image one for the blank card. It is postulated that the stories reveal certain personality traits.

5. *Social psychological aspects of bilinguality: culture and identity*

1 Although in this book we use the terms 'ethnolinguistic', 'cultural' and 'ethnic' group as interchangeable, they differ in that a linguistic group is defined by a

shared language, whereas an ethnic group is defined by a number of characteristics such as 'patrimony' and ancestry which may or may not include language, and a cultural group is defined by a number of cultural components such as values, norms, beliefs and customs and may also include language. In the present discussion we will use the terms 'cultural' and 'ethnic' groups as synonyms.

2 The objective of this technique is to map a set of objects into a set of points in multi-dimensional metric space, such that objects which are similar are close together in the space and objects which are dissimilar are distant from each other in the space. This technique enables the social scientist in our particular case to measure perceived social distances between groups and between self and other groups and to identify the relevant dimensions on which these perceptions vary. For details on MDS, see Kruskal & Wish, 1978.

3 Although there is no general agreement in social psychology about the following terms, a *social attitude* may be defined as a disposition to respond consistently in a favourable or unfavourable way to a class of social objects; a *belief* is defined as a person's perception of links between an object and its attribute; it is the cognitive component of an attitude; a *stereotype* is defined as a set of ideas or beliefs shared by members of a group about members of another social, cultural or ethnic group. The distinctive group features are exaggerated; the attribution of value judgements to these features, which add an emotive dimension to the stereotype, gives rise to *prejudices* towards another group. The function of a stereotype is to justify our conduct in relation to a group. For a recent discussion of social stereotypes see Hewstone & Giles, 1986.

7. *Multilingualism and intergroup relations*

1 'Ethnic identity is allegiance to a group – large or small, socially dominant or subordinate – with which one has ancestral links. There is no necessity for a continuation, over generations, of the same socialization or cultural patterns, but some sense of a group boundary must persist. This can be sustained by shared objective characteristics (language, religion, etc.) or by more subjective contributions to a sense of "groupness", or by some combination of both. Symbolic or subjective attachment must relate, at however distant a remove, to an observable real past' (Edwards, 1985, p. 10).

2 According to Ferguson (1959), 'DIGLOSSIA is a relatively stable language situation in which, in addition to the primary dialects of the language (which may include a standard or regional standards), there is a very divergent, highly codified (often grammatically more complex) superposed variety, the vehicle of a large and respected body of written literature, either of an earlier period or in another speech community, which is learned largely by formal education and is used for most written and formal spoken purposes but is not used by any sector of the community for ordinary conversation'.

3 It is noteworthy that in history periods of migrations, invasions or intergroup conflicts have often resulted in language shift and assimilation after a variable period of bilingualism.

4 The question of pidginization, creolization and decreolization is a vast and controversial subject which would require a whole book and, in any case, has received full treatment in a large number of studies, past and present; we can only refer the

reader to a recent and balanced account of these phenomena, i.e. Mühlhäusler, 1986.

9. *Bilinguality and second language acquisition*

1 Second language (L_2) acquisition includes any language(s) learned *after* the first. In this chapter 'acquisition' and 'learning' are used interchangeably.

2 AUX stands for 'auxiliary' and refers to the set of verbs which help to make distinctions in aspect, mood, voice, etc., e.g. English *do*, *be*, *have*, and the modal auxiliaries.

3 Functors, or function words, are words and bound morphemes whose role is grammatical, as opposed to lexical words, which carry the main semantic content.

4 MLU (Mean Length of Utterance): see Chapter 2, Note 2.

5 In the hook-word technique the learner uses key words in L_2 as memory aids; these key words are numbered and overlearned with their number so that the mere mention of the number evokes the words and its mental image. These words are then used to 'hook' new words via a mental imagery association. For more details the reader is referred to Paivio & Desrochers (1980).

GLOSSARY

NB The definitions given in this Glossary correspond to those used in the book and do not necessarily accord with commonly accepted ones. For further information the reader should consult the Subject Index.

acculturation (acculturated) The process by which an individual adjusts to a new culture; this usually includes the acquisition of the language(s) of that culture.

acrolect The speech variety closest to the standard on a *creole continuum* (*see continuum, decreolization*).

additive See bilinguality.

anomie A bilingual individual's state of anxiety resulting from an inability to resolve the conflicting demands made by his two cultures.

assimilation A process by which an individual or group *acculturate* (q.v.) to another group by losing their own ethnolinguistic characteristics (cf. *integration*).

   Fear of assimilation is a process by which an individual refuses to *acculturate* (q.v.) for fear of losing his own culture and language.

baby talk Distinctive linguistic characteristics found in the speech of adults when addressing very young children.

basilect The oldest and socially lowest speech variety on a *creole continuum* (*see continuum, decreolization*).

bicultural(ism) State of an individual or group who identify with more than one culture.

   A bicultural bilingual is one who has native competence in his two languages, identifies with both cultural groups and is perceived by each group as one of them.

bidialectal(ism) Proficiency in the use of more than one dialect of a language, whether regional or social.

   Principle propounded in sociolinguistics and educational linguistics wherein different speech varieties are accorded equal linguistic validity and used in their appropriate social contexts.

bilingual (noun) Individual who has access to two or more distinct *linguistic codes* (*see code*).

   (adjective) Refers to a bilingual individual or to a community who use two or more languages.

bilingual education Any system of education in which, at a given point in time and for a

264

varying length of time, simultaneously or consecutively, instruction is given in two languages.

bilingualism   The state of an individual (cf. *bilinguality*) or a community characterized by the simultaneous presence of two languages (cf. *contact*).

Diglossic bilingualism: a state of bilingualism in which two languages co-occur, each with a distinct range of social functions.

Individual or personal bilingualism: cf. *bilinguality*.

Territorial bilingualism: co-occurrence of two or more languages which have official status within a geographical area; or coexistence of two or more unilingual areas within a single political structure (e.g. unilingual regions in a multilingual state).

bilinguality   A psychological state of the individual who has access to more than one linguistic code as a means of social communication; this access varies along a number of dimensions.

Additive bilinguality: a situation in which a child derives maximum benefit from the bilingual experience for his cognitive development; this is usually the case where the two languages are highly valued in the child's environment.

Adolescent bilinguality: state of bilinguality reached after childhood but before adulthood.

Adult bilinguality: state of bilinguality reached after adolescence.

Balanced bilinguality: a state of bilinguality in which an equivalent competence is reached in both languages, whatever the level of competence; note that balance is not equally distributed for all domains and functions of language.

Childhood bilinguality: state of bilinguality reached before 10–12 years.

Compound bilinguality: a state of bilinguality in which two sets of linguistic signs have come to be associated with the same set of meanings; this type of bilinguality is usually linked to a common context of acquisition.

Consecutive early bilinguality: childhood bilinguality in which the second language is acquired before 5–6 years but after the acquisition of basic skills in the mother tongue (L_1, then L_2).

Coordinate bilinguality: a state of bilinguality in which translation equivalents in two languages each correspond to a distinct set of semantic representations; this type of bilinguality is usually linked to different contexts of acquisition.

Dominant bilinguality: a state of bilinguality in which competence in one language is superior to competence in the other; note that dominance is not equally distributed for all domains and functions of language.

Infancy bilinguality: state of bilinguality reached during early childhood.

Simultaneous bilinguality: infancy bilinguality in which the child develops two mother tongues from the onset of language (L_A, L_B).

Subtractive bilinguality: a situation in which the bilingual child's cognitive development is delayed in comparison with his monolingual counterpart; this usually occurs when the mother tongue is devalued in the environment.

borrowing   The taking over of linguistic forms (usually lexical items) by one language from another; such borrowings are known as loan words.

broken language   A communication strategy by which a speaker attempts to use his interlocutor's mother tongue though he has a limited competence in it.

code A set of social conventions making use of a system of signs which enable individuals who share these conventions to communicate with one another.

Linguistic code: a code composed of a system of linguistic rules known by the individuals who use it and stand in a similar relationship to it.

code alternation Generally speaking, a communication strategy used by bilinguals and consisting of the alternate use of two languages in the same utterance or conversation. Cf. *code-mixing* and *code-switching*.

code-mixing A communication strategy used by bilinguals in which the speaker of language x transfers elements or rules of language y to x (the base language); unlike *borrowing* (q.v.), however, these elements are not integrated into the linguistic system of x.

code-switching A bilingual communication strategy consisting of the alternate use of two languages in the same utterance, even within the same sentence; it differs from *code-mixing* (q.v.) in the sense that there is no base language. We distinguish between competence and incompetence code-switching.

competence Linguistic competence: an individual's knowledge of the system of rules which generate a linguistic code.

Bilingual competence: linguistic competence involving knowledge of the system of rules generating two or more linguistic codes.

Language or communicative competence includes linguistic competence and its social and psychological correlates.

Native speaker's competence: the language competence of an individual who knows a language like his mother tongue.

compound (*binguality*) *See binguality*.

contact (*languages in—*) Co-occurrence of two or more languages either in the individual (*binguality*, q.v.) or in society (*bingualism*, q.v.).

continuum Continuous linguistic variation between two or more languages or speech varieties; at each pole of this continuum are situated two distinct linguistic entities which may be mutually unintelligible.

A creole is a single continuous chain of varieties connecting the *basilect* (q.v.) at one pole to the *acrolect* (q.v.) at the other.

coordinate (*binguality*) *See binguality*.

creole/creolization A creole is commonly regarded as a *pidgin* (q.v.) which has become the first language of a new generation of speakers; this process, called *creolization*, is characterized by an expansion of linguistic functions and forms.

critical (*optimal/sensitive*) *age* Age at which acquisition or learning is achieved in an optimal way; before that age the individual has not reached the necessary maturation stage; after that age he has partially or totally lost the capacity for this acquisition or learning.

Optimal age for learning a second language, with the result that the learner acquires native-speaker competence in that language.

decreolization (*post-creole continuum*) The process by which a creole moves towards the dominant (standard) variety at the expense of its most distinctive characteristics.

deculturation The process by which an individual adapts to a new culture at the expense of his first. Extreme deculturation leads to *assimilation* (q.v.), which may involve loss of the first language.

development (*language—*) Refers to the child's language acquisition, including developmental correlates such as the relationship between language and cognitive, affective and social development.

Bilingual development: language development involving the acquisition of two or more languages and including the cognitive, affective and social correlates of this development (cf. *bilinguality*).

dialect   A regionally or socially distinctive variety of a language.

diglossia   A situation where two very different varieties of a language or two distinct languages co-occur throughout a *speech community* (q.v.), each with a distinct range of social functions.

Leaky diglossia: a situation where one variety or language spreads into the functions formerly reserved for another.

domain   A group of institutionalized social situations typically constrained by a common set of behavioural rules.

enculturation   A part of the socialization process by which a child acquires the rules of behaviour and the values of his culture.

endogenous (language)   A language that is used as mother tongue within a speech community (cf. *exogenous*).

ethnolinguistic   Refers to a set of cultural, ethnic and linguistic features shared by one social group.

exogenous (language)   A language not used as mother tongue but only as official or institutionalized language in a speech community (cf. *endogenous*).

foreigner talk   A bilingual communication strategy in which the speaker simplifies his mother tongue to make himself understood by another speaker who has limited competence in it.

handicap (linguistic/bilingual/cognitive—)   A disadvantage which prevents an individual from achieving expected norms in language or cognitive development.

identity (cultural/ethnic)   At the individual level: a psychological mechanism by which a child develops the dimension of his personality pertaining to his membership of a cultural or ethnic group.

At the group level: cultural or ethnic characteristics of the members of a group perceived as a social entity.

immersion (programs)   A type of *bilingual education* (q.v.) in which a group of learners is taught through the medium of a language different from their mother tongue, the latter being introduced later.

Early immersion: Immersion program in which a second language is used exclusively as a medium of instruction in the early years of schooling.

Late immersion: Immersion program in which a second language is introduced as a medium of instruction at a later stage.

Partial immersion: Immersion program in which both the first and the second language are used as media of instruction.

independence   A psychological state which enables a language mechanism or a linguistic code to function independently of another language mechanism or linguistic code (cf. *interdependence*).

integration   A process by which an individual *acculturates* (q.v.) to a new culture without losing his first culture and identity, including language (cf. *assimilation*).

integrative(ness)   Integrative orientation: reasons suggesting that an individual is learn-

ing a second language in order to form a closer liaison with the other language community.

Integrative motive: includes not only the orientation but also the motivation to
learn the second language for these reasons.

interdependence Relationship between two linguistic systems or psychological mechanisms which means that one cannot function or develop without reference to the
other.

interference In the field of learning, there is interference when one piece of learning or
one association inhibits another.

In second language learning: refers to learning problems in which the learner unconsciously and inappropriately transfers elements or rules from the first to the
second language.

May refer to any language behaviour in which a speaker calls upon elements and
rules from two or more linguistic codes in the same utterance or communication
interaction (cf. *code alternation, code-mixing, code-switching*).

interlanguage Refers to successive stages in the processes of acquisition of a second
language in which the linguistic productions of the learner represent systematic
approximations to the target language.

L An abstract language competence without reference to any specific language.

L_1 Denotes the mother tongue or first language.

L_2 Denotes a second language learned after the first.

L_A/L_B Denotes the co-occurrence of two mother tongues learned simultaneously.

L_X, L_Y, L_Z Denotes any natural language.

language Auxiliary language: a language which has been adopted by different speech
communities for purposes of communication, it being the native language of none of
them. Cf. *lingua franca*.

Community or heritage language: a minority language valued by the community
of its speakers who actively encourage its maintenance.

First language or mother tongue: the linguistic code(s) corresponding to the individuals first language experience; also the linguistic code(s) used as mother tongue
by most members of a speech community.

Foreign language: second and subsequently learned language(s) which are not
widely used by the speech community in which the learner lives.

International language: language of wider communication used beyond the
national boundaries of a linguistic community for specific purposes.

Majority or dominant language: a language used by a socio-economically dominant group in society, or one which has received a political or cultural status superior
to that of other languages in the community.

Minority or subordinate language: a language used by a socially subordinate
group, or one which has received a social or cultural status inferior to that of another
(dominant) language in the community.

National language: a language which may or may not have official (q.v.) status
but is used by an important section of the speech community.

Native language: the language or languages which have been acquired naturally
during childhood (also first language, mother tongue).

Official language: a language which is legally adopted by a state as its language of communication for all or some of its official transactions; this language may be endogenous or exogenous (q.v.).

Second language: (a) the language learned by an individual after acquiring his first or native language or mother tongue; (b) a non-native language which is the mother tongue of the speech community.

Source language: (a) the language in which a message is transmitted and which is decoded by the interpreter/translator with the aim of recoding it in another language (*target language*, q.v.); (b) the first language of the second language learner.

Standard language: a language variety which has been accorded a status which is socially and culturally superior to other varieties and is used officially.

Target language: (a) the language into which a message in another language is translated or interpreted; (b) the language which is the goal of second language acquisition.

language history The past and present data on the history of acquisition and use of one or more languages.

lect A collection of linguistic phenomena which has a functional identity within a speech community (Cf. *acrolect, basilect*).

lingua franca An auxiliary language (*see language*) used between groups of people who speak different native languages for the purpose of routine communication.

linguistic code See *code*.

linguistic community See *speech community*.

linguistic continuum A continuous linguistic variation between two languages or language varieties; at the opposite poles of this continuum are situated two distinct linguistic entities which may be mutually unintelligible.

Creole continuum: See *decreolization*.

linguistic handicap See *handicap*.

literacy State of an individual or community relating to the decontextualized use of language, especially in the written mode.

loan blend A type of *borrowing* (q.v.) in which the loan word is modified according to the rules of the borrowing language.

melting pot A policy of *assimilation* (q.v.) which reflected the dominant US ideology towards its ethnic minority groups before the Second World War.

monocultural/unicultural Individual/group identifying with and being identified by only one culture.

monolingual/unilingual Individual/group having access to only one linguistic code.

mother tongue See *language: first language*.

multilingual/multilingualism See *bilingual/bilingualism*.

native speaker An individual for whom a particular language is a 'native language' (*see language: first language*).

optimal age See *critical age*.

pidgin/pidginization A new language developed by two speech communities attempting to communicate and characterized by reduced grammatical structure and lexis; the process by which this language develops.

planning (*language—*) The official organization of the relations between languages within a given territory.

External/status planning: interference with the existing status relations between languages in contact in a given territory.

Internal/corpus planning: interference with the internal dynamic processes of a language.

pluralism A cultural and linguistic policy by which ethnolinguistic minority groups are integrated into the wider society while being allowed to maintain their linguistic and cultural characteristics to varying degrees.

preferred language The language chosen by a bilingual speaker in a given situation from among his *repertoire* (q.v.).

repertoire (speech—) The range of languages or varieties available for use by a speaker, each of which enables him to perform a particular social role: the range of languages or varieties within a *speech community* (q.v.).

second language See *L₂, language.*

segregation Process by which an individual or group is kept linguistically and culturally isolated within a society.

semilingualism A term used to denote a state in the language development of a bilingual who has reached native-speaker competence in none of his languages (cf. *bilinguality: subtractive*).

sensitive age See *critical age.*

separatism A political process by which an ethnolinguistic group chooses the solution of language nationalism to its linguistic and cultural problems.

shift (language—) Process in which a speech community gives up a language completely in favour of another one.

speech accommodation The process by which interlocutors modify their speech style (e.g. accent) or switch codes in order to converge towards, or diverge from, each other in communication interactions.

speech community Any regionally or socially definable human group identified by the use of a shared linguistic system(s) and by participation in shared sociolinguistic norms.

standard The prestige variety of language used within a speech community; the natural or artificial process by which a dialect becomes a standard language is called *standardization.*

submersion A form of education in which a child is schooled in a language other than his mother tongue.

subtractive See *bilinguality.*

switch (mechanism) psychological mechanism by which the bilingual is enabled to shut out one of his linguistic systems while using another.

translation equivalent A linguistic unit in one language corresponding to a linguistic unit in another language at the semantic level.

variety Any system of linguistic expression whose use is governed by situational variables, such as region, occupation, etc.

vernacular The indigenous language or dialect of a speech community.

vitality (ethnolinguistic—) That which makes an ethnolinguistic group likely to behave as a distinctive and active collective entity in intergroup relations.

REFERENCES

Abdulaziz Mkilifi, M. H. (1978) Trigglossia and Swahili–English bilingualism in Tanzania. In J. A. Fishman (ed.) *Advances in the Study of Societal Multilingualism.* The Hague: Mouton.

Aboud, F. E. (1976) Social development aspects of language. *Papers in linguistics,* 9, 15–37.

Aboud, F. E. & Mitchell, F. G. (1977) Ethnic role taking: the effects of preference and self-identification. *International Journal of Psychology,* 12, 1–17.

Aboud, F. E. & Skerry, S. A. (1984) The development of ethnic attitudes: a critical review. *Journal of Cross-Cultural Psychology,* 15, 3–34.

Adler, K. (1977) *Collective and Individual Bilingualism: A Socio-Linguistic Study.* Hamburg: Helmut Buske Verlag.

Aellen, C. & Lambert, W. E. (1969) Ethnic identification and personality adjustments of Canadian adolescents of mixed English–French parentage. *Canadian Journal of Behavioral Science,* 1, 69–86.

Albanese, J. F. (1985) Language lateralization in English–French bilinguals. *Brain and Language,* 24, 284–96.

Albert, M. L. & Obler, L. K. (1978) *The Bilingual Brain.* New York: Academic Press.

Allard, R. & Landry, R. (1986) Subjective ethnolinguistic vitality viewed as a belief system. *Journal of Multilingual and Multicultural Development,* 7, 1–12.

Altenberg, E. P. & Cairns, H. S. (1983) The effect of phonotactic constraints on lexical processing in bilingual and monolingual subjects. *Journal of Verbal Learning and Verbal Behavior,* 22, 174–88.

Amir, Y. (1969) Contact hypothesis in ethnic relations. *Psychological Bulletin,* 71, 319–42.

Andersen, E. A. (1985) Sociolinguistic surveys in Singapore. *International Journal of the Sociology of Language,* 55, 89–114.

Andersen, J. R. (1983) *The Architecture of Cognition.* Cambridge, Mass.: Harvard University Press.

Andersen, J. R. & Bower, G. H. (1973) *Human Associative Memory.* New York: Winston.

Andersen, R. B. W. (1976) Perspectives on the role of interpreter. In R. W. Brislin (ed.) *Translation: Application and Research.* New York: Gardner Press Inc.

Andersen, R. W. (1981) Two perspectives on pidginization as second language acquisition. In R. W. Andersen (ed.) *New Dimensions in Second Language Acquisition Research.* Rowley, Mass.: Newbury House.

271

Anisfeld, E. & Lambert, W. E. (1964) Evaluation reactions of bilingual and monolingual children to spoken language. *Journal of Abnormal and Social Psychology*, 59, 89–
97.

Anisfeld, M., Bogo, N. & Lambert, W. E. (1962) Evaluational reactions to accented
English speech. *Journal of Abnormal and Social Psychology*, 65, 223–31.

Arkwight, T. & Viau, A. (1974) Les processus d'association chez les bilingues. *Working
Papers on Bilingualism*, 2, 57–67.

Arnberg, L. (1984) Mother tongue playgroups for pre-school bilingual children. *Journal of Multilingual and Multicultural Development*, 5, 65–84.

Arnedt, C. S. & Gentile, J. R. (1986) Test of dual coding theory for bilingual memory.
Canadian Journal of Psychology, 40, 290–9.

Arsenian, S. (1937) *Bilingualism and Mental Development*. New York: Teachers College
Contribution to Education, Columbia University, 712.

Asher, J. & Price, B. (1967) The learning strategy of the total physical response: some
age differences. *Child Development*, 38, 1219–27.

Atkinson, R. C. (1975) Mnemotechnics in second language learning. *American Psychology*, 30, 821–8.

Atkinson, R. C. & Raugh, M. R. (1975) An application of the mnemonic keyword
method to the acquisition of a Russian vocabulary. *Journal of Experimental Psychology*:
Human Learning and Memory, 104, 126–33.

Auer, P. (1987) Le transfert comme stratégie conversationnelle dans le discours en L$_2$.
In G. Lüdi (ed.) *Devenir Bilingue–Parler Bilingue*. Tübingen: Niemeyer.

Babu, N. (1984) Perception of syntactic ambiguity by bilingual and unilingual tribal
children. *Psycho-Lingua*, 14, 47–54.

Baetens Beardsmore, H. (1980) Bilingual education in International Schools, European Schools and Experimental Schools: A Comparative Analysis. In Lim Kiat
Boey (ed.) *Bilingual Education*. Singapore: Singapore University Press.

Baetens Beardsmore, H. (1982) *Bilingualism: Basic Principles*. Clevedon, Avon: Multilingual Matters, 1.

Baetens Beardsmore, H. & Swain, M. (1985) Designing bilingual education: aspects of
immersion and 'European School' models. *Journal of Multilingual and Multicultural
Development*, 6, 1–15.

Bailey, N., Madden, C. & Krashen, S. (1974) Is there a 'natural sequence' in adult
second language learning? *Language Learning*, 24, 235–43.

Bain, B. (1975) Toward an integration of Piaget and Vygotsky: bilingual considerations. *Linguistics* 16, 5–20.

Bain, B. (1976) Verbal regulation of cognitive processes: a replication of Luria's procedure with bilingual and unilingual infants. *Child Development*, 47, 543–6.

Bain, B. & Yu, A. (1978) Toward an integration of Piaget and Vygotsky: a cross-
cultural replication (France, Germany, Canada) concerning cognitive consequences of biliguality. In M. Paradis (ed.) *Aspects of Bilingualism*. Columbia,
South Carolina: Hornbeam Press.

Balkan, L. (1970) *Les Effets du Bilinguisme Français–Anglais sur les Aptitudes Intellectuelles*.
Brussels: AIMAV.

Ball, P., Giles, H., Byrne, J. L. & Berechree, P. (1984) Situational constraints on the
evaluative significance of speech accommodation: some Australian data. *International Journal of the Sociology of Language*, 46, 115–29.

Ball, P., Giles, H. & Hewstone, M. (1984) Second language acquisition: the intergroup theory with catastrophic dimensions. In H. Tajfel (ed.) *The Social Dimension: European Developments in Social Psychology*, Volume 2, 668–94.

Bamgbose, A. (1984) Minority languages and literacy. In F. Coulmas (ed.) *Linguistic Minorities and Literacy*. Berlin: Mouton.

Bandura, A. (1977) *Social Learning Theory*. Englewood Cliffs, N.J.: Prentice-Hall.

Barik, H. C. (1973) Simultaneous interpretation: temporal and quantitative data. *Language and Speech*, 16, 237–70.

Barik, H. C. & Swain, M. (1978) A longitudinal study of bilingual and cognitive development. *International Journal of Psychology*, 11, 251–63.

Barth, F. (1970) *Ethnic Groups and Boundaries: The Social Organization of Culture Difference*. London: Allen and Unwin.

Bartlett, F. C. (1932) *Remembering: A Study in Experimental and Social Psychology*. Cambridge: Cambridge University Press.

Barton, M. I., Goodglass, H. & Skai, A. (1965) Differential recognition of tachistoscopically presented English and Hebrew words in right and left visual fields. *Perceptual and Motor Skills*, 21, 431–7.

Beaudoin, M., Cummins, J., Dunlop, H., Genesee, F. & Obadia, A. (1981) Bilingual education: a comparison of Welsh and Canadian experience. *Canadian Modern Language Review*, 37, 498–509.

Beebe, L. (1981) Social and situational factors affecting communicative strategies of communicative code-switching. *International Journal of the Sociology of Language*, 46, 139–49.

Belair Lockheed, J. (1987) Le Contact Inter-Ethnique: Antécédents, Processus et Conséquents. Unpublished Ph. D. dissertation. Ottawa: Université d'Ottawa.

Bentahila, A. & Davies, E. E. (1983) The syntax of Arabic–French code-switching. *Lingua*, 59, 301–30.

Bentolila, A. & Gani, L. (1981) Langues et problèmes d'éducation en Haïti. *Langages*, 61, 117–27.

Ben-Zeev, S. (1972) The Influence of Bilingualism on Cognitive Development and Cognitive Strategy. Unpublished Ph.D. dissertation. Chicago: University of Chicago.

Ben-Zeev, S. (1977a) Mechanisms by which childhood bilingualism affects understanding of language and cognitive structures. In P. A. Hornby (ed.) *Bilingualism: Psychological, Social and Educational Implications*. New York: Academic Press.

Ben-Zeev, S. (1977b) The effect of bilingualism in children from Spanish–English low economic neighborhoods on cognitive development and cognitive strategy. *Working Papers on Bilingualism*, 14, 83–122.

Bereiter, C. & Engelmann, S. (1966) *Teaching Disadvantaged Children in the Preschool*. Englewood Cliffs, N. J.: Prentice Hall.

Berger, C. R. (1986) Social cognition and intergroup communication. In W. B. Gudykunst (ed.) *Intergroup Communication*. London: Edward Arnold.

Berger, P. & Luckman, T. (1967) *The Social Construction of Reality*. London: Allen Lane.

Berkovits, R., Abarbanel, J. & Sitman, D. (1984) The effects of language proficiency on memory for input language. *Applied Psycholinguistics*, 5, 209–21.

Berk-Seligson, S. (1986) Linguistic constraints on intrasentential code-switching: a study of Spanish–Hebrew bilingualism. *Language in Society*, 15, 313–48.

Berry, J. W. (1980) Acculturation as varieties of adaptation. In A. Padilla (ed.) *Acculturation: Theory and Models*. Washington: AAAS.

Berry, J. W., Kalin, R. & Taylor, D. M. (1977) *Multiculturalism and Ethnic Attitudes in Canada*. Ottawa: Supply and Services Canada.

Bever, T. G. (1970) *Are there Psycho-Social Interactions that maintain a Low I. Q. Score of the Poor?* Unpublished mimeo. University of Columbia.

Bhatnagar, J. (1980) Linguistic behaviour and adjustment of immigrant children in French and English schools in Montreal. *International Journal of Applied Psychology*, 29, 141–58.

Bialystok, E. & Frohlich, M. (1977) Aspects of second language learning in classroom setting. *Working Papers on Bilingualism*, 13, 2–26.

Bialystok, E. & Ryan, E. B. (1985a) Toward a definition of metalinguistic skill. *Merrill-Palmer Quarterly*, 31, 229–51.

Bialystok, E. & Ryan, E. B. (1985b) A metacognitive framework for the development of first and second language skills. In D. L. Forrest-Pressley, G. E. MacKinnon & T. Gary Waller (eds.) *Metacognition, Cognition, and Human Performance*. New York: Academic Press.

Bickerton, D. (1975) *Dynamics of a Creole System*. Cambridge: Cambridge University Press.

Biedermann, I. & Tsao, Y. C. (1979) On processing Chinese ideographs and English words: some implications from Stroop-test results. *Cognitive Science*, 2, 125–32.

Birdwhistell, R. L. (1970) *Kinesics and Context*. Philadelphia: University of Pennsylvania Press.

Blanc, M. (1980) *Réflexions sur quelques Classes d' Immersion*. Unpublished mimeo. London: Birbeck College, University of London.

Blanc, M. (1986) Canada's non-official languages: assimilation or pluralism? *The London Journal of Canadian Studies*, 3, 46–56.

Blanc, M. (1987a) Préface/Foreword. In M. Blanc & J. F. Hamers (eds.) *Theoretical and Methodological Issues in the Study of Languages/Dialects in Contact at the Macro- and Micro-Logical Levels of Analysis*. Quebec: International Center for Research on Bilingualism, B–160, 3–8.

Blanc, M. (1987b) A project of community bilingual education: some theoretical and applied issues. In M. Blanc & J. F. Hamers (eds.) *Theoretical and Methodological Issues in the Study of Languages/Dialects in Contact at the Macro- and Micro-Logical Levels of Analysis*. Quebec: International Center for Research on Bilingualism, B–160, 191–201.

Blanc, M. & Hamers, J. F. (1982) *Social Networks and Multilingual Behaviour: The Atlantic Provinces Project*. Paper given at the Fourth Sociolinguistics Symposium, University of Sheffield.

Blanc, M. & Hamers, J. F. (1987) Réseaux sociaux et comportements langagiers. In A. Prujiner (ed.) *L'Interdisciplinarité en Sciences Sociales pour l'Etude du Contact des Langues*. Quebec: International Center for research on Bilingualism, B–158, 1–13.

Bloomfield, L. (1935) *Language*. London: Allen and Unwin.

Bogen, J. E. (1969) The other side of the brain II: an appositional mind. *Bulletin of the Los Angeles Neurological Society*, 34, 191–220.

Bond, M. H. & Yang, K. S. (1982) Ethnic affirmation vs. cross-cultural accommodation: the variable impact of questionnaire language. *Journal of Cross-Cultural Psychology*, 13, 165–85.

Bourhis, R. Y. (1982) Language policies and language attitudes: le monde de la francophonie. In E. B. Ryan & H. Giles (eds.) *Attitudes towards Language Variation: Social and Applied Contexts*. London: Edward Arnold.

Bourhis, R. Y. (ed.) (1984) *Conflict and Language Planning in Quebec*. Clevedon: Multilingual Matters.

Bourhis, R. Y. & Giles, H. (1977) The language of intergroup distinctiveness. In H. Giles (ed.) *Language, Ethnicity and Intergroup Relations*. London: Academic Press.

Bourhis, R. Y., Giles, H., Leyens, J. P. & Tajfel, H. (1979) Psychological distinctiveness: language divergence in Belgium. In H. Giles & R. N. Sinclair (eds.) *Language and Social Psychology*. Oxford: Blackwell.

Bourhis, R. Y., Giles, H. & Rosenthal, D. (1981) Notes on the construction of a 'Subjective Vitality Questionnaire' for ethnolinguistic groups. *Journal of Multilingual and Multicultural Development*, 2, 145–54.

Bourhis, R. Y., Giles, H. & Tajfel, H. (1973) Language as a determinant of Welsh identity. *European Journal of Social Psychology*, 3, 447–60.

Bourhis, R. Y. & Sachdev, I. (1984) Vitality perceptions and language attitudes: some Canadian data. *Journal of Language and Social Psychology*, 3, 97–126.

Brass, P. R. (1974) *Language, Religion and Politics in North India*. Cambridge: Cambridge University Press.

Brent-Palmer, C. (1979) A sociolinguistic assessment of the notion 'im/migrant semilingualism' from a social conflict perspective. *Working Papers on Bilingualism*, 17, 135–80.

Breton, R. J. L. (1976) *Atlas Géographique des Langues et des Ethnies de l'Inde et du Subcontinent*. Quebec: International Center for Research on Bilingualism / Presses de l'Université Laval, A–10.

Broadbent, D. E. (1958) *Perception and Communication*. London: Pergamon Press.

Brown, H., Sharma, N. K. & Kirsner, K. (1984) The role of script and phonology in lexical representation. *The Quarterly Journal of Experimental Psychology*, 36A, 491–505.

Brown, H. D. (1973) Effective variables in second language acquisition. *Language Learning*, 23, 231–44.

Brown, R. (1973) *A First Language: The Early Stages*. Cambridge, Mass.: Harvard University Press.

Brown, R. & Gilman, A. (1960) The pronouns of power and solidarity. In T. Sebeok (ed.) *Style in Language*. New York: Wiley.

Bruck, M. (1982) Language-impaired children's performance in an additive bilingual education program. *Applied Psycholinguistics*, 3, 45–60.

Bruck, M., Jakimik, J. & Tucker, G. R. (1975) Are French immersion programs suitable for working class children? A follow up investigation. *Word*, 27, 311–41.

Bruner, J. S. (1965) The growth of mind. *American Psychologist*, 20, 1007–17.

Bruner, J. S. (1966) *Towards a Theory of Instruction*. New York: Norton.

Bruner, J. S. (1971) *The Relevance of Education*. New York: Norton.

Bruner, J. S. (1973a) *Beyond the Information Given*. London: Allen & Unwin.

Bruner, J. S. (1973b) The growth of representational processes in childhood. In J. S. Bruner, *Beyond the Information Given*. London: Allen & Unwin.

Bruner, J. S. (1975a) The ontogenesis of speech acts. *Journal of Child Language*, 2, 1–20.

Bruner, J. S. (1975b) Language as an instrument of thought. In A. Davies (ed.) *Problems of Language and Learning*. London: Heinemann.

Bruner, J. S. & Sherwood, V. (1981) Thought, language and interaction in infancy. In J. P. Forgas (ed.) *Social Cognition*. London: Academic Press.

Bryson, S., Mononen, L. & Yu, L. (1980) Procedural constraints on the measurement of laterality in young children. *Neuropsychologia*, 18, 243–6.

Bull, W. (1964) The use of vernacular languages in fundamental education. In D. Hymes (ed.) *Language in Culture and Society*. New York: Harper & Row.

Burstall, C. (1975) Factors affecting foreign-language learning: a consideration of some recent research findings. *Language Teaching and Linguistics Abstracts*, 8, 1–18.

Buteau, M. (1970) Students' errors in the learning of French as a second language. *International Review of Applied Linguistics*, 7, 133–46.

Byrne, D. (1969) Attitudes and attraction. *Advances in Experimental Social Psychology*, 4, 35–89.

Calvet, J. L. (1974) *Linguistique et Colonialisme: Petit Traité de Glottophagie*. Paris: Payot.

Calvet, J. L. (1981) L'alphabétisation ou la scolarisation: le cas du Mali. In A. Martin (ed.) *L'Etat et la Planification Linguistique*. Québec: Editeur Officiel du Quebec, Volume 2, 163–72.

Canale, M. & Swain, M. (1980) Theoretical bases of communicative approaches to second language teaching and testing. *Applied Linguistics*, 1, 2–43.

Cancino, H., Rosansky, E. J. & Schumann, J. H. (1974) Testing hypotheses about second language acquisition: the copula and negative in three subjects. *Working Papers on Bilingualism*, 3, 80–96.

Cancino, H., Rosansky, E. J. & Schumann, J. H. (1975) The acquisition of the English auxiliary by native Spanish speakers. *TESOL Quarterly*, 9, 421–30.

Caporael, L. R. Lukaszewski, M. P. & Culbertson, G. H. (1983) Secondary baby talk: judgements by institutionalized elderly and their caregivers. *Journal of Personality and Social Psychology*, 44, 746–54.

Caramazza, A. & Brones, I. (1980) Semantic classification by bilinguals. *Canadian Journal of Psychology*, 34, 77–81.

Caramazza, A., Yeni-Komshian, G. & Zurif, E. (1974) Bilingual switching at the phonological level. *Canadian Journal of Psychology*, 28, 310–18.

Carpinteria Unified School District (1982) *Title VII Evaluation Report 1981–1982*. Carpinteria, Ca.: Unpublished report.

Carringer, D. C. (1974) Creative thinking abilities of Mexican youth: the relationship of bilingualism. *Journal of Cross-Cultural Psychology*, 5, 492–504.

Carroll, F. W. (1978a) *Cerebral Lateralization and Adult Second Language Learning*. Unpublished Ph.D. dissertation. Albuquerque: University of New Mexico.

Carroll, F. W. (1978b) Cerebral dominance for language: a dichotic listening study of Navajo–English bilinguals. In H. H. Key, G. G. McCullough & J. B. Sawyer (eds.) *The Bilingual in a Pluralistic Society*. Long Beach: California State University.

Carroll, F. W. (1980) Neurolinguistic processing of a second language: experimental evidence. In R. Scarcella & S. Krashen (eds.), *Research in Second Language Acquisition*. Rowley, Mass.: Newbury House.

Carroll, J. B. (1962) The prediction of success in intensive foreign language training. In R. Glazer (ed.) *Training, Research and Education*. Pittsburgh: University of Pittsburgh Press.

Carroll, J. B. (1965) The contribution of psychological theory and educational research to the teaching of foreign languages. *Modern Language Journal*, 49, 273–81.

Carroll, J. B. (1973) Implications of aptitude test research and psycholinguistic theory for foreign language teaching. *International Journal of Psycholinguistics*, 2, 5–14.

Carroll, J. B. (1978) Linguistic abilities in translators and interpreters. In D. Gerver & H. W. Sinaiko (eds.) *Language, Interpretation and Communication*. New York and London: Plenum Press.

Carroll, J. B. & Sapon, S. M. (1959) *Modern Language Aptitude Test. Form A*. New York: The Psychological Corporation.

Cattell, R.B. (1971) *Abilities: Their Structure, Growth and Action*. Boston: Houghton Mifflin.

Champagnol, R. (1973) Organisation sémantique et linguistique dans le rappel libre bilingue. *L'Année Psychologique*, 73, 115–34.

Champagnol, R. (1978) Effets des consignes de traitement 'perceptif' et 'sémantique' sur la reconnaissance et le rappel des mots français et anglais. *Psychologie Française*, 23, 115–25.

Champagnol, R. (1979) Reconnaissances interlangues et intermodalités avec indicateurs de transformation. *L'Année Psychologique*, 79, 65–85.

Chan, M. C., Chau, H. L. H. & Hoosain, R. (1983) Input/output switch in bilingual code switching. *Journal of Psycholinguistic Research*, 12, 407–16.

Charniak, E. & McDermott, D. (1985) *Introduction to Artificial Intelligence*. Reading. Mass.: Addison–Wesley.

Chernigovskaya, T. V., Balonov, L. J. & Deglin, V. L. (1983) Bilingualism and brain functional asymmetry. *Brain and Language*, 20, 195–216.

Chernov, G. F. (1973) Towards a psycholinguistic model of simultaneous interpretation. *Linguistische Arbeitsberichte*, 7, 717–26.

Cherry, C. (1953) Some experiments on the recognition of speech with one and two ears. *Journal of the Acoustic Society of America*, 5, 975–9.

Chesarek, S. (1981) *Cognitive Consequences of Home on School Education in a Limited Second Language: a Case Study in the Crow Indian Bilingual Community*. Ailie House, Va.: Paper presented at the Language Proficiency Assessment Symposium.

Cheshire, J. (1987) A survey of dialect grammar in British English. In M. Blanc & J. F. Hamers (eds.) *Theoretical and Methodological Issues in the Study of Languages/Dialects in Contact at Macro- and Micro-Logical Levels of Analysis*. Quebec: International Center for Research on Bilingualism, B–160, 50–8.

Chihara, T. & Oller, J. W. (1978) Attitudes and attained proficiency in EFL: a sociolinguistic study of adult Japanese speakers. *Language Learning*, 28, 55–68.

Child, I. L. (1943) *Italian or American? The Second Generation in Conflict*. New Haven: Yale University Press.

Chimombo, J. (1979) An analysis of the order of acquisition of English grammatical morphemes in a bilingual child. *Working Papers on Bilingualism*, 18, 201–30.

Chomsky, N. (1965) *Aspects of the Theory of Syntax*. Cambridge, Mass.: MIT Press.

Chun, J. (1979) The importance of the language-learning situation: is immersion the same as the 'sink or swim' method? *Working Papers on Bilingualism*, 18, 131–64.

Clark, M. J. (1978) Synonymity of Concreteness Effects on Free Recall and Free Association: Implications for a Theory of Semantic Memory. Unpublished Ph.D. dissertation. London, Ontario: University of Western Ontario.

Clay, M. M. (1976) Early childhood and cultural diversity in New Zealand. *Reading Teacher*, 29, 333–42.

Clément, R. (1978) *Motivational Characteristics of Francophones learning English.* Quebec: International Center for Research on Bilingualism/Presses de l'Université Laval, B–70.

Clément, R. (1980) Ethnicity, contact and communicative competence in second language. In H. Giles, W. P. Robinson & P. M. Smith (eds.) *Language: Social Psychological Perspectives.* Oxford: Pergamon Press.

Clément, R. (1984) Aspects socio-psychologiques de la communication inter-ethnique et de l'identité culturelle. *Recherches Sociologiques*, 15, 293–312.

Clément, R. (1987) *Meta-theoretical Comments on Language and Social Psychology: an Introduction to Theoretical Issues.* Bristol: Paper presented at the Third International Conference on Social Psychology of Language. Bristol, 20–23 July 1987.

Clément, R., Gardner, R. C. & Smythe, P. C. (1977a) Motivational variables in second language acquisition: a study of francophones learning English. *Canadian Journal of Behavioral Science*, 9, 123–33.

Clément, R., Gardner, R. C. & Smythe, P. C. (1977b) Inter-ethnic contact: attitudinal consequences. *Canadian Journal of Behavioral Science*, 9, 205–15.

Clément, R. & Hamers, J. F. (1979) Les bases sociopsychologiques du comportement langagier. In G. Bégin & P. Joshi (eds.) *Psychologie Sociale.* Quebec: Presses de l'Université Laval.

Clément, R. & Kruidenier, B. G. (1983) Orientations in second language acquisition: the effects of ethnicity, milieu and target language on their emergence. *Language Learning*, 33, 273–91.

Clément, R. & Kruidenier, B. G. (1985) Aptitude, attitude and motivation in second language proficiency: a test of Clément's model. *Journal of Language and Social Psychology*, 4, 21–37.

Clément, R., Smythe, P. C. & Gardner, R. C. (1978) Persistence in second language studies: motivational considerations. *Canadian Modern Language Review*, 34, 688–94.

Clyne, M. G. (1967) *Transference and Triggering.* The Hague: Nijhoff.

Clyne, M. G. (ed.) (1981) *Foreigner Talk. Special issue of International Journal of the Sociology of Language*, 28. The Hague: Mouton.

Clyne, M. (1982) *Multilingual Australia.* Melbourne: River Seine Publications.

Cobarrubias, J. & Fishman, J. A. (eds.) (1983) *Progress in Language Planning.* The Hague: Mouton.

Cohen, A. D. (1975) *A Sociolinguistic Approach to Bilingual Education: Experiments in the Southwest.* Rowley, Mass.: Newbury House.

Cohen, A. D. (1976) The acquisition of Spanish grammar through immersion: some findings after four years. *Canadian Modern Language Review*, 32, 572–4.

Commins, B. & Lockwood, J. (1979) The effect of status differences, favoured treatment and equity on intergroup comparisons. *European Journal of Social Psychology*, 9, 281–9.

Corballis, M. C. (1980) Laterality and myth. *American Psychologist*, 35, 284–95.

Corballis, M. C. & Morgan, M. (1978) On the biological basis of human laterality. *The Behavioral and Brain Sciences*, 1, 261–9.

Corder, S. P. (1967) The significance of learner's errors. *International Review of Applied Linguistics*, 9, 147–60.

Corder, S. P. (1975) Error analysis, interlanguage and second language acquisition. *Language Teaching and Linguistics Abstracts*, 8, 201–18.

Corder, S. P. (1981) *Error Analysis and Interlanguage*. London: Oxford University Press.

Cornejo, R. (1975) The acquisition of lexicon in the speech of bilingual children. In P. Turner (ed.) *Bilingualism in the Southwest*. Tucson, Arizona: University of Arizona Press.

Critchley, M. (1974) Aphasia in polyglots and bilinguals. *Brain and Language*, 1, 15–27.

Cummins, J. (1973) A theoretical perspective on the relationship between bilingualism and thought. *Working Papers on Bilingualism*, 1, 1–9.

Cummins, J. (1976) The influence of bilingualism on cognitive growth: a synthesis of research findings and explanatory hypotheses. *Working Papers on Bilingualism*, 9, 1–43.

Cummins, J. (1978) Bilingualism and the development of metalinguistic awareness. *Journal of Cross-Cultural Psychology*, 9, 139–49.

Cummins, J. (1979) Linguistic interdependence and the educational development of bilingual children. *Review of Educational Research*, 49, 222–51.

Cummins, J. (1981) The role of primary language development in promoting educational success for language minority students. In *California State Department of Education. Schooling and Language Minority Students: A Theoretical Framework*. Los Angeles: Evaluation, Assessment and Dissemination Center.

Cummins, J. (1984a) *Bilingualism and Special Education: Issues in Assessment and Pedagogy*. Clevedon, Avon: Multilingual Matters, 6.

Cummins, J. (1984b) Wanted: a theoretical framework for relating language proficiency to academic achievement among bilingual students. In C. Rivera (ed.) *Language Proficiency and Academic Achievement*. Clevedon, Avon: Multilingual Matters, 10.

Cummins, J. & Gulutsan, M. (1974) Some effects of bilingualism on cognitive functioning. In S. T. Carey (ed.) *Bilingualism, Biculturalism and Education*. Edmonton: The University of Alberta Press.

Cummins, J. & Mulcahy, R. (1978) Orientation to language in Ukrainian–English bilinguals. *Child Development*, 49, 479–82.

Cummins, J., Swain, M., Nakajima, K., Handscombe, J., Green, D. & Tran, C. (1984) Linguistic interdependence among Japanese and Vietnamese immigrant students. In C. Rivera (ed.) *A Communicative Competence Approach to Language Proficiency Assessment*. Clevedon: Multilingual Matters.

Curtiss, S. (1977) *Genie: A Psycholinguistic Study of a Modern Day Wild Child*. New York: Academic Press.

Cziko, G. A., Lambert, W. E. & Gutter, R. (1979) French immersion programs and students social attitudes: a multidimensional investigation. *Working Papers on Bilingualism*, 19, 13–28.

Cziko, G., Lambert, W. E., Sidoti, N. & Tucker, G. R. (1978) Graduates of Early Immersion: Retrospective Views of Grade 11 Students and their Parents. Unpublished research report. Montreal: McGill University.

Dalrymple-Alford, E. C. (1968) Interlingual interference in a color-naming task. *Psychonomic Science*, 10, 215–16.

Dalrymple-Alford, E. C. (1985) Language switching during bilingual reading. *British Journal of Psychology*, 76, 111–22.

Dalrymple-Alford, E. C. & Aamiry, A. (1967) Speed of responding to mixed language signals. *Psychonomic Science*, 9, 535–6.

Dalrymple-Alford, E. C. & Aamiry, A. (1970) Word associations of bilinguals. *Psychonomic Science*, 21, 319–20.

Dalrymple-Alford, E. C. & Budayr, B. (1966) Examination of some aspects of the Stroop color-word test. *Perceptual and Motor Skills*, 23, 1211–14.

d'Anglejan, A. (1978) Language learning in and out of classrooms. In J. C. Richards (ed.) *Understanding Second and Foreign Language Learning*. Rowley, Mass.: Newbury House.

Darcy, N. T. (1953) A review of the literature on the effects of bilingualism upon the measurement of intelligence. *Journal of Genetic Psychology*, 82, 21–57.

Das Gupta, J. (1975) Ethnicity, language and national development in India. In N. Glazer & D. P. Moynihan (eds.) *Ethnicity: Theory and Experience*. Cambridge, Mass.: Harvard University Press.

Da Silveira, Y. I. (1988) *Développement de la bilingualité chez l'Enfant Fon de Cotonou*. Unpublished Ph.D. dissertation. Quebec: Université Laval.

Dato, D. P. (1971) The development of the Spanish verb phrase in children's second-language learning. In P. Pimsleur & T. Quinn (eds.) *The Psychology of Second Language Learning*. Cambridge: Cambridge University Press.

de Beaugrande, R. (1987) Translation as text processing. *ALSED–LSP Newsletter*, 10, 2–22.

de Francis, J. (1984) *The Chinese Language: Fact and Fantasy*. Honolulu: University of Hawaii Press.

Deshaies, D. (1981) *Le Français Parlé dans la Ville de Québec: une Etude Sociolinguistique*. Quebec: International Center for Research on Bilingualism, G–1.

Deshaies, D. & Hamers, J. F. (1982) *Etude des Comportements Langagiers dans Deux Entreprises en Début de Processus de Francisation*. Quebec: International Center for Research on Bilingualism, G–3.

Desrochers, A. & Petrusic, W. M. (1983) Comprehension effects in comparative judgements. In J. C. Yuille (ed.) *Imagery, Memory and Cognition*. Hillsdale, N. J.: Erlbaum.

Deutsch, J. A. & Deutsch, D. (1963) Attention: some theoretical considerations. *Psychological Review*, 70, 80–90.

de Vos, G. & Romanucci-Ross, L. (1975) *Ethnic Identity*. Palo Alto: Mayfield.

de Vriendt, S. & Willemyns, R. (1987) Sociolinguistic aspects: linguistic research in Brussels. In E. Witte & H. Baetens Beardsmore (eds.) *The Interdisciplinary Study of Urban Bilingualism in Brussels*. Clevedon: Multilingual Matters.

Diebold, A. R. (1968) The consequences of early bilingualism in cognitive and personality information. In E. Norbeck, D. Price-Williams & W. M. McCord (eds.) *The Study of Personality: An Interdisciplinary Appraisal*. New York: Holt, Rinehart & Winston.

Dillard, J. L. (1978) Bidialectal education: Black English and Standard English in the United States. In B. Spolsky & R. L. Cooper (eds.) *Case Studies in Bilingual Education*. Rowley, Mass.: Newbury House.

Dillon, R., McCormack, P. D., Petrusic, P., Cook, M. & Lafleur, L. (1973) Release from proactive interference in compound and coordinate bilinguals. *Bulletin of the Psychonomic Society*, 2, 293–4.

di Vesta, F. J. & Gray, G. S. (1972) Listening and note-taking. *Journal of Educational Psychology*, 63, 8–14.

Dodson, K. (1981) A reappraisal of bilingual development and education. In H.

Baetens Beardsmore (ed.) *Elements of Bilingual Theory*. Brussels: Vrije Universiteit te Brussel.

Dodson, K. (1983) Bilingualism, language teaching and learning. *British Journal of Language Teaching*, 21, 3–8.

Dolson, D. P. (1985) The effects of Spanish home language use on the scholastic performance of Hispanic pupils. *Journal of Multilingual and Multicultural Development*, 6, 135–55.

Dorian, N. C. (1981) *Language Death: The Life Cycle of a Scottish Gaelic Dialect*. Philadelphia: University of Pennsylvania Press.

Dornic, S. (1978) The bilingual's performance: language dominance, stress and individual differences. In D. Gerver & H. W. Sinaiko (eds.) *Language, Interpretation and Communication*. New York: Plenum Press.

Doron, S. (1973) Reflexivity–Impulsivity and their Influence on Reading for Inference for Adult Students of ESL. Unpublished mimeo. Michigan: University of Michigan.

Doyle, A., Champagne, M. & Segalowitz, N. (1977) Some issues in the assessment of linguistic consequences of early bilingualism. *Working Papers on Bilingualism*, 14, 21–30.

Driedger, L. (1975) In search of cultural identity factors: a comparison of ethnic students. *Canadian Review of Sociology and Anthropology*, 12, 150–62.

Dubé, N. C. & Herbert G. (1975) Evaluation of the St John Valley Title VII Bilingual Education Program, 1970–1975. Unpublished report. Madawaska, Maine.

Dulay, H. C. & Burt, M. K. (1973) Should we teach children syntax? *Language Learning*, 23, 245–58.

Dulay, H. C. & Burt, M. K. (1974a) Natural sequences in child second language acquisition. *Language Learning*, 24, 37–53.

Dulay, H.C. & Burt, M. K. (1974b) A new perspective on the creative construction hypothesis in child second language acquisition. *Working Papers on Bilingualism*, 4, 71–98.

Dulay, H. C. & Burt, M. K. (1975a) A new approach to discovering universals of child second language acquisition. In D. Dato (ed.) *Developmental Psycholinguistics*. Washington, DC: Georgetown University Press.

Dulay, H. C. & Burt, M. K. (1975b) Creative construction in second language learning and teaching. In M. K. Burt & H. C. Dulay (eds.) *New Directions in Second Language Learning, Teaching and Bilingual Education*. Washington, DC: TESOL.

Dulay, H. C., Burt, M. K. & Krashen, S. (1982) *Language Two*. New York: Oxford University Press.

Duncan, S. E. & de Avila, E. A. (1979) Bilingualism and cognition: some recent findings. *NABE Journal*, 4, 15–50.

Dunn, L. M. (1959) *Peabody Picture Vocabulary Test*. Tennessee: American Guidance Service.

Dyer, F. N. (1971) Color-naming interference in monolinguals and bilinguals. *Journal of Verbal Learning and Verbal Behavior*, 10, 297–302.

Dyer, F. N. (1972) *The Stroop Phenomenon and its Use in the Study of Perceptual, Cognitive and Responses Processes*. US Army Medical Research Laboratory: Report 985.

Dyer, F. N. (1973) The Stroop phenomenon and its issue in the study of perceptual, cognitive, and response processes. *Memory and Cognition*, 1, 106–20.

Education For All (1985) *The Report of the Committee of Inquiry into the Education of Children from Ethnic Minority Groups*. London: Her Majesty's Stationery Office.

Edwards, H. P., Doutriaux, C. W., McCarrey, H. A. & Fu, L. (1976) Evaluation of Second Language Programs: Annual Report 1975–1976. Unpublished mimeo. Ottawa: Roman Catholic Separate School Board.

Edwards, J. (1982) Irish and English in Ireland. In P. Trudgill (ed.) *Language in the British Isles*. Cambridge: Cambridge University Press, 480–98.

Edwards, J. (ed.) (1984) *Linguistic Minorities, Policies and Pluralism*. London: Academic Press.

Edwards, J. (1985) *Language, Society and Identity*. Oxford: Blackwell.

Edwards, V. K. (1978a) Language attitudes and underperformance in West Indian children. *Educational Review*, 30, 51–8.

Edwards, V. K. (1978b) Dialect interference in West Indian children. *Language and Speech*, 21, 76–86.

Edwards, V. K. (1984) Language policy in multicultural Britain. In J. Edwards (ed.) *Linguistic Minorities, Policies and Pluralism*. London: Academic Press.

Edwards, V. K. (1986) *Language in a Black Community*. Clevedon: Multilingual Matters.

Ehri, L. C. & Ryan, E. B. (1980) Performance of bilinguals in a picture–word interference task. *Journal of Psycholinguistic Research*, 9, 285–302.

Eilers, R.E., Gavin, W. J. & Oller, D. K. (1982) Cross-linguistic perception in infancy: early effects of linguistic experience. *Journal of Child Language*, 9, 289–302.

Ekstrand, L. H. (1978) Migrant adaptation: a cross-cultural problem. In R. Freudenstein (ed.) *Teaching the Children of Immigrants*. Brussels: Didier.

Ekstrand, L. H. (1980) *Optimum Age, Critical Period, Harmfulness or what in Early Bilingualism? A Critical Review of Theories and Empirical Evidence*. Leipzig: Paper presented at the Twenty-Second International Congress of Psychology, 6–12 July 1980.

Ekstrand, L. H. (1981) Theories and facts about early bilingualism in native and migrant children. *Grazer Linguistische Studien*, 14, 24–52.

Ellis, R. (1985) *Understanding Second Language Acquisition*. Oxford: Oxford University Press.

Endo, M., Shimizu, A. & Hori, T. (1978) Functional asymmetry of visual fields for Japanese words in kana (syllable-based) writing and Japanese shape-recognition in Japanese subjects. *Neuropsychologia*, 16, 291–7.

Ervin, S. M. (1961) Semantic shift in bilingualism. *American Journal of Psychology*, 74, 233–41.

Ervin, S. M. (1964) Language and TAT content in bilinguals. *Journal of Abnormal and Social Psychology*, 68, 500–7.

Ervin, S. M. & Osgood, C. E. (1954) Second language learning and bilingualism. *Journal of Abnormal and Social Psychology*, Supplement, 49, 139–46.

Ervin-Tripp, S. M. (1964) An analysis of the interaction of language, topic and listener. *American Anthropologist*, 66, 86–102.

Ervin-Tripp, S. M. (1973) Identification and bilingualism. In A. Dil (ed.) *Language Acquisition and Communicative Choice*. Stanford: Stanford University press.

Ervin-Tripp, S. M. (1974) Is second language learning like the first? *TESOL Quarterly*, 8, 11–127.

Fang, S. P., Tzeng, O. J. & Alva, L. (1981) Intralanguage versus interlanguage: Stroop effects in two types of writing systems. *Memory and Cognition*, 96, 609–17.

Fantini, A. E. (1978) Bilingual behaviour and social cues: case studies of two bilingual children. In M. Paradis (ed.) *Aspects of Bilingualism*. Columbia: Hornbeam Press.

Fantini, A. E. (1985) *Language Acquisition of a Bilingual Child: A Sociolinguistic Perspective*. Clevedon: Multilingual Matters.

Fasold, R. (1984) *The Sociolinguistics of Society*. Oxford: Blackwell.

Fasold, R. & Shuy, R. W. (eds.) (1970) *Teaching Standard English in the Inner City*. Washington, DC: Center for Applied Linguistics. Urban Language Series.

Fathman, A. (1975) The relationship between age and second language productive ability. *Language Learning*, 25, 245–53.

Felix, S. W. (1981) The effect of formal instruction on second language acquisition. *Language Learning*, 31, 87–112.

Ferguson, C. A. (1959) Diglossia. *Word*, 15, 125–40.

Ferguson, C. A. & DeBose, C. E. (1977) Simplified register, broken language and pidginization. In A. Valdman (ed.) *Pidgin and Creole Linguistics*. Bloomington: Indiana University.

Fillmore, C. J. (1968) The case for case. In E. Bach & R. T. Harms (eds.) *Universals in Linguistic Theory*. New York: Holt, Rinehart & Winston.

Fishman, J. A. (1964) Language maintenance and language shift as a field of inquiry. *Linguistics*, 9, 32–70.

Fishman, J. A. (1965) Who speaks what language to whom and when? *La Linguistique*, 2, 67–8.

Fishman, J. A. (1967) Bilingualism with and without diglossia; diglossia with and without bilingualism. *Journal of Social Issues*, 32, 29–38.

Fishman, J. A. (1968) Nationality–nationalism and nation–nationism. In J. A. Fishman, C. A. Ferguson & J. Das Gupta (eds.) *Language Problems of Developing Nations*. The Hague: Mouton.

Fishman, J. A. (1972) *The Sociology of Language: An Interdisciplinary Social Sciences Approach to Language in Society*. Rowley, Mass.: Newbury House.

Fishman, J. A. (1977a) Language and ethnicity. In H. Giles (ed.) *Language, Ethnicity and Intergroup Relations*. London: Academic Press.

Fishman, J. A. (1977b) The sociology of bilingual education. In B. Spolsky & R. L. Cooper (eds.) *Frontiers of Bilingual Education*. Rowley, Mass.: Newbury House.

Fishman, J. A. (1980) Bilingualism and biculturalism as individual and societal phenomena. *Journal of Multilingual and Multicultural Development*, 1, 1–13.

Fishman, J. A. (1985) 'Nothing new under the sun': a case study of alternatives in language and ethnocultural identity. In J. A. Fishman, M. H. Gertner, E. G. Lowy & W. G. Milan (eds.) *The Rise and Fall of the Ethnic Revival: Perspectives on Language and Ethnicity*. Berlin: Mouton.

Fishman, J. A., Cooper, R. & Ma, R. (1971) *Bilingualism in the Barrio*. Bloomington: Indiana University Press.

Fishman, J. A. & Lovas, J. (1970) Bilingual education in sociolinguistic perspective. *TESOL Quarterly*, 4, 215–22.

Fitzpatrick, F. (1987) *The Open Door*. Clevedon: Multilingual Matters.

Forgas, J. P. (1981) What is social about social cognition? In J. P. Forgas (ed.) *Social Cognition: Perspectives on Everyday Understanding*. London: Academic Press.

Frasure-Smith, N., Lambert, W. E. & Taylor, D. M. (1975) Choosing the language of instruction for one's children: a Quebec Study. *Journal of Cross-Cultural Psychology*, 6, 131–55.

Fredman, M. (1975) The effect of therapy given in Hebrew on the home language of the bilingual and polyglot adult aphasic in Israel. *British Journal of Disorders of Communication*, 10, 61–9.

Gagnon, M. (1970) *Echelle d'Attitude à l'Egard de la Langue Seconde, Anglais pour Francophones: Manuel et Normes*. Montreal: Lidec Inc.

Gagnon, M. (1974) Quelques facteurs déterminant l'attitude vis-à-vis de l'anglais, seconde langue. In R. Darnell (ed.) *Linguistic Diversity in Canadian Society*. Edmonton: Linguistic Research Inc., Volume 2.

Gal, S. (1979) *Language Shift: Social Determinants of Linguistic Change in Bilingual Austria*. New York: Academic Press.

Galloway, L. (1980) *The Cerebral Organization of Language in Bilinguals and Second Language Learners*. Niagara Falls, Ontario: Paper read at the Symposium on Cerebral Lateralization in Bilingualism, BABBLE Conference.

Galloway, L. & Krashen, S. (1980) Cerebral organization in bilingualism and second language. In R. Scarcella and S. Krashen (eds.) *Research in Second Language Acquisition*. Rowley, Mass.: Newbury House.

Gans, H. (1979) Symbolic ethnicity: the future of ethnic groups and cultures in America. *Ethnic and Racial Studies*, 2, 1–20.

Gardner, R. C. (1979) Social Psychological aspects of second language acquisition. In H. Giles & R. St. Clair (eds.) Language and Social Psychology. Oxford: Blackwell.

Gardner, R. C. (1980) On the validity of affective variables in second language acquisition: conceptual, contextual and statistical considerations. *Language Learning*, 30, 255–70.

Gardner, R. C. (1985) *Social Psychology and Second Language Learning: the Role of Attitudes and Motivation*. London: Edward Arnold.

Gardner, R. C. & Lambert, W. E. (1959) Motivational variables in second-language acquisition. *Canadian Journal of Psychology*, 13, 266–72.

Gardner, R. C. & Lambert, W. E. (1972) *Attitudes and Motivation in Second Language Learning*. Rowley, Mass.: Newbury House.

Gardner, R. C. & Smythe, P. C. (1975) *Second Language Acquisition: A Social Psychological Approach*. London, Ontario: University of Western Ontario, Department of Psychology, Research Report 332.

Gass, S. (1979) Language transfer and universal grammatical relations. *Language Learning*, 27, 327–44.

Gass, S. (1984) A review of interlanguage syntax: language transfer and language universals. *Language Learning*, 34, 115–31.

Gaziel, T., Obler, L. & Albert, M. (1978) A tachistoscopic study of Hebrew–English bilinguals. In M. Albert & L. Obler (eds.) *The Bilingual Brain*. New York: Academic Press.

Geffner, D. S. & Hochbert, I. (1971) Ear laterality performance of children from low middle socio-economic levels on a verbal dichotic listening task. *Cortex*, 3, 193–203.

Gekoski, W. L. (1980) Language acquisition context and language organization in bilinguals. *Journal of Psycholinguistic Research*, 9(5), 429–49.

Gendron, J. D. (1972) *Rapport de la Commission d'Enquête sur la Situation de la Langue Fran-*

çaise et sur les Droits Linguistiques au Québec, Livre I. La Langue de Travail. La Situation de la Langue Française au Québec. Quebec: Editeur Officiel du Québec.

Genesee, F. (1976) The role of intelligence in second language learning. *Language Learning,* 26, 267–80.

Genesee, F. (1979) *Les Programmes d'Immersion en Français du Bureau des Ecoles Protestantes du Grand Montréal.* Quebec: Etudes et Documents du Ministère de l'Education du Québec.

Genesee, F. (1980) A Comparison of Early and Late Second Language Learning. Unpublished mimeo. Montreal: McGill University.

Genesee, F. (1981a) Cognitive and social consequences of bilingualism. In R. C. Gardner & R. Kalin (eds.) *A Canadian Social Psychology of Ethnic Relations.* London: Methuen.

Genesee, F. (1981b) Evaluation of the Laurenvale Early Partial and Early Total Immersion Program. Unpublished mimeo. Montreal: McGill University.

Genesee, F. (1984) French Immersion Programs. In S. Shapson & V. D'Oyley (eds.) *Bilingual and Multicultural Education: Canadian Perspective.* Clevedon: Multilingual Matters.

Genesee, F. & Bourhis, R. Y. (1982) The social psychological significance of code switching in cross-cultural communication. *Journal of Language and Social Psychology,* 1, 1–27.

Genesee, F., Hamers, J. F., Lambert, W. E., Mononen, L., Seitz, M. & Starck, R. (1978) Language processing in bilinguals. *Brain and Language,* 5, 1–12.

Genesee, F., Tucker, G. R. & Lambert, W. E. (1978) The development of ethnic identity and ethnic role taking skills in children from different school settings. *International Journal of Psychology,* 13, 39–57.

Gerver, D. (1971) Aspects of Simultaneous Interpretation and Human Information Processing. Unpublished Ph.D. dissertation. Oxford: Oxford University.

Gerver, D. (1972a) ASPA–Automatic speech-pause analyzer. *Behavioral Research Methods and Instrumentation,* 4, 265–70.

Gerver, D. (1972b) *Simultaneous and Consecutive Interpretation and Human Information Processing.* London: Social Science Research Council, Report HR566/1.

Gerver, D. (1976) Empirical studies of simultaneous interpretation. In R. W. Brislin (ed.) *Translation: Application and Research.* New York: Gardner Press.

Gerver, D., Longley, P., Long, J. & Lambert, S. M. (1980) Selecting Trainee Conference Interpreters. Unpublished mimeographed report. Stirling: University of Stirling.

Giles, H. (1970) Evaluative reactions to accents. *Educational Review,* 22, 211–27.

Giles, H. (1973) Accent mobility: a model and some data. *Anthropological Linguistics,* 15, 87–105.

Giles, H., Bourhis, R. Y. & Taylor, D. M. (1977) Towards a theory of language in ethnic group relation. In H. Giles (ed.) *Language, Ethnicity & Intergroup Relations.* London: Academic Press.

Giles, H. & Byrne, J. L. (1982) An intergroup approach to second language acquisition. *Journal of Multilingual and Multicultural Development,* 3, 17–40.

Giles, H., Hewstone, M. & Ball, P. (1983) Language attitudes in multilingual settings: prologue with priorities. *Journal of Multilingual and Multicultural Development,* 4, 81–100.

Giles, H. & Johnson, P. (1981) The role of language in ethnic group relations. In J. C. Turner & H. Giles (eds.) *Intergroup Behaviour*. Oxford: Blackwell.

Giles, H., Mulac, A., Bradac, J. J. & Johnson, P. (1986) Speech accommodation theory: the first decade and beyond. *Communication Yearbook*, 10, 8–34.

Giles, H. & Powesland, P. F. (1975) *Speech Style and Social Evaluation*. London: Academic Press.

Giles, H., Rosenthal, D. & Young, R. K. (1985) Perceived ethnolinguistic vitality: the Anglo- and Greek–Australian setting. *Journal of Multilingual and Multicultural Development*, 6, 253–69.

Giles, H. & Ryan, E. B. (1982) Prolegomena for developing a social psychological theory of language attitudes. In E. B. Ryan & H. Giles (eds.) *Attitudes towards Language Variation: Social and Applied Contexts*. London: Edward Arnold.

Giles, H. & Smith, P. M. (1979) Accommodation theory: optimal levels of convergence. In H. Giles & R. N. St Clair (eds.) *Language and Social Psychology*. Oxford: Blackwell.

Giles, H., Taylor, D. M. & Bourhis, R. Y. (1973) Towards a theory of interpersonal accommodation through speech: some Canadian data. *Language in Society*, 2, 177–92.

Glanzer, M. & Duarte, A. (1971) Repetition between and within languages in free recall. *Journal of Verbal Learning and Verbal Behavior*, 10, 625–30.

Glazer, N. (1966) The process and problems of language maintenance: an integrative review. In J. A. Fishman (ed.) *Language Loyalty in the United States*. The Hague: Mouton.

Glazer, N. & Moynihan, D. P. (eds.) (1963) *Beyond the Melting Pot*. Cambridge, Mass.: MIT/Harvard University Press.

Gleason, H. A. (1961) *An Introduction to Descriptive Linguistics*. Revised edition. New York: Holt, Rinehart & Winston.

Gliksman, L. & Gardner, R. C. (1976) *Some Relationships between Students' Attitudes and their Behaviour in the French Classroom*. London, Ontario: Language Research Group, Department of Psychology, University of Western Ontario, Research Bulletin, 5.

Goffman, E. (1959) *The Presentation of Self in Everyday Life*. New York: Doubleday.

Goggin, J. & Wickins, D. D. (1971) Proactive interference and language change in short-term memory. *Journal of Verbal Learning and Verbal Behavior*, 10, 453–8.

Goldman-Eisler, F. (1968) *Psycholinguistics: Experiments in Spontaneous Speech*. London: Academic Press.

Goldman-Eisler, F. (1972) Segmentation of input in simultaneous interpretation. *Journal of Psycholinguistic Research*, 1, 127–40.

Gonzales, G. (1970) The Acquisition of Spanish Grammar by Native Spanish Speakers. Unpublished Ph.D. dissertation. Austin: University of Texas at Austin.

Goodman, G. S., Haith, M. M., Guttentag, R. E. & Rao, S. (1985) Automatic processing of word meaning: intralingual and interlingual interference. *Child Development*, 56, 103–18.

Goodz, N. S. (1984) *Parent-to-Child Speech in Bilingual Families: Variables Influencing Parental language Mixing*. Boston: Paper presented at the Ninth Annual Meeting of the Boston University Conference on Child Development.

Goodz, N. S. (1985) *Parent-to-Child Speech in Bilingual and Monolingual Families*. Toronto: Paper presented at the Society for Research on Child Development.

Gordon, H. W. (1980) Cerebral organization in bilinguals. *Brain and Language*, 9, 255–68.

Gordon, M. M. (1981) Models of pluralism: the American dilemma. *The Annals of the American Academy of Political and Social Science*, 454, 178–88.

Gorrell, J. J., Bregman, N. J., McAllistair, H. A. & Lipscombe, T. J. (1982) A comparison of spatial role-taking in monolingual and bilingual children. *Journal of Genetic Psychology*, 140, 3–10.

Grammont, M. (1902) *Observations sur le Langage des Enfants*. Paris: Mélanges Meillet.

Gray, T. (1982) Bilingual program? What's that? *Linguistic Reporter*, 24.

Green, D. W. (1986) Control, activation, and resource: a framework and a model for the control of speech in bilinguals. *Brain and Language*, 27, 210–23.

Greenberg, J. H. (1956) The measurement of linguistic diversity. *Language*, 32, 109–15.

Gregg, K. R. (1984) Krashen's monitor and Occam's razor. *Applied Linguistics*, 5, 79–100.

Grégoire, A. (1947) *L'Apprentissage du Langage*. Gembloux: Duculot.

Grosjean, F. (1982) *Life with Two Languages: An Introduction to Bilingualism*. Cambridge, Mass.: Harvard University Press.

Grosjean, F. (1985a) The bilingual as a competent but specific speaker–hearer. *The Journal of Multilingual and Multicultural Development*, 6, 467–77.

Grosjean, F. (1985b) Polyglot aphasics and language mixing: a comment on Perecman. *Brain and Language*, 26, 349–55.

Grosjean, F. & Soares, C. (1986) Processing mixed language: some preliminary findings. In J. Vaid (ed.) *Language Processing in Bilinguals: Psycholinguistic and Neuropsychological Perspectives*. Hillsdale, N. J.: Erlbaum.

Gudykunst, W. B. (1986) Towards a theory of intergroup communication. In W. B. Gudykunst (ed.) *Intergroup Communication*. London: Edward Arnold.

Guiora, A. Z. (1972) Construct validity and transpositional research: toward an empirical study of psychoanalytic concepts. *Comprehensive Psychiatry*, 13, 139–50.

Gumperz, J. J. (1964a) Linguistic and social interaction in two communities. *American Anthropologist*, 66, 137–53.

Gumperz, J. J. (1964b) Hindi–Punjabi code-switching in Delhi. In H. Hunt (ed.) *Proceedings of the Ninth International Congress of Linguistics*. The Hague: Mouton.

Gumperz, J. J. (1968) The speech community. In D. L. Sills (ed.) *International Encyclopaedia of the Social Sciences*. New York: Macmillan, Volume 9.

Gumperz, J. J. (1971) *Language in Social Groups*. Stanford: Stanford University Press.

Gumperz, J. J. (1982) Social network and language shift. In J. J. Gumperz (ed.) *Discourse Strategies*. Cambridge: Cambridge University Press.

Gumperz, J. J. & Wilson, R. (1971) Convergence and creolization: a case from the Indo-Aryan/Dravidian Border in India. In D. H. Hymes (ed.) *Pidginization and Creolization of Language*. Cambridge: Cambridge University Press.

Guttentag, R. E., Haith, M. M., Goodman, G. S. & Hauch, J. (1984) Semantic processing of unattended words by bilinguals: a test of the input switch mechanism. *Journal of Verbal Learning and Verbal Behavior*, 23, 178–88.

Hakuta, K. (1976) A case study of a Japanese child learning a second language. *Language Learning*, 26, 321–51.

Hakuta, K. & Diaz, R. (1984) The relationship between bilingualism and cognitive ability: a critical discussion and some new longitudinal data. In K. E. Nelson (ed.) *Children's Language*. Hillsdale, N. J.: Erlbaum, Volume 5.

Halliday, M. A. K. (1975) *Learning how to Mean: Explorations in the Development of Language*. London: Edward Arnold.

Hamers, J. F. (1973) Interdependent and Independent States of a Bilingual's Two Languages. Unpublished Ph.D. dissertation. Montreal: McGill University.

Hamers, J. F. (1979) Le rôle du langage et de la culture dans les processus d'apprentissage et dans la planification éducative. *Recherche, Pédagogie et Culture*, 43, 24–31.

Hamers, J. F. (1981) Psychological approaches to the development of bilinguality. In H. Baetens Beardsmore (ed.) *Elements of Bilingual Theory*. Brussels: Vrije Universiteit te Brussel.

Hamers, J. F. & Bertrand, C. (1973) Interplay of the semantic aspect of the stimuli in a language naming task. *Rapport d'Activité de l'Institut de Phonétique*. Brussels: Université Libre de Bruxelles.

Hamers, J. F. & Blanc, M. (1982) Towards a social–psychological model of bilingual development. *Journal of Language and Social Psychology*, 1, 29–49.

Hamers, J. F. & Blanc, M. (1983) *Bilingualité et Bilinguisme*. Brussels: Mardaga. Série Psychologie et Sciences Humaines, 129.

Hamers, J. F. & Blanc, M. (1987) *Social Psychological Foundations of Bilingual Development*. Paper presented at the Third International Conference on the Social Psychology of Language, Bristol, 20–23 July 1987.

Hamers, J. F. & Deshaies, D. (1981a) Effets des contacts inter-groupes sur les attitudes envers la langue seconde et les membres de ce groupe culturel chez les élèves anglophones et francophones de la province de Québec. In J.-G. Savard & L. Laforge (eds.) *Actes du 5ᵉ Congrès de l'Association Internationale de Linguistique Appliquée*. Quebec: International Center for Research on Bilingualism/Presses de L'Université Laval, A–16, 141–9.

Hamers, J. F. & Deshaies, D. (1981b) Les contacts interethniques: qu'est-ce qui les rend efficaces? In J. D. Gendron & R. Vigneault (eds.) *Compte-Rendu du Colloque sur "Les mécanismes psychologiques sous-jacents à l'apprentissage d'une langue seconde"* – ACFAS 1980. Quebec: International Center for Research on Bilingualism/Presses de l'Université Laval, B–99, 15–27.

Hamers, J. F. & Deshaies, D. (1982) Les dimensions de l'identité culturelle chez les jeunes québécois. In J. D. Gendron, A. Prujiner & R. Vigneault (eds.) *Identité Culturelle: Approches Méthodologiques*. Quebec: International Center for Research on Bilingualism, B–113, 39–78.

Hamers, J. F. & Lambert, W. E. (1972) Bilingual interdependencies in auditory perception. *Journal of Verbal Learning and Verbal Behavior*, 11, 303–10.

Hamers, J. F. & Lambert, W. E. (1974) Bilingual reactions to cross-language semantic ambiguity. In S. T. Carey (ed.) *Bilingualism, Biculturalism and Education*. Edmonton: University of Alberta, Printing Department.

Hamers, J. F. & Lambert, W. E. (1977) Visual field and cerebral hemisphere preferences in bilinguals. In S. J. Segalowitz & F. A. Gruber (eds.) *Language Development and Neurological Theory*. New York: Academic Press.

Hammoud, R. (1982) Utilisation de l'Image Mentale et du Champ d'Association dans l'Enseignement du Vocabulaire Arabe à des Débutants Adultes Francophones. Unpublished Ph.D. dissertation. Quebec: Université Laval.

Hammoud, R. (1983) *Utilisation de l'Image Mentale et du Champ d'Association dans l'Enseignement du Vocabulaire d'une Langue Etrangère à des Débutants Adultes Francophones en Contexte Canadien.* Quebec: International Center for Research on Bilingualism, B–129.

Hamp, E. P. (1965) What a contrastive grammar is not, if it is. *Georgetown Round Table Monograph*, 21. Georgetown: University of Georgetown.

Hansen, J. & Stansfield, C. (1981) The relationship of field dependent–independent cognitive styles to foreign language achievement. *Language Learning*, 31, 349–67.

Hanson, G. (1979) The position of the second generation of Finnish immigrants in Sweden: the importance of education in the home language to the welfare of second generation immigrants. Split, Paper presented at the Symposium on the Position of Second Generation Yugoslav Immigrants in Sweden.

Harley, B. (1986) *Age in Second Language Acquisition.* Clevedon: Multilingual Matters, 22.

Harley, B., Hart, D. & Lapkin, S. (1986) The effects of early bilingual schooling on first language skills. *Applied Psycholinguistics*, 7, 295–322.

Harley, B. & Swain, M. (1977) An analysis of verb form and function in the speech of French immersion pupils. *Working Papers on Bilingualism*, 14, 31–46.

Harley, B. & Swain, M. (1978) An analysis of verb systems used by young learners of French. *Interlanguage Studies Bulletin*, 3, 35–79.

Harris, B. & Sherwood, B. (1978) Translating as an innate skill. In D. Gerver & H. W. Sinaiko (eds.) *Language, Interpretation and Communication.* New York and London: Plenum Press.

Hartnett, D. (1975) The Relation of Cognitive Style and Hemispheric Preference to Deductive and Inductive Second Language Learning. Unpublished Ph.D. dissertation. Montreal: McGill University.

Hasuike, R., Tzeng, O. & Hung, D. (1986) Script effects and cerebral lateralization: the case of Chinese characters. In J. Vaid (ed.) *Language Processing in Bilinguals: Psycholinguistic and Neuropsychological Perspectives.* Hillsdale, N. J.: Erlbaum.

Hatch, E. M. (1974) Second language learning-universals? *Working Papers on Bilingualism*, 3, 1–17.

Hatch, E. M. (ed.) (1978a) *Second Language Acquisition: a Book of Readings.* Rowley, Mass.: Newbury House.

Hatch, E. M. (1978b) Discourse analysis and second language acquisition. In E. M. Hatch (ed.) *Second Language Acquisition: a Book of Readings.* Rowley, Mass.: Newbury House, 401–35.

Hatch, E. M. (1983) *Psycholinguistics: a Second Language Perspective.* Rowley, Mass.: Newbury House.

Hatta, T. (1981) Differential processing of kanji and kana stimuli in Japanese people: some implications from Stroop-test results. *Neuropsychologia*, 19, 87–93.

Haugen, E. (1950) The analysis of linguistic borrowings. *Language*, 26, 210–31.

Hebb, D. O., Lambert, W. E. & Tucker, G. R. (1971) Language, thought and experience. *Modern Language Journal*, 55, 212–22.

Hébert, R. (1976) Rendement Académique et Langue d'Enseignement chez les Elèves Franco-Manitobains. Saint-Boniface, Manitoba: Centre de Recherches du Collège Universitaire Saint-Boniface.

Hechter, M. (1975) *Internal Colonialism: the Celtic Fringe in British National Development, 1530–1966.* London: Routledge and Kegan Paul.

Heidelberger Forschungsprojekt 'Pidgin-Deutsch' (1976) *Untersuchungen zur Erlernung des Deutsches durch ausländische Arbeiter.* Heidelberg: Germanistiches Seminar der Universität.

Heider, F. (1958) *The Psychology of Interpersonal Relations.* New York: Wiley.

Herbert, R. K. (1982) Cerebral asymetry in bilinguals and the deaf: perspectives on a common pattern. *Journal of Multilingual and Multicultural Development,* 3, 47–59.

Hernandez-Chavez, E. (1978) Language maintenance, bilingual education and philosophies of bilingualism in the United States. In J. E. Alatis (ed.) *International Dimensions of Bilingual Education.* Washington, DC: Georgetown University Press.

Hewitt, R. (1986) *White Talk Black Talk: Inter-racial Friendship and Communication amongst Adolescents.* Cambridge: Cambridge University Press.

Hewstone, M. & Giles, H. (1986) Social groups and social stereotypes in intergroup communications: a review and model of intergroup communication breakdown. In W. B. Gudykunst (ed.) *Intergroup Communication.* London: Edward Arnold.

Hink, R., Kaga, K. & Suzuki, J. (1980) An evoked potential correlate of reading ideographic and phonetic Japanese scripts. *Neuropsychologia,* 18, 455–64.

Hinnenkamp, V. (1982) *Foreigner Talk und Tarzanisch.* Hamburg: Helmut Buske Verlag.

Holmstrand, L. E. (1979) The effects on general school achievement of early commencement of English instruction. Uppsala: University of Uppsala Department of Education, Uppsala Reports on Education, 4, 1–45.

Homans, G. C. (1961) *Social Behavior: its Elementary Forms.* New York: Harcourt, Brace and World.

Hopper, R. (1977) Language attitudes in the job interview. *Communication Monograph,* 44, 346–51.

Hudson, R. A. (1980) *Sociolinguistics.* Cambridge: Cambridge University Press.

Hughes, E. C. (1970) The linguistic division of labor in industrial and urban societies. Georgetown Monograph Series on Language and Linguistics, 23, 103–19.

Hummel, K. M. (1986) Memory for bilingual prose. In J. Vaid (ed.) *Language Processing in Bilinguals: Psycholinguistic and Neuropsychological Perspectives.* Hillsdale, N.J.: Erlbaum.

Husband, C. & Saifullah Khan (1982) The viability of ethnolinguistic vitality. *Journal of Multilingual and Multicultural Development,* 3, 193–205.

Hymes, D. (1971) *On Communicative Competence.* Philadelphia: University of Pennsylvania Press.

Hynd, G. & Scott, S. (1980) Propositional and appositional modes of thought and differential speech lateralization in Navajo Indian and Anglo children. *Child Development,* 51, 909–11.

Hynd, G., Teeter, A. & Stewart, A. (1980) Acculturation and the lateralization of speech in the bilingual native American. *International Journal of Neuroscience,* 11, 1–7.

Ianco-Worrall, A. D. (1972) Bilingualism and cognitive development. *Child Development,* 43, 1390–400.

Ingram, R. M. (1985) Simultaneous interpretation of sign languages: semiotic and psycholinguistic perspectives. *Multilingua,* 4, 91–102.

Jakobovits, L. A. (1970) *Foreign Language Learning: a Psycho-linguistic Analysis of the Issues.* Rowley, Mass: Newbury House.

Jakobovits, L. A. & Lambert, W. E. (1961) Semantic satiation among bilinguals. *Journal of Experimental Psychology*, 62, 576–82.

Jakobovits, L. A. & Lambert, W. E. (1967) A note on the measurement of semantic satiation. *Journal of Verbal Learning and Verbal Behavior*, 6, 954–57.

James, C. (1980) *Contrastive Analysis*. Harlow: Longman.

Javier, R. A. & Alpert, M. (1986) The effect of stress on the linguistic generalization of bilingual individuals. *Journal of Psycholinguistic Research*, 15, 419–35.

Jones, E. E. & Davies, K. E. (1965) From acts to dispositions: the attribution process in perception. In L. Berkowitz (ed.) *Advances in Social Psychology*. New York: Academic Press, Volume 2.

Joreskog, K. G. & Sorbom, D. (1978) *LISREL: Analysis of Linear Structural Relationships by the Method of Maximum Likelihood*. Chicago: International Educational Services.

Kachru, B. B. (1978) Code-mixing as a communicative strategy. In J. Alatis (ed.) *International Dimensions of Bilingual Education*. Washington, DC: Georgetown University Press.

Kachru, B. B. (1982) The bilingual's linguistic repertoire. In B. Hartford, A. Valdman & C. R. Foster (eds.) *Issues in International Bilingual Education: the Role of the Vernacular*. New York: Plenum Press.

Kalin, R. (1982) The social significance of speech in medical, legal and occupational settings. In E. B. Ryan & H. Giles (eds.) *Attitudes towards Language Variation*. London: Edward Arnold.

Karmiloff-Smith, A. (1979) *A Functional Approach to Child Language*. Cambridge: Cambridge University Press.

Keller-Cohen, D. (1979) Systematicity and variations in the non-native child's acquisition of conversational skills. *Language Learning*, 29, 27–44.

Kelly, H. H. (1973) The process of causal attribution. *American Psychologist*, 28, 107–28.

Kendall, M. B. (1980) Radical grammars: interplays of form and function. In H. Giles, W. P. Robinson & P. M. Smith (eds.) *Language: Social Psychological Perspectives*. Oxford: Pergamon.

Kenyeres, A. (1938) Comment une petite Hongroise de sept ans apprend le français. *Archives de Psychologie*, 26, 321–66.

Kessler, C. & Quinn, M. E. (1982) Cognitive development in bilingual environments. In B. Hartford, A. Valdman & C. R. Foster (eds.) *Issues in International Bilingual Education: The Role of the Vernacular*. New York: Plenum Press.

Kessler, C. & Quinn, M. E. (1987) Language minority children's linguistic and cognitive creativity. *Journal of Multilingual and Multicultural Development*, 8, 173–86.

Khubchandani, L. M. (1978) Multilingual education in India. In B. Spolsky & R. L. Cooper (eds.) *Case Studies in Bilingual Education*. Rowley, Mass.: Newbury House.

Khubchandani, L. M. (1979) A demographic typology for Hindi, Urdu, Panjabi speakers in Northern India. In W. C. McCormack & S. A. Wurm (eds.) *Language and Society*. The Hague: Mouton.

Kintsch, W. (1970) Recognition memory in bilingual subjects. *Journal of Verbal Learning and Verbal Behavior*, 9, 405–9.

Kintsch, W. & Kintsch, E. (1969) Interlingual interference and memory processes. *Journal of Verbal Learning and Verbal Behavior*, 8, 16–19.

Kintsch, W. & Van Dijk, T. A. (1978) Toward a model of text comprehension and production. *Psychological Review*, 85, 363–94.

Kirp, D. (1983) Elusive equality: race, ethnicity, and education in the American experience. In N. Glazer & K. Young (eds.) *Ethnic Pluralism and Public Policy*. London: Heinemann.

Kirsner, K., Brown, H. L., Abrul, S., Chadha, N. K. & Sharma, N. K. (1980) Bilingualism and lexical representation. *Quarterly Journal of Experimental Psychology*, 32, 585–94.

Kiyak, H. A. (1982) Interlingual interference in naming color words. *Journal of Cross-Cultural Psychology*, 13, 125–35.

Klein, W. & Dittmar, N. (1979) *Developing Grammars*. Berlin: Springer Verlag.

Klima, E. S. & Bellugi, U. (1966) Syntactic regularities in the speech of children. In J. Lyons & R. J. Wales (eds.) *Psycholinguistic Papers: The Proceedings of the 1966 Edinburgh Conference*. Edinburgh: Edinburgh University Press.

Kloss, H. (1966) Conceptual background: an analysis of factors influencing language maintenance outcomes. In J. A. Fishman (ed.) *Language Loyalty in the United States*. The Hague: Mouton.

Kloss, H. (1969) *Research Problems in Group Bilingualism*. Quebec: International Center for Research on Bilingualism.

Kloss, H. & McConnell, G. D. (1974ff.) *Composition Linguistique des Nations du Monde*. Quebec: International Center for Research on Bilingualism/Presses de l'Université Laval.

Kolers, P. A. (1963) Interlingual word association. *Journal of Verbal Learning and Verbal Behavior*, 2, 291–300.

Kolers, P. A. (1965) Bilingualism and bicodalism. *Language and Speech*, 8, 122–6.

Kolers, P. A. (1966) Reading and talking bilingually. *American Journal of Psychology*, 79, 357–76.

Kolers, P. A. (1968) Bilingualism and information processing. *Scientific American*, March, 78–86.

Kolers, P. A. (1978) On the representation of experience. In D. Gerver & H. W. Sinaiko (eds.) *Language, Interpretation and Communication*. New York: Plenum Press.

Kolers, P. A. & Gonzales, E. (1980) Memory for words, synonyms and translation. *Journal of Experimental Psychology, Human Learning and Memory*, 6, 53–65.

Krashen, S. (1981) *Second Language Acquisition and Second Language Learning*. Oxford: Pergamon Press.

Krashen, S., Long, M. & Scarcella, R. (1979) Age, rate and eventual attainment in second language acquisition. *TESOL Quarterly*, 13, 573–2.

Krashen, S., Seliger, H. & Hartnett, D. (1974) Two studies in adult second language learning. *Kritikon Litterarum*, 3, 220–8.

Kreitler, H. & Kreitler, S. (1976) *Cognitive Orientation and Behaviour*. New York: Springer Verlag.

Kruskal, J. B. & Wish, M. (1978) *Multidimensional Scaling*. Beverly Hills & London: Sage Publications.

Kuo, E. C. Y. (1979) Measuring communicativity in multilingual societies: the case of Singapore and West Malaysia. *Anthropological Linguistics*, 21, 328–40.

Kuo, E. (1984) Mass media and language planning: Singapore's 'Speak Mandarin' campaign. *Journal of Communication*, 34, 24–35.

Kyle, J. G. & Woll, B. (1985) *Sign Language: The Study of Deaf People and their Language*. Cambridge: Cambridge University Press.

Lambert, W. E., Havelka, J. & Gardner, R. C. (1959) Linguistic manifestations of bilingualism. *American Journal of Psychology*, 72, 77–82.

Lambert, W. E., Hodgson, R. C., Gardner, R. C. & Fillenbaum, S. J. (1960) Evaluation reactions to spoken languages. *Journal of Abnormal and Social Psychology*, 60, 44–51.

Lambert, W. E., Ignatov, M. & Krauthamer, M. (1968) Bilingual organization in free recall. *Journal of Verbal Learning and Verbal Behavior*, 7, 207–14.

Lambert, W. E. & Jakobovits, L. A. (1960) Verbal satiation and changes in the intensity of meaning. *Journal of Experimental Psychology*, 60, 376–83.

Lambert, W. E., Just, M. & Segalowitz, N. (1970) Some cognitive consequences of following the curricula of Grades One and Two in a foreign language. *Georgetown Monograph Series on Languages and Linguistics*, 23, 229–79.

Lambert, W. E. & Klineberg, O. (1967) *Children's View of Foreign Peoples: A Cross-National Study*. New York: Appleton-Century-Croft.

Lambert, W. E. & Moore, N. (1966) Word-association responses: comparison of American and French monolinguals with Canadian monolinguals and bilinguals. *Journal of Personality and Social Psychology*, 3, 313–20.

Lambert, W. E. & Rawlings, C. (1969) Bilingual processing of mixed-language associative networks. *Journal of Verbal Learning and Verbal Behavior*, 8, 604–9.

Lambert, W. E. & Segalowitz, N. (1969) Semantic generalization in bilinguals. *Journal of Verbal Learning and Verbal Behavior*, 8, 559–66.

Lambert, W. E. & Taylor, D. M. (1981) *Language in the Education of Ethnic Minority Immigrants: Issues, Problems and Methods*. Miami: Paper presented at the Conference on the Education of Ethnic Minority Immigrants.

Lambert, W. E. & Tucker, G. R. (1972) *Bilingual Education of Children: The St Lambert Experiment*. Rowley, Mass.: Newbury House.

Landry, R. (1978) Le bilinguisme: le facteur répétition. *Revue Canadienne des Langues Modernes*, 34, 548–76.

Landry, R. & Allard, R. (1985) Choix de la langue d'enseignement: une analyse chez des parents francophones en milieu bilingue soustractif. *Canadian Modern Language Review*, 41, 480–500.

Larsen-Freeman, D. E. (1976) An explanation for the morpheme acquisition order of second language learners. *Language Learning*, 26, 126–34.

Lavandera, B. R. (1978) The variable component of bilingual performance. In J. Alatis (ed.) *International Dimensions of Bilingual Education*. Washington, DC: Georgetown University Press.

Lawler, J. & Selinker, L. (1971) On paradoxes, rules and research in second language learning. *Language Learning*, 21, 27–43.

Legaretta, D. (1979) The effects of program models on language acquisition by Spanish speaking children. *TESOL Quarterly*, 13, 521–34.

Lenneberg, E. H. (1967) *Biological Foundations of Language*. New York: Wiley.

Leopold, W. F. (1939–1949) *Speech Development of a Bilingual Child*. Evanston, Illinois: Northwestern University Press, 4 Volumes.

Le Page, R. B. (1964) *The National Language Question*. Oxford: Oxford University Press.

Le Page, R. B. (1968) Problems of description in multilingual communities. *Transactions of the Philological Society*, 189–212.

Le Page, R. B. (1978) *Projection, Focussing, Diffusion or Steps towards a Sociolinguistic Theory of Language, Illustrated from the Survey of Multilingual Communities, Stage I: Cayo District, Belize (Formerly British Honduras) and II: St. Lucia.* School of Education, St. Augustine's, Trinidad: Society for Caribbean Linguistics Occasional Paper No. 9. Reprinted in *York Papers in Linguistics,* 9, 1980.

Le Page, R. B. (1981) *Caribbean Connections in the Classroom.* London: Mary Glasgow Language Trust.

Le Page, R. B. & Tabouret-Keller, A. (1985) *Acts of Identity: Creole-based Approaches to Language and Ethnicity.* Cambridge: Cambridge University Press.

Lewis, G. (1972) *Multilingualism in the Soviet Union: Language Policy and its Implementation.* The Hague: Mouton.

Lewis, G. (1978) Types of bilingual communities. In J. E. Alatis (ed.) *International Dimensions of Bilingual Education. Georgetown University Round Table on Languages and Linguistics 1978.* Washington DC: Georgetown University Press.

Lewis, G. (1981) *Bilingualism and Bilingual Education.* Oxford: Pergamon Press.

Lieberson, P. (1970) *Language and Ethnic Relations in Canada.* New York: Wiley.

Lieberson, S. (1964) An extension of Greenberg's linguistic diversity measure. *Language,* 40, 526–31.

Lieberson, S. & Hansen, L. K. (1974) National development, mother tongue diversity, and the comparative study of nations. *American Sociological Review,* 39, 523–41.

Liedtke, W. W. & Nelson, L. D. (1968) Concept formation and bilingualism. *Alberta Journal of Education Research,* 14, 225–32.

Liepmann, D. & Saegert, J. (1974) Language tagging in bilingual free recall. *Journal of Experimental Psychology,* 103, 1137–41.

Light, L. L., Berger, D. & Bardales, D. E. (1975) Trade-off between memory for verbal items and their visual attributes. *Journal of Experimental Psychology: Human Learning and Memory,* 104, 188–93.

Lightbown, P. M. (1978) Question form and question function in the speech of young French L_2 learners. In M. Paradis (ed.) *Aspects of Bilingualism.* Columbia, South Carolina: Hornbeam Press.

Lightbown, P. M. (1984) The relationship between theory and method in second-language acquisition. In A. Davies, C. Crier & A. P. R. Howatt (eds.) *Interlanguage.* Edinburgh: Edinburgh University Press.

Lightbown, P. M. (1985) Great expectations: second-language acquisition research and classroom teaching. *Applied Linguistics,* 6, 173–89.

Lindholm, J. J. & Padilla, A. M. (1978) Language mixing in bilingual children. *Journal of Child Language,* 5, 327–35.

Linton, R. (1945) *The Cultural Background of Personality.* New York: Appleton-Century.

Long, J. & Harding-Esch, E. (1978) Summary and recall of text in first and second language: some factors contributing to performance differences. In D. Gerver & H. W. Sinaiko (eds.) *Language, Interpretation and Communication.* New York and London: Plenum Press.

Long, K. K. & Padilla, A. M. (1970) *Evidence for Bilingual Antecedents of Academic Success in a Group of Spanish–American College Students.* Unpublished research report. Bellingham: Western Washington State College.

Longley, P. (1978) An integrated program for training interpreters. In D. Gerver & H. W. Sinaiko (eds.) *Language, Interpretation and Communication.* New York and London: Plenum Press.

Miller, N. (ed.) (1984) *Bilingualism and Language Disability. Assessment and Remediation.* London: Croom Helm.

Milner, B. (1975) Psychological aspects of focal epilepsy and its neuro-surgical management. In D. P. Purpura, J. K. Penry & R. D. Walker (eds.) *Advances in Neurology*, New York: Raven Press.

Milon, J. P. (1974) The development of negation in English by a second language learner. *TESOL Quarterly*, 8, 137–45.

Milroy, L. (1980) *Language and Social Networks.* Oxford: Blackwell.

Minkowski, M. (1963) On aphasia in polyglots. In L. Halpern (ed.) *Problems of Dynamic Neurology.* Jerusalem: Hebrew University.

Mishkin, M. & Forgays, D. (1952) Word recognition as a function of retinal locus. *Journal of Experimental Psychology*, 43, 43–8.

Modiano, N. (1973) *Indian Education in the Chiapas Highlands.* New York: Rinehart, Holt & Winston.

Moerman, M. (1965) Ethnic identification in a complex civilization: who are the Lue? *American Anthropologist*, 67, 1215–30.

Mohanty, A. K. & Babu, N. (1983) Bilingualism and metalinguistic ability among Kond tribals in Orissa, India. *The Journal of Social Psychology*, 121, 15–22.

Moore, G. A., MacNamara, J. & Tucker, G. R. (1970) Interlingual Dichotic Interference. Unpublished research report. Montreal: McGill University.

Morrison, F. (1981) *Evaluation of the Second Language Learning (French) Programs in Schools of the Ottawa and Carleton Boards of Education: Eighth Annual Report.* Ottawa: Ottawa Board of Education Research Center.

Morrow, K. E. (1977) *Techniques of Evaluation of a Notional Syllabus.* London: Royal Society of Arts.

Morton, J. (1964) A preliminary functional model for language behaviour. *International Audiology*, 3, 216–25.

Morton, J. (1969) Categories of interference: verbal mediation and conflict in card-sorting. *British Journal of Psychology*, 60, 329–46.

Morton, J. (1979a) Word recognition. In J. Morton & J. Marshall (eds.) *Psycholinguistics 2: Structures and Processes.* Cambridge, Mass.: MIT Press.

Morton, J. (1979b) Facilitation in word recognition: experiments causing change in the logogen model. In P. A. Kolers, M. E. Wrolstad & M. Bouma (eds.) *Processing of Visible Language.* New York: Plenum Press.

Morton, J. (1980) The logogen model and orthographic structure. In U. Frith (ed.) *Cognitive Process in Spelling.* London: Academic Press.

Moscovici, S. (1984) The phenomenon of social representations. In R. M. Farr & S. Moscovici (eds.) *Social Representations.* Cambridge: Cambridge University Press/ Paris: Editions de la Maison des Sciences de l'Homme.

Moser, B. (1978) Simultaneous interpretation: a hypothetical model and its practical application. In D. Gerver & H. W. Sinaiko (eds.) *Language, Interpretation and Communication.* New York and London: Plenum Press.

MOTET (Mother Tongue and English Teaching Project) (1981) *Summary of Report 1 and 2.* Bradford: University of Bradford.

Mougeon, R. & Canale, M. (1978) Maintenance of French in Ontario: is education in French enough? *Interchange*, 9, 30–9.

Mougeon, R., Brent-Palmer, C., Belanger, M. & Cichocki, W. (1982) *Le Français Parlé en Situation Minoritaire.* Quebec: International Center for Research on Bilingualism B-105.

Mühlhäusler, P. (1986) *Pidgin and Creole Linguistics.* Oxford: Blackwell.

Mulac, A., Wiemann, J., Yoerks, S. & Gibson, T. W. (1983) Male/female language differences and their effects in like-sex and mixed-sex dyads: a test of interpersonal accommodation and the gender-linked language effect. Paper presented at the Second International Conference on Social Psychology of Language, Bristol, 18–22 July 1983.

Murray, D. J. (1986) Characteristics of words determining how easily they will be translated into a second language. *Applied Psycholinguistics, 7,* 353–72.

Naiman, N., Fröhlich, M., Stern, H. H. & Todesco, A. (1978) *The Good Language Learner.* Toronto: Ontario Institute for Studies in Education.

Neisser, U. (1966) *Cognitive Psychology.* New York: Appleton-Century-Croft.

Nelson K. (1981) Social cognition in a script framework. In J. H. Flavell & L. Ross (eds.) *Social Cognitive Development.* Cambridge: Cambridge University Press.

Nelson, K. & Gruendel, J. M. (1981) Generalized event representations: basic building blocks of cognitive development. In M. Lamb & A. L. Brown (eds.) *Advances in Developmental Psychology.* Hillsdale, N. J.: Erlbaum, Volume 1.

Nickel, G. (1971) Contrastive linguistics and foreign language teaching. In G. Nickel (ed.) *Papers in Contrastive Linguistics.* Cambridge: Cambridge University Press.

Nott, R. & Lambert, W. E. (1968) Free recall of bilinguals. *Journal of Verbal Learning and Verbal Behavior, 7,* 1065–71.

Obler, L. K. (1981) Right hemisphere participation in second language acquisition. In K. C. Diller (ed.) *Individual Differences and Universals in Language Learning Aptitude.* Rowley, Mass.: Newbury House.

Obler, L. & Albert, M. (1978) A monitor system for bilingual language processing. In M. Paradis (ed.) *Aspects of Bilingualism.* Columbia, SC: Hornbeam Press.

Obler, L., Zatorre, R., Galloway, L. & Vaid, J. (1982) Cerebral lateralization in bilinguals: methodological issues. *Brain and Language, 15,* 40–54.

Okoh, N. (1980) Bilingualism and divergent thinking among Nigerian and Welsh school children. *The Journal of Social Psychology, 110,* 163–70.

Oller, J. W. (1979) *Language Tests at School.* London: Longman.

Oller, J. W. Baca, L. & Vigil, A. (1977) Attitudes and attained proficiency in ESL: a sociolinguistic study of Mexican–Americans in the South-West. *TESOL Quarterly, 2,* 173–83.

Oller, J. W., Hudson, A. J. & Liu, P. F. (1977) Attitudes and attained proficiency in ESL: a sociolinguistic study of native speakers of Chinese in the United States. *Language Learning, 27,* 1–27.

Oller, J. W. & Perkins, P. (1978) Intelligence and language proficiency as sources of variance in self-reported affective variables. *Language Learning, 28,* 85–97.

O'Neil, W. & Dion, A. (1983) Bilingual recognition of concrete and abstract sentences. *Perceptual and Motor Skills, 57,* 839–45.

O'Neil, W. & Huot, R. (1984) Release from proactive inhibition as a function of pronunciation shift in bilinguals. *Canadian Journal of Psychology, 38,* 54–62.

Opoku, J. Y. (1983) The learning of English as a second language and the development of the emergent bilingual representational systems. *International Journal of Psychology, 18,* 271–83.

Politzer, R. L. (1974) Developmental sentence scoring as a method. *Modern Language Journal*, 58, 245–50.

Polomé, E. C. (1982) Sociolinguistically-oriented language surveys: reflections on the survey of language use and language-teaching in Eastern Africa. *Language in Society*, 11, 265–83.

Pool, J. (1969) National development and language diversity. *La Monda Lingo-Problemo*, 1, 140–56.

Poplack, S. (1980). Sometimes I'll start a sentence in Spanish y termino en español: toward a typology of code-switching. *Linguistics*, 18, 581–618.

Poplack, S. (1983) Intergenerational variation in language use and structure in a bilingual context. In C. Rivera (ed.) *An Ethnographic/Sociolinguistic Approach to Language Proficiency Assessment*. Clevedon: Multilingual Matters.

Poplack, S., Sankoff, D. & Miller C. (1987) The Social Correlates and Linguistic Consequences of Lexical Borrowing and Assimilation. Unpublished mimeo. Ottawa: University of Ottawa.

Porter, D. (1983) Assessing communicative proficiency: the search for validity. In K. Johnson & D. Porter (eds.) *Perspectives in Communicative Language Teaching*. London: Academic Press.

Potter, M. C., So, K.-F., von Eckhardt, B. & Feldman, L. B. (1984) Lexical and conceptual representation in beginning and proficient bilinguals. *Journal of Verbal Learning and Verbal Behavior*, 23, 23–8.

Powers, S. & Lopez, R. L. (1985) Perceptual, motor, and verbal skills of monolingual and bilingual Hispanic children: a discriminant analysis. *Perceptual and Motor Skills*, 60, 999–1002.

Preston, M. S. (1965) Inter-Lingual Interference in a Bilingual Version of the Stroop Colour-Word Task. Unpublished Ph.D. dissertation. Montreal: McGill University.

Preston, M. S. & Lambert, W. E. (1969) Interlingual interference in a bilingual version of the Stroop color-word task. *Journal of Verbal Learning and Verbal Behavior*, 8, 295–301.

Price, S., Fluck, M. & Giles, H. (1983) The effects of language of testing on bilingual pre-adolescents' attitudes towards Welsh and varieties of English. *Journal of Multilingual and Multicultural Development*, 4, 149–61.

Prujiner, A., Deshaies, D., Hamers, J. F., Blanc, M., Clément, R. & Landry, R. (1984) *Variation du Comportement Langagier lorsque Deux Langues Sont en Contact*. Quebec: International Center for Research of Bilingualism, G–5.

Quinn, T. J. (1981) Establishing a threshold-level concept for community language teaching in Australia. In M. Garner (ed.) *Community Languages: their Role in Education*. Melbourne/Sydney: River Seine Publications.

Raugh, M. R. & Atkinson, R. C. (1975) A mnemonic method for learning a second language vocabulary. *Journal of Educational Psychology*, 67, 1–16.

Raven, R. (1974) The development of Wh-questions in first and second language learners. In J. C. Richards (ed.) *Error Analysis: Perspectives on Second Language Acquisition*. London: Longman.

Redlinger, W. E. & Park, T. Z. (1980) Language mixing in young bilinguals. *Journal of Child Language*, 7. 337–52.

Reitz, J. G. (1974) Language and ethnic community survival. *Canadian Review of Sociology and Anthropology*. Special Issue, 104–22.

Reynell, J. (1969) *Reynell Development Language Scales Manual*. Windsor: NFER Publishing Co.

Ribot, T. (1882) *Diseases of Memory: an Essay in the Positive Psychology*. London: Paul.

Richards, J. C. (1971) Error analysis and second language strategies. *Language Sciences*, 17, 12–22.

Richards, J. C. (1972) Social factors, interlanguage and language learning. *Language Learning*, 22, 159–88.

Richards, J. C. (1974) A non-contrastive approach to error analysis. In J. C. Richards (ed.) *Error Analysis: Perspectives on Second Language Acquisition*. London: Longman.

Richards, J. C. & Sampson, G. P. (1974) The study of learner English. In J. C. Richards (ed.) *Error Analysis: Perspectives on Second Language Acquisition*. London: Longman.

Rivera, C. (ed.) (1983) *An Ethnographic/Sociolinguistic Approach to Language Proficiency Assessment*. Clevedon: Multilingual Matters.

Rivera, C. (ed.) (1984) *Language Proficiency and Academic Achievement*. Clevedon: Multilingual Matters.

Robinson, G. L. N. (1981) Bilingual education in Australia and the United States. In M. Garner (ed.) *Community Languages: Their Role in Education*. Melbourne/Sydney: River Seine Publications.

Rogers, L., Ten Houten, W., Kaplan, C. D. & Gardiner, M. (1977) Hemispheric specialization of language: An EEG study of bilingual Hopi children. *International Journal of Neuroscience*, 8, 1–6.

Rohner, R. P. (1984) Toward a conception of culture for cross-cultural psychology. *Journal of Cross-Cultural Psychology*, 15, 11–138.

Ronjat, J. (1913) *Le Développement du Langage Observé chez un Enfant Bilingue*. Paris: Champion.

Rose, R. G. & Carroll, J. (1974) Free recall of mixed language list. *Bulletin of the Psychonomic Society*, 3, 267–8.

Rose, R. G., Rose, P. R., King, N. & Perez, A. (1975) Bilingual memory for related and unrelated sentences. *Journal of Experimental Psychology: Human Learning and Memory*, 1, 599–606.

Rosier, P. & Farella, M. (1976) Bilingual education at Rock Point: some early results. *TESOL Quarterly*, 10, 379–88.

Ross, J. A. (1979) Language and the mobilization of ethnic identity. In H. Giles & B. Saint-Jacques (eds.) *Language and Ethnic Relations*. Oxford: Pergamon Press.

Roy, M. K. (1980) Peuplement et croissance démographique en Acadie. In J. Daigle (ed.) *Les Acadiens des Maritimes: Etudes Thématiques*. Yarmouth, NS: Lescarbot.

Royal Commission on Bilingualism and Biculturalism (1967–1970) Ottawa: Queen's Printer, 4 Volumes.

Rubin, J. (1968) *National Bilingualism in Paraguay*. The Hague: Mouton.

Ruke-Dravina, V. (1971) Word associations in monolingual and multilingual individuals. *Linguistics*, 74, 66–84.

Rupp, J. (1980) *Cerebral Language Dominance in Vietnamese–English Bilingual Children*. Unpublished doctoral dissertation. Albuquerque: The University of New Mexico.

Ryan, E. B. & Carranza, M. A. (1975) Evaluative reactions of adolescents towards

Simard, L. M., Taylor, D. M. & Giles, H. (1976) Attribution processes and interpersonal accommodation in a bilingual setting. *Language and Speech*, 19, 374–87.

Skehan, P. (1984) On the non-magical nature of second and foreign language acquisition. *Polyglot*, 5, A1.

Skehan, P. (1986) Where does language aptitude come from? *British Studies in Applied
Linguistics*, 1, 95–113.

Skutnabb, Kangas, T. (1981) *Bilingualism or Not: The Education of Minorities*. Clevedon:
Multilingual Matters.

Skutnabb-Kangas, T. & Toukomaa, P. (1976) *Teaching Migrant Children's Mother
Tongue and Learning the Language of the Host Country in the Context of the Socio-Cultural
Situation of the Migrant Family*. Tampere: UNESCO Report, University of Tampere,
Research Reports, 15.

Smolicz, J. J. (1979) *Culture and Education in a Plural Society*. Canberra: Curriculum Development Center.

Smolicz, J. J. (1981) Core values and cultural identity. *Ethnic and Racial Studies*, 4, 75–
90.

Smolicz, J. J. (1984) Multiculturalism and an overarching framework of values: some
educational responses for ethnically plural societies. *European Journal of Education*, 19,
11–23.

Snow, C. E. & Ferguson, C. A. (eds.) (1977) *Talking to Children*. Cambridge: Cambridge University Press.

Snow, C. E. & Hoefnagel-Hohle, M. (1978) The critical period for language acquisition: evidence from second language learning. *Child Development*, 49, 1114–28.

Soares, C. (1984) Left-hemisphere language lateralization in bilinguals: use of the concurrent activities paradigm. *Brain and Language*, 23, 86–96.

Soares, C. & Grosjean, F. (1981) Left hemisphere language lateralization in bilinguals
and monolinguals. *Perception and Psychophysics*, 29, 599–601.

Soares, C. & Grosjean, F. (1984) Bilingual in a monolingual and bilingual speech
mode: the effect on lexical access. *Memory and Cognition*, 12, 380–6.

Sridhar, S. (1981) Contrastive analysis, error analysis and interlanguage. In J. Fisiak
(ed.) *Contrastive Linguistics and the Language Teacher*. Oxford: Pergamon Press.

Srivastava, R. N. (1984a) Consequences of initiating literacy in the second language.
In F. Coulmas (ed.) *Linguistic Minorities and Literacy*. Berlin: Mouton.

Srivastava, R. N. (1984b) Literacy education for minorities: a case study from India.
In F. Coulmas (ed.) *Linguistic Minorities and Literacy*. Berlin: Mouton.

Starck, R., Genesee, F., Lambert, W. E. & Seitz, M. (1977) Multiple language experi-
ence and the development of cerebral dominance. In S. J. Segalowitz & F. A.
Gruber (eds.) *Language Development and Neurological Theory*. New York: Academic
Press.

Stenzl, C. (1982) Comment on H. C. Barik: *A Study of Simultaneous Interpretation*. Unpublished research report. London: Birkbeck College, Department of Applied Linguistics.

Stenzl, C. (1983) Simultaneous Interpretation: Groundwork Towards a Comprehensive Model. Unpublished MA dissertation. London: Birkbeck College, University of
London.

Stephenson, G. M. (1981) Intergroup bargaining and negotiation. In J. C. Turner &
H. Giles (eds.) *Intergroup Behaviour*. Oxford: Blackwell.

Street, R. L. (1982) Evaluation of noncontent speech accommodation. *Language and Communication*, 2, 13–31.

Street, R. L. & Giles, H. (1982) Speech accommodation theory: a social cognitive approach to language and speech behaviour. In M. Roloff & C. Berger (eds.) *Social Cognition and Communication*. Beverley Hills, Ca.: Sage.

Street, A. L. & Hopper, R. (1982) A model of speech style evaluation. In E. B. Ryan & H. Giles (eds.) *Attitudes towards Language Variation*. London: Edward Arnold.

Stroop, J. R. (1935) Studies of interference in serial verbal reactions. *Journal of Experimental Psychology*, 118, 643–61.

Sugishita, M., Iwata, M., Toyokura, Y., Yoshioka, M. & Yamada, R. (1978) Reading of ideograms and phonograms in Japanese patients after partial commissurotomy. *Neuropsychologia*, 26, 417–26.

Sussman, H., Franklin, P. & Simon, T. (1982) Bilingual speech: bilateral control? *Brain and Language*, 15, 125–42.

Swain, M. (1971) Bilingualism, monolingualism and code acquisition. Chicago: Paper presented at the Child Language Conference.

Swain, M. (1972) Bilingualism as a First Language. Unpublished Ph.D. dissertation. Irvine: University of California.

Swain, M. (1982) Immersion education: applicability for nonvernacular teaching to vernacular speakers. In B. Hartford, A. Valdman & C. R. Foster (eds.) *Issues in International Bilingual Education: the Role of the Vernacular*. New York: Plenum Press.

Swain, M. & Lapkin, S. (1982) *Evaluating Bilingual Education: A Canadian Case Study*. Clevedon: Multilingual Matters.

Swain, M. & Wesche, M. (1973) Linguistic interaction: case study of a bilingual child. *Working Papers on Bilingualism*, 1, 10–34.

Swan, M. (1985) A critical look at the communicative approach. *ELT Journal*, 31, 2–12 & 76–87.

Tabouret-Keller, A. (1968) Sociological factors of language maintenance and shift: a methodological approach based on European and African examples. In J. A. Fishman, C. A. Ferguson & Das Gupta (eds.) *Language Problems of Developing Nations*. New York: Wiley.

Tabouret-Keller, A. (1972) A contribution to the sociological study of language maintenance and language shift. In J. A. Fishman (ed.) *Advances in the Sociology of Language*. The Hague: Mouton, Volume 2.

Tabouret-Keller, A. & Luckel, F. (1981) Maintien de l'alsacien et adoption du français: éléments de la situation linguistique en milieu rural en Alsace. *Langages*, 61, 39–62.

Taeschner, T. (1983) *The Sun is Feminine*. Berlin: Springer Verlag.

Taft, R. (1977) Coping with unfamiliar cultures. In N. Warren (ed.) *Studies in Cross-Cultural Psychology*. London: Academic Press, Volume 1.

Tajfel, H. (1974) Social identity and intergroup behaviour. *Social Science Information*, 13, 65–93.

Tajfel, H. (ed.) (1978) *Differentiation between Social Groups: Studies in the Social Psychology of Intergroup Relations*. London: Academic Press.

Tajfel, H. (1981) *Human Groups and Social Categories: Studies in Social Psychology*. Cambridge: Cambridge University Press.

Tajfel, H. & Turner, J. C. (1979) An integrative theory of intergroup conflict. In W. G.

van Dijk, T. A. (1980) *Macrostructures: an Interdisciplinary Study of Global Structures in Discourse, Interaction and Cognition*. Hillsdale, N.J.: Erlbaum.

Verdoodt, A. (1972) The differential impact of immigrant French speakers on indigenous German speakers: a case study in the light of two theories. In J. A. Fishman (ed.) *Advances in the Sociology of Language*. The Hague: Mouton, Volume 2.

Vocate, D. R. (1984) Differential cerebral speech lateralization in Crow Indian and Anglo children. *Neuropsychologia*, 22, 487–94.

Voinescu, I., Vish, E., Sirian, S. & Maretsis, M. (1977) Aphasia in a polyglot. *Brain and Language*, 4, 165–76.

Volterra, V. & Taeschner, T. (1978) The acquisition and the development of language by bilingual children. *Journal of Child Language*, 5, 311–26.

Vygotsky, L. S. (1962) *Thought and Language*. Cambridge, Mass.: MIT Press.

Vygotsky, L. S. (1978) *Mind in Society: the Development of Higher Psychological Processes*. Cambridge, Mass.: Harvard University Press.

Walters, J. & Zatorre, R. J. (1978) Laterality differences for word identification in bilinguals. *Brain and Language*, 6, 158–67.

Wagner-Gough, J. (1975) Comparative studies in second language learning. *CAL-ERIC/CLL Series on Languages and Linguistics*, 26.

Wagner-Gough, J. (1978) Excerpts from comparative studies in second language learning. In E. M. Hatch (ed.) *Second Language Acquisition*. Rowley, Mass.: Newbury House, 155–71.

Ward, C. A. & Hewstone, M. (1985) Ethnicity, language and intergroup relations in Malaysia and Singapore: a social psychological analysis. *Journal of Multilingual and Multicultural Development*, 6, 271–96.

Wardhaugh, R. (1970) The contrastive analysis hypothesis. *TESOL Quarterly*, 4, 123–30.

Wardhaugh, R. (1986) *An Introduction to Sociolinguistics*. Oxford: Blackwell.

Weber, M. (1968) *Economy and Society: an Outline of Interpretive Sociology*. New York: Bedminster Press.

Webster (1961) *Webster's Third New International Dictionary of the English Language*. London: Bell & Sons.

Wechsler, A. (1977) Dissociative aphasia. *Archives of Neurology*, 34, 257.

Weinreich, U. (1953) *Languages in Contact*. The Hague: Mouton.

Welford, A. T. (1968) *Fundamentals of Skills*. London: Methuen.

Wells, C. G. (1981) *Learning through Interaction. The Study of Language Development*. Cambridge: Cambridge University Press.

Wells, C. G. (1985a) Preschool literacy-related activities and success in school. In D. R. Olson, N. Torrance & A. Hildyard (eds.) *Literacy, Language, and Learning: The Nature and Consequences of Reading and Writing*. Cambridge: Cambridge University Press.

Wells, C. G. (1985b) *Language Development in the Pre-school Years*. Cambridge: Cambridge University Press.

Whitaker, H. A. (1978) Bilingualism: a neurolinguistic perspective. In W. C. Ritchie (ed.) *Second Language Acquisition Research*. New York: Academic Press.

Whiteley, W. H. (1971) Introduction. In W. H. Whiteley (ed.) *Language Use and Social Change*. London: Oxford University Press.

Whiteley, W. H. (1973) Sociolinguistic surveys at a national level. In R. Shuy and

R. W. Fasold (eds.) *Language Attitudes: Current Trends and Prospects*. Washington, DC: Georgetown University Press.

Whorf, B. (1956) *Language, Thought and Reality*. Cambridge, Mass.: MIT Press.

Wiens, A. N., Manuagh, T. S. & Matarazzo, J. D. (1976) Speech and silence behaviour of bilinguals conversing in each of two languages. *Linguistics*, 172, 79–93.

Wilks, Y. (1975) Machine translation and artificial intelligence. In B. M. Snell (ed.) *Translating and the Computer*. Amsterdam: North-Holland.

Wilks, Y. (1981) A position note on natural language understanding and artificial intelligence. *Cognition*, 10, 337–40.

Willemyns, R. (1987) The investigation of 'language continuum and diglossia'. In M. Blanc & J. F. Hamers (eds.) *Theoretical and Methodological Issues in the Study of Languages/Dialects in Contact at Macro- and Micro-logical Levels of Analysis*. Quebec: International Center for Research on Bilingualism, B–160, 30–49.

Williams, C. H. (1984) More than tongue can tell: linguistic factors in ethnic separatism. In J. Edwards (ed.) *Linguistic Minorities, Policies and Pluralism*. London: Academic Press.

Williams, F., Whitehead, J. L. & Miller, L. M. (1971) Ethnic stereotyping and judgements of children's speech. *Speech Monographs*, 38, 166–70.

Williams, G. (1986) Language planning or language expropriation? *Journal of Multilingual and Multicultural Development*, 7, 509–18.

Winograd, E., Cohen, C. & Baressi, J. (1976) Memory for concrete and abstract words in bilingual speakers. *Memory and Cognition*, 4, 323–9.

Witelson, S. F. (1977) Early hemisphere specialization and interhemispheric plasticity: an empirical and theoretical review. In S. J. Segalowitz and F. A. Gruber (eds.) *Language Development and Neurological Theory*. Cambridge, Mass.: MIT Press.

Witte, E. & Baetens Beardsmore, H. (eds.) (1987) *The Interdisciplinary Study of Urban Bilingualism in Brussels*. Clevedon: Multilingual Matters.

Wode, H. (1976) Developmental sequences in naturalistic L_2 acquisition. *Working Papers on Bilingualism*, 11, 1–31.

Wode, H. (1978) The L_1 versus L_2 acquisition of English interrogation. *Working Papers on Bilingualism*, 15, 37–57.

Wode, H. (1983) *Learning a Second Language: 1. An Integrated View of Language Acquisition*. Tübingen: Narr.

Wode, H., Bahns, J., Bedey, H. & Frank, W. (1978) Developmental sequences: an alternative approach to morpheme orders. *Language Learning*, 28, 175–95.

Wong Fillmore, L. (1976) *The Second Time Around: Cognitive and Social Strategies in Second Language Acquisition*. Unpublished Ph.D. dissertation. Stanford University.

Wong Fillmore, L. (1979) Individual differences in second language acquisition. In C. J. Fillmore, D. Kempler & W. S.-Y. Wang (eds.) *Individual Differences in Language Ability and Language Behaviour*. New York: Academic Press, 203–28.

Wong Fillmore, L. (1980) Cultural perspectives on second language learning. *TESOL Reporter*, 14, 22–31.

Woolford, E. (1983) Bilingual code-switching and syntactic theory. *Linguistic Inquiry*, 14, 520–36.

Wrightsman, L. S. (1972) *Social Psychology in the Seventies*. Belmont, California: Wadsworth Publishing Company.

Chiapas (Mexico) 206-7
Chiapa-Spanish 206
Chicano 138
Chichewa (Bantu language) 34
Chichewa-English 34
childhood bilinguality*
  consecutive* 9, 10, 17, 75-6, 80, 224
  simultaneous* 9, 10, 32, 74, 79-80, 224
China 169-70, 172
Chinese 41, 46, 49, 87, 88, 138, 139, 140, 169-
  70, 173, 218, 220, 234
Chinese Australians 167
Chinese Canadians 167
Chinese-English 41, 49, 87, 88, 103, 139, 140,
  173, 218, 220, 234
Chinese-Thaï 138
class (social) 156, 159, 162, 165, 168, 204
clinical studies 39, 108 ff, 121
cloze test 16, 266
Cockney 130
code* 2 and *passim*
  linguistic 6 and *passim*
code alternation* *see* code-switching
code choice/selection 144-7, 173, 178
code-mixing* 1, 21-2, 35-6, 39, 88, 111, 112,
  144, 148, 149, 152-3, 183
code-switching* 19, 21-2, 35, 75, 88, 92, 95,
  107, 111, 112, 138, 144, 148-52, 162, 178,
  183
cognitive 2, 6
  advantage 9, 11, 15, 22, 51-5, 56-7, 79-80,
    224
  control 68-9, 78, 79, 80, 91
  development 11, 22, 47-55, 56, 57, 78-82,
    216, 219
  disadvantage 9, 15, 22, 48, 51, 52, 53-4, 56-
    7, 78-80
  function(ing) 63 ff., 73, 75, 76, 77, 78-82,
    196
  organization 8, 9, 61, 75, 77-8, 230
  structures 84
  styles 234
colonialism 167-8, 169, 172, 177, 188, 191
common underlying proficiency (CUP) 55, 78
communal groups 158-9
communication
  function 6, 62 ff., 73, 75, 77, 82, 170
  modes 233-4
communicativity index 27
community
  language(s) 206, 211-12
  speech* 6, 9, 10, 11, 12, 26, 152, 166, 173,
    178, 180, 183
competence
  analytic 63, 69, 80
  bilingual 149, 252-3 *see also* balanced;
    dominant

communicative 16, 17, 69, 229-30, 240
  language 14, 16, 17-20, 53-55, 69, 126, 130,
    229-30
  linguistic 6, 7, 8, 9, 14, 17, 69, 122, 141, 142,
    143-4, 229-30
  metalinguistic 47, 50, 55, 68, 75, 78, 80
  sociolinguistic 230
  strategic 230
  transitional 216
compound bilinguality* 8-10, 20, 93-6, 102,
  109
concept-mediation hypothesis 103
confidence (in use of L₂) 240
  measures 23
Conseil de la Langue Française 161
constraint
  equivalence 150-1
  free-morpheme 150-1
contact* (languages in) 1, 2, 4, 5, 6 and *passim*
context
  of acquisition 8, 9, 10, 11, 12, 20-1, 37-9,
    44-5, 93-6, 221-2, 227-8
  embedded v. reduced 55
  non-verbal 92
  of situation 145, 151, 179
  sociocultural 56-8, 79-82, 236
  verbal 91
contextualized *see* decontextualized language
continuum*
  additive-subtractive 80
  bilingual-monolingual 143
  compound-coordinate 93-6
  sociolinguistic 2, 7, 9, 12, 157, 173, 184
  methodological 2, 155, 170
  post-creole continuum* *see* decreolization
contrastive analysis 216, 224-5
convergence 2, 151, 152, 160, 182
  see also speech accommodation
conversation 68-9
coordinate bilinguality* 2, 8-10, 20, 93-6,
  102, 109, 253
Cotonou (capital of Benin) 11
creativity
  creative thinking 49-50, 78
  sociolinguistic 157, 182
creole 146, 131, 162, 180-81, 209, 211
creolization* 179-81
cross-cultural *see* intercultural
Crow (North-American Indian language) 45,
  209
Crow-English 45, 209
Cuba 191
Culham (UK) 197
cultural differences 18, 24, 106-8, 121
cultural identity *see* identity
cultural imagery 102, 232-3
culturation 115, 123-4